A PHILOSOPHY OF STRUGGLE

A PHILOSOPHY OF STRUGGLE: THE LEONARD HARRIS READER

PHILOSOPHIA NATA EX CONATU

Edited by Lee A. McBride III

BLOOMSBURY ACADEMIC
LONDON • NEW YORK • OXFORD • NEW DELHI • SYDNEY

BLOOMSBURY ACADEMIC
Bloomsbury Publishing Plc
50 Bedford Square, London, WC1B 3DP, UK
1385 Broadway, New York, NY 10018, USA

BLOOMSBURY, BLOOMSBURY ACADEMIC and the Diana logo are trademarks
of Bloomsbury Publishing Plc

First published in Great Britain 2020

Cover patterns © Alamy Stock Photo / Getty Images
Portrait of Leonard Harris © Chris Sowe (chrissowe.com)

A catalogue record for this book is available from the British Library.

A catalog record for this book is available from the Library of Congress.

ISBN: HB: 978-1-3500-8420-9
PB: 978-1-3500-8419-3
ePDF: 978-1-3500-8421-6
eBook: 978-1-3500-8422-3

Typeset by Newgen KnowledgeWorks Pvt. Ltd., Chennai, India

To find out more about our authors and books visit www.bloomsbury.com
and sign up for our newsletters.

CONTENTS

Contents

ACKNOWLEDGMENTS

I am indebted to the Philosophy Born of Struggle Association (PBOS), the Alain Locke Society, and the World Congress of Philosophy, Fédération Internationale des Sociétés de Philosophie (FISP), for holding me up when I was certain that I had fallen down; for the Indian Council of Philosophical Research (ICPR), Ministry of Human Resources and Development, Government of India, 2012; Actes du Colloque International, Université Felix Houphouët-Boigny, Abijan, Senegal, 2016; University of KwaZulu Natal, Centre for Critical Research on Race and Identity, 2016; World Ethical Institute, Peking University, 2017; Institute for Interdisciplinary Studies of World Literature, Zhejiang University, Hangzhou, China, 2018; and the University of Science and Technology, Wuhan, China, 2018, for hosting me and allowing me to enter your houses of enlightenment. For my wife, Linda F. Harris; our children, Leonard N. Harris, Jarrard L. Harris, Jamila R. Grant, Samiayah Ncube; daughter-in-law Christine Harris; son-in-law Mthulisi Ncube and grandchildren, Jaliyah R. Grant, Jade R. Grant, Jameson L. Harris, Isaac Reeves, Ilijah Ncube and Champion Ncube.

Leonard Harris

SOURCE ACKNOWLEDGMENTS

The editor and publisher gratefully acknowledge the permission granted to reproduce the copyright material in this book. All efforts have been made to trace copyright holders. In the event of errors or omissions, please notify the publisher in writing of any corrections that will need to be incorporated in future editions of this book.

Chapter 2: Harris, Leonard. 1998. "The Concept of Racism: An Essentially Contested Concept?" *Centennial Review* 42 (2, Spring): 217–31. Reproduced by permission of Michigan State University.

Chapter 3: Harris, Leonard. 1999. "What, Then, Is Racism?" In *Racism*, edited by Leonard Harris, 437–50. Amherst, NY: Humanity Books. Reproduced by permission of Prometheus Books.

Chapter 4: Harris, Leonard. 2018. "Necro-Being: An Actuarial Account of Racism." *Res Philosophica* 95 (2): 273–302. Reproduced by permission of *Res Philosophica*.

Chapter 5: Harris, Leonard. 1992. "Autonomy under Duress." In *African-American Perspectives on Biomedical Ethics*, edited by Harley Flack and Edmund Pellegrino, 133–49. Washington, DC: Georgetown University Press. Reproduced by permission of Georgetown University Press.

Chapter 6: Harris, Leonard. 1992. "Honor: Emasculation and Empowerment." In *Rethinking Masculinity*, edited by Larry May and Robert Strikwerda, 191–208. Lanham, MD: Rowman & Littlefield. Reproduced by permission of Rowman & Littlefield.

Chapter 7: Harris, Leonard. 2003. "Tolerance, réconciliation et groupes." *Guerre et Réconciliation, Jounée de la Philosophie àl UNESCO* 5: 59–94. Reproduced by permission of the United Nations Educational, Scientific and Cultural Organization (UNESCO).

Chapter 8: Harris, Leonard. 2016. "Dignity and Subjection." *Présence Africaine* 193 (1): 141–59. Reproduced by permission of *Présence Africaine*.

Chapter 9: Harris, Leonard. 1999. "Honor and Insurrection or A Short Story about Why John Brown (with David Walker's Spirit) Was Right and Frederick Douglass (with Benjamin Banneker's Spirit) Was Wrong." In *Frederick Douglass: A Critical Reader*, edited by Bill E. Lawson, 227–42. Oxford: Blackwell. Reproduced by permission of John Wiley & Sons.

Chapter 10: Harris, Leonard. 2002. "Insurrectionist Ethics: Advocacy, Moral Psychology, and Pragmatism." In *Ethical Issues for a New Millennium*, edited by John Howie, 192–210. Carbondale: Southern Illinois University Press. Reproduced by permission of Southern Illinois University Press.

Source Acknowledgments

Chapter 11: Harris, Leonard. 2018. "Can a Pragmatist Recite a *Preface to a Twenty Volume Suicide Note*? Or Insurrectionist Challenges to Pragmatism—Walker, Child, and Locke." *The Pluralist* 13 (1, Spring): 1–25. Reproduced by permission of *The Pluralist*.

Chapter 12: Harris, Leonard. 1998. "Universal Human Liberation: Community and Multiculturalism." In *Theorizing Multiculturalism*, edited by Cynthia Willett, 449–57. Oxford: Blackwell. Reproduced by permission of John Wiley & Sons.

Chapter 13: Harris, Leonard. 2002. "Community: What Type of Entity and What Type of Moral Commitment." In *the Quest for Community and Identity*, edited by Robert E. Birt, 243–55. Lanham, MD: Rowman & Littlefield. Reproduced by permission of Rowman & Littlefield.

Chapter 15: Harris, Leonard. 1992. "The Horror of Tradition or How to Burn Babylon and Build Benin While Reading a *Preface to a Twenty Volume Suicide Note*." *Philosophical Forum* 24 (1–3, Fall–Spring 1992–3): 94–119. Reproduced by permission of John Wiley & Sons.

Chapter 16: Harris, Leonard. 2014. "Telos and Tradition: Making the Future – Bridges to Future Traditions." *Philosophia Africana* 16 (2): 59–71. Reproduced by permission of *Philosophia Africana*.

EDITOR'S INTRODUCTION

This volume draws together select writings representative of Leonard Harris's influential career as a critical philosopher, featuring trenchant essays on philosophy born of struggle, immiseration and racism, honor and dignity, insurrectionist ethics, and the building of tradition. In these introductory remarks I replicate the structure of this volume as indicated in the table of contents, hoping to give a window into Harris's oeuvre.

Prolegomenon

Part I of this volume offers a critical introduction to Harris's philosophical worldview. "What, *then*, is 'Philosophy Born of Struggle'? *Philosophia nata ex conatu*" (Chapter 1) offers a conception of philosophy, contrary to the classical conception of philosophy as the pursuit of wisdom using pristine reasoning methods addressing perennial vexing questions and concepts. Rather, philosophy is defined with a normative claim and a fallibilist/contextual approach to epistemology—always situated in philosophy as a human, contra-transcendental project. This distinctively Harrisian approach is heavily influenced by the critical pragmatism of Alain Locke, the materialism and concerns of Angela Y. Davis, and the virtue ethics of such authors as David Walker and Lydia M. Child.

In "What, *then*, is 'Philosophy Born of Struggle'? *Philosophia nata ex conatu*"[1] the classical meaning of "philosophy" is eschewed; a new meaning with an avowedly value-laden dimension is proffered. Philosophy, on Harris's account, does not begin with souls seeking release from their earthly corporeal existence—a practice in dying.[2] Philosophy neither begins with high-caste leisurely men seeking eternal truths (for their own sake) nor with anonymous reasonable beings behind a veil of ignorance working autonomously in a cooperative venture for mutual advantage.[3] Philosophy, as Harris conceives it, begins with the full range of human experiences (including genocide, slavery, exploitation, misery, degradation, cognitive dissonance, cynicism, etc.). This philosophy, born of struggle, should help people assess their situation and facilitate the mitigation of struggles and misery, the actual experiences of surviving human populations. Harris posits an amoral universe. No cosmic teleology to give purpose and direction. No inherent arc bending toward justice, no promise of redemption for the abused and wretched, and no Redeemer (albeit a deity, the wise, Being qua Being, or corporal or incorporeal selves that know themselves). In this sense, Harrisian philosophy begins in a thoroughly disenchanted universe.[4] It begins with a humanism—it begins with the experiences, capacities, and needs of human beings.[5] It is a philosophy born of struggle; human beings striving to survive (*philosophia nata ex conatu*).

Because Harris postulates an amoral universe—no god, no divine plan, no cosmic teleology to give purpose and direction, and no cosmic principle (e.g., karma) systematically meting out reward and punishment—he is in opposition to a host of philosophers and theorists, not just classical authors but also scholars and activists such as Edward W. Blyden, Martin Luther King Jr., and Cornel West. Blyden, for instance, believes that the colonial plundering of Africa, the subjugation of "the African race," and that population's forthcoming dignified ascension beyond its previous glory was predestined.[6] In other words, Blyden postulates a teleological universe, a universe that gives goal- or telos-oriented purpose to immiserated African peoples.[7] In a different context, yet in a similar vein, King reassures African Americans,

> We're going to win our freedom because both the sacred heritage of our nation and the eternal will of the almighty God are embodied in our echoing demands. And so, however dark it is, however deep the angry feelings are, and however violent explosions are, I can still sing "We Shall Overcome."
>
> We shall overcome because the arc of the moral universe is long, but it bends toward justice.[8]

For King, the struggles of African Americans bear the eternal will of the Almighty; the universe is moral and there will be justice in the end. With such an outlook, West gives high esteem to "engaged gaiety, subversive joy and revolutionary patience, which works for and looks to the kingdom to come."[9] That is, African Americans should defiantly find joy in the face of oppression; they should persevere patiently because justice will eventually be dealt, if not here, then in the kingdom to come. Harris argues that such illusions should be abandoned. In stark contrast, he posits an amoral universe that offers no cosmic teleology or promise of redemption for the abused and wretched. In this sense, Harrisian philosophy begins in this perilous, contingent universe, warts and all. It begins with human ideals and foibles and the perplexities of organic persistence within particular social and natural environments. It is a philosophy arising from strenuous effort (*philosophia nata ex conatu*).

This Harrisian position is pointedly anti-absolutist (or anabsolutist). Harris rejects the notion that there is one grand narrative, an unbiased epistemic objectivism from a god's-eye-perspective. His ontology, for example, contends that social kinds are anabsolute—class, race, and gender categories are seemingly objectively real and can be used for purposes of explanation; however, they are actually unstable, contingent, and not well bounded. Harris rejects dogmatism and various forms of cultural imperialism that often rest upon stereotypes, overdetermined generalizations, or some other form of fallacious reasoning. He suggests that we cannot escape provincialism, perspectivism, a limited picture—our depictions, our explanations, our values are always context-bound, always influenced by a particular set of historically contingent intervening background assumptions. Our classifications and social groupings almost always contain anomalies and outliers. Social entities (e.g., ethnic groups and racialized groups) change over time. And, within our social groups, our conceptions of human nature and virtue do not reveal one true, authentic mode of being. Rather, human nature, our esteemed character traits (i.e., our virtues), and even the ways that we conceive dignity manifest in differing ways in accord with varying values and cultural variables. Thus, Harris is a pluralist, recognizing the various modes or traditions in which human beings construe humanity, virtue, and dignity. Harrisian philosophy offers a critical position, cognizant of its limitations, and wary of its enlisted stereotypes, myths, and provincial fabrications.[10] It is a "philosophy" that both proffers what it is to do philosophy and what "philosophy" qua "philosophy" should mean.

Immiseration and Racism (Oppression as Necro-Being)

Part II of this volume features three articles on immiseration and racism. "The Concept of Racism: An Essentially Contested Concept?" (Chapter 2) queries whether racism is indeterminate, visceral, or essentially contested. Harris, contrary to nominalist accounts, contends that even if we disagreed about whether racism is a species of objective reality or constructed, we should make a normative claim and "decide what account or explanation is most efficacious for reasons of good evidence and defensible morals." In "What, Then, Is Racism?" (Chapter 3), Harris discusses numerous conceptions of racism and problems of definition. Racism, on this view, is caused by numerous variables—a "polymorphous agent of death, premature births, shortened lives, starving children, debilitating theft, abusive larceny, degrading insults and insulting stereotypes forcibly imposed." "Necro-Being: An Actuarial Account of Racism" (Chapter 4) depicts racism as a particular form of necro-tragedy, irredeemable misery. Harris offers an account of explanation couched in actuarial description, which offers a view of the "anabsolute," that which is often concealed in volitional, institutional, structural, or racial contract accounts of racism.

Having traveled extensively and having taken account of the various ways in which people are oppressed and immiserated around the globe, Harris has a pointed interest in disclosing unnecessary misery and thinking through potential means of shaping different futures. To this end, Harris has devoted considerable attention to race-based oppression, or racism. Harris begins with a query about whether racism is an inherently controversial concept. Harris sees racial groupings/categorizations as odious social constructions, nefarious tropes (initially) imposed upon a population to facilitate dehumanization or subjugation. (This places Harris at odds with theorists such as Lucius Outlaw and Chike Jeffers.[11]) Nevertheless, Harris argues that a normative dimension is required even if the concept of racism is essentially contested; to ameliorate the real material disparities of racialized populations, racially oppressed populations will have to form communities of resistance.

An Ethics of Insurrection; Or, Leaving the Asylum

Part IV features three articles on insurrectionist ethics and virtues of tenacity. "Honor and Insurrection or A Short Story about Why John Brown (with David Walker's Spirit) Was Right and Frederick Douglass (with Benjamin Banneker's Spirit) Was Wrong" (Chapter 9) offers an argument in favor of the character virtues promoted by David Walker (such as tenacity and indignation). Contrary to absolute pacifism, Harris advocates an ethics of insurrection. In "Insurrectionist Ethics: Advocacy, Moral Psychology, and Pragmatism" (Chapter 10), Harris argues that a crucial condition of any adequate philosophy is that it provide the type of intuitions, strategies, and motivations common among insurrectionists, particularly, slave insurrections. If a philosophy's normative dimension cannot tell us that a slave should revolt, it is inadequate. Classical pragmatism fails this test. "Can a Pragmatist Recite a *Preface to a Twenty Volume Suicide Note*? Or Insurrectionist Challenges to Pragmatism—Walker, Child, and Locke" (Chapter 11) suggests that reasoning strategies that assume a well-ordered world are deeply misguided. Yet, Harris contends that a philosophy should provide resources for people conflicted or besieged in a world of paradoxes and dilemmas within which it is impossible to reasonably predict outcomes or where unwanted outcomes are almost guaranteed.

Harrisian philosophy born of struggle supports an ethics of insurrection. There are four basic tenets to the position. First, there is a willingness to defy accepted norms and authority figures when they cause or maintain immiseration. These practitioners of insurrectionist ethics see reason to disrupt relatively stable social orders, if those social orders countenance oppressive practices or necro-being. To this end, they may endorse acts of resistance, which can take various forms, including irreverent outspoken protest, acts of civil disobedience, or physical violence. Second, there is a marshaling of the social and political force of porous and variegated social collectives on behalf of the subjugated. Harris maintains that human cognition relies heavily upon representative heuristics. Representative heuristics is understood as a reasoning strategy crucial to cognition but prone to stereotypes and fallacious inferences. Nevertheless, it is through representative heuristics that social entities are assembled. These particular social entities are not understood as stable categories or natural kinds; rather, these socially constructed groups of resistance are understood as porous, evolving communities with contingent futures. Third, there is a conception of humanity or personhood that recognizes all human beings as members of the moral community or potential bearers of honor, that is, a notion of shared humanity that does not presuppose an innately unredeemable subhuman group. Dignity is thus afforded to all persons. Fourth, there is a valorizing of insurrectionist character traits (e.g., indignation, enmity, tenacity, or irreverence). Harris gives high esteem to the character traits evinced by David Walker and Lydia Maria Child. These insurrectionist character traits make possible the sorts of authoritative voices and postures that will demand the liberation of the oppressed. They and outliers. Social entities (e.g., ethnic groups and racialized groups) change over time. And, within our social groups, our conceptions of human nature and virtue do not reveal one true, authentic mode of being. Rather, human nature, our esteemed character traits (i.e., our virtues), and even the ways that we conceive dignity manifest in differing ways in accord with varying values and cultural variables. Thus, Harris is a pluralist, recognizing the various modes or traditions in which human beings construe humanity, virtue, and dignity. Harrisian philosophy offers a critical position, cognizant of its limitations, and wary of its enlisted stereotypes, myths, and provincial fabrications.[10] It is a "philosophy" that both proffers what it is to do philosophy and what "philosophy" qua "philosophy" should mean.

Immiseration and Racism (Oppression as Necro-Being)

Part II of this volume features three articles on immiseration and racism. "The Concept of Racism: An Essentially Contested Concept?" (Chapter 2) queries whether racism is indeterminate, visceral, or essentially contested. Harris, contrary to nominalist accounts, contends that even if we disagreed about whether racism is a species of objective reality or constructed, we should make a normative claim and "decide what account or explanation is most efficacious for reasons of good evidence and defensible morals." In "What, Then, Is Racism?" (Chapter 3), Harris discusses numerous conceptions of racism and problems of definition. Racism, on this view, is caused by numerous variables—a "polymorphous agent of death, premature births, shortened lives, starving children, debilitating theft, abusive larceny, degrading insults and insulting stereotypes forcibly imposed." "Necro-Being: An Actuarial Account of Racism" (Chapter 4) depicts racism as a particular form of necro-tragedy, irredeemable misery. Harris offers an account of explanation couched in actuarial description, which offers a view of the "anabsolute," that which is often concealed in volitional, institutional, structural, or racial contract accounts of racism.

Having traveled extensively and having taken account of the various ways in which people are oppressed and immiserated around the globe, Harris has a pointed interest in disclosing unnecessary misery and thinking through potential means of shaping different futures. To this end, Harris has devoted considerable attention to race-based oppression, or racism. Harris begins with a query about whether racism is an inherently controversial concept. Harris sees racial groupings/categorizations as odious social constructions, nefarious tropes (initially) imposed upon a population to facilitate dehumanization or subjugation. (This places Harris at odds with theorists such as Lucius Outlaw and Chike Jeffers.[11]) Nevertheless, Harris argues that a normative dimension is required even if the concept of racism is essentially contested; to ameliorate the real material disparities of racialized populations, racially oppressed populations will have to form communities of resistance.

In "What, Then, Is Racism?" (1999), Harris describes racism as "a polymorphous agent of death," a destroyer of lives and futures. Racism, on this view, denotes a network of interrelated forces and barriers that systematically strip a racialized population of its humanity, typically involving demeaning stereotypes, unspeakable terrors, and humiliation. Racist practices and institutions invariably deny a racialized population ownership of, or access to, material resources, stunting that population's ability to accumulate and transfer assets across generations. Thus, racism is a polymorphous network of forces and barriers that allows groups to empower themselves by not only stigmatizing and dehumanizing a racialized group but also stripping that group of its assets and material resources. Racism thus captures more than race-based ill will or self-delusion.[12] It does not reduce racism to a merely anthropological, economic, or political structural phenomena.[13] It links racism with material disparity and the denial of basic human dignity, explaining how racialized populations are stripped of honor and assets. It captures both the terror and brutality as well as the material losses of racism. It emphasizes the actual destruction of life, and thereby futures, of racialized populations.

In "Necro-Being: An Actuarial Account of Racism" (2018), Harris deploys the notion of *necro-being*.[14] Necro-being denotes "that which makes living a kind of death—life that is simultaneously being robbed of its sheer potential physical being as well as non-being, the unborn." Here, Harris emphasizes the relation between racism and undue ill-health and death; the ability to empirically verify unnecessary perpetuation of shortened lives, physical pain, debilitating diseases, and premature deaths in racialized populations takes center stage. This actuarial account of racism is a minimalist, descriptive approach that evades the excesses and impediments readily evident in competing explanatory models: (1) the misguided use of rational-intentional explanations, (2) the limitations of believing social kind racial realism, and (3) the misguided view that racism exists as one global logical system. Construing racism as necro-being and approaching it with actuarial analyses—statistical models, risk assessment, life expectancy rates, and so on—allow us to imagine a way of morally condemning racism without committing to the view that racism can be reduced to one logical form, without the need for a comprehensive explanation of its causes. It allows us to imagine condemning racism without committing to the categorization of racial kinds as transhistorical, objective social entities.

Honor and Dignity (Reason and Efficacious Agency)

Part III of this volume offers four articles on honor and dignity. In "Autonomy under Duress" (Chapter 5), Harris argues that there is a limit to what a "concept" of autonomy and health can provide, correlatively, and that reasoning methods from principles to action can justify utter misery for citizens of democracies. "Honor: Emasculation and Empowerment" (Chapter 6) considers the importance of a moral community, problems of representative heuristics, and the difficulties of African American males being respected. "Tolerance, Reconciliation and Groups"

(Chapter 7) argues for a radically different set of virtues, inclusive of indignation and tenacity, against the view that tolerance is as an intrinsic virtue. It considers the way tolerance has sustained terror and contributed to misery. In "Dignity and Subjection" (Chapter 8), Harris argues that dignity is a common-denominator value due persons because they are human. The "precondition for the possibility of dignity is efficacious agency and viable aspirations." Dignity is thus antithetical to subjection.

For Harris, moral philosophy is neither simple nor straightforward. Given the amoral universe and his anabsolutist approach to knowledges and categories, Harris is barred from drawing upon universal transcendental moral principles or some set of virtues intrinsic to the entire species. Harris suggests that our moral values and conceptions of virtue are tacitly influenced by intervening background assumptions that inform discursive judgments within a particular epoch, within a particular order of things. These intervening background assumptions are what Foucault terms an "épistémè."[15] Hence, an episteme lays behind our practical rationality, our quotidian moral reasoning, our application of moral principle to action or behavior. Historically, particular epistemai have conditioned and given warrant to awful valuations, egregious stereotypes. Groups of people have been dehumanized, excluded from the human family, rendered unworthy of dignity, incapable of receiving honor—and this would seem *de rigueur*, even rational within this order of things. In some epistemai, some racialized/oppressed groups are metaphorically rendered eunuchs—impotent, debilitated, confounded, unable to assertively shape their own future. But, given the nature of tacit background assumptions, discursive values and biases are seldom scrutinized. (This may motivate Harris's challenge to classical pragmatism.)

Harris suggests that the current episteme in the United States excludes African Americans from the human family. It tacitly denies African Americans full personhood, rendering this population a perpetual subordinate group. Implicit bias and degrading stereotypes pervade interracial interactions—with loan officers, with law enforcement, with doctors, and the like. This, in turn, perpetuates preventable misery, ill-health, and shortened lives—necro-being. In "Autonomy under Duress" (1992), Harris argues that the episteme must be challenged. He argues that we need a new conception of personhood; we need a conception of humanity that affords basic dignity to all human beings. We need a notion that does not presuppose or necessitate a subordinated human population. Harris assumes that rebellious communities or traditions of resistance will have to engage in transvaluation; they will have to assert new value imperatives and discern new virtues. But these values and virtues should be understood as revisable even if considered inalienable. Dignity and reciprocity, while central to Harris's position, can be depicted, bestowed, and practiced in various forms depending on the cultural context. Tenacity and indignation can be understood as pragmatic virtues rather than intrinsic virtues, especially if they bolster confidence in those who have been terrorized, help sustain just feelings of being wronged, or motivate oppressed people to bind together in communities of resistance.

An Ethics of Insurrection; Or, Leaving the Asylum

Part IV features three articles on insurrectionist ethics and virtues of tenacity. "Honor and Insurrection or A Short Story about Why John Brown (with David Walker's Spirit) Was Right and Frederick Douglass (with Benjamin Banneker's Spirit) Was Wrong" (Chapter 9) offers an argument in favor of the character virtues promoted by David Walker (such as tenacity and indignation). Contrary to absolute pacifism, Harris advocates an ethics of insurrection. In "Insurrectionist Ethics: Advocacy, Moral Psychology, and Pragmatism" (Chapter 10), Harris argues that a crucial condition of any adequate philosophy is that it provide the type of intuitions, strategies, and motivations common among insurrectionists, particularly, slave insurrections. If a philosophy's normative dimension cannot tell us that a slave should revolt, it is inadequate. Classical pragmatism fails this test. "Can a Pragmatist Recite a *Preface to a Twenty Volume Suicide Note*? Or Insurrectionist Challenges to Pragmatism—Walker, Child, and Locke" (Chapter 11) suggests that reasoning strategies that assume a well-ordered world are deeply misguided. Yet, Harris contends that a philosophy should provide resources for people conflicted or besieged in a world of paradoxes and dilemmas within which it is impossible to reasonably predict outcomes or where unwanted outcomes are almost guaranteed.

Harrisian philosophy born of struggle supports an ethics of insurrection. There are four basic tenets to the position. First, there is a willingness to defy accepted norms and authority figures when they cause or maintain immiseration. These practitioners of insurrectionist ethics see reason to disrupt relatively stable social orders, if those social orders countenance oppressive practices or necro-being. To this end, they may endorse acts of resistance, which can take various forms, including irreverent outspoken protest, acts of civil disobedience, or physical violence. Second, there is a marshaling of the social and political force of porous and variegated social collectives on behalf of the subjugated. Harris maintains that human cognition relies heavily upon representative heuristics. Representative heuristics is understood as a reasoning strategy crucial to cognition but prone to stereotypes and fallacious inferences. Nevertheless, it is through representative heuristics that social entities are assembled. These particular social entities are not understood as stable categories or natural kinds; rather, these socially constructed groups of resistance are understood as porous, evolving communities with contingent futures. Third, there is a conception of humanity or personhood that recognizes all human beings as members of the moral community or potential bearers of honor, that is, a notion of shared humanity that does not presuppose an innately unredeemable subhuman group. Dignity is thus afforded to all persons. Fourth, there is a valorizing of insurrectionist character traits (e.g., indignation, enmity, tenacity, or irreverence). Harris gives high esteem to the character traits evinced by David Walker and Lydia Maria Child. These insurrectionist character traits make possible the sorts of authoritative voices and postures that will demand the liberation of the oppressed. They make the shaping of alternative futures possible. Harris also suggests that the virtues of compassion, tolerance, and serenity may in fact reinforce immiseration and necro-being within subordinated populations.

In "Insurrectionist Ethics: Advocacy, Moral Psychology, and Pragmatism" (2002) and "Can a Pragmatist Recite a *Preface to a Twenty Volume Suicide Note*? Or Insurrectionist Challenges to Pragmatism—Walker, Child, and Locke" (2018), Harris poses insurrectionist challenges to pragmatism. Concerned with the inherent conservatism in classical pragmatism and its intervening background assumptions, Harris prods us to think about the limitations of the pragmatist orientation. Can pragmatism, in one of its classical iterations, give rise to rebellious voices that seek to challenge the episteme? Can pragmatism offer ameliorative concepts, reasoning strategies, coping mechanisms for those who are immiserated, those who are struggling to survive? Harris argues that an insurrectionist spirit is needed to leave the confines of "the Asylum."[16] But Alain Locke's critical pragmatism, read as a response to a world of paradoxes and dilemmas, is helpful in situating that insurrectionist disposition/spirit.

Bridges to Future Traditions

Part V of this volume contains five articles focusing on community, the building of traditions, and the possibility of shaping the future. In "Universal Human Liberation: Community and Multiculturalism" (Chapter 12), Harris contends that "Universal human liberation is freedom from the very boundaries of the names through which freedom is sought." Liberation from boundaries, whether national, racial, or class, involves destroying and escaping. "Community: What Type of Entity and What Type of Moral Commitment?" (Chapter 13) rejects the existential and phenomenologist use of the concept "the Other" and offers a view of the moral community. Rejecting communities as neat ontological entities, the article considers what type of moral commitments are involved in being a member of a community. "Tradition and Modernity: Panopticons and Barricados" (Chapter 14) depicts the barricado—the fence separating slaves from the ships' crew, allowing the crew to subjugate slaves and forcing slaves to become parasitic and vicious toward one another in order to survive—as a fitting paradigm for both slavery and modernity. Harris argues for cultural reciprocity and against the use of "reason" as a sufficient resource for thinking. In "The Horror of Tradition or How to Burn Babylon and Build Benin While Reading a *Preface to a Twenty Volume Suicide Note*" (Chapter 15), conceptions of tradition are described. The account rejects views of tradition that require norms of regeneration, redemption, vindication, and self-realization to define warranted traditions. The article confronts horrors of traditions but recognizes crucial role they play in establishing norms, drawing boundaries, and setting the stage for forms of cooperation. "Telos and Tradition: Making the Future—Bridges to Future Traditions" (Chapter 16) suggest that, even in an amoral universe (without an ultimate telos or purpose), we can build traditions and set goals for our disparate communities. In a meaningless universe, a meaningful future is possible.

In the nonmoral universe Harris postulates, there is no immanent teleology, no grand narrative, no redemption for necro-tragedy. Modern European Enlightenment thinking is understood as one type of reasoning among many. Human reason is provincial and susceptible to error and fallacious inferences. This is a thoroughly disenchanted world. But we can build communities of trust. We can manufacture traditions and archives for the next generations. Traditions, on this account, are conceived as inherently conservative. And, because of this, traditions are susceptible to comic or horrific manifestations. Hence, Harris suggests that we engage in community and the building of progressive traditions, remaining fully cognizant that we (or those who come later) will likely need to tear down and recreate our traditions as we build. That is, we should engage in progressive traditions that remain keen on transvaluation.

In "Universal Human Liberation: Community and Multiculturalism" (1998), Harris argues that substantive liberatory changes, the potential shaping of the future, always occurs through the struggles of particular communities. Through representative heuristics, social entities can form as socially constructed coalitions and adversarial groups (e.g., workers, feminists, and racialized ethnic groups). These adversarial groups can strive for universal human liberation, all the while fully anticipating the disbanding of these socially constructed adversarial groups. Resistance traditions can be built, which offer affectual and intellectual bulwarks that help make sense of our transnational reality and promote ascendency beyond abjection. In a world replete with unnecessary misery and necro-being, Harris marks ascendency with dignity as a praiseworthy goal and a good reason for creating bridges to the future.

Biographical Note

Leonard Harris was born in Cleveland, Ohio, April 12, 1948, the son of Eugene Harris Sr. and Agnes Chapel Harris. Graduating from Glenville High School in 1966, Harris attended Central State University (Wilberforce, Ohio), receiving a bachelor's degree in English and philosophy in three years. During the 1969–70 academic year, Harris completed a master's degree in philosophy at Miami University (Oxford, Ohio), spurred on by Robert Harris, Rick Momeyer, Martin Benjamin, Carl Hedman, and faculty from his undergraduate school (Central State University), Marian Musgrave and Francis Thomas. The following year, Harris matriculated at Cornell University, where he studied with Allen Wood, David Lyons, Norman Kretzman, Nicholas Sturgeon, and James Turner. Harris received his PhD in philosophy from Cornell in 1974. Harris held teaching positions at Central State University (1973–4), Livingston College, Rutgers University (1974–8), and the University of the District of Columbia (1978–80) before securing a position at Morgan State University (1980–90), where he received tenure and rose the level of Full Professor. In 1991, Harris accepted a position at Purdue University; he has taught philosophy and trained graduate students at Purdue for twenty-nine years.

Harris was arguably the first person to publish a noted anthology of African American philosophy, namely, *Philosophy Born of Struggle* (Kendall Hunt, 1983/2000). By 1993, J. Everet Green (Rockland Community College) and Leonard Harris had established the Philosophy Born of Struggle annual conference, which aims to "bring together philosophers who share an interest in the philosophy of the Black experience and in the public philosophy concerning issues of racial justice and human liberation." Harris has subsequently created the largest video archive (at Purdue University) of philosophers giving lectures in the bent of philosophies born of struggle. Harris founded the Alain L. Locke Association in 1996, which sponsors biannual conferences on the critical pragmatism of Locke. Harris is also known for his numerous contributions to the earnest study of the history of African American philosophers and the revival and exposition of Alain Locke scholarship.

Harris had edited three volumes on Locke: *The Critical Pragmatism of Alain Locke* (1999), *The Philosophy of Alain Locke: Harlem Renaissance and Beyond* (1989), and, coedited with Jacoby A. Carter, *Philosophical Values and World Citizenship* (2010). Harris coedited with Anne S. Waters and Scott Pratt *American Philosophies* (2002) and coauthored with Charles Molesworth a biography of Locke, *Alain L. Locke: Biography of a Philosopher* (2008). He also edited a volume on racism, titled *Racism* (1999).

Harris has lectured at such universities as the following: College for Girls, Jaipur, Panjab University, Chandigarh, India; Osmania University, Hyderabad, India; University of Rajasthan, Jaipur, India; Indian Council of Philosophic Research, Lucknow, India; New Age Girl Postgraduate College, Lucknow, India; Jadavpur University, Kolkata, India; Gauhati University, Assam, India; Jawaharlal Nehru University, New Delhi, India; Zhejiang University, Hangzhou, China; Dianzi University, Hangzhou, China; Zhejiang Yuexiu University of Foreign Languages, Shaoxing, China; Huazhong University of Science and Technology, Wuhan, China; Wuhan University, Wuhan, China; Peking University, Beijing, China; University of KwaZulu Natal, Durban, South Africa; Université Félix Houphouët-Boigny, Abidjan, Côte d'Ivoire; and Université Cheikh Anta Diop, Dakar, Senegal.

In 2014, Harris was awarded the Caribbean Philosophical Association's Frantz Fanon Outstanding Achievements Award. In 2018, he was awarded the Society for the Advancement of American Philosophy's Herbert Schneider Award, which recognizes a career-long achievement of distinguished contributions to the understanding of American philosophy.

Notes

1. The Latin phrase *Philosophia nata ex conatu* translates to "philosophy born from the endeavor/struggle."

2. See Plato, *Phaedo* ln. 64a, in *Plato: Complete Works*, ed. John Cooper. Indianapolis: Hackett, 1997; Michel Montaigne, "That to Philosophize is to Learn to Die," in *The Complete Essays of Montaigne*, trans. Donald Frame (Stanford, CA: Stanford University Press, 1958), 56–68.

3. John Rawls, *A Theory of Justice*, revised edition (Cambridge, MA: Belknap Press, 1999), 4.

4. Cf. Bernard Williams, "The Human Prejudice," in *Philosophy as a Humanistic Discipline* (Princeton, NJ: Princeton University Press, 2006), 137.

5. See Leonard Harris, "Humanism, Reason, and Emotion," in *The Black Humanist Experience: An Alternative to Religion*, ed. Norm R. Allen Jr. (Amherst, NY: Prometheus Books, 2003), 23–30.

6. Edward W. Bylden, *A Vindication of the African Race Being a Brief Examination of the Arguments in Favor of African Inferiority* (Monrovia: G. Killian, 1857); and Edward W. Blyden, *Christianity, Islam and the Negro Race* (New York: Black Classic Press, 1887).

7. The term "telos" denotes an end, goal, or purpose. Thus, "teleology" refers to goal-oriented theories, explanations, and accounts of natural phenomena.

8. Martin Luther King Jr., "Remaining Awake Through a Great Revolution," in *A Testament of Hope*, ed. James W. Washington (New York: HarperCollins, 1986), 277.

9. Cornel West, "Subversive Joy and Revolutionary Patience in Black Christianity," *The Cornel West Reader* (New York: Basic Civitas Books, 1999), 439.

10. It's like (Richard) Rorty, *without* the bourgeois American exceptionalism. See Richard Rorty, "The Contingency of Language," in *Contingency, Irony, and Solidarity* (Cambridge: Cambridge University Press, 1989); Richard Rorty, "Postmodernist Bourgeois Liberalism," in *Objectivity, Relativism, and Truth* (New York: Cambridge University Press, 1991); and Richard Rorty, "Globalization, the Politics of Identity and Social Hope," in *Philosophy and Social Hope* (New York: Penguin, 1999).

11. See: Lucius Outlaw, "Conserve Races? In Defense of W.E.B. Du Bois," *Critical Social Theory in the Interests of Black Folks* (Lanham, MD: Rowman & Littlefield, 2005), 139–62; Lucius Outlaw, "Rehabilitate Racial Whiteness?," in *What White Looks Like*, ed. George Yancy (New York: Routledge, 2004), 159–71; Chike Jeffers, "Du Bois, Appiah, and Outlaw on Racial Identity," in *The Oxford Handbook of Philosophy and Race*, ed. Naomi Zack (Oxford: Oxford University Press, 2017), 204–13; and Chike Jeffers, "The Cultural Theory of Race: Yet Another Look at Du Bois's 'The Conservation of Races'," *Ethics* 123 (April 2013): 403–26.

12. Jorge L. A. Garcia, "The Heart of Racism," in *Racism*, ed. Leonard Harris (Amherst, NY: Humanity Books), 398–434; Lewis Gordon, "Antiblack Racism and Ontology," in *Racism*, ed. Leonard Harris (Amherst, NY: Humanity Books, 1999), 347–55.

13. Pierre L. Van den Berghe, "Ethnicity as Kin Selection: The Biology of Nepotism," in *Racism*, ed. Leonard Harris (Amherst, NY: Humanity Books, 1999), 50–73; Etienne Balibar, "Class Racism," in *Racism*, ed. Leonard Harris (Amherst, NY: Humanity Books, 1999), 201–12; Charles Mills, *The Racial Contract* (Ithaca, NY: Cornell University Press, 1997).

14. Cf. J. Achille Mbembé, "Necropolitics." *Public Culture* 15 (1): 11–40.

15. For more on the term "episteme," see Michel Foucault, *The Archaeology of Knowledge*, trans. A. M. Sheridan Smith (New York: Vintage Books, 2010), 191; Samuel Talcott, "Episteme," in *Understanding Foucault, Understanding Modernism*, ed. David Scott (New York: Bloomsbury, 2017), 241–3.

16. See the closing section of "Can a Pragmatist Recite a *Preface to a Twenty Volume Suicide Note?* Or Insurrectionist Challenges to Pragmatism—Walker, Child, and Locke."

PART I
PROLEGOMENON

CHAPTER 1
WHAT, *THEN*, IS "PHILOSOPHY BORN OF STRUGGLE"?: *PHILOSOPHIA NATA EX CONATU*: (PHILOSOPHY AS, AND SOURCED BY, STRIFE, TENACIOUSNESS, ORGANISMS STRIVING)

In "What, *then*, is 'Philosophy Born of Struggle'? *Philosophia nata ex conatu*," Harris articulatses a distinctively Harrisian conception of philosophy. Harris begins with an account of humanity's future in the universe, defining philosophy as a *philosophia nata ex conatu*—an organic striving for survival, which forefronts life experiences, a pluralverse of voices always underpinned by values. Harris rejects the classical tradition of metaphysical and theocratic definitions of philosophy from Vasubandhu of Purusapura in Gandhara, Priscianus of Lydia, Aristotle of Stagira, and Averroes the Andalusian, whose orientations rely on misconceptions of the self, simultaneity, unity of universality and particularity, and what Harris terms "monsters"—categorically impossible beings. He also rejects the definitions of philosophy offered by more contemporary thinkers: Martin Heidegger, Gilles Deleuze, Felix Guattari, Friedrich Nietzsche, Giorgio Agamben, Paulin Hountondji, V. F. Dordova, and Enrique Dussel. This philosophy born of struggle requires an avowed normative dimension—it emphasizes the negation of necro-being (life as a living death) and reasoning methods warranted as critically pragmatic, contra reasoning methods as sacrosanct tools for pursing abstract universal truth. Harris posits an amoral universe—no arc trending towards justice, no grand narrative, no assured redemption for the tragic, no single teleology for humanity. However, there is an inspiring future. Philosophy, of this Harrisian bent, is inspired by such thinkers as Frederick Douglass, Lydia M. Child, and Alain L. Locke; it recognizes the plurality of peoples, knowledges, and traditions. We can create philosophies and value traditions without monsters fostered by classical traditions.

Let me give you a word of the philosophy of reform. The whole history of the progress of human liberty shows that all concessions yet made to her august claims, have been born of earnest struggle. ...

This struggle may be a moral one, or it may be a physical one, and it may be both moral and physical, but it must be a struggle. Power concedes nothing without a demand. It never did and it never will. ...

> If we ever get free from the oppressions and wrongs heaped upon us, we must pay
> for their removal. We must do this by labor, by suffering, by sacrifice, and if needs
> be, by our lives and the lives of others.
>
> Frederick Douglass, *"If There Is No Struggle, There Is No Progress"* (1857)[1]

Prior to 150 million years from 2019, humanity will have to leave the earth because el Sol (the sun) will deteriorate and make the earth's atmosphere and temperature uninhabitable for humans. Alpha Centauri is the nearest star after the sun to the earth in the Milky Way. It lies roughly 4.37 light-years away. It may take approximately 30,000–100,000 years traveling in a conventional spacecraft at average speeds of current spacecrafts to reach a planet around Alpha Centauri. Traveling 30,000 years or more on a spacecraft will mean the travelers have only themselves to evolve and could at best receive continually antiquated messages from the earth. If two separate populations traveled to different planets near the same star on different spacecrafts, given altered genes, random mutations, unpredictable mating habits, and environmental influences on the separate spacecrafts, they will become radically atypical from the population they left behind and from one another, let alone any traveling populations heading toward other stars.

It will take approximately 2.5 million years traveling near the speed of light to reach Andromeda, the nearest galaxy to the Milky Way. At least 2.5 million years of normal human history will be absolutely lost to the travelers. Because of time dilation, time slows for the travels. At best, the travelers will age only a few years and humanity on the earth will have aged for 2.5 million years when the travelers reach Andromeda, receiving, at best, antiqued messages from populations left behind. If different populations travel at near the speed of light to different regions of the universe, escaping both the Milky Way and Andromeda galaxies, they will evolve in radically different ways with no substantive shared history.

Herein sits the problem: Traveling at near the speed of light or conventional speeds, different populations will always develop and be fundamentally different and not in substantive communications. Humanity's best effort to escape termination, whether traveling near the speed of light or conventional speeds, results in atypical separated generations of travelers always entrapped in their provincialism and radical differences.[2] No conjoined communities, single telos, common species being, or evolutionary tract. Amoebas were not destined to become dinosaurs, let alone one sort of dinosaur. Their history prior to the emergence of dinosaurs from them was no predictor pointing to the future existence of dinosaurs. Provincialism and difference are inescapable; a pluralverse.[3] Historicism is wrong. This is where I begin to philosophize: facing eternal provincialism, given that historicism is wrong, pleased with the challenge of starting anew, and hoping for well-being and continuity. "When we ask, 'What is philosophy?' then we are speaking *about* philosophy. By asking in this way we are obviously taking a stand above and, therefore, outside of philosophy. But the aim of our question is to enter into philosophy, to tarry in it, to conduct ourselves in its manner, that is, to '*philosophize.*'"[4]

Let me begin to tarry by not "taking a stand above and, therefore, outside of philosophy," as if "philosophy" has a meaning as a noun bespeaking a way of life represented by persons who love or pursue wisdom, or as an adjective defined by a depiction of a soul or what is predicated of the self, namely, knower of true knowledge, but tarry. Philosophy, defined as the pursuit of wisdom and wisdom defined by knowledge of grand abstractions, is misguided. Universal forms and structures will not tell us what we need to know about sentient beings; there is no derivation manual from knowing the structure of a contradiction to knowing that kale is better than spinach. The precondition for the possibility of knowledge, and a necessity for well-being, is health. Without health, nothing follows. In a pluralverse it is not the discovery of absolute truth, objective categories, abstract principles, laws, or pristine methods of reasoning, but a making that is the hallmark of philosophies. Philosophies born of struggle, I contend, should include corporeality of health and avowed valuations. Thus, as a constitutive feature of what it is to do philosophy, necro-being (that which makes living a kind of death and the unheralded sorrow of the unborn, necro-tragedy) is taken into account. [5] The very structure of philosophy should provide tools, poetry, imagery, evidential reasoning, and openness about its deep structural values and norms.

I will begin the discussion by describing a definition of philosophy offered by Priscianus of Lydia, a refugee from Athens, Greece (530 CE). His definition provides a conceptual map of how philosophy has been defined across a broad range of languages, cultures and religions. I then distance my view from the type of definition offered by Priscianus of Lydia. The intent is to both philosophize philosophy born of struggle and philosophize an account worthy of its name as a noun token.

I

Priscianus of Lydia was a guest at the Sāsānian court at Seleucia-Ctesiphon of Khosrow II, Khosrow Parvīz—Khosrow the Victorious, King of Persia (reigned 590–628 CE). Priscianus of Lydia was one of seven non-Christians fleeing the reign of the Eastern Roman Emperor Justinian I (527–565 CE) who initiated a purge of non-Christian religions and philosophies. The court was, as Ganeri put it, the "Crossroads Court of Chosroes."[6] The Sāsānian-controlled empire stretched from what is now Syria, across Afghanistan, Pakistan, India, China, Iran, Iraq, Turkey, Croatia, Egypt, Yemen, and Saudi Arabia. At a now historic court meeting, Priscianus answers the question allegedly posed by Chosroes, "What is philosophy?" *Solutionum ad Chosroes*? ("Answers to the Questions of the Persian King Chosroes"). Priscianus of Lydia was thus on the run from the Christians, promoting a way of thinking that was not itself a religion and being sagacious at a royal court before Zoroastrian clergy.

The *Solutionum ad Chosroem* is divided into ten chapters. The first chapter concerns the soul, *io ipso*, philosophy. It begins with an argument in favor of the immortality of the soul, the manner by which the soul is connected to the body, and a claim that the soul is separable from the body but internal to itself. Philosophy is "to lead a pure life without contamination by matter and, at the same time, to acquire insight, without error, into true being."[7] "The point of departure for the demonstration [in the *Solutionum ad Chosroem*] is a definition of philosophy."[8] Philosophical activity is *operatio*.

> That which knows itself, however, must be incorporeal, for self-knowledge means that the object is directed towards itself and, as it were, coincides with itself in the act of knowing. Such an activity is impossible for a corporal being because the body consists always of parts alongside of and outside of each other. Therefore, it can never coincide with itself.[9]

The soul, if it knows itself, must be incorporeal.

The agent that knows, namely, the "self," is going to be ideally synonymous with the thing, the noun, knowledge. That is, the knowing agent is undifferentiated and conjoined with the thing known, not only the correlative traits of the self (virtues), but with its core such that the self and the "truth" are united. This requires what Priscianus needs—a unified self in itself, not outside looking in but an inside that is self-conscious and simultaneously not separated from what it is conscious of. The practice of alethic discrimination whereby there is a unity of the self with its abstraction (i.e., soul), or a self that cultivates itself always moving toward the abstraction—the essence of the noun— requires what cannot exist. Priscianus postulates a categorically impossible being:[10] a corporal self that knows itself but cannot be a self-knowing self (soul). Yet the two are conjoined, simultaneously, separate. What cannot exist is simultaneity that is not simultaneity. This is the wish-dream of phenomenologists.

Priscianus of Lydia brought to his presentation a wealth of references that spanned the ancient world, making his answer not just a well-informed neo-Platonic approach— categorizing the world in terms of parts and wholes, distinctions, defining entities in terms of what the entity does and searching for the ultimate forms—but his answers were in a world that confronted and defined reality in radically different ways.[11]

The essence of a "self" may be described in radically different ways. That is, the singular self may be considered a singular soul eternally individuated (e.g., as in Zoroastrianism, Egyptian Mystery Systems, Christianity), a reincarnated soul prior to its ascension into eternal bliss (e.g., as in Hinduisms' Atman/Brahman/knowable ultimate reality) or a no-self such that individuated "selves" are delusions and ultimate reality is unknowable such that even "reality" is meaningless (e.g., the anatta of Buddhism, mysticism). Competing definitions of the self are *ipso facto* competing definitions of philosophy.[12] This is so when philosophy, as a noun, as in the *Solutionum ad Chosroem*, is simultaneously a thing (*circa*, wisdom, truth, knowledge) and its embodied knower or pursuer, a "self."

II

Priscianus of Lydia presumed that self-knowledge is the source of right practice and right practice is the doing of philosophy. The lack of self-knowledge presumably leads to mistakes. This picture is at odds with quite a few other pictures. A contrary picture is expressed in the text *Abhidharmakośa-Bhāsya* (ca. 380–390) of Vasubandhu (ca. 350–430) from what is now India, Purusapura in Gandhara:[13]

Vasubandhu, rejection of Vatsiputriyuas' thesis that the "self" exists

1. If the person is a real entity, it will be other [*anya*] than the aggregate, because its nature exists [then] on its own [*svabhavatvat*], since each of the aggregates is other than the others; [in that case], either
   i. it will be produced by causes [*karana*] [and then it will not be eternal as you say, and you will have to state its causes]; or else;
   ii. it will be unconditioned (*asamskria*); and this is a non-Buddhist false doctrine (*tirthikadrsiprasangah*); if it were unconditioned, the person is not able to "function [or 'be affected by anything or produce effects']" (*nihprayojanatva*).

   It is thus fruitless to believe that the person is a real entity.
2. But if you admit that the person exists only on the level of a provisional designation, you abandon your doctrine and you side with our opinion.

By "stream" (samtana) he meant the material and mental aggregates (skandhas) succeeding one another without interruption in a life.[14]

Unlike Priscianus of Lydia, Vasubandhu of Purusapura in Gandhara rejected the existence of an individuated self-knower. "The delusion in question involves the idea of ownership. What Vasubandhu claims is that the picture of this turning-in on itself, of the self-attending to its own states—surely the picture at work in Priscian—is itself a delusion." For Vasubandhu, there is no "self" to know; if the individuated self is considered provisional in some sense, it is at best epiphenomenon and transient.

As long as one is prey to that illusion, one is alienated from oneself. For the idea of ownership implies, among other things, that one is in control of one's thoughts, that one is their agent, and can choose to think them or not, choose to acquire, retain or dispose of them at will. This, for Vasubandhu, is dangerous nonsense.

Humans are agents always under the influences of habits, others, feelings, desirers and their material environment. "In sum, philosophy, as a practice of estrangement, is the elimination of a false phenomenology of ownership which leads to delusions about self-control."[15]

In either the case of Priscianus of Lydia or Vasubandhu of Purusapura in Gandhara, the corporal self is not an agent with a mission of terminating human misery; that mission, if it is one, is tributary to its prime telos, namely, unity with, disappearance within, or perpetual cultivation in reverence to a monstrous categorically impossible being.

Philosophy has been a science of making the obvious disappear and that which we know to be hidden, submerged, or overgeneralized, apparent. "Philosophy is a practice of estrangement from the corporeal."[16] We know causation and correlation requires a series of events or states of affairs linked together over time. Too often the conceptual world of philosophy has been a place where murder, rape, and pillage are accidental or fleeting events in a larger scenario where evolution, or some other system portends well-being for all and sundry in some future scenario. Misery is nestled and hidden behind some purposeful condition that assures progress and future well-being. If the scenario considers life, in general it is a bane, the existence of the immiserated in such philosophic worlds is the least meaningful.

There is no transcendental realm where the misery we cause in the past is nonexisting hurt. The hurt cannot be rewarded by future benefits that make the past hurt nonexisting in the past, transcendental phantasmagoric realms of redemptive joy notwithstanding.

The Argentinian Jorge Luis Borges in *Labyrinths*, "Averroes' Search," revealed that Averroes (Abū l-Walīd Muḥammad Ibn ʾAḥmad Ibn Rušd [1126–1198 CE]), an Andalusian Muslim philosopher, could not know what Aristotle (384–322 BCE) of Stagira, Chalkidiki, Greece, meant by tragedy and comedy because neither were defined in the holy book of Islam, the Koran. For Aristotle, comedy originated with the existence of the kosmos, males frolicked around an image of a phallus; while tragedy expressed universal or abstract principles creating fear, pity, and sympathy in the audience. There were simply no concepts Averroes found in the Koran that matched this. Averroes could not translate what Aristotle meant because there was no conceptual basis in the text of authority, the Koran, that matched what Aristotle meant. What Aristotle meant if he were to be an authority had to have an associated meaning. Borges's literary license imagines that "Aristu (Aristotle) gives the name of tragedy to panegyrics and that of comedy to satires and anathemas. Admirable tragedies and comedies abound in the pages of the Koran and in the *mohalacas* of the sanctuary."[17] Averroes may not have had a good copy of Aristotle's *Poetics*, but he certainly had enough Aristotelian resources to know that tragedy and comedy had an enigmatic meaning when that meaning had to be consonant with the Koran.

There is no reason to believe that every conceptual world is, or should be, reducible to some "true" universality. Analogously, every misery and community of the subjugated has individual character; individual hurt, irreducible. Common traits are certainly informative, and simultaneously, so too are unique particular features. Correlatively, translations may be unspeakable. There may be no neat analogues between any two texts or any two forms of misery. Averroes could not translate Aristotle. An approach of equiprimordiality, rather than considering original texts sacrosanct, affords translations valuable status.[18] Averroes should have appreciated Aristotle's meaning of comedy and tragedy and the Koran's meaning, separately. These are reasons for why we should abandon "philosophy" as rhetoric, dialectic reasoning, and analytic clarifications as definitive of what sort of reasoning should be accorded warrant.

No one reasoning method or translation manual is assured to give us the appropriate inferences of the sort required by Averroes:

As the Law emphasizes the knowledge of God and His creation by inference, to learn the kinds of inference, their conditions and that which distinguishes philosophy from dialectic and exhortation from syllogism. This is impossible unless one possesses knowledge beforehand of the various kinds of reasoning and learns to distinguish between reasoning and what is not reasoning. This cannot be done except one knows its different parts, that is, the different kinds of premises.[19]

This is the same sort of problem al-Ghazālī (ca. 1056–1111), from Tabarân-Tûs, Iran, the great Muslim philosopher who ushered in Sufism and rejected the Aristotelian influenced tradition of *falsafa* addressed in *The Incoherence of the Philosophers* (*Tahâfut al-falâsifa*):

The philosophers have agreed, just as the Mu'tazila have agreed, on the impossibility of affirming knowledge, power, and will for the First Principle ... it is not permissible to affirm attributes that are additional to His essence in the way it is allowable in our case for our knowledge and power to constitute a description of ourselves that is additional to our essence.[20]

Anthropocentric attributes, like frolicking or having a will leaves impossible beings less than omnipotent or transcendental; their transcendence must in some way be established as separate from the limitations of human reality. Zeus, the Hellenic God, in effect, cannot turn out to be just a great seducer of women like Leda that he seduced while in the form of a Swan; the Asantehene, God incarnate among some Asante of Ghana, cannot be just a mortal. al-Ghazālī was right. There is an incommensurability and non-translatability between pure abstract being attributes and anthropocentric traits. Analogously, there is an incommensurability between the self and the soul.

If reason is the sole evidential route to any form of warranted belief, there can be no guttural emotions, leaps of faith, or normative choices on this route. The preponderance of evidence suggests that slave revolts or slave attacks on their masters fail; every woman and man engaged in such activities is acting against, on reflection, reasoned judgment, empirical evidence of probable success and utilitarian considerations. Almost no slave could have empirical evidence at their disposal to make such evaluations in any event. Nonetheless, they should revolt; they should escape.

Priscianus avoided resting the definition of the soul on an attachment to, or feature of, corporal reality. Corporal reality requires the physics of death—motion, energy, mass, space, and time. The universe is a cauldron of constant death. Every corporal entity is destined to die. Energy, mass, and space admit of no virtues. They are the layers upon which the death of all entities rest. Chaos exists. Humans are violent killers of all other species and of their own kind—violence workers (e.g., armed overseers, police, guards, soldiers, assassins)—are always highly respected and fairly well-paid overlords of slaves, serfs, peasants, plebeians, wage workers, prisoners, and soldiers. Priscianus was wise not to define philosophy as an activity that comes natural to humanity; otherwise, philosophical life would be implicated in the viciousness of human reality. Abstractions could not then be as pristine as Priscianus wanted. I, however, will sink into the mud.

III

I contend, as a normative claim, that genuine philosophy is *Philosophia nata ex conatu* (philosophy as, and sourced by, strife, tenaciousness, organisms striving), *ex intellectualis certamen cum sit* (the result of intellectual struggle with real corporal existence), always inclusive of undue duress—it is sentient beings that can be afflicted, and thereby no concept of form, dialectic rationality, phenomenology, sagacious insight, confessions, testimonial, or witnessing is warranted without the expressed inclusion of the afflicted seen as such. The universe is purposeless, and hooves are no better than feet, but undue misery is not just a consequence of evolution and maladaptation, Malthusian necessity, class conflicts, or limitations and benefits made possible by geographic conditions but also malevolent intentions and structures, desires, objectives, social group conflict, institutions, identities, communities, and misguided values. The killing of Tasmanians, all, can be described as a feature of their evolution, which involved ineffective adaptation to disease and mismanagement of the confrontation with the advanced weapons of invaders and poor communication techniques. It can also be described as Christian-led genocide in pursuit of wealth. Both descriptions are inescapably value-laden. There are choices to be made that are not simple algorithms, calculations and formal derivatives from grand abstractions, true pictures of objective material conditions, eternal principles, forms, or structures. Simple algorithms, for example, can be used effectively by the ruling or working class, saint or sinner.[21] Evidential claims should be subject to discourse—whether dialectic, analytic, dialogic, discursive, rationalist, intuitive, abductive, rhetorical, syllogistic, pragmatic, utilitarian, or instrumental. The revaluation, transvaluation, and transposition of reasoning methods and philosophies, always entrapped to some degree in unknowable values and norms, can be nonetheless discussed as openly as possible and choices made. One of those choices involves our view of the "self" and its constitutive character as an agent.

The unity theory of virtue is wrong as well as the unity theory of the self. The unity theory of virtue is any theory of virtue that contends virtues such as piety or courage is a good and if genuinely possessed by an individual that virtue pervades their being and influences in appropriate ways relevant attitudes and acts. Virtues on this view are *intestinius*, constitutive of the agent. There are no such beings. Persons are always influenced by a myriad of variables, some internal to their character and some external influences on their behavior. The brightness of lights in a room influences everyone's choices. Vasubandhu of Purusapura in Gandhara was right. Humans are agents with habits, feelings, and desires, all subject to a myriad of influences.

Alain Locke (1885–1954), the African American philosopher and author of critical pragmatist, put it succinctly:

There is nothing in the universe that consists of virtues, principles, ideas, thoughts, feeling, and beliefs as material features that themselves reproduce themselves, see themselves, know themselves to be memories, beliefs, virtues or principles. [W]hether we call the logical feelings "feelings of relation" with [William] James, or of "certainty and doubt" with [Gerhard] Kruger, or of "acceptance and rejection" with numerous others, after [Franz] Brentano, the author of this distinction originally, or what not. True and false, whatever else they express in addition, at least register, in the most abstract possible way, the positive or the negative character of such logical attitudes, regarding them formally by implication as all claiming to be based on an identical qualitative and universally applicable distinction. This we know to be a "normative fiction," whatever may be our opinion about its function and justification.[22]

Dead matter, molecules, and atoms do not carry personal memories and virtue traits. The virtues of piety, benevolence, altruism, humility, obedience, compassion and patience nor the virtues of tenacity, enmity, indignation, resentment, guile or audacity are qualities. In addition, virtues are not entities created or sustained by forms, structures nor attributes such as coherence or consistency.[23] Virtues embodied by travelers are always decidable, revisable and embodied. Products of creation, not discovery; not instances of an abstraction but there content makes what can count as an abstraction. Reasons for why we should live one way or another or act one way or another are not 'reasons' etched in the wily world of transcendental codes hiding in plain view or with the help of a derivation manual taking our minds step by step from grand principles or tacit contracts to loving cats rather than dogs.

There are no unified "selves" that are simple cognitive machines, possessed of a singular consciousness. Racists, murderers, executioners, police, and assassins need not violate any intrinsically held knowledge that their victims are persons and should not suffer undue harm; they can be very kind to their neighbors in the morning, burn Jews and Communists or use machetes and hack to death pregnant Tutsi women in the evening, and respect their wives and husbands at night. The Akan Ghanaian Kwasi Wiredu's defense of evidential rationalism noted not only that reason can be fallible but also that vigilance is a feature of what it is to be reasonable.[24] It is a stanch bulwark against arbitrary assumptions. However, his picture is a bit too rosy. Efficacious vigilance and evidential reason have served colonizers, photographers that insulted the people they were photographing, racists historians, physicians that used Africans for experiments, pedophiles, serial rapists, dictators, and authors of war machines well. There is nothing in the nature of reason, understood as logic, abductive reasoning, and avoidance of fallacies, that assure defensible beliefs, let alone a mode of thinking that guides behavior.

Unified selves are the ideal monsters of delusional philosophers romanticizing their male and female heroes and sheroes of pure perfection, monsters we are to imitate and always necessarily fail to be sufficient carbon copies. This is not just the wish-dream of Edward W. Blyden, the Pan-African nationalist who imagined a world where each race could live according to their true racial personalities in harmony.[25] The world that has to exist to make the unified "self" possible is one where the "self" is individuated and its constituent traits form a model being.[26] This world assures that all humanity for *ad infinitum* share at least one trait: lack. Always lack. The model is rigged. The *philosophia* upon which it is based is an entrapment. When a philosophy is grounded in this rigged *philosophia* and contends that the self is a fiction and then tells us that the only real beings are a pristine kind definitive of civilization, for example, the racist Immanuel Kant (1724–1804), then the *philosophia* upon which it was founded has reemerged—it must find its monster.[27] Defining the source of knowledge as created by imagination, intuition, mysterious faculties of epistemic insight, or emotions created by local experiences does not warrant the positing of pristine beings void of ambiguity and uncertain claims who know universal truth. One way to see the entrapment is to consider a philosophy that appreciates the importance of listening to the voices of the immiserated but is nonetheless committed to an ontology of absolute agency and unified selves.

Philosophy born of struggle should always make possible epistemologies, metaphysics, and aesthetics that include the excluded. The excluded can only be tangential, additive, or an ontologically exceptional aggregate when what it is to do philosophy is to presuppose the supremacy of abstract ideal nothingness, relations, principles, no self, no being, beyond being, a categorically impossible being of the shifting knower and stable known, the known and the knower as synonymously corporeal, the transcendental unknowable known or transfigured self-known noncorporeal being. These are conceptual locations making impossible real beings; the voices of real people cannot be heard because they are, *o ipso*i, outside, under, lower, other, abject, entrapped in their bane temporality, particularity, singularity, encrusted in their inferior race, trapped in their gender gowns, and forged in the wrong religion, nation, language, or culture. Analogous to Priscianus's definition of philosophy, "to lead a pure life without contamination by matter and, at the same time, to acquire insight, without error, into true being," the Japanese philosopher Kitaro Nishida searched in the same vein for epistemic truth. In the process he expressed tremendous care for the well-being of humanity; however, he ends the search with the valorization of nothingness. We disappear. Certainly, care for the immiserated can be expressed by anyone, despite their philosophy. The Tibetan Dalai Lama, Lhamo Dondrub (1935–) of the Gelug school of Buddhism, considered a living Buddha of compassion, a reincarnation of the bodhisattva Chenrezig who renounced Nirvana in order to help mankind, is arguably the world's most compassionate living representative of the least of us. There is no necessity that using a Priscianus type of understanding of philosophy will generate malevolence; atheist and religionist can be equally concerned with human well-being. The point here is that real people should not be derivative of what it is to do philosophy but constitutive. They should be constitutive in a way that recognizes discordance rather than unity of the self, soul, or Being. As Alain Locke put it, "All philosophies, it seems to me, are in ultimate derivation philosophies of life and not of abstract, disembodied 'objective' reality; products of time, place and situation, and thus systems of timed history rather than timeless eternity."[28] Given that there are no *a priori* normative truths, and no normative truths are derivative from abstractions by mystical, magical, or pristine reasoning methods, cast into an abyss, I choose a philosophy born of struggle that structures a doing that requires we exist and matter. We do not disappear.

There are various ways that populations and people disappear when philosophy is defined in the way of Priscianus, the neo-Platonist.

IV

In Plato's utopian city-state of Kallipolis, "philosophers [must] become kings ... or those now called kings [must] ... genuinely and adequately philosophize."[29] Philosophers, in an admittedly simplified description of Plato's views, are to be the rulers and guardians because they have a passion for truth, wisdom, and knowledge of the Good. Plato assumes that actions and choices by philosophers are directed by wisdom arrived at through reason. In his view, the best possible world would be the result of a knowledge regime under the guidance of aristocratic philosophers because they are motivated by truth, wisdom, and the Good. These are Plato's dangerous delusions.

If Plato had access to modern research on how people actually think and behave, he might have rejected the idea of individual authors as the font of right reason and wisdom that gives them due authority over others. Reason is rarely the motivating force for actions. The heuristics of normal reasoning incline people—including philosophers—to be provincial and to imagine that their provincialism is actually universal.[30] Possibly, if Plato considered his lack of freedom when he was a slave, he might have denounced his loyalty to a supremacist knowledge regime and to aristocratic philosopher kings because they function as masters over troves of degraded slaves.[31] With an appreciation of how the structure of communities influences philosophies and of how misguided persons who believe they possess certain truth can be, Plato might have accepted Alain Locke's pluralist theory of value approach as found in *When Peoples Meet*, placing his hopes in a democracy of pluralist philosophers.

Whoever defines the "knowledge of knowledge" owns and controls what can be thought of as authorized knowledge. The persons that define the "knowledge of knowledge" also decide which authors are considered worthy of study and, *mutatis mutandis*, which individuals profit from publishing the books of authors considered authorial and historically canonical. Networks of authors and publishers define, decide, and promote particular schools of thought. In so doing, they help create and sustain traditions that thereby form well-defined markets. The persons credentialed by ruling educational institutions are, in effect, the agents for a regime of prescribed knowledge and well-defined markets.

Books that are not under copyright protection, including ancient texts, are important resources for maintaining traditions. Such readily available books make it possible for generation after generation of scholars to study the same books, comment on the same authors, and thereby utilize the same categories of thought to form controversies within narrow matrices of ideas. A given collection of ideas—for example, those ideas regarding vitalism or monotheism—form schools of thought such as phenomenology or Idries

Abutahir Shah's sufism. The schools that are considered worthy of study are determined by credentialed scholars. Rarely are authors such as Immanuel Kant (1724–1804) or Karl Marx (1818–1883) defined simply as instantiations of "Europeans," but it is common to read the works of Japanese, African, or Chinese authors as paradigmatic of "Japanese," "African," or "Chinese" kinds of persons. The empiricism, value pluralism, determinism, or vitalism of Japanese, African, or Chinese authors is reduced to nothing more than an expression of their ethnic, national, or racial kind. They are less worthy of study from the standpoint of the regime of knowledge (ruling educational institutions) that consider Kant and Marx to be real agents of wisdom.

Africa, for example, consists of several large language communities, including Arabic, Portuguese, French, and English, and traditional language groups such as Xhosa, Zulu, Akan, and Amharic. "A philosopher who writes in a language other than English (or, to a lesser but ever decreasing extent, French or German) has very little chance of achieving global recognition unless by some miracle he or she has the opportunity of being translated, whereas the most prominent US philosophers become *eo ipso* prominent world philosophers."[32] One of the saddest commentaries on the colonial heritage is that the former colonized tend to grant high honors, in the form of financial rewards, titles, and awards for books to scholars of the former colonizer. Of fifteen honored lecturers at the Centre for Logic, Epistemology and the History of Science at Universidade Estadual De Campinas, Brazil, by 2007, thirteen were from Europe and two from Latin America. It would be difficult to find a university in Europe that spends its money or time to honor any philosopher from Latin America unless it were a special ethnic award. "In the age of Japanese colonialism of Korea, people said that philosophy means Dekansho, that means [René] Descartes [1596-1650], Kant and [Johanna] Schopenhauer [1766–1838]."[33] In 2008, Hyung Chul Kim "estimate[d] that on average, the ratio of western to oriental philosophy [faculty] in Korean universities [was] about 7:3."[34] In addition, "many philosophers in different Asian countries, like Cambodia, Thailand, or Japan [were asked] to name ten philosophers from their culture, and in many countries they [couldn't] think of anyone[;] they [could] only name European philosophers."[35] The language of authorship and publishers with an English-speaking market are, at the very least, unintentionally complicit in the regime of knowledge that promotes single-language provincialism.

V

If I read Priscianus as giving preeminence to the self as a knower, a being but not the "Being," he anticipates the German philosopher Martin Heidegger's (1889-1976) way of escaping provincialism in *What Is Philosophy?* Given that the history of the term "philosophy" has changed and that different definitions will not yield a single meaning because definitions are genuinely different, Heidegger insists that the answer to the question "What is philosophy?" requires engaging in doing philosophy: "But in truth, we are considering the future nature of philosophy." Not, according to Heidegger, just its past history of different definitions. Rather, "We are trying to listen to the voice of Being … What we come across is only this—various turnings of thinking."[36] Doubt, despair, fear, anxiety, hope, and confidence obscure contemporary "turnings of thinking" preventing direct access to "Being." "We are introduced to and become acquainted with what philosophy is only when we learn how, in what manner, it is."[37] And "Being" includes *ousia* (Beingness), Plato's idea, and *energeia* of Aristotle (actuality). "The Being of being rests on this Beingness." True knowledge, logos, and wisdom reside within Being. Being is an irreducible aggregate, a phenomenon made from individuals but constituting a different kind of entity not identical to one of its members.[38]

Heidegger's philosophical answer, unfortunately, recommends doing philosophy in a way that moves toward, even if we do not reach, an impossible phenomenological entity. Being of being. Escape. We are off, if we follow Heidegger, on a search leading nowhere. A "Being" synonymous with an undifferentiated sphere of knowledge. An abstraction that has no agency, no influence on our daily lives, accessible at best to a privileged sort of person that could not achieve unity with "Being" and return to establish its presence. Analogously, Chenrezig renounced Nirvana. He did not go because he knew he could not come back; there would be no Chenrezig to enlighten humankind.

We are encouraged to revere a monster, Being of being. The whole that is separate from its parts, an asymmetry whereby an individual can conceivably ascend to Being but Being is irreducible to any individual. The well-fare of beings in this world is, at best, derivative. Accidental. Life itself considered a bane stepping stone. The learned, the wise, these are persons due our highest esteem. The monster is pristine. Let us make the monster disappear. The telos is already here.

Humans, for phenomenologists, exist in a condition of lack, if not in the Buddhist sense of life as inherently suffering the trauma of desirer and need or in the view of Christians that consider humanity inheriting a horrible sin, a condition nonetheless in need of redemption. Contrary to this view of humanity as bane, corporality is what we have, and it should not be afflicted with undue suffering—including being burdened with a self-concept of inextricable lack. The philosophizing that begins with humanity as entrapped in a condition of eternal lack is not born of the human drama to overcome limitations and undue pain but of excursions in search of the categorically impossible and revering all sorts of "Being" as the assemblage of one or another abstract, absolute, or transcendental monster. Monsters, however, are not the only impediment to escaping the trope of philosophy defined as synonymous with an inquiry into true being.

The project for Francophones Gilles Deleuze and Felix Guattari's *What Is Philosophy?* is to relate singularities to one another, not, however, in search of a universal or absolute similarity. Creation of concepts is always immanent, and they simultaneously provide stability. "The conceptual persona and the plane of immanence presuppose each other."[39] Philosophy is concept creation, not as a definition or a description of what it is philosophers do, but as an engagement in the sort of activity associated with what it is that philosophers do. "Deleuze's analytic 'concept' introduces *the pure form of time* into concepts, in the form of what he calls "continuous variation" or "pure variability."[40] "The aim," he says, "is not to rediscover the eternal or the universal, but to find the conditions under which something new is produced (*creativeness*)."[41] All folds differ, and this difference is primary; however, they resemble each other in the concept. Concepts exist in a flow; a sort of historical continuum of ideas created by persons engaged in avoiding chaos and evaluating their reality. As Deleuze contends, "it is not at all a matter of bringing things together under one and the same concept [universals], but rather of relating each concept to the variables that determine its mutations [singularities]." [42] Incessant becoming is always interrupted, stability exists, if only delusional, but variation continues. Similar to the Germanic Friedrich Nietzsche,

> Let us still give special consideration to the formation of concepts. Every word immediately becomes a concept, inasmuch as it is not intended to serve as a reminder of the unique and wholly individualized original experience to which it owes its birth, but must at the same time fit innumerable, more or less similar cases—which means, strictly speaking, never equal-in other words, a lot of unequal cases.

Given this picture of concepts, Nietzsche ends with "What, then, is truth? A mobile army of metaphors, metonyms, and anthropomorphisms."[43] Trafficked women brutalized by a veritable army of men who are rarely punished, raped boys by women, victims of misandry, humiliated underpaid workers—they are not linguistic formations; 71 percent of sex-trafficked victims around the world are women and girls, and 29 percent are men and boys—they are real persons.[44] Whether in Estonia, Latvia, or Lithuania, the subject disappears in the "category," the statistical numeration, the abstraction, or may be subsumed under such heading as "trafficked victims." Their bodies are not analogs of words. And descriptions of their misery are not identical with their misery nor sufficiently conveyed by language. What we should count, see, and believe as truth are hardly reducible to concepts well codified as metaphors, metonyms, and anthropomorphisms.[45]

Deleuze's picture transforms philosophy into a game. It is navel gazing. Deleuze's approach does not direct us to search for or reveal true being; in fact, there may be no true being. However, we are left with no imperatives as a function of what "philosophy" means and no structure intrinsic to its meaning that directs us along any given line of concepts other than simply gazing at the barren picture of endless varieties of concepts. Listening to Deleuze or Nietzsche may help us escape philosophy as an inquiry into the truth, self, the soul, or being, but we escape into an endless abyss, or in Nietzsche's case, a trope about pursuing empowerment for those of us fortunate enough not be terrorized by the Lord's Resistance Army (noted for kidnapping children and making them soldiers, hacking off limbs, and offering the sayings of their prophet), drug lords in Southern France, or official police. Leaving a philosophical world that is committed to a search for unmitigated truth through a singular reasoning method, and arguably Deleuze and Nietzsche left that world, we are still faced with the task of building a viable world knowing that our definitions have limitations and that the self is an historical agent. Noting that there are metaphors, metonyms, and anthropomorphisms, or that

concepts create new ways of seeing (percepts) and new ways of feeling (affects), is not enough. Given this world of sentient cognition and behavior, now the solely dominant species on the planet, we are stuck with the metaphysics of nouns. What, then, "should philosophy mean" is not adequately answered by navel gazing.

Alain Locke considered the need to avowedly assert norms when he considered the conflict between value anarchy (i.e., value relativism) and monism (i.e., principle considered absolutely true). The first implies that all values are equally arbitrary and no value, norms included, can be given warranted preference; its contrary for Locke, monism, implied that there was only one warranted set of norms. Locke rejected monism but insisted that "in de-throning our absolutes, we must take care not to exile our imperatives, for after all, we live by them."[46] Consequently, Locke ventured the need for the normative values of tolerance, reciprocity and respect. Analogously, what are the imperatives for the meaning of a term deeply entrenched in our lexicon of being—philosophy? What should it be born of? These questions are arguably due an answer, *circa*, if not an imperative, most certainly a warranted preference.

Giorgio Agamben's *What Is Philosophy?* moves from an analysis of concepts, phonemes, letters, syllables, and words that come together to make inquiries into being, soul, and the self in pursuit of universal answers to what are impossible or inexhaustible questions in philosophical writing. Characteristic of Agamben, he leaves open ways of living in community and seeking answers to questions.[47] "What is philosophy?" is, consequently, for Agamben, vexing questions.

Paulin Hountondji, the philosopher from the People's Republic of Benin, in *African Philosophy: Myth & Reality* defends a definition of philosophy as the use of abductive rationalist reasoning and critiques ethnophilosophy (popular beliefs redescribed as if consciously formulated as philosophic principles and conversely considered the basis of a people's sagacious views). Hountondji insists on the need for African experiences and the actual history of philosophy to be taken into account.[48] Philosophies are defined by their reasoning methods, evaluative foundational assumptions, and argument designs by individuals but not depictions of popular cultural beliefs or the expressions of sagacious pronouncements. The sort of discourse developed by Henry Odera Oruka, the Kenyan, in *Sage Philosophy: Indigenous Thinkers and Modern Debate on African Philosophy*, is considered ethnophilosophy and thereby rejected as genuine philosophy.[49]

Both Hountondji's and Agamben's philosophies are arguably not entrapped in defining philosophy as a way of life in pursuit of a singular self or limited to an analysis of concepts or indefensible normative ideations. However, given that meanings change over time, there may be no family of definitions of philosophy that provide a coherent meaning. In a world of vexing questions or a world where we suffer the delusion that all questions have neat answers and make sense, we are nonetheless confronted with the same task: building a viable world, inclusive of "philosophy" as itself a noun (in the manner of Priscianus) or noun token (in the manner of value relativist such as Locke).

Karl Marx, the German, was right in his brief note entitled *Theses on Feuerbach* (1845): "The philosophers have so far *interpreted* the world. The point, however, is to *change* it."[50] However, Marx, like a good philosopher, having long since completed his doctoral disputation *The Difference between the Democritean and Epicurean Philosophy of Nature* in 1814, ventures to explain the world. The explanation has been a catalyst substantively responsible for helping to change the world. That is, his explanation of capitalism has been so profound that it must be credited with helping to provide the concepts, percepts, reasoning methods, poetic terms, and motivations that have been a resource for generations of successful activists. Deleuze's Guattari's *Capitalism and Schizophrenia* (1972) introduces concepts such as code, lines of flight and body without organs to capture the character of capitalism in the world that comes after the world Marx pictured. Their explanation, however, does not rely on picturing irreconcilable contradictions of material class interests being likely resolved in the establishment of universal human interest such that workers produce in freedom and become self-conscious producers of themselves.[51] The world is explained by Marx in terms of the forces of contradictory class interest, which are likely resolved in a way that propels change in a direction of progress because the immediate interest of the working class and universal human interest are identical: simultaneity. The resolution of contradictions is concrete; contractions of interest get resolved in this world analogous to logical contradictions and contraries getting resolved, that is, the logos of human interest and history. This is the simultaneity of the particular and the universal, the abstract and the concrete, the patterns of the past producing or causing achievement of an imagined telos. Analog between the form (dialectic, contradiction) and the concrete (conflicting class interests). There has to be some logos, dialectic, resolution of contradictions; some abstract concrete real, some law doing the work. That is what is real. We are here as conduits of ontological social kings (classes)—agents of the real—representatives of a kind. Otherwise, we disappear.

VI

If I read Priscianus as appreciating the need for the self to cultivate itself and is thereby changing over time, he anticipated what the Spanish philosopher José Ortega y Gasset discussed in "Philosophy Contracts and Expands. The Drama of the Generations. The Imperial Triumph of Physics. Pragmatism," namely, that what issues philosophers address change over time as the self changes.[52] It would seem that with this understanding of the self the self does not disappear.

Ortega y Gasset considered what is perennial in what philosophers do and it turns out that for him what is perennial involves the categories of life, "The first category of our lives is 'to find oneself', 'to understand oneself', 'to be transparent',... it is not merely the self which is the subject, but also the world."[53] The self, extended to mean what and how to live, involves considering individuated being as simultaneously a being identical to all persons. This, for Ortega y Gasset, has the glow of eternality: "Whether we like it or not, our life is in its very essence futurism."[54] Ortega y Gasset, in concert with Heidegger, believed that we are constantly deciding what "'we' are going to be."[55] That is, each individual is simultaneously, even if unintentionally, helping to decide what humanity will be in the future by deciding what to do and be at each moment of the present.[56] The "self" is individuated, and like Priscianus's self, it provides a basis for the emergence of a wholly different, irreducible, being, namely, the "whole" of humanity. The categorically impossible being, that is, humanity, is imagined having an agency of its own, or rather, its agency is variously described according to which authority rules the definition and tells us what it is to be "human." The ethereal self of Priscianus is analogous to the anthropocentric self in Ortega y Gasset and Heidegger because both require the same *a priori* condition for their meaning of philosophy: a coherent kind, indivisible in its essence—a self, its virtues capable of being *intestinīus*, definitive, stable, inside and shaping moral emotions.

Priscianus of Lydia and Vasubandhu of Purusapura in Gandhara assume that individuation becomes aggregated, parts join the whole; however, the whole is indivisible and irreducible to any particular part; the whole is an ontological Being that either is postulated as existing (Priscianus) or is no longer speakable (Vasubandhu). False. Social aggregates are anabsolute. That is, social groups can appear solid and well defined, like classes, races or ethnic groups, but they are not well defined in reality.[57] They are immanently objective. They can be conceived as ontological for purposes of explanation, but they are not objectively stable kinds; they are not material objects. Abstractions are misleading, including conceptions of the self as a kind of coherent abstract being.

The philosopher's job has been to convince us that the thing in itself, Being, the self, the class dialectic, the social role of "something" is explainable in such a way that it sounds like a depiction of a galaxy whereby the galaxy is moving under its own laws without any stars. It is the laws governing the galaxy that matters. That's what is real. Being, the self or the soul, as such. Human traits such as piety, compassion, justice, or courage become synonymous, simultaneous, identical, subsumed, and, with a little philosophical magic, eternal and universal. The African American assassinated pacifist and civil rights leader Martin L. King Jr. (1929–1968) contended in his "Remaining Awake through a Great Revolution" (1968), having witnessed scores of beatings of peaceful marchers protesting racial segregation, "The arc of the moral universe is long, but it bends towards justice."[58] He was just wrong. There is no arc. Those beaten may well have died before the end of *de jure* racial segregation, those living rarely received its benefits, and protesters often were harmed. There is no assured justice for those suffering the agony of injustice, let alone a moral universe that would include all sentient beings everywhere receiving justice. Racial segregation, *de jure*, eventually came to an end in the United States, but that consequence had no correlation to an inclination for justice. Cases of contemporary types of fairness between African Americans and white Americans are not a replacement for the types of unfairness visited on past generations of African Americans by white Americans. My father was denied approval to be an electrician because he was told no Negroes were qualified, despite his performance on a standardized test that outperformed white applicants. Nothing that happens to me will replace his hurt, feeling of depression, powerlessness, income not acquired, and loss of business opportunity. I have never taken a standardized test for admission to anything or for any certification of a skill. Insidious and material harms existed. Sorrow songs are just that, songs that express lament, hurt, and irredeemable agony. But most philosophers do not tarry here. Instead of seeing the misery of past generations, the thought of misery disappears and is replaced by a law, rule, or picture of the "moral universe," as if there was such a thing, making "justice" happen. Good philosophical magic. The tragic exists, that is, no future for those that suffered, and their progeny may not be repaired or rewarded as a function of their suffering—total loss, necro-tragedy.

Philosophers have often postulated the existence of groups as theoretical or ontological entities—ethnic group, class, race, or conditions such as patriarchism, racism, or authoritarianism. Then they forget that the postulates, their categorization, were tools and things that are not solid states. They forget that there are real people that make the linguistic mark, the concept, make sense. It is easy to move from a realism about material objects and stable patterns to a realism of immanent objects and unstable patterns. Let us imagine a corporation without any people and think of it like a galaxy without any stars; it acts but no one agent does the acting. The trick is to follow in the vein of Priscianus of Lydia's way of doing philosophy, live as if we were the embodiment of the corporation, or, in philosophic terms, Being, soul or humanity, irreducible to any individual or star. It is the laws that matter in such a picture; correlatively, institutional patterns, tendencies, repeated outcomes, unintentional outcomes, or collective behavior forming social entities can be well used to explain aggregate collective behavior. However, groupings constantly change, boundaries are never stable, and groups come in and out of existence. That's why they are anabsolute. Another aspect of the philosopher's job has been to make us believe that our provincial condition is just an instantiation of something else (institutional pattern, etc.), thereby the brutality of authorities and suffering undeserved is explained away. The self disappears. This too easily occurs in the search for a logic in human history, that is, a simultaneity of logos and being, a force, ontological kind, or a mission driving toward or exhibiting an already realized telos.

VII

According to the noted Argentinian champion of liberation, rooted in Latin American struggles for liberation, Enrique Dussel (1934–), it is arguable that "philosophy of liberation is rising from the periphery, from the oppressed, from the shadow that the light of Being has not been able to illumine."[59] It is to discover the facts of domination, whether the grouping is "The people," the dominated, the massacred Amerindian, the Black slave, the Asiatic of the opium wars, the Jew of the concentration camps, the woman as sexual object, the child under ideological manipulation. Persons are always in need of l'estime de soi (self-esteem). "Liberation, the act of the oppressed by which they express or realize themselves … is to leave the prison (deny the denial) and affirm the history that was anterior and exterior to the prison."[60] Persons and groups are agents and the oppressed are invested with interests, motivations, and are compelled by their condition and their intestinius character toward freedom.

I have avoided a marriage of hermeneutical phenomenology and Marxism in the spirit of Dussel's *Philosophy of Liberation* in which persons are understood in terms of a "self versus other" dichotomy. One reason of importance is that I begin from a concept of the person as a dialogical and interrelated social being. Thus, characterizations of "self" and "other" already misconstrues the human. The "self" is always, already, encoded in the "other." Juxtaposing oppositionality as a matter of "self" and "other" conceptually negates the reality of commonality. Dussel seems to recognize this problem. He emphasizes the importance of respecting unique social locations and struggle. "The people," in effect, do not exist as a coherent singular voice nor as a chorus of voices that we can be sure that a given philosophy expresses their voices. However, "The ultimate intention is to justify the struggle of victims, of the oppressed, for their liberation: reason is only 'the cunning of life.'"[61] Dussel returns to the base: committed to a fairly strict "either-or" positionality of "self–other" and a liberation that requires a directing social formation. "The method of philosophy of liberation knows that politics—the politics of the exploited—is the first philosophy [philosophy of the praxis of liberation] because politics is the center of ethics as metaphysics (ethico-metaphysical exteriority is concretized in a privileged way in politics; thus surpassing mere ontology."[62] There is a hierarchy of valuable forms of action, politics at the top even without a singular social agent, and reason stays encoded in agency, hiding behind, the rule of which our corporal being is both the expression and its agent; it is the real.

Let me be earnest: There is no one "philosophy born of struggle," no one representative aggregated social kind that embodies as its sole interest universal human liberation and well-being, no one voice that is driven by its nature or its location to speak for all, that is, one voice of the people, women, men, or humanity.

Humanity is not an organism simply trying to survive in a sea of other organisms whereby nothing is actually decidable. If humanity were, its history of cannibalism, ethnocide, genocide, rape, and pedophilia have all been justified or at least understandable. Current and future forms of social terror should be praised because they could be quite beneficial, utilitarian, instrumental, and productive for the purpose of species survival and empowerment—so long as past hurts and genocides do not count. But this is tortured reasoning. The organ of our being is not reducible to a single or singular kind of driving imperative. This is another wish dream of every inheritor of the Aristotelian or Vasubandhu type of *philosophia* legacy—materialist, evolutionist, sagacious, phenomenologist, or existentialist. There must be some Being, some determinate, some ontology representing a categorical kind where parts disappear into the whole or the parts exist in relative isolation as individuated pure kinds, some imperative like brute survival or actualized universal human interest, some self or nonself that is the historical agent, or some aggregated ontology that is the embodiment of surety, progress, realization, freedom from something, and ascension to liberation, liberty, or the best possible being without substantive remainder.

The organ of our being, arguably, involves a continual struggle with hard-won moments of well-deserved accomplishments. We can have hope without entrapment in undue delusions, progress without the pretense of having arrived at a location beyond provincialism, traditions without the pretense that traditions are purely inherited and we have no role in inventing our sacred rituals, and insurrectionist ethics without the feeling that our actions are all justified by an algorithm of pure reason; we can acknowledge the use of representative heuristic in the formation of identities without portending that our social identities are instantiation of objective forms awaiting realization, admit our fallibility and remain excellent scientists, and pursue "our" eternity in a finite universe.

Philosophies arguably welled in a form of philosophy born of struggle speak with unique voices, not with one voice, picture of reality, or standpoint from one set of moral emotions. Exceptionalism is always dangerous. It involves categorizing people and attributing ubiquitous fonts of truth to them. Exceptionalism may also involve treating an individual or type of person as the source of true revelations beneficial to all, for example, a sadhu in Rishikesh, India, by the waters of the holy Ganges River; Pope Francis, the Catholic at the Vatican, Rome, or the Kumari Devi of Kathmandu, Nepal, the living Hindu Goddess of Durga, with Taleju, an unseen force, font of revelatory insight and healing. Which community of experience and conception of truth and religious belief system is to be given preeminence? I will focus on the former sorts of exceptionalism. The voices of African American women and men, for example, may be very different from the voices of Dalit women and men.[63] The religions of the Native Americans as understood by, for example, V. F. Cordova in *How It Is: The Native American Philosophy* and those of the Aboriginal people of Australia may well share an interest in preserving their religious heritages and defending themselves against discrimination; however, there is no reason to assume that the phantasmagoric of each faith is a basis for exceptionalism of the sort that justifies a hierarchy of kinds.[64] That is, each faith should not provide the believers an ethnic pristine self that leaves other people inferior or lesser. A provincial condition is at best a temporary surcease. Arguably, all existing identities will be transvalued: mother into parent, Yugoslavian into European, and so on. The future is not likely to be a simple picture of the present. Locations matter, but they are hardly sacrosanct sources of pristine unambiguous knowledge regimes. An inclusive preservationist approach requires the rejection of absolutism. It is dangerous to pick a sample of the voices considered representative of a kind—the sample necessarily excludes voices that, on reflection, may have been included, *ad infinitum*. This is one reason why philosophy born of struggle is not one philosophical orientation that portends to voice, see, express, and encompass. Magobo More's, Chielozona Eze's, Angela Davis's, Rozenna Maart's, Tommy Curry's, and Richard Jones's razor sharp revealing of race, class, cultural traditions, and women and men's agency within the context of their philosophy born of struggle are not identical depictions of agency or normativity.[65] Their philosophies born of struggle pictures what any one focus would miss. We are not absolved from rigorous consideration and evaluation of each account, just assuming an *a priori* pristine position of observation and revelation. The problems of exceptionalism are not restricted to issues of provincialism and categorization.

Exceptionalism too often involves treating social groups as surreal entities, for example, the people, the natives, the Negro, or the working class. Conversely, individuals are surreal unless understood in terms of their bonds, links, and similarities that form groups. And neither the suffering nor the accomplishments of groups require treating them as stable well-defined historical agents, aggregates, or objective forces. Anabsolutes cannot be made into singular undifferentiated, unchanging, material agents. Language can help with clarifications, distinctions, and definitions, and provide caveats intended to help avoid overgeneralizations, confirmation bias, conjunction fallacy, conservation bias, availability heuristics, or surrogation, but language cannot fix this.[66] Nor can tricky reasoning strategies escape being reasoning strategies; reasoning itself, its very being, is inherently engineered cognition; reason cannot step outside itself; reasoning cannot fix this. Any form of cognition requires overgeneralized categories, some form of stereotypes, representative heuristics and exceptionalist thinking to explain or describe patterns. Evidential, dialectic, revelatory, pragmatic, epideictic, or discursive reason is an escape route into a realm of the real. At best we are faced with perpetual corrections and improved computations, not an end-state of self-known knowers of the real.

If philosophy is no longer a singularity, a well-bounded noun, a search for simultaneity of self and alt-self, the place to find simultaneity of the universal and the particular, philosophy's boundary would be thereby sufficiently porous and unchartered. Philosophy should provide tools of poetry, imagery, evidential reasoning, inclusion of real people, and norms incommensurable with philosophy as a science. Philosophy is not an algorithm but a walkway. The philosophical theology of Wallace Thurman, Anthony Neal, James Cone, Eboni Marshall-Thurman, or Kelly Brown Douglas may well be confronted by the atheism/agnosticism of Norm Allen, Alice Walker, Angela Davis, or John McClendon; the existentialism of Jane and Lewis Gordon is substantively concerned with human liberation but at odds on numerous grounds with the Marxism of Nkolo Foé and Stephan C. Ferguson, both equally concerned with human liberation. Maria Lugones's revelation of what counts as oppression as a voice from a defined feminist standpoint or Sylvia Wynter's conception of "being human" can be compatible, and at points incompatible, with Tommy Curry's focus on misandry, yet each allows us to see what has often been unseen and consider ways of being (not Being). Neither Judith Green's nor Dwayne Tunstall's form of pragmatism is neatly compatible with that of Alain Locke; however, the community of pragmatists is enriched by their voices. The life of the mind is enriched by conceptions of tradition and modernity homed in the world of Gauhati, India, by Sauraypran Goswami, or Buenos Aires, Argentina, by Ricardo Malinandi. [67] David Walker, Lydia M. Child, Maria W. Stewart, and Henry D. Thoreau did not speak with one voice, other than the voices of afflicted, even if sometimes entrapped in the ligaments of Priscianus's ideal of philosophy.[68]

Philosophy, considered a science like chemistry or physics and promising an epistemic logos route to pristine wisdom, should share the same space as alchemy and divination as a cure to HIV. Let us dispense with the pursuits of Priscianus of Lydia, Aristotle, Vasubandhu of Purusapura in Gandhara, and Averroes and their derivatives nestled in worlds that make reality disappear. We cannot escape provincialism. But we should try. We cannot escape the use of cognitive categories or some variegates of nouns and monsters. But we should try. The trying is affirming the value of life; it is a good worth having, a good we want more of; and in the trying it is possible to live without the egregious monsters of simultaneity and create increased forms of well-being. At the very least, health, the precondition for the possibility of our being. So, let us applaud our hard-earned progress and take a stand, here, inside of corporal reality born of earnest struggle.[69]

"And who will join this standing up

....

we are the ones we have been waiting for."[70]

("Poem for South African Women." Commemoration of the forty thousand women and children who, on August 9, 1956, presented themselves in bodily protest against the "dompass" in the capital of apartheid. June Jordan)

Notes

1. Paragraphs in Section IV are excerpts from "Philosophy of Philosophy: Race, Nation and Religion," *Graduate Journal of Philosophy* 35 (1–2): 1–12, esp. 1–2, 2–3, and 5.
   The full quote from Douglass ("If There Is No Struggle, There Is No Progress," July 1857):

   > Let me give you a word of the philosophy of reform. The whole history of the progress of human liberty shows that all concessions yet made to her august claims, have been born of earnest struggle. The conflict has been exciting, agitating, all-absorbing, and for the time being, putting all other tumults to silence. It must do this or it does nothing. If there is no struggle there is no progress. Those who profess to favor freedom and yet depreciate agitation, are men who want crops without plowing up the ground, they want rain without thunder and lightning. They want the ocean without the awful roar of its many waters …

   > This struggle may be a moral one, or it may be a physical one, and it may be both moral and physical, but it must be a struggle. Power concedes nothing without a demand. It never did and it never will. Find out just what any people will quietly submit to and you have found out the exact measure of injustice and wrong which will be imposed upon them, and these will continue till they are resisted with either words or blows, or with both. The limits of tyrants are prescribed by the endurance of those whom they oppress. In the light of these ideas, Negroes will be hunted at the North, and held and flogged at the South so long as they submit to those devilish outrages, and make no resistance, either moral or physical. Men may not get all they pay for in this world; but they must certainly pay for all they get. If we ever get free from the oppressions and wrongs heaped upon us, we must pay for their removal. We must do this by labor, by suffering, by sacrifice, and if needs be, by our lives and the lives of others.

2. The anticipation of human demise in a galactic catastrophe assumes that humanity will not be destroyed by an asteroid slamming into the earth or any other celestial sphere we inhabit, or that humanity everywhere will not be destroyed by an incurable infectious decease, catastrophic climate change, or that nuclear warfare causes the extinction of humanity.

3. The term "pluralverse" comes from William James, *A Pluralistic Universe* (Lincoln, NE: University of Nebraska Press, [1909] 1996). However, I mean to it to point to only the human pluralverse, not the phantasmagoric of transcendental mythology that James treats as if it could be real. See Christopher Hitchens, *God Is Not Great: How Religion Spoils Everything* (New York: Hachette Book Group, 2007); and Alain Locke's view of the fluidity of reality in

"Values and Imperatives," in *The Philosophy of Alain Locke: Harlem Renaissance and Beyond*, ed. Leonard Harris (Philadelphia, PA: Temple University Press, 1989), 31–50; and his doctoral dissertation, *The Problem of Classification in the Theory of Value* (Cambridge, MA: Harvard University Press, 1918).

4. Martin Heidegger, *What Is Philosophy?*, trans. William Kluback and J. T. Wilde (Tübingen: Twayne, [1955] 1958), 21.

5. See, for the unborn, Dorothy Roberts, *Killing the Black Body: Race, Reproduction and the Meaning of Liberty* (New York: Vintage Books, 1997); Stephanie E. Jones-Rogers, *They Were Her Property: White Women as Slave Owners in the American South* (New Haven, CT: Yale University Press, 2019); Leonard Harris, "Necro-Being: An Actuarial Account of Racism," *Res Philosophia* 95 (2, April 2018): 273–302.

6. Jonardon Ganeri, "What Is Philosophy? A Cross-Cultural Conversation in the Crossroads Court of Chosroes," *Harvard Review of Philosophy* 24 (2017): 1–8.

7. Steel, Carlos G., *The Changing Self: A Study on the The Soul in Later Neoplatonism: Iamblichus, Damacius and Priscianus* (Brussels: Paleis Der Academien-Hertogsstraat I, 1978), 15.

8. Ibid., 121–54.

9. Ibid., 15.

10. See Leonard Harris, "The Horror of Tradition or How to Burn Babylon and Build Benin While Reading a *Preface to a Twenty Volume Suicide Note*," *Philosophical Forum* 24 (1–3, Fall–Spring 1992–3): 94–119.

11. Priscianus Lydus. "*Solutiones eorum de quibus dubitavit Chosroes Persarum rex*," in *Supplementum Aristotelicum* I, 2, ed. I. Bywater (Berlin: George Reimer, 1886), 39–104; Victoria Erhart, "The Context and Contents of Priscianus of Lydia's Solutionum ad Chosroem," *Medieval Philosophy* (1998): https://www.bu.edu/wcp/Papers/Medi/MediErha.htm. F. A. JI. De Haas, "Priscian of Lydia and Pseudo-Simplicius on the Soul," *The Cambridge History of Philosophy in Late Antiquity*, vol. 2 (Cambridge: Cambridge University Press, 2011), 756–64. Priscian mentions: Plato's *Timaeus*, *Phaedo*, and *Phaedrus*; Aristotle's *Politics*, *Physics*, *On the Heavens*, *Generation and Corruption*, *On Dreams*, and *On Prophesying by Dreams*; Hippocrates, Strabo's *Geography*, Ptolemy's *Almagest*, Iamblichus' *On the Soul* and the works of Plotinus and Proclus. The list is a catalog of Neoplatonic works on cosmology and natural history.

12. Ganeri, "What Is Philosophy?," 2.

13. *Abhidharmakośa-Bhāsya of Vasubandhu*, trans. Louis de La Vallée Poussin, vol. 4 (Delhi, India: Motilal Banarsidass, 2012).

14. Ibid., 2526.

15. Ganeri, "What Is Philosophy?," 3.

16. Ibid., 2.

17. Jorge Luis Borges, *Labyrinths* (New York: New Direction Books, [1962] 2007), 155.

18. See Ibrahim Marazka, "Translation beyond Empire: On the Equiprimordiality of Original and Translation," *Word and Text* 4 (2): 84–97.

19. Mohammad Jamil-ur Rehman, *The Philosophy and Theology of Averroes* (Baroda, India: A.G. Widgery, 1921), 16.

20. Abū Ḥāmid Muḥammad ibn Muḥammad al-Ghazālī, *The Incoherence of the Philosophers*, trans. Michael E. Marmura (Provo, UT: Brigham Young University Press, 1997), 97.

21. See for an account of the need for value imperatives from the standpoint of value relativism Locke, "Values and Imperatives," 31–50. See as an example of how algorithms negate freedom Yuval Noah Harari, *Homo Deus: A Brief History of Tomorrow* (New York: HarperCollins, 2007).

22. Locke, *The Problem of Classification in the Theory of Value*, 243. Also see Ernest Mason, "Deconstruction in the Philosophy of Alain Locke," *Transactions of the Charles S. Peirce Society: A Quarterly Journal in American Philosophy* 24 (1): 95–6.

23. See for an example of error theory and moral principles distinct from physical reality: Locke, "Values and Imperatives," 34–50.

24. See Kwasi Wiredu, "Knowledge, Truth and Fallibility," in *The Concept of Knowledge: The Ankara Seminar*, ed. Ioanna Kucuradi and Robert S. Chohen (Dordrecht, The Netherlands: Kluwer Academic, 1995), 127–48.

25. See Edward W. Blyden, *Christianity, Islam and the Negro Race* (London: W. B. Whittingham, [1887] 1994).

26. See Leonard Harris, "Can a Pragmatist Recite a *Preface to a Twenty Volume Suicide Note?* Or Insurrectionist Challenges to Pragmatism—Walker, Child, and Locke," *Pluralist* 13 (1, Spring 2018): 1–25; Leonard Harris, "Walker: Naturalism and Liberation," *Transactions of the Charles S. Peirce Society: A Quarterly Journal in American Philosophy* 49 (1): 93–111.

27. See Julie K. Ward and Tommy L. Lott (eds.), *Philosophers on Race: Critical Essays* (London: Blackwell, 2002).

28. Locke, "Values and Imperatives," 31. Also see Cleavis Headley, "Locke's Value and Imperatives: Values as Normative Fictions and as Regulative Ideals," unpublished, presented at the Alain Locke Conference & Insurrectionist Ethics Roundtable, Department of Philosophy, Howard University, April 12, 2019.

29. Plato, *Republic*, trans. Allan Bloom (New York: Basic Books, 1991), 473D.

30. See Hilary Kornblith, *Naturalizing Epistemology* (Cambridge: MIT Press, 1985).

31. See Page DuBois, "The Slave Plato," in *Slaves and Other Objects* (Chicago, IL: University of Chicago Press, 2003), 153–68.

32. William L. McBride, "The Global Role of US Philosophy," *Diogenes* 51 (3): 94. See also William L. McBride, "Consumerist Cultural Hegemony within a Cosmopolitan Order—Why Not?," in *From Yugoslav Praxis to Global Pathos: Anti-Hegemonic Post-Post Marxist Essay* (New York: Rowman & Littlefield, 2001), 177–89.

33. Julian Baggini, "The Mind of Korea," *Philosophers' Magazine* 43 (4): 85.

34. Ibid.

35. Julian Baggini, "Uniting Nations?," *Philosophers' Magazine* 43 (4): 97.

36. Heidegger, *What Is Philosophy?*, 90–1.

37. Ibid., 91.

38. Ibid., 55.

39. Gilles Deleuze and Felix Guattari, *What Is Philosophy?*, trans. Hugh Tomlinson and Graham Burchill (New York: Verso, 1996), 7.

40. Ibid., 67.

41. Daniel Smith, "The Nature of Concepts," *Parallax* 18 (1, February 2012): 67 (italics in original).

42. Ibid., 67. Gilles Deleuze and Claire Parnet, *Dialogues*, trans. Hugh Tomlinson and Barbara Habberjam (New York: Columbia University Press, 1987), vii.

43. Friedrich Nietzsche, "On Truth and Lies in an Extra-Moral Sense," in *The Portable Nietzsche*, ed. and trans. Walter Kaufman (New York: Penguin Books, 1976), 46–7.

44. www.stopthetraffik.org. Also see Tommy Curry, *The Man-Not: Race, Class, Genre, and the Dilemmas of Black Manhood* (Philadelphia, PA: Temple University Press, 2017).

45. Tommy J. Curry, Ebony A. Utley, "She Touched Me: Five Snapshots of Adult Sexual Violations of Black Boys," *Kennedy Institute of Ethics Journal* 28 (2): 205–41.

46. Locke, "Values and Imperatives," 34. See for the difference between Locke and William James regarding absolutes, realism and values: Neil W. Williams, "Absolutism, Relativism and Anarchy: Alain Locke and William James on Value Pluralism," *Transactions of the Charles S. Peirce Society: A Quarterly Journal in American Philosophy* 53 (3): 400–24; Leonard Harris, "Conundrum of Cosmopolitanism and Race: The Great Debate between Alain Locke and William James," in *Philosophical Values and World Citizenship*, ed. Jacoby A. Carter and L. Harris (New York: Lexington Books, 2010), 56–77.

47. Giorgio Agamben, *What Is Philosophy?* (Stanford, CA: Stanford University Press, 2018).

48. Paulin Hountondji, *Philosophy African: Myth & Reality* (Bloomington: Indiana University Press, 1983). On ethnophilosophy and sages, see Henry Odera Oruka, *Sage Philosophy: Indigenous Thinkers and Modern Debate on African Philosophy* (Nairobi: African Center for Technological Studies [ACTS] Press, 1991); Gail Presbey, "Who Counts as a Sage? Problems in the Further Implementation of Sage Philosophy," *Quest: Philosophical Discussions* 11 (1–2): 53–65.

49. Hountondji revised his view of philosophy and has expressed deep appreciation for ethnophilosophy. See for the debates Tsenay Serequeberhan, *African Philosophy* (London: Paragon House, 1991). Franziska Dübgen and Stefan Skupien, *Paulin Hountondji: African Philosophy as Critical Universalism* (New York: Palgrave Macmillian, 2019).

50. Karl Marx, "Theses on Feuerbach" (1845), in *Ludwig Feuerbach and the End of Classical German Philosophy*, ed. Friedrich Engels (Peking: Foreign Languages Press, 1976), 65 (italics in original).

51. Gilles Deleuze and Félix Guattari, *Anti-Œdipus*, vol. 1 of *Capitalism and Schizophrenia*, trans. Robert Hurley, Mark Seem, and Helen R. Lane (London: Continuum, [1972] 2004; first published, Paris: Les Editions de Minuit); Gilles Deleuze and Félix Guattari, *A Thousand Plateaus*, vol. 2 of *Capitalism and Schizophrenia*, trans. Brian Massumi (London: Continuum, [1980] 2004; first published, Paris: Les Editions de Minuit).

52. José Ortega y Gasset, "Philosophy Contracts and Expands. The Drama of the Generations. The Imperial Triumph of Physics. Pragmatism," in *What Is Philosophy?*, trans. Mildred Adams (New York: W.W. Norton, 1964), 29–46.

53. Ibid., 236.

54. Ibid., 247.

55. Heidegger, *What Is Philosophy?*, 88–9.

56. Gasset, *What Is Philosophy?*, 249.

57. I read the term "anabsolute" in an article by Ishmael Reed, just after I read his novel *Yellow Back Radio Broke Down* (Champaign, IL: Dalkey Archive Press, 1969). A major theme depicted by the story is the struggle between a pluralistic African-American culture and an intolerant pluralist white culture.

58. Martin L. King Jr., "Remaining Awake Through a Great Revolution," in *A Testament of Hope: The Essential Writings and Speeches of Martin L. King, Jr.*, ed. James M. Washington (San Francisco: HarperSanFrancisco, [1968] 1991), 268–78.

59. Enrique Dussel, *Philosophy of Liberation*, trans. Aquilina Martinez and Christine Morkovsky (New York: Orbis Books, 1980), 14.

60. Ibid., 62.

61. Ibid., 56.

62. Enrique Dussel, *Ethics of Liberation*, trans. Eduardo Mendieta, C. P. Bustillo, Y. Angulo and N. Maldonado-Torres (Durham, NC: Duke University Press, 2013), 170.

63. See Sharmila Rege, "Dalit Women Talk Differently: A Critique of 'Difference' and Towards a Dalit Feminist Standpoint Position," *Economic and Political Weekly* (October 31, 1998): 39–46. Also see Achille Mbembe, *A Critique of Black Reason*, trans. Laurent Dubois (Durham, NC: Duke University Press, 2017).

64. Preservationism and universality: V. F. Cordova, *How It Is: The Native American Philosophy of V. F. Cordova*, ed. Kathleen Dean Moore, Ted Jojal, Amber Lacy, and Linda Hogan (Tucson: University of Arizona Press, 2007).

65. Magobo P. More, *Looking Through Philosophy in Black* (New York: Rowman & Littlefield, 2018); Chielozona Eze, *Ethics and Human Rights in Anglophone African Women's Literature: Feminist Empathy* (New York: Palgrave Macmillian, 2016); Interview with Angela Davis, February 25, 2015, https://www.youtube.com/watch?v=q6Mfgl-5dd4; Rozena Maart, "Philosophy Born of Massacres. Marikana, the Theatre of Cruelty: The Killing of the 'Kaffir,'" *Acta Academia* 46 (4): 1–28; Curry, Tommy J. and Leonard Harris (eds.), *Radical Philosophy Review* 18 (1), includes guest editors' introduction: Curry, Tommy J., and Leonard Harris, "Philosophy Born of Struggle: Thinking through Black Philosophical Organizations as Viable Schools of Thought," 1–10; Curry, Tommy J. and Richard Jones (eds.), *Radical Philosophy Review* 17 (1), includes guest editors' Introduction: Curry, Tommy J., and Richard A. Jones. "The Black Radical Tradition as an Inspiration for Organizing Themes of Radical Philosophy," 1–16.

66. See for a discussion of this problem: Leonard Harris, "The Concept of Racism: An Essentially Contested Concept?," *Centennial Review* 42 (2, Spring 1998): 217–32.

67. Anthony S. Neal, *Howard Thurman's Philosophical Mysticism: Love against Fragmentation* (Lanham, MD: Rowman & Littlefield, 2019); James Cone, *Black Theology and Black Power* (New York: Harper & Row, 1969); Eboni Marshall-Turman, *Toward a Womanist Ethic of Incarnation: Black Bodies, the Black Church, and the Council of Chalcedon* (New York: Palgrave Macmillan, 2013); Kelly Brown Douglas, *Stand Your Ground: Black Bodies and the Justice of God* (New York: Orbis Books, 2015); Norm R. Allen Jr., *Black Humanist Experience: An Alternative to Religion* (New York: Prometheus, 2003); Angela Y. Davis, *Are Prisons Obsolete?* (New York: Seven Stores Press, 2003); John McClendon III, *Philosophy of Religion and the African American Experience: Conversations with My Christian Friends* (Boston, MA: Brill-Rodopi, 2017); Lewis R. Gordon, *Existentia Africana* (New York: Routledge, 2000); Nkolo Foé, "Pragmatism as a Vision of the World and as a Method: A Philosophical Examination of the Challenges Presented to Contemporary Social Research by Subjective Idealism," in *Readings in Methodology: African Perspectives*, ed. Jean-Bernard Ouedraogo and Carlos Cardoso (Dakar: CODESRIA, 2011), 3–35; Sauravpran Goswami (ed.), *Dimensions of Philosophy: Tradition and Modernity* (Gauhati, India: Publication Cell, Department of Philosophy, Gauhati University, 2010); Ricardo Maliandi, *Etica: conceptos y problemas*, 4th ed. (Buenos Aires: Biblos, 2009); Stephen C. Ferguson, *Philosophy of African American Studies: Nothing Left of Blackness* (New York: Palgrave Macmillian, 2015); Maria Lugones, *Pilgrimages/Peregrinajes: Theorizing Coalition Against Multiple Oppressions (Feminist Constructions)* (Lanham, MD: Rowman & Littlefield, 2003); Sylvia Wynter, Katherine McKittrick (eds.), *On Being Human as Praxis* (Durham, NC: Duke University Press, 2015); Curry, *The Man-Not*; Judith M. Green, *Deep Democracy: Community, Diversity,*

and Transformation (Lanham, MD: Rowman & Littlefield, 1999); Dwayne A. Tunstall, *Doing Philosophy Personally: Thinking about Metaphysics, Theism, and Antiblack Racism* (New York: Fordham University Press, 2013).

68. See Lee McBride, "Symposium on Insurrectionist Ethics," *Transactions of the C. S. Peirce Society* 49 (1, Winter 2013): 27–111.

69. One way to consider the importance of "struggle" is consider its use in various conceptual schemes: see the history of the Philosophy Born of Struggle Association, conference programs, and archives at http://bit.ly/2dhplBT and an interview at the Centre for Critical Research on Race and Identity, University of KwaZulu Natal, June 30, 2016, https://www.youtube.com/watch?v=GGFpFzqr3aY.

   See for example George Yancy, "African-American philosophy: Through the lens of socio-existential struggle," *Philosophy and Social Criticism*, 37(5)551–574. Murray, Jessica, "She had agony written all over her face: representations of rape in the work of Rozena Maart," *Journal of Literary Studies*, Dec. 2011, Vol.27(4), p.36. Stephen C. Ferguson, John McClendon, *African American Philosophers and Philosophy: An Introduction to the History, Concepts and Contemporary Issues*, London: Bloomsbury Publishing, 2019. Also see Jacoby A. Carter's account of Alain Locke in *African American Contributions to the America's Culture*, New York: Palgrave Macmillian, 2016.

70. June Jordan (2005), "Poem for South African Women" (c. 1980), in *Directed by Desire: The Collected Poems of June Jordan*, ed. Jan Heller Levi and Sara Miles (Port Townsend, WA: Copper Canyon Press), 279.

PART II
IMMISERATION AND RACISM (OPPRESSION AS NECRO-BEING)

CHAPTER 2
THE CONCEPT OF RACISM: AN ESSENTIALLY CONTESTED CONCEPT? (1998)

In "The Concept of Racism: An Essentially Contested Concept?" Harris considers what counts as essentially contested and thereby entrapped in undecidable competing meanings. Harris gives an orienting taxonomy of competing conceptions of racism, contending that racism, even if essentially contested, requires a decision regarding what it means. Notably, Harris favors constructivist explanations of race. Races, on this account, are odious social constructions, misleading tropes—not ontologically "real" wholes. Yet, whether or not we conceive of races as contrived or real, "the assets, statuses, and ownership patterns created by the history of racial oppressions leaves raciated populations with [real, objective] disadvantages ... There is a need for racially excluded and exploited populations to acquire the real material resources for sustaining flourishing lives."

Racism can be understood, metaphorically, as a noun if it names a particular group of circumstances, beliefs, and effects. Metaphorically, as a noun, racism is like a "thing" of social reality.[1] A number of authors, for example, Alexander Crummell, Jacques Barzun, Franz Boas, Ruth Benedict, Michael Banton, Barry Gross, Sidney Hook, Thomas Sowell, and numerous others, define racism as a thing of social reality. They offer definitions of racism with fairly clear boundaries, although they offer different definitions. Michael Banton, for example, in "The Concept of Racism" expands on Ruth Benedict's famous 1940 definition in *Race and Racism*.[2] According to Benedict, "racism is the dogma that one ethnic group is condemned by nature to congenital superiority." Banton defines racism as "the doctrine that a man's behavior is determined by stable inherited characters deriving from separate racial stocks having distinctive attributes and usually considered to stand to one another in relations of superiority and inferiority."[3] Banton uses a race-relations paradigm and, contrary to Benedict, argues that people often appeal to ideas of racial superiority without beliefs about biologies.

Approaches that consider racism as a noun—naming a thing of social reality—I will generally categorize as "objective realism." Objective realism, for my purposes, is the view that (1) social entities are objectively knowable (true relatively independent of subjective judgments) and (2) terms such as "race" or "racism" can be fairly determinant, referring to specific "real" entities or enduring social arrangements. Objective realism supports the idea that "the group is just as real as the person."[4] Objective realists are endurantists. Endurantists believe that objects exist wholly present at a single moment.

Comte, Herder, and Spencer, for example, understood groups in this fashion. Durkheim, when he treats groups as empirically verifiable entities, defines groups as social facts. Social facts are real ontological beings, although Durkheim never completely divorced groups from their rootedness in individual consciousness.[5]

One way to see why the belief that social entities exist and exist objectively is so important to understanding racism is by considering what happens when "races" are not considered objective entities. Racialism is the belief that "races," as objective biological kinds, exist. An objective realist can believe that racialism is a racist belief if "races" do not exist, that is, if the term "race" does not refer, pick out, or stand for an objective feature of persons. However, if "race" does refer to an objective feature of persons, a belief in the existence of races is not thereby inherently racist. The difference is strictly dependent on the ontological status of races and on how reasonable, rather than prejudicial, it is to believe that races exist. In addition, metaphysicians might argue that races invariably have, or are associated with, ontological essences.

A radically opposing approach to objective realism proceeds as if racism is a type of predicate or floating attribute. This approach is constructivist. What is real for a constructivist is very different than for an objectivist.[6]

Racism, as a metaphorical predicate or floating attribute, describes a wide range of circumstances, beliefs, and effects. Racism for a constructivist does not name an object of social reality. There are "racisms" on this approach because all such terms are necessarily indeterminate, visceral, or essentially contested. That is, all terms that purport to pick out or refer to an ontologically stable, well defined, enduring objective social entity such as a race, class, or nation actually do not name social things but a phenomenon of predication; predications best describe the vicissitude of valuations we apply to mentally constructed groups.[7] An example of this view, which emphasizes differences in historical circumstances and thereby the impossibility of a singular definition of racism, is Stuart Hall's view that

> Racism is always historically specific. Though it may draw on the cultural traces deposited by previous historical phases, it always takes on specific forms. It arises out of present—not past—conditions. Its effects are specific to the present organization of society, to the present unfolding of its dynamic political and cultural processes—not simply its repressed past.[8]

On another account based on the same idea, Paul Gilroy contends that

> there is no racism in general and consequently there can be no general theory of race relations or race and politics ... a perspective that emphasizes the need to deal with racisms rather than a single ahistorical racism also implicitly attacks the fashionable over identification of race and ethnicity with tradition.[9]

As Anthony Appiah argues in "Racisms," "much of what we say about it [racism] is, on the face of it, inconsistent."[10] The inconsistencies, not particularly unusual for most concepts, are particularly appalling for Appiah. A more empirically warranted and rational approach for Appiah is one that embraces the idea of racisms and rejects all forms of racialism.

Racism, for constructivists, is shaped, caused, and defined by beliefs about race. The belief that biological racial groups are coterminous with the way we define social groups as races, for constructivists, is often considered an important cause and definition of racism. Amy Gutmann and Anthony Appiah's *Color Conscious*, Ellis Cose's *Color-Blind*, and Jim Sleeper's *Liberal Racism* each consider the belief in the existence of races, and its associated practices, an important feature of racism.[11] In another orientation to this issue, critical race theorists reject the idea that there is a single right interpretation of texts, a universal truth embedded in text awaiting discovery, and the notion that texts, words, or laws have a singular meaning.[12] Critical race theory holds that concepts are indeterminate and normally subject to competing interpretations. Thus, moral choices must be made that are not contingent on the unfiltered meaning of texts, rules, precedents, and laws. Consequently, racism as an indeterminate or an essentially contested concept depicts visceral circumstances and effects.

There are numerous approaches and positions fitting between the poles of objectivism and constructivism. A person might believe, for example, that racism is like a noun because it refers to a circumstance best understood as well defined. However, this person might also believe that there are no objective entities and certainly no races. Max Weber and numerous structuralists may be interpreted as holding this view. Another person might believe that racism is like a predicate and that races do not exist, yet believe that objective entities exist and that such entities as classes or nations are best understood as nouns. Such a person might be a classical Marxist or a social Darwinist. In addition, some authors might reject the idea that racialism is true for logical and empirical reasons. Such authors may believe in the existence of objective entities but simply deny that "race" is such an entity.

John Dewey is noted for rejecting the idea that social entities exist as well as the idea that there is an unbridgeable dichotomy between objective reality and subjective constructions. The dichotomy was rejected because, in part, he considered it to be another false dualism like "good" versus "bad" or the is/ought dichotomy. W. V. O. Quine, a more contemporary naturalist, also rejects these dichotomies. Quine requires that we investigate existential conditions and evidence for depicting ontological entities.[13] Evaluating the heuristic roles of beliefs and using defensible criteria are the sort of pragmatist conditions Quine supports.

One way to contrast the poles of objectivism and constructivism is by contrasting them with controversial ways of deciding whether races exist. Some authors believe that races exist (euphemistically termed "splitters" because they categorize minor differences as defining races), and others deny that races exist (euphemistically termed "lumpers" because they deny that minor differences define races). Splitters and lumpers differ for reasons having to do with debates about evidence and classification, particularly gradations over genetic variations, rather than existence in general.[14] "A racist can only be a splitter, a lumper can only be an egalitarian, but an egalitarian has the choice of being a lumper or a splitter."[15]

Naturalists can be splitters or lumpers. The choice is contingent on views of evidence rather than existence in general. The dichotomy between objectivists and constructivists, like that between splitters and lumpers, provides a framework for considering at least one controversial notion that even naturalism does not escape: whether racism is an essentially contested concept.

Essentially Contested Concepts

I will first consider what is meant by an essentially contested concept and then argue that racism is not such a concept. My intention is to use this argument to explore the genuinely controversial features of racism as a concept. I argue that there are genuine philosophical differences over the meaning of racism that are not a function of confusion, indeterminacy, or an essentially contestable character.

An essentially contested concept is the sort of concept that makes conflicting meanings a condition of what it entails. Concepts that are usually salient, ambiguous, or imprecise lend themselves to being sites of conflict over meaning. W. B. Gallie's *Philosophy and the Historical Understanding* provides a rich explication of such concepts.[16] On his account, an essentially contested concept is appraisive because "its worth is attributed to it as a whole … the accredited achievement is *initially* variously describable" but ultimately traits belong to the whole; "to use an essentially contested concept means to use it against other uses."[17] Gallie used the view of essentially contested concepts to argue, among other things, that metaphysics was a misguided field of study because it was contingent on positing wholes that were invariably contested.[18] What metaphysical essences existed, if any, were as undecidable as what ontological wholes existed. Gallie also argued that many moral disagreements were not resolvable in some final sense of having absolutely certain right answers because some moral conflicts were contingent on essentially contested concepts. In addition, Gallie considered the concepts of champion, democracy, art, and religion as essentially contested.

It has been argued that Gallie's definition of an essentially contested concept does not allow for distinguishing when a concept is simply confused or socially contested because persons have fundamentally different goals or intentions for its use.[19] Concepts with indeterminate meanings are not necessarily essentially contested; they are indeterminate. Concepts are subject to revision, reformation, and contestation. In addition, concepts such as democracy and justice are contested because, in part, criteria used to decide what they should mean are the subject of controversy.

Concepts, it seems to me, can be contested whether absolutely clear or completely confused; whether appraisive, variously describable, oppositional, or posited as a way of capturing a whole phenomenon. If the criteria for answering questions or if the character of the question presupposes an answer (e.g., the question "what is the nature of groups" presupposes that groups have a knowable nature), then a question may be essentially contestable. Concepts that are central to such questions are thereby suspect. Gallie's approach, however, strikes an interesting chord when I consider whether racism fits what he considers as essentially contested: racism seems not to be an essentially contested concept although, ostensibly, it seems to have all of the requisite requirements. The primary reason for this is that there are a family of ideas associated with the term "racism" that cut across competing schools of thought. Nonetheless, I believe that there are legitimate conflicts.

Racists, objectivist and constructivist, may be committed to the belief in the existence of races—as objective biological kinds and/or social constructions hierarchically arranged as superior/inferior kinds. It is conceptually necessary that racists are splitters. Racists, consequently, proffer egregious, unnecessary, or heinous dichotomies and hierarchies. Whether we should see racism as a type of noun or predicate, however, is contingent on a variety of other views besides the family of ideas we find most frequently associated with the term. A brief review of the many ways that "race" has been used will exemplify its complexity and role in deciding whether racism should be treated, metaphorically, as a noun or a predicate.

Definitions of Race

Race can refer to a belief in the existence of biological kinds, represented by inherited, ancestral, or folk traits; inherited through blood, genes, or a mystical spirit. (The list of races in the world is simply mind-boggling.) In this sense, the members of a race can be a part of any family, nation, or religion.

Race, in another sense, can refer to bonds of kinship, tribal identity, and spiritual essence. Gauls, Franks, Celts, Teutons, Southern Italians, Hutus, and Tutsis were once widely considered separate races. Classical Hinduism, for example, requires clear lines of familial demarcation: Brahman on one side and untouchable on the other. Each caste is meaningful as a function of its spiritual import, that is, caste identity is determined by spiritual essences. Race stands as a trope invested in, but not defining, caste.[20] Race as a biological kind is coterminous with spiritually inherited essences; its causal character is compatible with deeper spiritually dictated causes. An untouchable, for example, has a blood inheritance lower than that of a Brahman from the standpoint of a Brahman; blood inheritance is an epiphenomenon, a marker, of the deeper spiritual divide.

In yet another sense of race, ethnic and national standing may be treated as synonymous and coterminous with racial taxonomies. Thus, the child of an Irish and German couple would be considered inherently inauthentic, a mutant, and condemned from birth as an ingenuine being. References to a "Japanese race," a "Spanish race," or an "African race" are examples that use kinship, national character, and geography as racial kinds. They are names defining race membership to national and other geographical factors rather than biological or spiritual heritage. There are, for example, no biological tests used to determine if a French citizen is purely Gaelic or tainted with the blood of Celts even if there is an underlying notion that the French are a Gaelic race and the Irish, Celtic. Balibar and others may be wrong in holding that the concept of race is embedded in nationalism, but they are certainly correct when they make the weaker claim that racial being is often tied to the ideology of nationalism.[21]

Although the above is in no way exhaustive of the ways race is used, in each case, notions of group identity of a kind are involved. Racial traits are considered inheritable in each use, whether determined by biology, spiritual nature, or family heritage. Races are considered as "wholes" of some sort, and what is true of the whole is taken as inferentially true of each individual member. Whether belief in the existence of races is morally defensible, however, is contingent on one's definition of racism. If, for example, race is understood as synonymous with ethnicity, racism involves judgments of inferior/superior kinds of ethnic groups. The moral status of beliefs in race are radically at variance, given the broad differences in views of racism.

Racialists may not intend to entail moral connotations of inferior or superior rankings by their belief in the existence of races. That is, a racialist can intend to consider the use of race as morally benign. Richard Goldsby contends, "A race is a breeding population of individuals identifiable by the frequency with which a number of inherited traits appear in that population. A breeding population is one which for reasons of geography or culture mates largely within itself." In most modern sociobiologist accounts, uniformity of inherited traits is denied. Comparative frequency in one population of a species as opposed to other populations defines racial groups. Thus, for Goldsby, "the concept of race has biological meaning when it is applied to populations rather than to individuals."[22] Moreover, races breed "for themselves," as distinct from some of the ways women are perceived, as surrogate vessels or incubators that breed "for males."[23] That is, races are self-interested agents. Although a racialist may not intend degrading connotations, even the depiction of persons as breeding populations is encoded in value-laden language. Goldsby seems oblivious to the valuative character of persons as breeders and thus renders unnoticed the ostensibly neutral organic notions that have been saturated with valuative force. Consequently, race, even when the intention is to use it strictly as a scientific concept, does not escape having moral and evaluative status.

In what amounts to the converse of racialism, one can believe that races do not exist yet demean persons constructed as racially other.[24] Such persons deny that races exist but contend that culturally infused natures roughly parallel categories of race. The "new racism" is of this sort.[25] As Ryan Williams states, "The new ideology attributes defect and inadequacy to the malignant nature of poverty, injustice, slum life and racial difficulties. The stigma that marks the victim ... is an acquired stigma, a stigma of social rather than genetic origin."[26] Another feature of new racism is its symbolic character. Symbols stand for, present, or are codes for already constituted forms of absolute otherness. The defect resides within the raciated agent, embedded, unremovable, and at best controlled by the untainted, the defect-free, and the non-depraved agents of truth, justice, and the way of the right rather than the laws of racial natures or evolution's unerring march toward improved civilizations.

Ashley Montague and others have argued persuasively that the concept of race is simply unnecessary. Human variability can be well depicted without the use of race.

Supporters of Montague suggest that even if there are biological differences between groups of "breeding" populations, and such differences are significant causes of social standing or behavior, we can replace the morally charged term of race with more useful scientific terminology. Montague's contention, however, was much stronger: race is simply meaningless except as a valuative term invariably denoting hierarchies, chains of being, stereotypes, and useless social constructions.

The appraisal feature of race is contested, whether it is meaningless because it does not refer and is thereby objectionable, or whether it does refer and is therefore without moral approbation for referential reasons. Thus, race as a concept is not essentially contested. It is a source of dispute because what counts as its existence is debatable and what role, if any, it should play in our web of beliefs is morally contestable. Race, as well as racism, retain contested appraisal features across competing positions. Whether racism is essentially contested, however, requires additional considerations.

Explanations

Given that races are some form of a social entity with heritable traits, either biological or biological-like, racism would seem to involve some form of ranking races in a hierarchical fashion of irredeemable or relatively stable inferior/superior kinds. This "appraisive" feature of racism, as indicative of inferior or superior kinds, is retained across various uses of the term "racism," if not directly, at least inferentially. These are arguably minimal features for a definition of racism. However, there are explanations of racism that do not treat the belief in the existence of races and racial hierarchical rankings as significant causal forces. "Racist beliefs" are, when institutional rules and practices are considered the primary cause of racism, a relatively insignificant causal variable. In addition, accounts that focus on institutional rules may not treat beliefs in existence of racial groups as causal forces. Racist practices, circumstances, or effects on such accounts are not the doxastic mirror of beliefs in the existence of races or hierarchical rankings of racial groups. Moreover, racialized groups are not necessarily causal agents in explanations of racism.

Institutional rules and practices may be racist, or cause racism, because they match, fit, promote, or function to sustain stringent differentiations of race coterminous with socially constituted races. Institutional rules and practices produce, thereby, racially egregious consequences. Structuralists, post-structuralists, critical race theory authors, and persons that use Stokely Carmichael's and Charles V. Hamilton's idea of institutional racism proceed in this fashion.[27] Such an approach, concerned with describing institutional racism, neither describes how groups behave nor describes racism as the result of the belief that races exist and the prejudicial attitudes based on this view. The approach is dependent on descriptions of outcomes for following usually color-blind rules and regulations. Institutional accounts, however, can incorporate how groups behave as substantive variables. Michael Omi and Howard Winant's *Racial Formation in the United States: From the 1960s to the 1980s* substantively considers both white supremacy and color-blind institutional rules as causal variables.[28] Lucius Outlaw's *On Race and Philosophy* also considers both institutional rules and racial group behavior as substantive variables.[29] Outlaw, in addition, is concerned with the way philosophy and philosophers have treated the reality of race.

Logic-based accounts are another way of explaining racism with variables other than the belief in the existence of races. I roughly group as "logic-based" accounts the following: Cashmore's *Logic of Racism*, C. Delcampagne's *L'invention du racisme*, Lewis Gordon's *Bad Faith and Antiblack Racism*, Michel Wieviorska's "Racism and Modernity in Present-Day Europe," Joel Kovel's *White Racism: A Psychohistory*, and the classic, Gordon W. Allport's *The Nature of Prejudice*.[30] Although the authors of these accounts have different views about whether races exist and whether racialism is a form of racism, they discuss racism in terms of various logical or psychological dimensions. Inconsistencies, contradictions, attitudes of self-deception, deceit, living in bad faith, living in avoidance of reasoned judgment, and so on are the primary notions used to explain, describe, and condemn racism. These accounts may rely on a Hegelian notion of dialectics or some version of relativism or rationalism. The common thread is that there is something wrong with the way one thinks that is the primary focus of discussion. The play of consciousness, reasoning, and intellectual honesty are the focus of these works.

Interest-group approaches, which differ from both institutional and logic-based accounts, contend that racism is best understood as a function or consequence of real underlying pursuits and advantages. These accounts may focus on class, nation, or status interests as the real, underlying causes or conduits for the qualitatively different attribute of racism. Marxists characteristically proceed in this fashion.

There are also interest-group accounts that utilize the sociobiologists' view of society in order explain groups as biological kinds. Such accounts may conceive society as an organism of competing groups. There are, in addition, interest-group approaches that consider racial groups as essentially psychological groups, with racial identity as tropes of group identity based on substantive traits such as family, religion, and neighborhood. Society, in such views, may be considered a set of interacting groups, forming different, competing, and overlapping networks.[31] What counts as paradigmatically "racist" in interest-group accounts is not contingent on what people believe about the superiority or inferiority of others nor on biological or social races as substantively causal agents. Rather, the character of consequences, real interests, and networked interactions define when situations count as racist. The beliefs normally understood as racist are thus epiphenomenal rather than primary causal conduits. The real crux of racism is the arrangement of working interests that gives rise to such beliefs.

The above accounts in no way provide a comprehensive categorization of explanations of racism that do not rely on the belief in the existence of races or races as causal variables. However, all of the above separate the meaning of race from racism. We must, however we construe the relationship between race and racism, make pragmatic judgments informed by some notion of how we should treat social entities and what sorts of entities should hold what status. This is the case whether one is an objectivist, constructivist, or a naturalist falling somewhere between these options.

Noun, Predicate, or Just Essentially Contested?

Racism and race arguably exhibit Gallie's criteria of essentially contested concepts, that is, appraisive, variously describable, oppositional, and positing itself as a whole. The concepts of racism and race nonetheless remain genuinely controversial. Whether racism is best understood as a noun or a predicate is decidable. Controversies concerning whether "racism," "racisms," or "race" exist are contingent on deciding an array of philosophical issues about ontology, morality, and explanatory notions of agency, evidence, and causation. Moreover, criteria for making decisions about competing background assumptions often involve morally appraisive beliefs.

Even if racism is considered an indeterminate concept, best understood as a predicate, we must decide when we are faced with an instance of *a* racism, among the infinite variety of racisms. That is, when we are, for heuristic and practical purposes, required to act in an endurantist fashion—when an object is wholly present at a single moment—we are entrapped. We are entrapped in making moral decisions about persons as if their race was a stable category. We are compelled to proceed as if the definitions we use for when a person is Black or white, for example, are stable. We know that *Who is Black* in America is defined by the one-drop rule—one drop of sub-Saharan African ancestry makes a person Black.[32] This definition is peculiar to a certain period in American history and has little to do with the myriad of ways races are defined in other parts of the world. When prejudice occurs, it affects enduring persons living under social definitions of their identity, contrived, real, or strictly limited to a particular community.

In order to institute social policies, we must have an account of groups as enduring entities or social facts. Institutional rules and regulations apply to individuals understood as instantiations of types, if not kinds. Why, and what, institutional rules and practices perpetuate human misery require explanations of group behavior. These explanations direct us in suggesting solutions that are at least reasonable to consider. Thus, assuming that there are no ontologically stable, enduring, and causing group agents, we use heuristic categories to account for why, and what, rules and practices sustain human misery.

Even if we reject metaphysical or ontological debates about racial essences and existence, we still need to know what sorts of things count as racially heinous; we still need to decide what account or explanation is most efficacious for reasons of good evidence and defensible morals. Whatever explanation of racism we tender is not sufficiently decided by whether or not we believe in the existence of races. The reality of antiblack racism, for example, in no way disappears because we acknowledge that social definitions of race are fabrications and in no way match the biologies of persons. If we are agnostic about the existence or nonexistence of objective social entities, in order to explain dichotomies deemed the consequence of prejudice, we cannot be agnostic about the pragmatic questions of how we should treat social entities (real or imagined).

Splitters and lumpers have competing issues of morality to decide because the evidence can never decide for us.

We must decide how to act as if social groups behave with essencelike qualities, that is, how to act as if individuals were instantiations of types, if not kinds. If it is false that "women" are historical agents, intentionally causing social events in ways that are not reducible to biological causations, it does not follow that we should ignore the oppression of women as a group because they lack ontological status. We can, and must, decide how to treat social wholes enduring long enough to suffer across generations. Ethnic groups, classes, and categories such as woman, homosexual, or aboriginal people, for example, have histories and forms of immiseration associated with their existence.

Racialism, I believe, has already totalized the world. Every space already belongs to a nation; every nation is already stigmatized in a racialized world as an instantiation of a racial category. We do not escape a racialized world by color blindness, thereby allowing it; nor can we defeat egregious dichotomies by valorizing transitory categories of racial identity. Charles W. Mills's *Racial Contract* persuasively argues that racial domination, and how it structures politics, is clarified when we posit a nonideal contract[33]—that is, when we treat white supremacy, and arguable other forms of racial cohesion, as a tacit contract between persons. Such a methodological approach helps account for the perpetuation of racial prejudice and exploitation, in part, because it foregrounds the type of group cohesion necessary to sustain racial domination.

If there were no loan, college admission, or scholarship application that used racial categories, if no one identified themselves or others as racial, and if the American census did not use racial categories, the reality of stereotypes, exclusions, and radically different economic standings would nonetheless match reproducing populations. Blindness to the consequences of historical immiseration is hardly a way to confront and seek its transformation.

The battle against racialism, as a facticity, I believe, has long been lost—there is nothing to contest about this. Even if no one uses the concept of race or picks out others as racial kinds with hidden essences, the assets, statuses, and ownership patterns created by the history of racial oppressions leaves raciated populations with disadvantages. Those disadvantages include an inheritance of racial oppression and diminished assets. What is to be contested involves other forms of authentic presence among differentiations, contrived and real. There is a need for racially excluded and exploited populations to acquire the real material resources for sustaining flourishing lives. We are, I believe, confronted with a world crime against humanity that requires the attention of humanity, regardless of the preconditions for believing in the existence of social entities.

Notes

1. I am indebted to comments at Michigan State University, East Lansing, Michigan, and the Critical Theory Collective, Purdue University, 1995. I have argued elsewhere that this view can be understood as "racism simplex": "Justice and the Concept of Racism," in *Exploitation and Exclusion: Race and Class in Contemporary US Society*, ed. Abebe Zegeye, Julia Maxted, and Leonard Harris (London: Hans Zell, 1991), 28–44.

2. Banton, Michael. "The Concept of Racism," in *Race and Racialism*, ed. Sami Zubaida (New York: Tavistock, 1970), 17. Ruth Benedict, *Race and Racism* (London: Routledge, 1940). For an excellent debate over definitions of racism, see Robert Miles, *Racism* (New York: Routledge, 1989), and his criticism of the race–relations paradigm in *Racism After 'Race Relations'* (New York: Routledge, 1993).

3. Banton, "The Concept of Racism," 18.

4. Charles K. Warriner, "Groups Are Real: A Reaffirmation," *American Sociological Review* 21 (1956): 550–1.

5. See Emile Durkheim, *Suicide* (Glencoe, IL: The Free Press, 1951), for a case of treating social groups as objective entities. He is at least ambivalent in *Rules of Sociological Methods* (Illinois: The Free Press, 1950), treating social currents as currents of opinion and social facts as entities, without ontological status, but experienced as objective entities. For an excellent discussion of "social facts," see George Ritzer, *Sociology: A Multiple Paradigm Science* (Boston, MA: Allyn and Bacon, 1975), 35–82.

6. I explore this distinction in *Racism* (Amherst, NY: Humanity Books, 1999).

7. A classical phenomenological approach to social entities is Alfred Schutz, *The Structure of the Life World* (Evanston, IL: Northwestern University Press, 1973).

8. Stuart Hall, "Racism and Moral Panics in Post-war Britain," in *Five Views of Multi-Racial Britain: Talks on Race Relations Broadcast by BBC TV*, ed. Commission for Racial Equality (London: Commission for Racial Equality, 1978).

9. Paul Gilroy, "One Nation under a Grove," in *Anatomy of Racism*, ed. David Theo Goldberg (Minneapolis: University of Minneapolis Press, 1990), 265.

10. Anthony Appiah, "Racisms," in *Anatomy of Racism*, ed. David Theo Goldberg (Minneapolis: University of Minneapolis Press, 1990), 3.

11. Amy Gutmann and Anthony Appiah, *Color Conscious: The Political Morality of Race* (Princeton, NJ: Princeton University Press, 1996); Ellis Cose, *Color-Blind: Seeing Beyond Race in a Race-Obsessed World* (New York: HarperCollins, 1997); Jim Sleeper, *Liberal Racism* (New York: Viking, 1997).

12. Richard Delgado, "Critical Race Theory," *Sage Race Relations Abstracts* 19 (2): 3–28. Also see Art Berman, *From the New Criticism to Deconstruction: The Reception of Structuralism and Post-structuralism* (Urbana: University of Illinois Press, 1988).

13. I am here thinking of W. V. O. Quine's "Natural Kinds," in *Ontological Relativity* (New York: Columbia University Press, 1969), 114–38.

14. Leonard Lieberman, "The Debate over Race: A Study in the Sociology of Knowledge," *Phylon* 29 (2): 127–42.

15. Ibid., 138.

16. W. B. Gallie, *Philosophy and the Historical Understanding* (New York: Schoken, 1964).

17. Ibid., 161.

18. Ibid., 223–4.

19. See John Kekes, "Essentially Contested Concepts: A Reconsideration," *Philosophy and Rhetoric* 10 (2, Spring 1977): 71–89.

20. See Oliver Cox, *Caste, Class, and R7ce: A Study in Social Dynamics* (New York: Doubleday, 1948). Also see Vernon Williams, *From a Caste to a Minority: Changing Attitudes of American Sociologists toward Afro-Americans, 1896-1945* (New York: Greenwood Press, 1989).

21. See Etienne Balibar and Immanuel Wallerstein's *Race, Nation, Classe: Les identites ambiques* (Paris: Editions la Decouverte, 1988).

22. Richard A. Goldsby, "The Reality and Significance of Human Races: A Biological Perspective," in *Biological Differences and Social Equality: Implications for Social Policy*, ed. Masako N. Darrough and R. H. Blank (Westport, CT: Greenwood Press, 1983), 17.

23. See Masako N. Darrough, "Biological Differences and Economic Equality: Race and Sex," in *Biological Differences and Social Equality: Implications for Social Policy*, ed. Masako N. Darrough and R. H. Blank (Westport, CT: Greenwood Press, 1978), 109–36. Also see Audrey Smedley, *Race in North America* (Boulder: Westview Press, 1993). Also see Paul T. Baker, "The Biological Race Concept as a Research Tool," *Physical Anthropology* 27 (1, July 1967): 21–5. See for an excellent deconstruction of the concept of race Naomi Zack's *American Mixed Race* (Maryland: Rowman and Littlefield, 1995).

24. See Pierre L. Van der Berg, *Race and Racism* (New York: Wiley, 1967).

25. See Martin Barker, *The New Racism: Conservatives and the Ideology of the Tribe* (Westport, CT: Greenwood Press, 1981).

26. William Ryan, *Blaming the Victim* (New York: Pantheon Books, 1971) 7.

27. See as examples Charles V. Hamilton and Stokely Carmichael, *Black Power: The Politics of Liberation* (New York: Random House, 1967); Joyce A. Ladner, *Death of White Sociology* (New York: Random House, 1973); Derrick Bell, *Faces at the Bottom of the Well: The Permanence of Racism* (New York: Basic Books, 1992).

28. Michael Omi and Howard Winant, *Racial Formation in the United States: From the 1960s to the 1980s* (New York: Routledge and Kegan Paul, 1986). Also see Omi and Winant's "Biographic Essay: Racial Theory in the Post War United States: A Review and Critique," *Sage Race Relations Abstracts* 12 (2, May 1987): 3–45.

29. Lucius Outlaw, *On Race and Philosophy* (New York: Routledge, 1996).

30. Ernest Cashmore, *The Logic of Racism* (London: Allen & Unwin, 1987); Delcampagne, *L'invention du racisme* (Paris: Fayard, 1983); Lewis Gordon, *Bad Faith and Antiblack Racism* (Amherst, NY: Humanities Press, 1993); Michel Wieviorska, "Racism and Modernity in Present-Day Europe," *Thesis Eleven* 35 (1994): 51–61; Joel Kovel, *White Racism: A Psychohistory* (New York: Pantheon Books, 1970); Gordon W. Allport, *The Nature of Prejudice* (Cambridge: Addison-Wesley, 1954).

31. See Jitsuichi Masuoka and Preston Valien (eds.), *Race Relations: Essays in Honor of Robert E. Park* (Chapel Hill: University of North Carolina Press, 1961); Bob Blauner, *Racial Oppression in America* (New York: Harper & Row, 1972); Phyllis A. Katz, *Towards the Elimination of Racism* (New York: Paragon Press, 1976); and Randall Collins and Michael Makowsky, *The Discovery of Society* (New York: Random House, 1972).

32. See James Davis, *Who Is Black?: One Nation's Definition* (University Park: Penn State University Press, 1991).

33. Charles W. Mills, *The Racial Contract* (Ithaca, NY: Cornell University Press, 1997).

CHAPTER 3
WHAT, THEN, IS RACISM? (1999)

In "What, Then, Is Racism?" Harris articulates both his conception of racism and his conception of race. He depicts racism as a polymorphous agent of death, misery, and destroyed futures. Insulting stereotypes, humiliation, and brutality are often utilized to stigmatize and dehumanize a population. This is a moderately objectivist view, since the effects of racism and the influence of stable transhistorical groups can be checked against material realities. Yet, in regard to race, Harris holds a constructivist view. Like Alain Locke (1885–1954), Harris argues that races, understood as biological kinds matching social kinds, do not exist; racial groups, as social kinds, are fabrications. There is nothing inherently redeemable about racial categorizations. Nevertheless, Harris maintains that those terrorized by race have pragmatic reasons to bind together as a racial group and work on behalf of themselves, if their agency as a group negates the hegemonic conditions that impose racial categorization. Furthermore, Harris calls on us to marshal our forces in communal unity between and among the oppressed and immiserated populations of the world to destroy racism and commit it to history's trash heap.

What, then, is racism? Racism is a polymorphous agent of death, premature births, shortened lives, starving children, debilitating theft, abusive larceny, degrading insults, and insulting stereotypes forcibly imposed.[1] The ability of a population to accumulate wealth and transfer assets to their progeny is stunted by racism. As the bane of honor, respect, and a sense of self-worth, racism surreptitiously stereotypes. It stereotypes its victims as persons inherently bereft of virtues and incapable of growth. Racism is the agent that creates and sustains a virulent pessimism in its victims. The subtle nuances that encourage granting unmerited and undue status to a racial social kind are the tropes of racism. Racism creates criminals, cruel punishments, and crippling confinement, while the representatives of virtue profit from sustaining the conditions that ferment crime. Systemic denial of a population's humanity is the hallmark of racism.

Integral to race-based denials of humanity are unspeakable terrors, holocausts, vicious rapes, cruel beatings, tortures, and maiming rituals. It is never enough, in racist societies, to exploit and degrade. Humiliation and symbolic subjugation of even the dead of the suppressed population are required to sustain a sense of superiority, honor, healthiness, purity, and control in the dominant population. And too often, self-effacement, inferiority complexes, insecurity, and hopelessness are features developed by segregated and stereotyped persons. Thus, for example, in 1904 Vicksburg, Mississippi, when the two Negroes were captured, they were tied to trees and while the funeral pyres were being prepared they were forced to suffer the most fiendish tortures. The blacks were forced to hold out their hands while one finger at a time was chopped off. The fingers were distributed as souvenirs. The ears of the murderers were cut off. Holbert was beaten severely, his skull was fractured, and one of his eyes, knocked out with a stick, hung by a shred from the socket … The most excruciating form of punishment consisted in the use of a large corkscrew in the hands of some of the mob. This instrument was bored into the flesh of the man and woman, in the arms, legs and body, and then pulled out, the spirals tearing out big pieces of raw, quivering flesh every time it was withdrawn.[2]

The Holbert family was accused of defending their home against white intruders—the actual criminals. Since they were perceived as inherent criminals, and bereft of the entitlements accorded to persons considered members of the moral community, no trial was needed. Quivering flesh, taken by avid corkscrewers, was thrown to the crowd for souvenirs. The bodies were burned, and after cooling, pieces of charred flesh were taken from the ashes by men, women, and children for souvenirs. Shopkeepers and women of class occasionally used severed hands as ornamentation. This ritual of violence was not isolated to Mississippi. Corkscrewing flesh, bodily souvenirs, and public burning were reserved rituals for Blacks. With the invention of cameras, photographs of the crowd gloating over the bodies became a common feature of the ritual. Whether the madness occurs in Cambodia, Rwanda, Germany, Croatia, Guatemala, or America, when persons are described, ascribed, stereotyped, and symbolized as racially abject, the fact of one's phenotype—imagined or apparent—is used to warrant degrading representatives of the subjugated population. Each individual is either treated, or subject to be treated, in every social and business environment as a representative of a kind—a kind, the embodiment of which is always subject to humiliation—from conception to beyond death. Under British colonial domination, Welsh children were seen as born dirty, mired in eternal filth, and beyond concern except as workers; Japanese leather workers, Burakumin, are incapable, from the standpoint of "pure" Japanese, from parenting worthy children, and they are condemned from conception; Australian adoptive mothers and fathers separated light- and dark-skinned Aborigine siblings, showered foster parental love on light-skinned children, and abandoned dark-skinned children in accordance with public policy intended to systemically destroy the darker population. Racism is a mother demanding that her servants kill her child, immediately upon its issue from her womb, because "it" is of the wrong race; or when a country's president, such as Thomas Jefferson, keeps his interracial children as slaves; or a Cherokee chief trades his half-castes for horses. Racism is the degradation and humiliation of a population as a totally abject collective, beyond redemption.

When "real" means social realities that are historically inevitable, natural, or invariably a feature of every society, then races are not real. Universal and transhistorical human traits, such as agnate love or the ability to think in past and future tenses, do not necessarily cause the existence of racial identity or any particular racial identity. Races, as biological kinds matching social kinds, do not exist. That is, there are no necessary correlations between racial biologies and cultures. The science of ethnology is not one that describes character traits according to racial biologies. Rather, ethnology is a science that can describe the relationship of character traits to values, heritage, and practices. Racial groups, as social kinds, are constructions.

Groups are real in the sense that they are historically inevitable, natural, and invariably a feature of every society. Transhistorical groups, such as women, men, families, or workers, are always biological kinds closely matching social kinds.[3] There are universal character traits associated with such formations. There are, in effect, gender, age, capacities, and patterns associated with transhistorical kinds. And none of these kinds are racial kinds.

If there were only one person on the planet, that person would not have a biological race. That is, they would not have a nonadaptive, genetically determined character trait caused by a stable population of common descent.[4] If that person believed that they had a biological race, they would be mistaken. If their biology or genetic makeup was affected by this mistaken belief, they nonetheless remain malleable. That is, they remain capable of having different beliefs and behaviors.

If the only person on the planet believed that acquired cultural characteristics are transmitted in a racially significant way, they would be wrong. If that one person could use an artificial incubator and the resources of a sperm/egg bank, the next generation need not manifest cultural or character traits identical to their forbearers outside of the same social situation.

Constructions, socially and individually created, influence our lives. Some constructions are morally odious. Racial identities, especially when such identities are treated as inherent to every member, transhistorical, natural, and inevitable, are odious. Such racial identities are inextricably tied to, and invariably indebted to, degrading, demeaning, and misguided stereotypes. There simply are no virtues or any sense of self-worth that could not be better achieved than through the pernicious idea of race.

There are compelling reasons for persons terrorized by race to bind together, define themselves, and work on behalf of themselves. There are, for example, compelling reasons for such persons to marry within networks of the same social kind because such networks provide support and sustenance. The idea that Africans, for example, should unite to end destructive national identities and unnecessary boarders that divide geographically, politically, and culturally similar peoples is warranted. Moreover, Africans should defeat the continuing remnants of foreign elitism. Alexander Crummel, Edward Wilmot Blyden, and Kwame Nkrumah were right: Pan-African unity is a positive good. Seeking Pan-African unity for the reason of Negro uplift, however, has gone the way of seeking Wolof, Welsh, and Tasmanian uplift through Wolof, Welsh, and Tasmanian national unity—impossible accomplishments. The background reality within which language groups as racial kinds, such as Wolof, Welsh, and Tasmania, could become nation-states no longer exists. Analogously, a world in which relatively isolated groups can be reasonably counted as races, or as having the possibility of race-based nations, no longer exists. Moreover, native speakers are entrapped in a limited world of opportunity unless they also know a world dominant language. It is the terror of history, and the malleability of humanity, that destroys the security of closed raciated networks and makes the realization of racial ideals, such as an all-white Europe, all-yellow Japan, or an all-Black Africa, superfluous.

It is misguided to believe that English-speaking Jamaicans, Arabic-speaking Turks, and French-speaking Polynesians are unauthentic, free only if they could return to the time before colonialism or move into a time when the colonial culture is completely shed; or a time when alien religions, languages, or racial kinds are purged from an imagined pure cultural background.

Alain L. Locke's argument that victims of racism need a racial identity as a source of unity and as a resource to defend themselves has strong appeal, as long as the source of their victimization is racial and its destruction is aided by racial union among victims. That is, so long as the oppression is arguably caused by, or is strongly correlated to, the sort of racism in which the racial identity of the oppressor is a substantive variable determining the misery of the oppressed. Background realities change. Neither mulattoes, mestizos, nor mixed Asians are transhistorical. What they are, as groups, is far too unstable, transitory, continually redefined, and always disappearing to warrant commitment in the way that commitment to transhistorical realities can gain such warrant. Racial preservationists, that is, those who believe that existing groups are a sort of natural community and their members entitled to sustain whatever identity they currently foster, are analogous to environmentalists who believe "nature" is the static, unchanging, and unaffected physical surrounding they immediately inhabit. That is, they are analogous to persons who support completely untenable pictures of themselves and others.

The death of racial identity is no bellwether that racism is dead. Yet, liberation of any social race from oppression by racism requires ending the racial identity of the oppressor and the oppressed. For a racist, the goal of imagined superior races is always to dominate or destroy all others. For an anti-racist, the goal should include the negation of all institutions, interests, and benefits that sustain oppression by race. In addition, for an anti-racist, it should also include the negation of race as such—the negation of the social construction that links biology and culture, biology and character, biology and potential, and biology and rights.

Antiblack, anti-Welsh, or anti-colored racism necessarily has as their ultimate interests and objects ending the need for "anti," leaving nothing in its wake. The primary interest of any social race, if its members are to be liberated from debilitating stereotypes, is the negation of all identity by race and empowerment through control of assets.

In a nonracist world, social races would not exist. No one would be obligated for nonmoral reasons, such as fear of ostracism or the need for self-protection from prejudice, to marry within a predetermined racial group; no one would be born into a race; no one would have a nonmoral duty to be the representative of a race. Even if racialism continued in a nonracist world, through default (e.g., because socially like constructed kinds preferred their own), that would not warrant a description of such a society as racist. If 70 percent of every existing raciated population married internally, that would tell us the obvious—these people like themselves and those they know the most about. It would also hide what we know—racial groups come and go out of existence, and the definition of membership in such groups is continually redefined. In a racist world, however, the oppressed have obligations to one another. Without some form of internal unity, Gypsies, Jews, Kurds, Black South Africans, or numerous other groups would be unable to protect themselves from unspeakable horrors and holocausts.

History's terror, its seemingly careless concern for the wishes of the vanquished, makes hopes for stable racial kinds the erotica of necrophilia. History's intentional and unintentional terrors—its mutations, destructions, genocides, and assimilations—often leaves languages, cultures, and races as museum relics.

Racial constructions divide the world. The divisions often rest on perceptions of cultures as representing different races. Locke frequently criticized the conflation of race and culture—treating cultures as if they were the sole creation of a race and treating nations as if their justification should be based on promotion of a racial ideal. Cultural kinds can gain regard and cultural exchanges and transitions can occur without seeing peoples as the elixir of a race. The pathology of self-hatred, for example, associated with the high rate of Asian American women who marry white American men, is not solved by romanticizing an ideal pure Asian race and promoting Asian-only marriage. If the pursuit of status is one strong motivating force in deciding on one's mate, it is predictable that pathologies of self-hatred would accompany the degrading reality of white American racism. Ending "white" as a status marker may have a far greater impact on ending race-based pathologies than achieving a numerical arrangement of same-racial-kind marriages. Ending the perception of Asians as a pure racial kind, and thereby contributing to the negation of the idea of people as representing the elixir of a race or culture, may generate far more regard for Asian culture as a living reality—assimilable, malleable, and complex.

Racism is one of humanity's egregious and unnecessary forms of terrorizing. Social reality always changes. Various practices used to generate status—such as scarification, ownership of eunuchs, displaying enemy skulls, and various institutions such as slavery, serfdom, male suffrage, and caste-based rights—have slowly, grudgingly declined. Racism, contrary to a pessimist view of future possibilities, is not a permanent feature of future societies.

The answer to "What, then, is racism?" is disconnected in a complex way from the answer to "Why, then, does race or racism exist?" If the concept of race exists because people frequently mistake phenotypes for natures, that does not tell us why the concept of race persists, especially when phenotypes are a minor feature of racial differentiations. If racism exists because of kin nepotism, the current cause of racism is in no way answered. The current cause of racism, for example, may be the consequence of class struggle. Racism might exist because humans are irrational egotists, because kin nepotism is ubiquitous, or because racial mythology is a convenient trope in the service of nation-state formations to unite trading partners. The current cause of racism may have nothing to do with its origin. Moreover, answers to "what" questions require depictions of what exists—pictures of individuals and groups—and what subtle, salient, coercive, compelling, and enigmatic variables contribute to how the "what" functions now and how it is likely to function in the future.

Our beliefs about what will happen in the future often condition, if not determine, what beliefs we have now and what we do now. Our attitude toward reality differs, for example, depending on whether we believe racism is permanent or whether it is a defeatable social condition. Explanations, whether they use a notion of mechanical causation or teleological causation, whether pragmatist, historical materialist, structuralist, or otherwise, invariably help us imagine what we believe will happen in the future. The explanation form we prefer influences how we understand change, for example, whether we believe that change occurs for purposeful reasons or whether we believe that the world is dysteleological; whether change proceeds through random chaos, dialectically or rationally, whether change is fundamentally the result of intentional action and explained by accounts of intentionality, and so on. Moreover, the ontological elements that we believe exist, for example, races, classes, nations, civilizations, or peoples, influence what we believe can happen.

The explanation we prefer, and its ontological elements, should be based on strongly warranted belief, if not certain truth. We should neither risk our lives, as police, soldiers, or nurses, nor place the lives of our loved ones at risk without a genuine belief that our actions are at least strongly warranted. We should not risk the lives of current persons or future generations on the basis of weak accounts or for instrumental reasons that are not based on reasoned beliefs about what will happen.

I argue for a moderate form of objectivism, one that takes seriously explanations that consider groups real ontological entities. An objectivist believes at least that there are facts about the human world independent of contingent cultural or social ideas. Groups, for an objectivist, can exist independently as objective causal agents. That is, the cause or influential force of group phenomenon is engined by variables that are not strictly contingent for their power on fleeting ideas. Evolutionists or historical materialists are examples of philosophic orientations that are objectivist in orientation. Our biologies or material interests, in substantive and salient ways, drive group events. Races do not exist as transhistorical objective entities, and insofar as that is the case, I consider constructivist views of race to be valuable contributions to our understanding of reality.

Constructivists believe that facts about the human world are absolutely dependent on contingent cultural or social ideas. Groups do not exist for the constructivist independent of cultural or social ideas. The causal agency of groups is dependent on constructed ideations, that is, groups are in some substantive way a feature of individual or social ideas. Phenomenologists, existentialists, and vitalists are examples of constructivist-oriented philosophies. Even if social entities are considered real by philosophers with these orientations, they are not real in any substantive way independent from uncaused choices, phenon, or some form of unexplainable indeterminacies rooted in consciousness. Intentions are thus crucial, salient, and coercive variables.

Objectivists have, in my opinion, an interesting theoretical advantage over constructivists: given their respective theories of explanation, such as functionalist or structuralist, they proffer what the future holds. The future can be presaged, if not predicted, because material reality shapes, in a substantive way, events independent of unpredictable modes of consciousness. Who lives and dies, how long they live, what diseases they are subject to suffer from without adequate health care, who owns and profits from businesses, and thus whose children have bright futures are all shaped by the egregious fiscal realities in racist societies. Victims of racism, for example, live more often than not near toxic waste sites, drink industrially polluted water, and suffer preventable ill-health. People are born into these disadvantages and struggle, heroically, to overcome daily humiliation and the expropriation of their wealth. Evolutionists, for example, believe that fitness, adaptation, mutation, and survival are the sorts of conceptions needed to explain what groups have survived in the past and which sort will likely succeed in the future—usually without telling us which group will invariably succeed. Definite methods for shaping future societies can be plausibly inferred from such explanations. Neither individual existential moments of choice nor phenomenological forms of sense experience drives social change on evolutionary accounts. Biologies, geographies, and a host of variables inclusive of sense experience drive what evolutionists see as possible human futures. Marxists, as another example, often believe that risking their lives on behalf of the working-class struggle to overthrow the bourgeoisie means risking their lives in ways that will benefit the enhancement and thriving of all future persons. Thinking in terms of how objective, real groups or forces will shape the future is characteristic of objectivist approaches.

Philosophies that cannot proffer what traits and what sort of groups shape the future are at best parasitic on philosophies that purport to tell us what will happen. Where, for example, hospitals should be located or what the criteria should be for college admission are influenced by explanations of group behavior. Where to place a hospital is not given by philosophies that offer no substantive guidance to believe that our selection will have short- and long-term desired effects. Such philosophies can react to where the socialists, communists, capitalists, Muslims, Christians, or Buddhists place a hospital, but they cannot offer strong guidance concerning where to place one's loyalties for the purpose of creating a definitive future. Objectivists can argue that a given recommended community is preferred across fleeting, contextual, and constructed identities and will come into existence. It is parasitic to simply condemn the realities created or predicted by others while remaining agnostic about the efficacy of such predictions. Every society is already compelled to react to, and be affected by, universally influential social entities—religious communities, multinational corporations, class interests, regionally united nations—that define their teleology and community in objectivist terms. Given that social entities are often egregiously treated as metaphysical absolutes and undifferentiated wholes, there are nonetheless no viable explanations that reasonably offer projections that do not use some array of social entities as explanandum.

Anti-racists are always in the position of reacting to a world of dominant powers in hopes of creating an alternative world. Anti-racists who can affect the variables with the greatest impact on the future arguably can have a substantive impact. It is not, then, immaterial to know as best as we can what variables will affect what happens in the world and what social entities will have the greatest impact on abating conditions of misery.

A good deal of what happens in the world and what affects us, unfortunately, has nothing to do with our social constructions—including constructed racial social kinds. This is one reason why, I have suggested, that the death of racial identities is no bellwether for the death of racism. How we construct racial kinds is not sufficient to explain substantively what happens to such groups. That is, ideation of racial kinds may have little or nothing to do with what happens to those kinds or what affects those kinds have. Intentions, desires, purposes, choices, and heuristic categories may be relatively benign. Perceiving persons as freely choosing agents, independent selves, unencumbered by antecedent ties or obligations, may not be of much value for explanatory efficacy.

As a way of seeing why racial social kinds may be relatively weak causal variables as well as relatively weak agents in pursuit of teleological interests, imagine that Alain L. Locke, a constructivist, was right in believing that races, as biological kinds, are not real. Further, assume that social race—the beliefs, habits, customs, and informal institutional regulations defining racial groups—are significant causal variables. In addition, assume that races can have teleologies (e.g., a race can be said to contribute to a multicultural society if it also the bearer of an enriching culture). Assume also that Locke was right in believing that civilizations and peoples (i.e., ethnic groups, nations, tribes, linguistic groups), when they can sustain themselves, shape history. It is then arguable that civilizations and peoples, and the traits that define their success, will help us in substantively deciding what traits to support when faced with hard decisions over scarce resources.

Civilizations and peoples are not, however, coterminous with races. If civilizations and peoples cause historical change, race is a trope within those historical forces. As social constructions, it is not just that social race membership criteria radically change over relatively short periods of time, but that as causal variables they are subordinate to much more compelling and salient forces, for example, a civilization's march to standardize production, a people's effort to sustain territories identified as owned by that people, material class interests, or the pursuit of status by ownership and control of revered symbols or sources of wealth. If particular civilizations or peoples shape history, they can be said to do so if they are contiguous, continuous, and ontologically transhistorical. As Locke recognized, however, races do not have such historical coherency. The analysis of race in France, for example, tells us nothing about race in China or postcolonial Algeria if we accept a constructivist picture of reality. Constructivists see reality in nonsequential fashion, that is, historical epochs, social races, and forms of identity are unique. The multitude of races that have come and gone out of existence has not left any social race as a viable historical entity. The convergence of incipient variables, independent of race markers, perpetuates forms of racism, that is, rules, regulations, practices, codes, and modes of transferring wealth often function to sustain lower-class statuses, poor health services, and greater exposure to dangerous waste products for a social race, while the same variables favor another race. It is not race that is the cause of the misery. The vicious force of white supremacy, for example—given that St. Clair Drake and Martin Bernal are right in believing that white supremacist ideology has continued unabated for over a thousand years—is not a "race" with inherent causal traits but a polymorphic arrangement of incipient variables that conjoin to make possible the completely inhumane force of white supremacist ideology and behavior.[5] The disjunctions between race, civilization, and peoples renders race not as a salient variable but at best a contributor. Possibly, this is why explanations and predictions that rely on stable and assumed transhistorical races—stable entities—have been notoriously wrong.

There are no real essences that hold races together, that is, there are no natures that create or dictate the unity of racial identities across time. The effects of ascriptions, descriptions, and depictions in no way create the desire in people to want more goods than fewer, have a need for collective identities, or find expropriation of their creations egregious.

Populations oppressed, terrorized, exploited, and degraded by race are not invested with world historical missions any more than the populations engaged in demonic racial oppression.[6] Locke's view, if interpreted to mean that races contribute to social growth by manifesting a racial historical mission, is misguided. The teleology of race, even if a racial identity can be said to have contributed to a culture, is the negation of racial identity. One way to see this is the following: if there are historical agents such as the working class, moral consciousness, or civilizations, then such agents seek to create a reality and thereby satisfy their teleologies. That is, historical agents have, as an abiding interest or mission, the creation of a certain situation that embodies their goals. The historical mission of the working class, on Marx's account, for example, is the creation of a world in which the working class's interest is realized universally. The working class would then, in effect, cease to exist as a class since there would be no other classes. Analogously, the interest of the oppressed by race is the ending of race-based oppression. Minimally, this includes ending the conditions that create racial disparity and what it is to be stereotyped—inclusive of the negation of race. Consequently, if, as Locke believed, races can make contributions in some way distinguishable from cultural ones, such contributions or missions make sense solely within a limited, short-term, historical context. The sense of self-worth racial unity offers and its use as a bulwark against egregious racism has at best temporary pragmatic merit—no virtues are inculcated, no one can actualize their natures, no one gains union with good faith, no liberated consciousness is gained, and no tragedy is avoided. Racial identity is, as Locke notes, a temporary surcease.

There are no arguments that could justify making hard decisions about allocating scarce resources for the long term on preferential treatment of specific races. If our explanation of social races as causal variables is cogent, we cannot make the sort of inference about how to allocate scarce resources the way that we can use ideas about civilizations or peoples as causal variables to help inform decisions. Civilizations and peoples do not carry the sort of odious identification with degrading prejudice that is integral to race.

Racism is explained by objectivist criteria in a more convincing fashion than constructivist criteria, and it can offer long-term suggestions for creating community. Yet, without constructivist insights into how visceral race is, objectivist explanations can mistake anabsolutes for more substantive social objects, discount the influence of social constructions, and mistake contingent communities for natural communities.

Constructivist accounts are analogous to cautionary tales. Cautionary tales foreshadow terrible consequences if we fail to weigh appropriately competing motivations. If, as in the ancient Egyptian *Instruction of Ani*, motivation springs from our hearts, the seat of intuitive wisdom, then it is opposed to the certainty of tradition. The intuitions of each generation are not likely the same across generations. Khonshotep, the son, is committed to applauding instructions of his heart, and his father, the certain truth of tradition. Analogously, constructivists advise of the deeply important role our hearts play in shaping reality. If, as in Goethe's *Faust*, intuited religious faith and the search for certain knowledge are in conflict, the warning is that a probable decline of the soul will occur because the desire for certain knowledge is itself misguided. The warning of the constructivist, in a similar way, is that absolute access to an unmediated social reality is itself misguided. Statuses, for example, may be accorded through legal institutions in one society but through family lineage in another, making the nature of honor or racist insult contingent on the context—an important constructivist insight. Constructivist accounts help picture the web of significations and marks of exclusion and inferiority with attention to the personal, the daily, and concrete specificity.

It is objectivist criteria of what exists, across contexts, that I suggest we use to decide when situations count as racist. It is not just humiliations, stereotypes, and false forms of categorizing persons that define racism; it is the racial slavery of children, the hunger of the starving, and the charred remains of racial populations designated for extermination. If, for example, we define racism in historical materialist terms, there is a way to define racism whether the society uses institutional rules or family lineage to accord status. A historical materialist will consider the material sources that influence behavior. In addition, in the absence of adequate information about whether a situation is racist—and it is arguable that we rarely have adequate information—appeal to stable definitions has advantages that subjective definitions lack. Stable definitions offer, for example, criteria we can use to evaluate changes, such as whether the conditions creating racial misery are increasing or decreasing.

The ineffable character, and incongruous nature, of multiple identities that normally inhabit human consciousness is never stable and always subject to change. Constructivist explanations picture the vicissitudes of constantly shifting identities and efforts to avoid, or cop out of, forms of identity.

> As a culture, we call ourselves Spanish when referring to ourselves as a linguistic group and when copping out. It is then that we forget our predominant Indian genes … We call ourselves Hispanic or Spanish-American or Latin American or Latin when linking ourselves to other Spanish-speaking peoples of the Western Hemisphere and when copping out. We call ourselves Mexican-American to signify we are neither Mexican nor American, but more the noun "American" than the adjective "Mexican" (and when copping out).[7]

Mestizo may affirm both Indian and Spanish heritage; *raza* may refer to a Chicano's racial identity; *tejanos* may be Chicanos from Texas, *metis* or *metissage*, as the racial base of Euro-Asians, but Euro-Asians as mixed, in some form, with Europeans by definition. Simultaneously, Europeans, misconceived as paradigmatically white, are seen as white on a foreground of Bosnian, Slavic, Belarussian, and numerous other ethnic identities. That fact that racial realities are contingent on subjective or social ideation is compatible with a constructivist picture of what exists. However, all forms of identity involve copping out. Some forms are pathological, for example, forms that engender self-hatred. The reality of copping out is not a tragic or inherently debilitating feature of social reality. There are no authentic racial kinds hiding beneath our skins and no static social reality that requires a romantic racial solution.

What, then, is oppression? Or, rather, what is non-contextual oppression? Objectivists can answer both questions with something other than claims about contextual identities, feelings, local descriptions, and fleeting ascriptions. An objectivist can contend that class, nation, and gender identities are more likely to be identities rooted in, caused by, or closely associated with invariant human features. That is, an objectivist can contend that such entities are features not strongly contingent on constructions, such as ascriptions, descriptions, and depictions of group membership, but exist and function in certain ways regardless of constructions. Racist practices might be understood as completely unnecessary, never a feature of a truly liberated consciousness, and always dysfunctional.

Quaint platitudes about the importance of democracy, dialogue, critical thinking, and communal discourse, as well as romantic appeals to the obligations of the wealthy, are grossly inadequate solutions to the sinister motives of racists and the egregious joys and power secured by the monetary profit from situations of racism—the wages usurped from death and shattering lives. In a world that has increasingly destroyed substantive distinctions between peoples, while simultaneously maintaining contrived divisions of race, it is relatively easy to ignore the suffering of persons stigmatized as abject and beyond redemption while applauding cultural pluralism. The existing arrangement of assets—who owns factories, who controls health care, who gains from disposing of toxic waste in poor neighborhoods and underdeveloped countries, who profits from the sale of policing supplies—already structures differential life chances along lines of racial constructions. Directly changing these arrangements requires far more than the paternalism associated with maintaining racially and culturally segregated enclaves. Quaint platitudes, hoped-for changes in corrupt intentions, and shifts of intuited ideology are extremely weak causal variables as sources for change—changed ownership, control, participation, and access to material reality will have a far greater impact on creating a deraciated and socially viable world.

Racial oppression allows us to ignore the suffering of the oppressed by race, because the immiserated are tucked away in prisons, rural hovels, illegal drug dens, and communities that offer their members little to no real opportunity for gainful employment, let alone ownership or control. The death of racist oppression, regardless of the context or transient form of identity construction, requires creating fiscally empowered oppressed populations, new realities, and the actualization or blossoming of the deep-seated, warranted traits that unit humanity.

The Holberts, lynched but not forgotten, burned and dismembered but not bereft of honor, should have defended their homes—the killing of vicious aggressors and the enmity of an amoral community notwithstanding. No person should be encouraged to develop traits of submissiveness, especially those faced with living their lives in a world that marks them as abject, wretched, and inherently inferior. There is no reason to be self-effacing or complacent, whether one is a pacifist or not.[8] Anti-racists should be confident, demanding, uncompromising, and aggressive. Destroying racism will require more revolutions. They may be violent revolutions or they may be nonviolent, direct-action movements, based on philosophies of pacifism and the power of conscience. In either case, power concedes nothing without demand, compulsion, expropriation, and radical redistribution of control over the resources that make life possible.

There are competing views of racism that would not approach explanations in the above way. However, I do not believe that other explanatory approaches should depict the miseries any less vividly or recommend any milder actions to destroy the terror of race and racism.

Race is a trope undergirding North and South American, African, Asian, and European identities. Without communal unity between and among populations of these regions, a unity that subordinates and negates supremacist racial realities, the creation of universal human liberation is stunted.

Racism is one of history's unnecessary, fickle terrors. The forces that unite humanity—such as common dominators of class interest, inclinations to pursue status, and disdain for injustice to members of one's perceived community—can be marshaled to aid the destruction of sinister, unintentional, and structural racial formations of oppression. If attacked vigilantly and without compromise, racism will also be one of history's irretrievable terrors.

Notes

1. By death, I mean the actual destruction of life and thereby futures, exemplified in Joseph C. Miller's *Way of Death: Merchant of Death and the Angolan Slave Trade, 1730–1830* (Madison: University of Wisconsin Press, 1988). The social import of death, I believe, is well explored in Orlando Patterson's *Slavery and Social Death: A Comparative Study* (Cambridge, MA: Harvard University Press, 1982).

2. Trudier Harris, *Exorcising Blackness: Historical and Literary Lynching and Burning Rituals* (Bloomington: Indiana University Press, 1984), 2.

3. See Donald E. Brown, *Human Universals* (Philadelphia, PA: Temple University Press, 1991). Also see Alain Locke, "Values and Imperatives," in *The Philosophy of Alain Locke: Harlem Renaissance and Beyond*, ed. Leonard Harris (Philadelphia, PA: Temple University Press, 1989), 34–50. I am indebted to Frank Kirkland, Hunter College, for his 1992 critical comments on my views of ontology, "Race and the Nature of Social Entities: Or Trying to Make It [Race] Real Compared to What," unpublished. Also see Richard J. Bernstein. *Beyond Objectivism and Relativism: Science, Hermeneutics, and Praxis* (Philadelphia: University of Pennsylvania Press, 1983).

4. See Richard C. Lewontin, *Not in Our Genes: Biology, Ideology, and Human Nature* (New York: Pantheon Books, 1984).

5. See St. Clair Drake, *Black Folks Here and There: An Essay in History and Anthropology* (Los Angeles, CA: Center for Afro-American Studies, 1987); and Martin Bernal, *Black Athena: The Afroasiatic Roots of Classical Civilization* (New Brunswick, NJ: Rutgers University Press, 1987).

6. See my arguments against racial teleologies in "Agency and the Concept of the Underclass," in *The Underclass Question*, ed. Bill E. Lawson (Philadelphia, PA: Temple University Press, 1992), 33–56; and "Historical Subjects and Interests: Race, Class, and Conflict," in *The Year Left*, ed. Michael Sprinkler et al. (New York: Verso, 1986), 91–106. Also see the argument against colorblind romanticism in "Postmodernism and Racism: An Unholy Alliance," in *I Am Because We Are: Readings in Black Philosophy*, ed. Fred L. Hord and J. S. Lee (Amherst, NY: University of Massachusetts Press, 1995), 367–82.

7. Anzaldua, Gloria, *Borderlands/La Frontera: The New Mestiza* (San Francisco, CA: Spinsters/ Aunt Lute, 1987), 63.

8. An excellent example of the stalwart character of pacifists with deep moral commitments to human uplift is explored in Greg Moses, *Revolution of Conscience: Martin Luther King, Jr. and the Philosophy of Nonviolence* (New York: Guillford Press, 1997).

CHAPTER 4
NECRO-BEING: AN ACTUARIAL ACCOUNT OF RACISM (2018)

In "Necro-Being," Harris describes racism as an instantiation of necro-being (i.e., that which makes living a kind of death), a seminal form of oppression, its corporal being. Racialized populations are subjected to conditions of life that confer upon them the status of living dead; necro-tragedy (utter suffering and irredeemable loss). Despite races being anabsolute (unstable groups often treated as objectively stable entities), populations can be seen to suffer unduly. Harris offers an actuarial approach, which stands as an alternative to rational-intentional explanations, social kind racial realist explanations, and explanations that rely upon a comprehensive racial contract or a global (racial) logic. The actuarial approach provides a way of seeing, portraying, or depicting vast arrays of race-based miseries without positing a view of racism that fits a logical system. Thus, the actuarial account of racism is an attenuated explanatory model, which limits itself to the depiction (or making plain) of statistical correlations, patterns, and trends in risk, ill-health, and undue death for particular racialized populations in particular contexts. As such, this actuarial account "need not pretend to be an explanation that purports to cover all cases or offer a ubiquitous characterization of racism." The mode, form, type, and salience of racial necro-being will differ depending on the context.

Necro-Being

Racism is a form of necro-being: it kills and prevents persons from being born. It is absolute necro-tragedy. There is no redemption for the worst of its victims. Dominant groups acquire longer lives, assets, and high senses of self-worth at the cost of the extinction or sustained subordination of the subjugated. Racism kills as a function of the way especially health and wealth benefits occur to the communities for which racists belong through the aegis of fatal inventions of race. Racism is a polymorphous agent of death, premature births, shortened lives, starving children, debilitating theft, abusive larceny, degrading insults, and insulting stereotypes forcibly imposed (Harris 1999, 437). Racism persists because it works sufficiently well in an imperfect world to ensure a confluence of benefits, especially the most important benefit—namely, health benefits—for enough people over generations. It effects the preconditions for the possibility of embodied wellbeing. In addition, recursive and compounded benefits allow for sustaining vast differences in life chances. The relationship between dominant and subjected groups is one in which health can be understood as transferred from one to the other. Racism, as polyhedron, is only one variable in a vast range of sometimes ambiguous and multifarious influences of different saliences making necro-being.

There are anomalies associated with accounts of racism as a logic—that is, accounts that provide a neat picture of its causes and simultaneously provide reasons, consonant with its explanation, for its moral wrongness, whether the explanation is volitional, institutional, structural, or racial identities. I offer an actuarial picture of necro-being to help see misery that is missed by anomalies associated with these logics of explanation—that is, volitional, institutional, structural, and racial identities as a primal cause. Examples of logical world systems of racism are Marx and Engels (1848, 2001), Blyden ([1888] 2016), Goldberg (1990), Bowser (1995), Garcia (1996), Mills (1997), Loury (2002), Shelby (2008), and Bonilla-Silva (2014). The approach is intended to help see race-based misery, whether the folk conception of race is peculiar to Tasmania, Rwanda, the United States, or Burma. The approach foregrounds realities where contradictions are not resolved, true interests are not realized, and neither human nature nor powers, abilities, or capacities realized.

An actuarial account, as a descriptive account, foregrounds racism as undue death by providing a way of seeing, portraying, comporting, and depicting vast arrays of race-based miseries. The benefit of an actuarial account is that it helps us to see a vast range of miseries in ways that explanations fail to convey. The account is not comprehensive, but hopefully its philosophical contours are sufficiently suggestive to recommend viable future avenues of empirical research and sufficiently rich to support the thesis of racism as necro-being. In addition, the account is sometimes conveyed in poetic terms rather than the usual method of philosophical analytic distinctions and clarifications because I believe that poetic forms can convey subtle emotions, innuendoes, and images that well-structured arguments and analytic distinctions fail to convey.

One way to see the polyhedron terror of racism is to think about what it is to face the misery of injustice, unredeemable: necro-being. Necro-being, as I mean it, is always that which makes living a kind of death—life that is simultaneously being robbed of its sheer potential physical being as well as nonbeing, the unborn. Necro-being is nonbeing, categorically impossible beings (Harris 2017). Not invisible but nonexisting. Dead ghosts. The situation of necro-being is hardly the sole consequence of racism, and the situation can exist under conditions effected by, for example, only ethnic or status variables. I focus here on racism. Achille Mbembé developed a feature of Michel Foucault's concept of biopolitics (the use of sovereign power to control the use and meaning of bodies) and contends that "the function of racism is to regulate the distribution of death and to make possible the murderous function of the state" (Mbembé 1992, 17). It is, [Foucault] says "the condition for the acceptability of putting to death" (Foucault 1997, 228). The consequence for the immiserated according to Mbembé is that "vast populations are subjected to conditions of life conferring upon them the status of living dead" (Mbembé 1992, 3). Foucault's picture of racism requires a state and civil society with established codified institutional rules. However, suffering, humiliation, and physical abuse are not always conditions of forces of the state or institutions of well-codified rules in a civil society. Feudal societies, aristocracies, Saharan nomadic societies, and acephalous populations can be the site of racism. Immigrant women and trafficked slaves between different countries do not have social networks of community, marriage, or commonly owned businesses yet suffer similar miseries. Their lives are not influenced by a single state or civil society but by a myriad of states and civil societies of which they may have fragmented membership. Whether antiblack racism or racialized Islamophobia, persons can suffer harm that cannot be neatly tracked to the laws or institutional rules of a single society the same way that failure to treat a woman with breast cancer with high regard may not be tracked to one care giver.

Racism, despite the social formation within which it resides, creates a living death for masses of its victims. The working class, for example, may gain power in the future, but those who suffer now are not relieved by whatever ceremonies future generations hold in honor or memory of former workers. That's one reason why necro-being is a living death—being that in no way will receive substantive forms of relief, justice, recognition, or compensation. Given that there is no moral universe, injustice, suffering, good, bad or malevolence is nowhere recorded in the universe. During American slavery, "mistresses sometimes coupled physical violence with psychological violence. Slave children in the white household were introduced to these practices from an early age. The same hands, tongs, and shovels used in violence against adults were applied to children." The violence against slave women by a mistress included "Bible-stumping threats of hell for disobedience, verbal abuse, pinches and slaps, severe beatings, burnings, and murder" (Glymph 2008, 35). Mistresses gained status, enjoyed sadistic pleasures, avoided life-destructive labor assigned to their subjects, acquired wealth, and obtained relatively better health care than their subjects. Contemporary violence workers, such as police, soldiers, prison guards, and slave traffickers are well versed in the use of violence, receiving very often excellent salaries, awards, and community popularity. Physicians and nurses involved in removing, buying, and selling illegally obtained organs, such as eyes or livers, from the desperate and destitute usually live comfortable lives; the desperate and destitute frequently suffer and die prematurely.

The virtues of the victims of racism, as necro-being, do not add to a universe of goodness. That is one reason why indignant or forgiving normative traits have no import, save their role in the lives of the subjugated; the world is not a better or worse place because there is no moral universe where the traits of the powerless and completely isolated shape reality—such traits do not form some mystical social force that somehow magically help to terminate the conditions sustaining injustice. Even if forgiving and altruist traits, for example, on balance are preferable traits because they promote trust, valuable communication, and peaceful social change benefiting the least well-off, none invariably occur to any subjugated person, class, race, or ethnic group. There is no warrant for them to be sacrificial. There is no salvation, redemption, reparations, or recompense during their lifetime. There is no recognition of the suffering that, *ipso facto*, terminates their suffering. There is very little grieving for those that are robbed of coming into existence and very little sanctuary for the living.

Individuals are not instruments in a cosmic story, but even if they were unwitting tools, the story never provides them a role where they are redeemed and their suffering rewarded or ill-health replaced with good health. Stories that picture a moral universe are at best stories that provide solace. There are no instantiations of embodied pure abstract transcendental goodness that relieve suffering and no journeys that end in the salvation of shamed individuals. There is no world where they get to be appreciated for stalwart character or courage. The unborn have no such benefits and the living, in the midst of necro-being, are the embodiment of absolute tragedy.

The Tragic

The tragic is absolute irredeemable and meaningless affliction: necro-tragedy. Tragedy is neither Aristotelian nor Hegelian, neither ancient nor modern. It is not understandable as a collective understanding exemplified by the sadness of wayward human ways nor the collective trauma before a resolution making life well for all. It is not a dialectic resolution of conflict mysteriously inclined to be solved and terminate with congenial results. And even if the arc of the universe bends toward justice—that is the ideal Martin L. King Jr. so staunchly affirmed in his "Letter from Birmingham City Jail" (King 1963)—the arc's structure, teleology, and consequence are useless other than as a mythology for the immiserated as a source of solace and motivation to sonder on. The members of a necro-being universe never are the beneficiaries of justice, and no future condition in any way compensates those that have suffered or were never born. The virtuous and innocent suffer. There is no realization of universal interest or human nature. There is no memory. Millions of slave children, for example, raped, beaten, and killed leave no living record of their misery. This is not Nietzschean "beyond tragedy" as a state awaiting resolution or a state that ushers in a new sense of mission. This is a world where those who suffer are not available to be persons for whom moral emotions apply. One way to see this is to consider how the subjugated are not just implicated in their own misery but also unintentionally involved as parasites in the misery of others.

Racism

What the family of properties, meanings, and contours that "racism" entails in a Black/white binary America hardly has the same features and saliences when "Black" is a part of the tectonic of imperialist oppression and consumer products (e.g., cultural goods such as boxing matches, skin-lightening creams, Evangelical missionaries promoting gospel music, minstrelsy, Motown rhythm and blues albums, stereos, Zoot suits, bell-bottom blue jeans, miniskirts, and curling irons). "Black" as a racial nomenclature comes with material and cultural referents, images, practices, and products. Black identity participates in creating boundaries, cultural impositions, and categories.[1] Necro-being as I conceive it is not made palatable by thinking of African Americans as a population with an exceptional history or teleology. Black identity and African American cultural, class, and status formation have in various ways contributed to features of human misery. There are no innocent historical agents, that is, there are no identities, modes of consciousness, or class formations that function as conduits for the salvation of necro-being.

The very identity of "Black" spelled a death knell for the ethnic identity of all Ganga speakers. The identity caused no one's death; it was a tectonic tool in the arsenal of subjection forces. Ganga speakers suffered not just a holocaust but also total genocide. Their wooden spears were no match for metal knives, guns, and sailing ships. Their homeland, stretching between what is now Sierra Leone and Liberia along the Atlantic coast was devastated by a combination of whites who raided their villages—like afternoon hunting parties—and Mandingo or Fulani slave owners who used them for export, trade, or local purposes. What culture remains of these Ganga speakers is in court documents, ship ledgers, or religious practices and scattered terms in such locations as Palo Mayombe or Palo Mayoma in Cuba, Haiti, Dominica, Brazil, and Puerto Rico. Those cultural remains have long since lost any connection to the dead and tortured natives of the language, religion, and culture. An analog on a larger numerical scale would be the disappearance of every native English speaker, Christian, white, and Black American without any currently living persons having any appreciable sense of any language, national, cultural, racial, ethnic, or religious inheritance. Effectively, total annihilation; their descendants exist but with no memories or behaviors from ancestors of any significance.

What the progeny of the Ganga achieves, now understood as Black, whether mayor, lawyer, engineer, or computer scientist in no way aids their dead ancestors. Inherited features of cultural heritage are at best props, examples of historical remnants that living persons feel good having inherited but that perform no role in determining what they own or control. Analogously, unborn children who do not exist because their conceivable parents were sterilized, castrated, or suffered undue incarceration have no body to inherit ancestral cultural traits.

General features of racism do not neatly map to particular conditions. That is one reason why explanations of miseries in radically different societies should vary; a logic fails to make substantive distinction between what life means to different populations even if structures are identical. How can I see the racism that helped kill Tasmanians by 1843 and Tutsis in the Rwandan holocaust in 1994 without assuming that there is a single general cause or identical structure of emotions or forms of production? I could not see the intricacies of the miseries for themselves as themselves if I presume a logical social structure and a well-defined derivation manual that maps particular circumstances or events to the structure. How can I see the racism faced by the Rohingya of Myanmar, particularly when entrapped in Burmese refugee camps caged in animal pens, and the racism that is causative of the exceedingly high rate of suicide among African American males in 2017? How can I see the racism that helped kill the Ganga, suppressed indigenous nationalities of South Africa under apartheid, and killed Black Americans when "Black" is an identity used to help destroy indigenous nationalities, promote modernity (which includes African American culture as a model of modernity often imitated by Africans), and create deep senses of loss?

Racist violence workers do not see their subjects as victims let alone worthy of sympathy. But that common feature of violence workers neither does explain why Tutsi women were considered morally irredeemable and racially inferior cockroaches by Hutu perpetrators of genocide nor does it explain why white prison guards brutalize African American males more than white males. Comprehensive knowledge of anti-Rohingya racism may tell us nothing about antiblack racism in the United States. Why Dalit or Rohingya women are considered un-rapeable (their spiritual being makes them tainted lowly animals) and why Black American boys are considered un-rapeable (lying wretches invested with bestial natures and always agents of harm to others) may be understandable only if we see unique social stereotypes, not just similarities.

How can I see misery as a function of race without assuming a ubiquitous logic—that is, a set of volitions, explanations, opaque moral emotions, identical structures producing identical results, and virtuous properties embedded intrinsically in every agent? How can I see at least some contours of such a vast array of radically different forms of reality without simultaneously assuming a logic or singular causative account?

Imagine a way of morally condemning racism that is free of presenting racism as having a logical form. Racism, explained as having a logical form, is likely to be considered an epiphenomenon of class conflict, a subcategory of nepotism, the result of institutional rules, a consequence of intentional avarice, malfeasance, ill-will, disrespect, or irrationality. In all the above approaches to explanation, racism may be considered an independent variable in at least special cases shaping social and material relations. A moral criticism of racism gains efficacy if the explanation of its cause associated with the criticism is cogent; conversely, an explanation of racism always entails, like all explanations, value judgments, and the explanation gains cogency if the value judgments are defensible.

Imagine a way of morally condemning racism without the need for a corresponding explanation of its causes, or on my account, its polymorphic array of forces. We would not need to treat as anomalies every case of racial discord that fails to fit an explanatory account. If, for example, racism is caused by class exploitation, we must treat an individual case of racial harm not well explained as a reaction to or function of class positions; if racism is explained as a function of hoarding behavior, we must treat cases of racial harm motivated by malevolence and against an agent's better interest as an outlier. If racism is explained as a consequence of structures, such an account is inadequate unless it at least recognizes that emotions, beliefs, and values are important variables defining why individuals abide the rules that define the structure. And if the explanation relies on psychological states, such an account is inadequate unless it recognizes that there can be cases of racism that do not rely on invidious mental states but color-blind rules that may have never been intended as discriminatory.[2]

In addition, imagine a way of morally condemning racism that does not commit us to categorizing racial kinds as objective communities. "Objective communities" are communities that exist relatively independent of our choices. They are communities that social kind racial realists contend sustain raciated communities. Social kind racial realist believe that races are relatively stable social inbreeding populations that form communities.[3]

Races follow endogamy rules. Some significant force or forces, such as kinship or clan nepotism, the history of segregation, or ancestral heritage networks may be considered the dominant force determining the existence of racial communities. Raciated communities encumber communal bonds sustained through networks over generations (Harris 1997, 1998b, 2000, 2002. Also see, for debates regarding natural or objective communities and ontology, Sabia Jr. and Wallulis 1983; Harris 1998a).

In my imagined scenario, we could condemn anomalies without the need to treat them as outliers, accidents, epiphenomena of class conflict, ill-wills, malicious intentions or oddities, or the usual functioning of institutional rules. Every relevant anomaly, if it is racially encoded, will affect health. It is health that is always influential in the relevant way—it harms. If a racist ill-will has the result of benefiting an individual for example, given my admitted priority of death and health, it does not matter. I will not consider it "racism." The anomalies of explanation, such as individual cases of racial antipathy or disregard when racism is defined as a function of institutional rules or a consequence of class conflict, are not described as anomalies. It will be whether there are health and death desiderata. If someone finds that racial antipathy influences an individual such that their health is not ill effected, such an anomaly will not appear as "racist." Whether the antipathy is motivated by racial disregard is irrelevant. Admittedly, on this account the unity theory of virtue does not hold—that is, possessing one virtue does not assure the possession of other virtues. A virtue does not invariably pervade a persons' character or produce the same undifferentiated or consistent behavior; Thomas Aquinas and others were wrong (Porter 1993). Antipathy may have a wide range of utilities, not all invariably destructive, given that "intrinsic" goodness is completely irrelevant save in its individual or social role at a given time and place. The boundary, in virtue of what makes a condition at the very least a feature of racism, is undue ill-health and death as a function of raciation.

When I imagine thinking about racism in the above way, I segue into picturing, depicting, and describing racism rather than explaining racism. "Explaining" involves proving causes, and "describing" involves providing a picture. A problem with describing racism is that it needs fairly narrow parameters; a description based on the definition could help to provide direction to pick out appropriate cases and conditions. Even if "definitions" are considered a family of propositions, features, and images, they provide some boundary guidelines. A fairly narrow definition always fails to capture a variety of forms of prejudice, exclusions, and subjugations by race, which in one context may have a low salience and in another context, high salience, let alone a myriad of possible causes. This is one reason authors sometimes prefer to discuss "racisms" (Bonilla-Silva 2014).

"Racism," ostensively, is an essentially contested concept. That is, it is a concept we use to do more work than any concept can accomplish or be susceptible to a neat definition; for example, it is used as approbation, moral depiction, explanation, or description. It is appraisive, variously describable, oppositional, and often used to capture a whole phenomenon (Urquidez 2016).[4] However, it is a viable definable concept, given a range of caveats about definitions for various purposes. Some properties of racism seem standard, given radical differences in salience. For example, racism sustains egregious, unnecessary, and heinous dichotomies and hierarchies; it makes possible undue ill-health and death; and it tends to promote undue feelings of inferiority in its victims. Such lists of consequences and conditions can be unduly extensive, lending to its frequently seemingly porous and contestable character. But there are realities. Racial identities, always transitory, endure for periods sufficient to be objects of dereliction and loathing; lives are effected, communities are influenced, and death occurs.

Races are, I believe, historical contrivances, anabsolute, but have real being in each context. "The instability of the noun race proves that classification reflects historical context rather than defining it. The problem is that the noun race has become too contaminated by the political practices of segregation and extermination to be used by researchers unreflectively" (Bethencourt 2013, 7). Race has been a synonym for castes, distinction between pagan/gentile, peoples as ethnos (i.e., nations as races), plants, animals, descents, languages, nationality, religions, phenotypes, and genotypes. In general, "Racism attributes a single set of real or imaginary physical and/or mental features to the precise ethnic groups, and believes these features to be transmitted from one generation to generation" (Bethencourt 2013, 7–8). Racism "is channeled by a complex web of collective memories and sudden possibilities—a web that can change the forms and targets of racism" (Bethencourt 2013, 6). Whether in Oakland, California, or in Beijing, China, racism has broad definable traits that always need to be adjusted and informed by the relevant context (Dikötter 1997; Robb 1997; Hall 2011).

Racism, like death, is real, and the concept is especially well defined when it helps us to consider what is needed to negate its existence. I will proffer a definition, or rather a range of features that can be understood as a definition. Features of the definition will not pick out an essence, unmitigated fact, pure being, or the truth about all forms of racist misery without any caveats. It defines, shows. Given that all definitions have embedded referents, causal accounts, and normative values that are never sufficiently opaque—and all explanations use definitions—by subsumption, the definition of racism I offer entails normative values never sufficiently opaque. The traits I argue are the most salient indicators of racism are health transfers and death.

Contrary to Garcia and Mills, there may be nothing that is of "prime moral and explanatory importance" about racism (Garcia 1996, 404). That is, there may be nothing that will provide a comprehensive theory or logic of racism or provide a neat picture of its causes and simultaneously provide reasons, consonant with its explanation, of its moral wrongness. I doubt, but do not argue here, that there is an explanation of racism that matches a social logic of which it follows. And I doubt that the world is a place of social structures well designed in a way analogous to variables in symbolic logic equations—whether dialectic or analytic. I also doubt that we need a single thing, in virtue of which, racism is morally wrong. The popular meaning of "racism" has come to entail that it is implicitly and morally heinous, but the nature of the wrongness is not thereby simply conveyed.

In the following section, I first consider the advantages of giving an account of racism that pictures, depicts, and describes rather than explains. I also provide a narrow definition of racism.

Collective Intentions in a Nonracist World

Rational-intentional, causal, and interpretive explanations are broad categories of explanatory types (Hindess 1977; Little 1991). Rational-intentional theories presuppose that individual or group choices are crucial, salient features shaping circumstances and event series; causal accounts picture event series as determinant and shaped by direct forces, usually material or institutional; and interpretive accounts consider the goals of agents, meanings of events, and motivations as explanatory. Systematic torture, terrorism, and rape by use of humiliation, degradation, and dehumanization can be understood as a function of dispositions (virtues), situations (institutions and networks), or systems (logical global systems), whether rational-intentional, causal/materialist or interpretive (Zimbardo 2007).

Each method is substantively different. The irreducibility of the explanatory methods to one another is reflected in how they each depict virtues. Rational-intentional accounts tend to emphasize virtues or the lack thereof as salient causes (institutions and forms of production are subordinate variables); institutional accounts tend to emphasize the role of a race or race-blind rule (virtues and forms of production are subordinate variables); and materially determinant accounts emphasize ubiquitous common forms of production and consequences (virtues and institutions are subordinate variables). This hardly covers all forms of explanation; however, it provides a starting point.

I will focus on the limitations of rational-intentional explanations of why racism persists. I explore what it means to depict racism, rather than explain racism, in terms of necro-being—racism as a killing machine. An actuarial account does not exist. I argue that an actuarial account could allow us to depict racism as a life-and-death exchange: victims as corpses, cumulatively persons being robbed of their body parts and hosts for parasites of the same species.[5]

An actuarial account is a broad theoretical approach. It advocates using the tools of actuaries to see who lives or dies, health risks, and related probabilities by race to see differences of mortality and morbidity related to or correlated by race with environments, employment, and ownership. It avoids the misguided use of rational-intentional explanations, the limitations of social kind racial realism, and the misguided view that racism exists as a global logical system. If an actuarial way of describing and morally condemning racism is at least a useful addition to the rational-intentional way of proceeding, it may also be an attractive addition to institutional, materialist, and interpretive explanations.

The disagreements between Mills and Garcia have a long history (Garcia 2001, 27–42; Mills 2002; Headley 2000, 2006). Of particular note is that they each predicate their views on a different assumption about the relationship between individuals and groups. Individuals (existential indefeasible singulars) are for Garcia the explanation of collective behavior, and collective behavior for Mills is a function of institutions and systems. Mills is committed to an ontology, at least in the sense of a "historically" existing "social kind" that (1) has empirical measurable reality and/or (2) can be treated as having such a reality for us to think about the "racial contract" in ways that generate reasonable principles that we want to map onto an existing world. If the existing world is substantively different from the measurable existing world in (1), then we would need a new argument for why a thought experiment should be the source of recommendations for a world for which the thought experiment lacks substance.

The divide between Garcia and Mills is irreconcilable because their views of ontology are fundamentally at odds. An Aristotelian ontological essence of being and an existential view of being warrant fundamentally different views of social kinds. Individuals, on an Aristotelian approach, are instantiations of collective group or objective structural forms; objective structures and collective groups are always defined by existential individuals and their intentions. Contrary to Martinot's view, there is no middle position between an ontology that makes the individual its agent of being and one that makes some form of a collective group its agent of being such that what exists—and not just what is explained as a heuristic device—is the core of reality (Martinot 2007). Garcia and Mills are not just expressing different beliefs—both consider race itself a social construction—but different ways of seeing humanity. What the criticism of racism looks like is at least partially conditioned on what "it" is and "why" it functions through the aegis of individual traits and social abstracta or entities.

There are various kinds of racism. In this regard, Mills and Garcia have a point: there are racisms. Given various kinds of racism, and whether individual prejudice or institutionally driven, Garcia's contention is well reasoned. "What it is in virtue of which each is a form of racism" is a query that is not answered by simply explaining that racisms exist (Garcia 1996, 403). Garcia is arguably asking the same question that, according to Plato, Socrates asked Euthyphro: What is the form of piety, and by what is it that makes any particular act an act of piousness? This is a category question. At the very least, its answer requires that we have some sense of what makes an act a member of the kind. We need some way to link particular events to the category even if our derivation manual— the manual that tells us how to map a particular event to its membership in a general category—is imperfect. The "what it is" has to be mapped onto "what" (an ontology of being, weighted salience to individuals or structures) as its agential conduit; the category is an agent that not only defines reality but also can be said to influence and shape reality. Max Weber, Robert Parks, and Gordon Allport believed that intentions, habits, tastes, stereotypes, and misguided beliefs are of the greatest salience in sustaining racism (Stone and Routledge 2003).

Their different explanations for the persistence of racism were volitional; each author considered intentions as important causal variables and offered a rational-intentional explanatory form (e.g., individual intentions are gathered together as a swarm and treated as a common kind agent, creating structures, social pressure, institutional rules). It is "explaining from the intentional stance" (Dennett 1987; also see Tilly 1999, 2002; Hull 1992; Hacking 1994; Cummins 2000). Such stances can come to stand over a social order, having such a powerful history and seemingly ubiquitous practice that they are taken as natural. Explaining from the intentional stance is commonly thought of as moving from volitions, desires, beliefs, and intentions to actions. In this vein, Glenn C. Loury's *The Anatomy of Racial Inequality* (2002) is an example of explaining from an intentional stance. Loury terms his approach as one in the social–cognitive tradition. Race, for him, is to be explained in terms that embody social significance (Loury 2002; also see Garcia et al. 2002). Individual intentions coalesce in some form to shape collective intentions and their social agency. The divide between the volitional account of racism by Jorge Garcia and the institutional account of racism by Charles Mills will be used to consider the advantages of an actuarial account that avoids important limitations of both rational-intentional explanations of collective intentions and institutional accounts that rely on positing social kind racial entities.

Collective Intentions and Structural Violence

According to Garcia, the moral core of racism involves virtues. "Racism, then, is something that essentially involves not our beliefs and their rationality or irrationality, but our wants, intentions, likes and dislikes and their distance from the moral virtues" (Garcia 1996, 400). The moral virtues of importance are benevolence, malfeasance, and inadequate care for others. That is, the racists harbor a "vicious kind of racially based disregard for the welfare of certain people" (Garcia 1996, 399). The virtues explain. Institutional racism is a function of individual failings. "Institutional racism exists, as we said, when the racism in individuals becomes institutionalized" (Garcia 1996, 423).

The link between individual proclivities and institutions is direct. "Unless an institution is corrupted (in its ends, means, priorities, or assumptions) by a prior and independent racism in some individual's heart, however, institutional racism can never come to exist" (Garcia 1996, 424; also see Bonilla-Silva 2014).

Garcia's volitional account mistakenly treats intentions as the root of structures. Individual vices—ill-wills, disregard, malfeasance, malevolence—taken cumulatively or collectively never amount to a social stereotype, social structure, or institution. Blacks are, for example, more so than whites portrayed by American news media as uncontrollably violent. It is necessarily the case that some individuals must have invidious and malevolent intentions over time to portray Blacks in this way for the stereotype to be persistent; it is false that the stereotype is explained as a function of each individual invidious and malevolent intention. One reason for this that is relevant here is that each individual invidious intention could be significantly distinct, but the collective result could be the popular stereotype of Blacks as uncontrollably violent. The similarities between individual invidious intentions that are characteristically the basis for antiblack stereotypes do not form a coherent collective social agent.

One way to think about the difference between individual intentions and collective group behavior is to consider the character of intentions in relationship to survival. Individuals may be concerned with trying to stay alive and healthy, but it is false that the species is intentionally trying to stay alive and healthy as a function of collective intentions (cumulative or compounded). If no one were trying to stay alive, the species, as a function of the kinds of animals we happen to be, would be best explained as trying to stay alive. Ontogenetic causal motivations are not identical to phylogenetic behavior causes. A clear majority of individuals may be intentionally trying to survive, but the species does not have a collective will. It is only metaphorical that the species can be said to be trying to survive. The relationship between the collection of individual intentions to the collective behavior of survival is asymmetric. Unintentional consequences are not intentions. Just as it is false that frogs are trying to stay alive as a function of the individual intentions of each frog, if one accepts the idea that humans are at base an animal species, then we do not need collective intentions to explain why as individuals we are trying to stay alive.

Another way to think about collective intentions as the explanation for racism is to think about how to explain not the desires, beliefs, and intentions of racists but the desires, beliefs, and intentions of the oppressed. It may not be fruitful to say that the response to deprivation, inequalities, and insults is the collective intentional response of "feeling despised." There are no human populations incapable of, or not, feeling despised when suffering structural violence (Galtung 1969, 1990; Khan 1978; Scheper-Hughes 1992; 1996; Mamdani 1996; Uvin 1998). Structural violence—arrangement of category boundaries, income, asset, ownership, employment, and legal rules coupled with a general social perception of the oppressed as despised (not just poor, lowly, or subordinate)— produces highly predictable results. Racialized structural violence produces race-based responses of ethnocide and gerrymandered communities whether in Rwanda, South Africa, Brazil, or Australia. Analogously, slavery produces maroon societies, revolts, and populations forced to sustain self-subservience and self-deprecation (Anno 1991; Smidley et al. 2001; Ferguson 2014. Also see Anno 1996; Global Slavery Index 2016).[6]

Responses to structural violence, ranging from marooning to ethnocide, are not a matter of gathering together individual intentions to see how they coalesce into collective intentions that then translate, via some account of reasons or emotions causing behavior, into action. It is always the case that Pareto's maximum is true, especially in relationship to life and health. People want more health than less, independent of collective intentions. It is hard to think of the persistent struggles against racism as a matter of isolated individual existential beings deciding to feel despised and then cooperating with others to resist racist practices. "Being despised" exists as a social condition—that is, senses of being lowly occur in a context of what one knows or feels what it is to be lowly: loss of face, loss of bodily privacy, and so on. Certainly, the oppressed and oppressors intentionally engage in actions, but the point is that persistent struggles against racism and persistent feelings of being despised under racist regimes can be fruitfully thought of in ways other than segregated individual intentions or intentions coalescing together to form collective intentions.

Racial communities only appear as stable, static, well-defined, naturally given, or communal bastions driven by invariable human natures; that is why they are anabsolute. Anabsolute social groups are unstable, contingent, and constantly changing groups frequently interfaced with far more stable classes, nations, or ethnic groups. Anabsolute groups display anomalies: Black people everywhere, for example, arguably have a common moral interest to combat antiblack racism, and they are all the object of antiblack racism, yet there is no ontologically stable social "Black" race forming an ontological kind nor a logic of racism such that the salience of antiblack racism is constitutive. Antiblack racism in South Africa, given a vast array of populations with ethnic identities, is not identical to antiblack racism in the United States, where "Black" people almost never define themselves nor are defined in ethnic terms. There is no need to think of communities of races as historical populations that can escape the vagaries of history and context. Rather, constructivist views of community—namely, that communities are anabsolute entities of evolving modes of association and bonding—shape a defensible approach to racial and ethnic identity (Harris 2002).

African Americans are a breeding population, in evolutionist terms, but not a "race" in the sense of being a population consisting of an isolated gene pool. They are a "race" in the sense of being neatly socially identifiable by color and complexion coding that has only a socially defined sense. However, a socially defined sense of race is not adequate. There must be some objective kin selection project that allows hoarding and transfers across generations. The integrative structures of family, language, and so on, for Blacks are ethnic structures, not racial ones. The inseparable link between race and ethnicity in this regard suggests that reliance solely on race as defining community fails. Arguably, Mills's racial divide in the racial contract fails to explain adequately because race does not account for ethnic structures. That is, the racial contract in the actual world—Mills is committed to a racial "relationship" as an empirical fact—is always bifurcated in a myriad of ways by ethnic divides (Mills 2001, 19). For Mills, we can understand world racism as a contract, albeit a racial contract in which the terms of the relationship are ones that sustain antiblack racism. It is historically and descriptively explanatory because it "explains how society was created or crucially transformed" (Mills 1998, 4). However, the salient, ethnic and racial variables are neither identical nor reducible to one another. The suffering of young African American males in Gary, Indiana, may not be well captured by a single theory or logic of racism that also purports to capture the suffering of Yoruba-speaking young immigrant men from Nigeria, in the slums of Johannesburg. Both have suffered from antiblack racism, but to explain their worlds under one rubric arguably requires an unlimited number of caveats, such as noting their different statuses—immigrant or citizen, taking account of national heritage, class status, religious histories, language specific meanings, and educational resources.

Vicente Morales, the Creole captain of the slave ship *Jesus Maria* had a 15-year-old Spanish cabin boy, Juan Bufo, who was ordered to serve him a glass of rum aboard the slave ship during its voyage between Sierra Leone and Puerto Rico between December 1840 and January 1841. "When Bufo accidentally dropped the bottle, Morales tortured him for two or three days, little by little breaking his limbs and disfiguring his face with sharp instruments. He then pitched the lad overboard, though he had not yet expired" (Dorsey 2003, 302). Of the ninety-four surviving women, nearly all had been raped, but the Ganga-speaking *bozal* (Spanish for muzzle, novice, raw simpleton, wild animal like a horse or a dog; used to describe non-Creole Africans) were repeatedly raped, and the Spanish-speaking Africans were the least violated. "He [Morales, had] already murdered a [slave] girl named Boyce, for fear that her cries might attract anti-slave patrols in Caribbean waters" (Dorsey 2003, 308). Morales had experience terrorizing women, so when it came to "#169 Mania, a girl about 13 years of age, examined, states that the captain of 'Jesus Maria' held her nose and mouth to keep her from screaming and had connexion [rape] with her, she was hurt very much at the time" (Dorsey 2003, 304). Save for one 21-year-old woman, all the slaves were between 10 and 15 years old, the average age being 11 years. The rapists included Black seamen. Individual dispositions as a function of bad faith, ill-will, and choice certainly helped to make rape exist on this ship. However, Morales was described as mild-mannered, devoted to the well-being of his crew, and sadistically cruel.

The system of slavery made possible the *Jesus Maria*. The institutions of profit in human cargo, race-based patriarchy, the benefits of rape without punishment, and legal and informal rules governing commerce help to make rape a common occurrence. Institutional practices and the moral character of individuals might both be informative. However, if the explanation of miseries is a function of individual lack of virtues, the criticism of their agency is different than one that explains these miseries as a function of institutions.

If, as William J. Wilson and Charles Tilly contend, institutions function at best in the selfish predatory interest of members (real, perceived, structural, or accidental), then the hoarding behavior of persons in advantaged positions in these institutions is rewarded. They gain independent of their moral character (e.g., status, security, etc.). If, as many social Darwinists contend, it is in the nature of individuals to function in their own self-preserving interest (real, perceived, structural, or accidental), then it is the nepotism, endogamy, and institutional rules allowing persons in advantaged positions to acquire benefits and transfer assets that allow a given group to dominate (Wilson 1996; Tilly 1999).

It would seem, consequently, that if either conception of social agency is cogent (i.e., institutional or evolutionary), transfer of assets over generations is more effective by populations in advantaged positions than those in subordinate conditions, independent of whether a particular person in the advantaged position is the cause of misery. This occurs in the same way that people who live in communities with a myriad of health services gain whatever their social status independent of the intentions of persons in lower or higher positions. Under the regime of either explanatory type, we can always measure who dies and how long they lived.

Imagine a nonracist world. Such a world would be without intentional or unintentional racist beliefs, prejudices, or stereotypes, and with no behaviors corresponding to racist intentions, beliefs, prejudices, or stereotypes. Further, workers will be in a sociopolitical position for reasons other than intentional, unintentional, or institutional causes associated with racism in their society (Oliver and Shapiro 1995). Yet, in a nonracist world, the subjugated population of the formerly raciated world—that population without assets—would be in the position of the least well-off, the object of expropriation and subjugation, and continually seen as the least likely to achieve. If there were no individual racists, the reality of racism as a form of race-based expropriation and divide could persist in a nonracist world.

"Racism," applied to a nonracist world, is used here to specify the persistence of boundaries, whether recognized or not, which persists for reasons associated with race-based boundaries. Intended results are thereby irrelevant to the persistence of the difference. The compounded benefits whites have acquired, for example, from special privileges and inherited life insurance policies, trust funds, savings bonds, copyrights on computer parts, patents for name brands of guns, and so on, form a tremendous advantage over minority populations that lack such inherited benefits. The sheer fact of compounding—the added benefits over time of multiple benefits such as owning savings bonds and owning trademarks, copyright, and patents—means that the owners have compounded individual and collective advantages over persons without such benefits. In addition, the recursive benefits, especially those that reoccur on a scheduled basis, such as interest payments on outstanding loans or incremental value increases on farm property, provide inevitable advantages to the owners of such assets. Such assets are the preconditions that make possible good health and access to health-providing resources. Cumulative effects of asset accumulation in the portfolios of empowered racial groups provide them with options under conditions of scarcity, hardship, and personal indiscretions to hold sufficient resources to overcome untoward difficulties. The lack of cumulative benefits makes disadvantaged racialized populations invariably subject to hardships, such as the inability to pay for advance medical treatments; therefore, they experience shortened lives and produce fewer healthy progeny. Individuals of the formerly exploited and victimized group would remain behind the asset-holding group, although not recognized as such a group in a nonracist world.

A zero-sum game is one that supposes that there is only a defined array of assets available. However, we know that assets are not entrapped in a zero-sum game. Anomalies, inventions, unexpected asset-creating resources, and new desires are only a few reasons that assets are not entrapped in a zero-sum game. It is possible, consequently, that a subjugated population can ascend, for reasons having nothing to do with ending the causes of their subjection. Given rejection of the above unreasonable assumption, the former oppressed racial group (no longer identified or separated as a race in my imagined nonracist world) could not accumulate to the point of parity with a former racist oppressor without it being said that the "group" acquired assets and accumulated benefits. How and why they did so could be accidental or untoward.

Slavery became a crime in August 2007 in Mauritania. Approximately 40 percent of the current population are "black Moors"[7] or *Haratin*, who have served for generations "white Moors" or *Bidban*, approximately 30 percent of the population. *Haratin* means, in its folk usage, a despised population. Slave masters are not likely to willfully turn over all their material advantages to their former slaves and live as equals—neither a change in the character of their virtues nor institutional change is very likely to produce such a result. Inherited status forms a stigma, badge, and label of inferiority. Since racial identity as a public badge of identity is deeply anathema, contrary to the way racial identity in the modern West is embraced as a badge of culture, heritage, and solidarity, few courageous accounts, such as *Le Manifeste du Negro-Mauritanien Opprimé* ("Manifesto of the Oppressed Black Mauritanian") in 1986, have emerged from the voices of the enslaved (African Liberation Forces of Mauritania 1986). The response to the *Manifesto*, authored primarily by *Haritin* from the Toucouleur, included replacing government and military officials with Black Africans from the Wolof or Soninké groups. Ethnicity is bifurcated by race. Very rarely have Western-based African, Black, Christian, and/or romance language–based communities made the liberation of the *Haratin* their cause célèbre. Black Mauritanians, African Americans, and Afro-Brazilians are not a racial breeding population with integrated institutional structures, such as commonly owned businesses or religious institutions. Even if Mauritania becomes immediately a nonracist world, the *Haratin* and their children for generations to come will have shorter lives and worse health than the *Bidban*. Persons generally transfer privileges and assets to their progeny; communal forms of guardianship (e.g., marital patterns, neighborhood associations) help to secure these transfers. Given significantly different existing guardianship institutions, the future of the descendants of each population, even in a nonracial world, would differ significantly unless untoward asserts were acquired in a nonmoral world not confined to a zero-sum game.

Although *Haratin* Mauritanians, African Americans, and Afro-Brazilians are not a racial breeding population, and cannot thereby form a race understood as a clan or a family, they are all nonetheless the object of antiblack racism. Raciated communities, sustained by networks and maintaining encumbered bonds, do not form a world of racial bonds across different locations. Antiblack racism suffering has different saliences and histories.

The existence of Black people as objective raciated communities fails to make them, collectively, an ontological entity (i.e., stable group) or a singular historical agent instantiated with a common undifferentiated interest within a logical system of well-ordered social influences. Anomalies are too common. The variables shaping the martial networks of the Nuer is hardly connected to or identical with the variables shaping the marital networks of Afro-Brazilians. Shared senses of racial exclusion and experiences of prejudice certainly help make a world picture of racism, but not a neat system. I will, for example, face some form of racial antipathy no matter where I travel, thanks to the effectiveness of America's worldwide racist culture, yet the mode, form, type, and salience will always differ dependent on the context. Even if the racial realist is right about the existence of objective racial communities, it would be mistaken to suppose that the collective of racial communities across lines of nation, ethnicity, and class form an ontological kind. Intentions may not account for disparities within or between populations even in a nonracist world (Lemelle et al. 2011). An actuarial approach begins with the proposition that avoiding risk to life depicts. Conceptions of how humans can flourish, whether communitarian or libertarian, presuppose communities of individuals engaged in activities from farming to lovemaking at maximum levels of embodied well-being. Devising a life plan, even one that is Hobbesian self-interested, enlivened by a Nietzschean desire for empowerment or Léopold Sédar Senghor's existential self-making, agents are dependent on preconditions making plans possible. The first and foremost precondition is health.

Racism is always a function of the undue loss of life and health. It is, as I have argued elsewhere, a polymorphous agent of death, premature births, shortened lives, starving children, debilitating theft, abusive larceny, degrading insults, and insulting stereotypes forcibly imposed (Harris 1999). The probability of death defines racism: who dies, who benefits from their death, who suffer undue short lives, and who are the targets of life shorting acts. It is a polyhedron—racism is only one variable in a vast range of possible variables of different saliences; therefore, a vast array of possible influences and associated impacts constitute the best possible explanation for a given social reality. Given that how a race is defined, lived, and treated, tracking the death rates of a race by looking at disparities between competing populations, for example, is tracking a moving target (Lemelle et al. 2011). It is always contextual; therefore, race and racism are always entrapped in the need for heuristic definitions and boundaries. Death, however, is not a moving target; it is real.

My definition of racism is intended to be narrow and useful for helping to depict and see a picture. Admittedly, sadists will not see the wrongness. The definition presupposes that undue death and ill-health will fit somewhere as an unwanted mode of being in a defensible explanatory and moral account. Whether initiated or caused by an individual, structure, or rule, or whether intentional, accidental, or unintentional, there is no reason to think that any picture, explanation, or moral account will have some queer feature such that once seen or accepted will produce appropriate agreement or action. Even if Locke was right—that it is possible to discern common denominator values, value equivalences, and functional constraints (i.e., traits that all normal persons share sufficiently similar preferences amid ostensibly different value categories and ways that values consistently functions)—it is still the case that outliers and free riders are likely to exist. And even if well-being tends to always include a Pareto optimality (i.e., that people will tend to want more health than less), that desire is not absolutely common, and there are likely to be various definitions of health.[8]

On Glasgow's account, racism is racial disrespect, Blum considers racism either racial antipathy or racial inferiorization, Garcia considers racism a fundamentally vicious kind of racially based disregard for the welfare of certain people, Mills considers racism in terms of inappropriate contracts and institutions, Shelby considers racism as a function of exploitation and associated systems, Benedict considers racism a "dogma that one ethic group is condemned by nature to congenital superiority," and Banton considers racism a doctrine that situates stable inherited character traits derived from separate racial stocks having distinctive attributes (Benedict 1945, 87; Banton 1970, 17; Garcia 1997, 6; Mills 2001; Blum 2002, 2004; Shelby 2002; 2008; Glasgow 2009, 92–3).

I will take it as given that a moral wrong of racism is the unnecessary race-based sustaining of shortened lives, physical pain, debilitating diseases, and premature deaths—a moral wrong made possible, sustained, and perpetuated by the conditions that make embodied well-being possible. It is the absolute necessity of embodied well-being that bespeaks a substantive harm of racism. Racism can be thought of as one way of sustained undue harm by harming the preconditions that make possible the well-being of a raciated group. Health and life are assets independent of revaluation and transvaluation. There are important differences between populations regarding the definition of what counts as health, but none on whether having more of it is good; there are no differences of moment between populations on what counts as physical death—a completely decayed body at the very least counts.

Actuarial

I offer an actuarial account as a way of not explaining but depicting, describing, and picturing. A causal picture is not identical to a depicted picture. A depicted picture exists as a representation. A depiction portrays, surveys, shows, and makes plain (Hamon 1982). I avoid "explaining" using a logic or a world order whether in the form of a worldwide racial contract or a global system. I also avoid attributing racism to a fundamental cause whether driven by evolution, material interest, malfeasance, or lack of benevolence.

The situation of necro-being in not neatly mapped across different communities. Death happens in broad daylight, but an assemblage of social conditions makes its vicious death-creating existence variegated differently in different populations. African Americans with prognoses for breast cancer in Iowa do not form an ontological community of victims with the same misery in Florida, let alone Bahia, Brazil.

An actuarial account has limited scope. It is intended to do the job of both making apparent the terror of racism and showing how it works to create generation after generation of misery. It is a model providing a way of making apparent terrors that are too often poorly pictured. It pictures accidents, cumulative results, compounded accumulations, and networks of differential exchanges. An actuarial theory is analogical, not determinist; it uses correlations without supporting either upward or downward causation; probabilities are trends, not predictions. From the standpoint of an actuarial account, individual racist wills and acts coalesce to form core institutions and forms of production; conversely, individual racist wills and acts emerge from core institutions and forms of production. There is no commitment to either form of causal emergence. Consequently, whether capitalist, socialist, feudalist, fascist, or aristocratic, racism can emerge; white, Black, Arab, African, Indian, and others can be the source of racisms' undue death and ill-health mapped to context dependent definitions of race and ethnicity. The typical donor of a kidney in the Philippines is 28.9 years old with an average income of $480 a month in 2017; the typical recipient in Israel is 48.2 years old with an income of $53,000.[9] Class can work in tandem with national, ethnic, and racial divides.

An actuarial approach to racism describes and depicts racism as a species of racialism; actuarial functions depict racism. Racism is the terror of assessing and expropriating assets for sustaining health and life; it is the living social science of assuring poor health and premature death. Actuaries for slave ship voyages calculated, based on the probability of death, how much should be paid for slaves; how many slaves should be placed in the cargo hold of slave ships; how many could be expected to die; how much should be spent on each slave during the voyage from Africa to the West Indies; the relevant costs associated with men, women, and children adjusted for age; and how much each slave should be sold for to ensure a profit (Patterson 1982; Miller 1988).

How much should be invested in a slave and what the return should be was the province of actuaries. The return on investment was always twofold—in terms of transferable wealth such as gold or stable currencies and the status and honor that power allowed. The analog is that racism can be understood by adopting the language of actuaries and thinking in terms of social functions acting *as if* they were engaged in ruthless calculations. By so doing, it helps us to see why racism is not ineffable but persistent while simultaneously capturing egregious harms.

The explanation for the persistence of racism is obvious: it benefits every member of a dominant group fortuitously, independent of malevolent and malicious intentions or structures; poor health and premature death limit the ability of those oppressed by race to accumulate and transfer assets to their progeny; and progeny face greater dangers to their health than populations that do not inherit the results of parental miseries and egregious stereotypes visited upon all members of its social kind. A paradigm of evil, once seen, provides a platform for moral judgments—that is, we can think of it as totally unacceptable using a range of conceptions that would consider undue death morally wrong.

An actuarial account tracks premature death and thereby makes undue death and its accompanying conditions depict; it foregrounds death and ill-health. The issues important in an actuarial account include the following: how long a given sort of person lives, what illnesses are they subject to, and the costs associated with medical care for those illnesses. When applied to racism, this helps to create a picture of racism and discloses the axis of power, knowledge, and ethics endemic to its reality. This disclosure is especially important to dispense with the idea that racism is sufficiently explained by a Black/white social contract, volitions, interpretations, or relations of production. That is, by a logic. It is certainly the case that some instances of racism are caused by individuals with despicable character, and other instances are caused by institutional practices. An actuarial account tracks consequence, despite their "ultimate" casual origin. That is, if more smokers live in neighborhood x, then we can expect a greater rate of cancer, but only the actual consequences tell us probabilities and kinds because at the very least some form of a multiple variable analysis will be needed to provide a viable probability picture. Smoking cigarettes is correlated to high rates of death, and it is known to be a cause of death for reasons other than job type or home location. Job type and home location are indicators.

We need to know which individuals smoke to predict their likelihood of having cancer. Being Black and living in a Black neighborhood means that such a person is more likely to develop cancer than being white and living in a white neighborhood—but it is totally false that which individual Black person living in a Black neighborhood is likely to develop cancer is thereby predictable. Racist life and health insurance companies have used the first generalization to extract predatory profit by charging costs based on race and neighborhood. It is the reality of abnormal variations in health and life expectancy of miseries between populations over generations that tell us something is wrong. It is also the impossibility of knowing what individual will be at what risk that helps to make setting insurance costs to individuals according to their neighborhood and race so predatory—it uses a stereotype to set prices.

Often African Americans are trapped in a criminal legal system that makes it nearly impossible to escape because of the cost of legal counsel, loss of employment, and loss of employment opportunities. One harm generates a series of harms; harms and disadvantages are multiplied exponentially. In addition, felony convictions often defeat the possibility of many young men and women ever acquiring education or employment that pays retirement benefits. Felons cannot vote, and potential employers can easily learn whether an applicant has a felony record, making a job applicant with a felony record an unattractive employee. Any potential employer can legally refuse to hire a qualified applicant because of a felony record, and any institution of higher education can deny admission to a person with a felony record. Their ability to acquire assets and thereby transfer assets to their progeny is thereby confronted with massive obstacles. High blood pressure, kidney failure, obesity, and early-onset breast cancer bedevil the African American population. Preventable diseases such as malaria and river blindness bedevil a range of African populations. The health miseries of these populations—in relationship to their historical, national, and language locations—helps us to see the consequences of antiblack racism and see the reality of the various matrices and networks of immiseration.

There is, however, no single indicator invariably establishing the existence and degree of racism, death included. The Hispanic Paradox helps to create a picture of the polymorphic reality of racism. The Hispanic Paradox is that the health outcomes of Hispanics compare favorably with whites in the United States. Consequently, and paradoxically, the lower income and status of Hispanics compared with whites do not correlate to lower health outcomes. Even if the paradox does not exist because statistical information about mortality, morbidity, and actual health conditions is unreliable because Hispanics include immigrants that return to their place of origin when facing death, hide their true medical condition to avoid deportation, or because of variables associated with frequent use of medical resources, family support, or eating habits, it is still the case that disparities and similarities of health outcomes can be misleading.

I favor a life-course perspective and cumulative disadvantages. That is, we should consider the total number and kinds of disadvantages and illnesses encumbered over a lifetime (Bonilla-Silva 1987, 2014; Golash-Bozal 2015). Actuarial accounts can use multivalence comparisons. Death is the most obvious result; higher-than-usual rates of illness and a vast range of disparities are also results. What can thereby be pictured is a life of *viva negativia*—necro-being entrapment.

There may be individuals who earnestly want to commit suicide or choose ill-health to enjoy an opiate form of happiness. No matter the reason for their desire, they are not examples that defeat any theory of well-being. Their well-being exists when doing what they will. Their goal of death, if achieved, does not count as a state of being, *eo ipso*; death itself does not count as a state of ill- or well-being for the nonexisting consciousness of the dead. If unwanted ill-health is accepted as an unwanted condition, but other conditions thereby are accepted, then the consequence of death is still not a state of being. Desiring what is almost universally avoided only makes such individuals anomalies, not defeaters. Neither as goal nor consequence is death a state of being for the agent.

The disability paradox is analogous to the happiness paradox: paradoxically, in some cases, persons suffering from a health disability, such as congenital blindness or autism, do not feel as unhappy as persons with no disabilities, and some persons with low incomes and assets, such as the average person in such a condition in Bhutan, may not feel as unhappy as a person with much higher incomes and assets (Moller 2011). A relatively high sense of happiness may exist whether disabled or with a low income and asset holding. Death, among all groups and populations, however, is never a welcomed condition. It is always a bane to happiness. It is also a bane to populations in which happiness is not the ideal good but a conception of living according to natural or spiritual essence; death is a bane to workers transforming nature and to ascetics, such as a sadhu, seeking to avoid sensual goods in deference to a meditative holy state.

One reason that racism persists from an actuarial account is because it works sufficiently well in an imperfect world to ensure a confluence of benefits, especially the most important benefit—namely, health benefits for a sufficient number of people over generations and the preconditions for the possibility of embodied well-being. This picture is not causal; it is simply a correlation, and correlations do not explain; they picture. Socially constructed racial groups maximize reproductive benefits; they can hoard opportunities, transfer wealth across generations in a relatively controlled manner, and ensure progeny status and life-sustaining resources. This provides a well-managed accounting method by which individuals can reasonably be ensured a sense of self-worth at the expense of others and be able to transfer that sense of self-worth across generations with little to no cost to the agents of domination. Racism persists, and its persistence can be depicted, if not explained, by looking at how recursive and compounded benefits allow for sustaining vast differences in life chances.[10]

The "transfer" here is partly metaphorical. There is no direct, unmediated transfer of health harms and benefits. That is one difficulty with trying to depict networks or use a network social theory. There is no ultimate cause or sacrosanct metanarrative that provides a coherent logical picture with neat causal chains and dimensions. However, if racism is the sort of phenomenon that is best understood as various forms of racisms, then this result may not provide a neat picture that satisfies a desire for a world system, but it does provide a way of seeing anomalies. The miseries suffered by victims of racisms happen even if there is no neat causal chain from individual invidious behavior to the misery of an individual or the workings of institutional rules to the misery of a whole population. They happen through the aegis of a vast range of associations, probabilities, propensities, and relationships. Parents, for example, are not invariably caused to favor their children over strangers when deciding whom to transfer their assets to upon their untimely demise, but they often do so.

Actuarial accounts of all types are burdened with submerged ideological components (Simon 1988). Ideological components are unstated assumptions that fit congenitally with some set of ideas about reality. "Insurance classifications differentiate people in ways that would normally be considered offensive. The ideological power of actuarial practices is their ability to neutralize the moral charge carried by these forms of difference" (Simon 1988, 794). Analogous to criminalizing language, such as "habitual offender" or "high-rate offender" and making categories of kinds that then warrant blanket condemnations and treatment, actuaries create categories of "frequency of hospitalization" or age brackets that shape eligibility for benefits, costs, and rewards to all its members, assemblage and undifferentiated. Actuarial accounts provide statistical knowledge of populations regarding health conditions, such as rates of cancer, high blood pressure, and heart attacks, used to distribute costs, such as health and life insurance premiums, and benefits such as discounts given probabilities of risk. Patterns can be discerned according to relevant demographics. What and how costs and benefits are distributed is not a matter of profiles somehow "telling" the reader what moral to conclude, as if humanity consisted of minds with a common set of moral intuitions and virtues across lines of ethnicity, class, race, nation, or language community, but is always a matter of moral debate.

Marx was wrong. There is no explanation that fails to be ideological— pejoratively so— and no explanation that simply reveals or conveys truths matching reality. Data can mislead, and small data can be uninformative. Pure empiricism and pure idealism are romantic illusions. Descriptions are complex existential quantifiers, event identity, genuine referring expressions, semantically ambiguous between quantification and referential interpretations, communicate a speaker's meaning. The incongruities between the illocutionary acts of meaning, interpretation, and action always accompany the world of speech.

Descriptions of racist misery are more vivid and accurate with appropriate statistical information. Neither descriptions nor explanations, however, escape the burden of being pejorative. Descriptions can be scrutinized for what moral assumptions they entail. The best we can do is to provide descriptions, admittedly invested with unspeakable and unseen norms, that help to convey. Death is not relative. The body decays. Even if an author defines the meaning of racism with well-delineated boundaries and stringent features of what counts as racism such that we know in virtue of what it is wrong, I take it as given that undue death and ill-health will be counted.

There is no viable moral or explanatory theory that makes undue loss of life and death other than intuitively heinous. Whatever makes racism morally wrong, it will certainly include, even if it is not reducible to, undue loss of life or prevention of existence.

One benefit of an actuarial account is that it need not pretend to be an explanation that purports to cover all cases or offer a ubiquitous characterization of racism. Differential death rates between the Nuer and the Dinka in Southern Sudan are not well depicted as the result of racism. The demographics under conditions of war shifts the sources of misery, and the salience of ancient ethnic conflicts has far more agency than the influence of a relatively modern concept of biological race.

The tortures during the Black War in Austria, rapes in Nanking, Argentina's committing systematic murder and disenfranchisement of its African population, the genocide in Rwanda, or the Abu Ghraib prison may not be sufficiently seen by discussing dysfunctional virtues or social contracts and rules gone awry. Racial communities enlivened by individual malicious intentions, gathered together into a collective swarming intention as well as social structures, delinked from individual malicious intentions but forming rules shaping outcomes may misguide rather than offer a picture of the loss of life and life chances that racism creates. The features of racism embedded in torture regimes—whether the colonial regime of Rhodesia, the colonies in North and South America, or ancient civilizations constituted as newly formed nation states, such as China, Japan, or Southern Sudan, with their own internal histories of raciation in existence long before the Black/white imposition of Euro/American regimes—may not be subject to a singular explanatory formula. In a nonracist world, interpretive and volitional accounts of disparities leave no one responsible for unintended or willed inherited disparities; institutional accounts leave every rule a culprit.

If epistemic injustice, class exploitation, prejudice, exclusion by race, clan, ethnicity, war, or victimization by malice and ill-will are considered the moral core or the principle cause of racism, death, and the probability of death are always absolute indicators. Arguably, it may be best to think in terms of "racisms," yet, for any form and in every context, death, premature death, and ill-health accompany that form and reside in that context. Death is the shadow that no interpretation escapes; no property of ill-will, disrespect, disdain, loathing, or irrational judgment survives the termination of life; no epistemic or subjective feelings of trauma eludes; and every imposition of institutional rules and every mode and means of production has as its consequence the indicator of death.

Statistical categories such as "suicide victims" or "murdered victims of rape" do not form a community of lived experience—that is, a statistical collective of a kind *ipso facto* does not entail that the kind has collective agency.[11] The dead do not get to feel that they have lived a good life any more than suicide victims get to know that their misery or pain no longer exists. The suffering of the imprisoned is not replaced by the life of the free in the future. Feelings of relief and the joy of freedom occur only while alive. Short of feeling relieved, after being tortured, there is no redemption or salvation. The dead have no sickness. That is why necro-being is beyond being; it makes the dismembering of the bodies of victims of racism an industry in which their body parts are often for sale. Living less long, their progeny inherit less. Hoarding is less effective among agnates and associates of their social kind. The dead do not get paid. Their progeny cannot collect what their dead agnates lacked. Their being form no community networks. Patterns of their misery can be mapped, but the mapped are never a conjoined community of high blood pressure, stress, early-onset breast cancer, or fetal alcoholism sufferers confronting their myriad of disadvantages together.

The struggle against racism in various parts of the world is rarely led by institutions staffed predominantly by the worst of its victims—they are being raped, beaten, killed, underemployed, jailed, and so on. Rather, a myriad of local and international associations of skilled individuals champion the struggle, always needing to be sensitive to local variations of how races are defined and what local moral emotions, stereotypes, institutions, and forms of production exist.

The negation of racism, I suggest, is the negation of the impossibility of ascendency of a racially subjugated population in a given social world (capitalist, feudal, socialist, or otherwise). Death for racism is the death of the agental efficacy of the raciation; status, wealth, class, and health are no longer "transferred." The negation of racism requires the death of necro-being—a mapping by race that no longer shows the polymorphic being of undue death and ill-health, whether caused by class structures, hoarding, ill-wills, fraudulent social contracts, intuitions, dysfunctional biases inherited from evolutionary stratagems, willful ignorance, bad faith, or weak wills. Kill necro-being by race; cast its memory into the dustbin of absolutely forgotten history.

Acknowledgments: I am indebted to critical comments and insights from my 2012 and 2014 Philosophy of Social Science classes, Purdue University; Lee McBride, The College of Wooster; Allen Wood, Indiana University; Amy Pommerening, Texas State University; Jacoby A. Carter, John Jay College of Criminal Justice; and Alberto Urquidez, Gustavus Adolphus College.

Notes

1. An analog for this is Mudimbe 1988, in which conceptions of "Africa" have a complicated history, and also Mbembe 2017, in which the paradox of "Black" as a name for people, race, and kind has a tortured history.

2. A structural account, for example, can recognize that psychological states have causative roles (Haslanger 2015) and a volitional psychological account can recognize that structures can be causative without psychological state explanations (Machery et al. 2010).

3. Social kind racial realists: Mallon 2016, 2004; Glasgow 2007; Mills 1998; Root 2000; Sundstrom 2001, 2002; Taylor 2000, 2004; and Outlaw 1996.

4. For Harris's approach to essentially contested concepts see Harris 1998a.

5. For pictures of differential health and race discussions and pictures of racism see Washington 2006; Roberts 2011; Sullivan 2013, 190–218; Scott 1985; Randall 2006; Donoghue 2008; Black 2003.

6. The Global Slavery Index 2016. https://www.globalslaveryindex.org. Accessed 2017.

7. Wikipedia contributors, "Moors," *Wikipedia, The Free Encyclopedia*, https://en.wikipedia.org/w/index.php?title=Moors&oldid=831753490. Accessed 2017.

8. I am indebted to Lee McBride, The College of Wooster, for suggesting that embodied "well-being" may be a common denominator value.

9. Coalition for Organ Failure Solutions, Organs Watch, ESOT. http://cofs.org/home/. Accessed 2017.

10. An implication of this account is that racism between any two populations can be ended or abated by a radical change in asset holdings and transference abilities, assuming all else is equitable.

11. I am indebted to Tommy Curry, Texas A&M, and Gwenetta Curry, Georgia State University, at the 2016 Philosophy Born of Struggle Conference, Texas A&M University, for drawing attention to the alarming rates of suicide among especially African American males.

References

Anno, B. Jaye. 1991. *Prison Heath Care: Guidelines for the Management of an Adequate Delivery System*. Chicago: National Commission on Correctional Health Care.

Anno, B. Jaye. 2001. *Correction Heath Care: Guidelines for the Management of an Adequate Delivery System*. Washington, DC: U.S. Department of Justice, National Institute of Corrections. https://nicic.gov/correctional-health-care-guidelines-management-adequate-delivery-system.

Banton, Michael. 1970. "The Concept of Racism." In *Race and Racialism*, edited by Sami Zubaida, 17–34. New York: Tavistock.

Benedict, Ruth. 1945. *Race and Racism*. London: Routledge and Kegan Paul.

Bethencourt, Francisco. 2013. *Racisms: From the Crusades to the Twentieth Century*. Princeton, NJ: Princeton University Press.

Black, Edwin. 2003. *War against the Weak: Eugenics and America's Campaign to Create a Master Race*. Washington, DC: Dialogue Press.

Blum, Lawrence. 2002. *"I'm Not a Racist, But..." The Moral Quandary of Race*. Ithaca, NY: Cornell University Press.

Blum, Lawrence. 2004. "Systemic and Individual Racism, Racialization, and Antiracist Education: A Reply to Garcia, Silliman, and Levinson." *Theory and Research in Education* 2 (1): 49–74.

Blyden, Edward W. [1888] 2016. *Christianity, Islam and the Negro Race*. Mansfield Center, CT: Martino.

Bonilla-Silva, Eduardo. 1987. "Rethinking Racism: Toward a Structural Interpretation." *American Sociological Review* 62 (3): 465–80. http://dx.doi.org/10.2307/2657316.

Bonilla-Silva, Eduardo. 2014. *Racism without Racists*. Lanham, MD: Rowman & Littlefield.

Bowser, Benjamin. 1995. *Racism and Anti-Racism in World Perspective*. London: Sage.

Cummins, Robert. 2000. "'How Does It Work?' versus 'What Are the Laws?': Two Conceptions of Psychological Explanation." In *Explanation and Cognition*, edited by Frank C. Keil and Robert A. Wilson, 117–44. Cambridge: MIT Press.

Dennett, Daniel C. 1987. *The Intentional Stance*. Cambridge: MIT Press.

Dikötter, Frank, ed. 1997. *The Construction of Racial Identities in China and Japan*. London: Hurst.

Donoghue, Edward. 2008. *Black Breeding Machines: The Breeding of Negro Slaves in the Diaspora*. Bloomington, IN: Author House.

Dorsey, Joseph C. 2003. "'It Hurt Very Much at the Time': Patriarchy, Rape Culture, and the Slave Body-Semiotic." In *The Culture of Gender and Sexuality in the Caribbean*, edited by Linden Lewis, 294–322. Gainesville: University Press of Florida.

Ferguson, Robert A. 2014. *Inferno: An Anatomy of American Punishment*. Cambridge, MA: Harvard University Press.

Forces de libération africaines de Mauritanie (FLAM). 1986. *Le Manifeste du Négro-Mauritanien Opprimé*.

Foucault, Michel. 1997. *Il faut defender la societie: Cours au College de France, 1975–1976*. Paris: Seuil.

Galtung, Johan. 1969. "Violence, Peace, and Peace Research." *Journal of Peace Research* 6 (1): 167–91. http://dx.doi.Org/10.1177/002234336900600301.

Galtung, Johan. 1990. "Cultural Violence." *Journal of Peace Research* 77 (3): 291–305. http://dx.doi.Org/10.1177/0022343390027003005.

Garcia, Jorge. 1997. "Current Conceptions of Racism: A Critical Examination of Some Recent Social Philosophy." *Journal of Social Philosophy* 28 (2): 5–42. http://dx.doi.org/10.1111/j.1467-9833.1997.tb00373.x.

Garcia, Jorge. 1999. "The Heart of Racism." In *Racism*, edited by Leonard Harris, 398–435. Amherst, NY: Humanity Books.

Garcia, Jorge. 2001. "The Racial Contract Hypothesis." *Philosophia Africana* 4 (1): 27–42. http://dx.doi.org/10.5840/philafricana20014115.

Garcia, Jorge, John McWorter, and Glenn C. Loury. 2002. "Race and Inequality: An Exchange." *First Things* 123: 22–40.

Glasgow, Joshua. 2007. "Three Things Realist Constructionism about Race—or Anything Else—Can Do." *Journal of Social Philosophy* 38 (4): 554–68. http://dx.doi.0rg/lO.llll/j. 1467-9833.2007.00398.X.

Glasgow, Joshua. 2009. "Racism and Disrespect." *Ethics* 120 (1): 64–94. http://dx.doi. org/10.1086/648588.

Glymph, Thavolia. 2008. *Out of the House of Bondage*. Cambridge: Cambridge University Press.

Golash-Bozal, Tanya M. 2015. *Race and Racism*. New York: Oxford University Press.

Goldberg, David. 1990. *Anatomy of Racism*. Minneapolis: University of Minnesota Press.

Hacking, Ian. 1994. "Entrenchment." In *GRUE!*, edited by Douglas Stalker, 193–224. Chicago, IL: Open Court.

Hall, Bruce A. 2011. *A History of Racism in Muslim West Africa, 1600–1960*. Cambridge: Cambridge University Press.

Hamon, Philippe. 1982. "What Is a Description?" In *French Literary Theory Today*, edited by Tzvetan Todorov, 147–78. Cambridge: Cambridge University Press.

Harris, Leonard. 1997. "Alain Locke: Community and Citizenship." *The Modern Schoolman* 74 (4): 337–46. http://dx.doi.org/10.5840/schoolman199774430.

Harris, Leonard. 1998a. "The Concept of Racism: An Essentially Contested Concept?" *Centennial Review* 42 (2): 217–32.

Harris, Leonard. 1998b. "Universal Human Liberation: Community and Multiculturalism." In *Theorizing Multiculturalism*, edited by Cynthia Willett, 449–57. Oxford: Blackwell.

Harris, Leonard. 1999. "What, Then, Is Racism?" In *Racism*, edited by Leonard Harris, 437–51. Amherst, NY: Humanity Books.

Harris, Leonard. 2000. "Community: What Type of Entity?" In *The Quest for Community and Identity*, edited by Robert Birt, 243–55. New York: Rowman & Littlefield.

Harris, Leonard. 2002. "Universal Human Liberation and Community: Pixley Kaisaka Seme and Alain Leroy Locke." In *Perspectives in African Philosophy*, edited by Samuel W. Yohannesm and Claude Sumner, 150–9. Addis Ababa: Addis Ababa University.

Harris, Leonard. 2017. "Looking for Locke." In *Oxford Handbook of Philosophy and Race*, edited by Naomi Zack. Oxford: Oxford University Press.

Haslanger, Sally. 2015. "Social Structure, Narrative, and Explanation." *Canadian Journal of Philosophy* 45 (1): 1–15. http://dx.doi.org/10.1080/00455091.2015.1019176.

Headley, Clevis. 2000. "Philosophical Approaches to Racism: A Critique of the Individualist Perspective." *Journal of Social Philosophy* 31 (2): 223–57. http://dx.doi. org/10.1111/0047-2786.00043.

Headley, Clevis. 2006. "Philosophical Analysis and the Problem of Defining Racism." *Philosophia Africana* 9 (1): 1–16. http://dx.doi.org/10.5840/philafricana2006917.

Hindess, Barry. 1977. *Philosophy and Methodology in the Social Sciences*. Atlantic Highlands, NJ: Humanities Press.

Hull, David. 1992. "Biological Species: An Inductivist's Nightmare." In *How Classification Works: Nelson Goodman among the Social Sciences*, edited by Mary Douglas and David Hull, 42–68. Edinburgh: Edinburgh University Press.

Khan, Rasheeduddin. 1978. "Violence and Socio-economic Development." *International Social Science Journal* 30 (4): 834–57.

King, Martin L., Jr. 1963. "Letter from Birmingham City Jail." In *A Testament of Hope: The Essential Writings and Speeches of Martin Luther King, Jr.*, edited by James M. Washington, 289–302. New York: HarperCollins.

Lemelle, Anthony J., Wornie Reed, and Sandra Taylor, eds. 2011. *Handbook of African American Health*. New York: Springer.

Little, Daniel. 1991. *Varieties of Social Explanation: An Introduction to the Philosophy of Social Science*. Boulder, CO: Westview Press.

Loury, Glenn C. 2002. *The Anatomy of Racial Inequality*. Cambridge, MA: Harvard University Press.

Machery, Edouard, Luc Faucher, and Daniel R. Kelly. 2010. "On the Alleged Inadequacies of Psychological Explanations of Racisms." *The Monist: An International Quarterly Journal of General Philosophical Inquiry* 93 (2): 228–54.

Mallon, Ron. 2004. "Passing, Traveling and Reality: Social Constructionism and the Metaphysics of Race." *Nous* 38 (4): 644–73.

Mallon, Ron. 2016. *The Construction of Human Kinds*. Oxford: Oxford University Press.

Mamdani, Mahmood. 1996. *Citizen and Subject*. Princeton, NJ: Princeton University Press.

Martinot, Steve. 2007. "Race and the Ghosts of Ontology." *APA Newsletters* 6 (2): 4–10. https://cdn.ymaws.com/www.apaonline.org/resource/collection/950518C1-3421-484C-8153-CDA6ED737182/v06n2BlackExperience.pdf.

Marx, Karl, and Frederick Engels. [1848] 1962. *The Manifesto of the Communist Party*. In *Karl Marx and Frederick Engels: Selected Works*, vol. 1. Moscow: Foreign Languages.

Marx, Karl, and Frederick Engels. 2001. *On Colonialism*. San Francisco, CA: University Press of the Pacific.

Mbembé, Achille. 2017. *Critique of Black Reason*. Durham, NC: Duke University Press.

Mbembé, J. A. 1992. "Necropolitics." *Public Culture* 15 (1): 11–40.

Miller, Joseph C. 1988. *Way of Death*. Madison: University of Wisconsin Press.

Mills, Charles. 1997. *The Racial Contract*. Ithaca, NY: Cornell University Press.

Mills, Charles. 1998. *Blackness Visible: Essays on Philosophy and Race*. Ithaca, NY: Cornell University Press.

Mills, Charles. 2001. " 'Heart Attack': A Critique of Jorge Garcia's Volitional Conception of Racism." *Journal of Ethics* 7 (1): 29–62. http://dx.doi.Org/10.1023/A:1022874712554.

Mills, Charles. 2002. "Reply: The Racial Contract as Methodology (Not Hypothesis)." *Philosophia Africana* 5 (2): 75–99. http://dx.doi.org/10.5840/philafricana20025119.

Moller, Dan. 2011. "Wealth, Disability, and Happiness." *Philosophy and Public Affairs* 39 (2): 177. http://dx.doi.Org/10.1111/j.1088-4963.2011.01205.x.

Mudimbe, V. Y. 1988. *Invention of Africa*. Bloomington: Indiana University Press.

Oliver, Melvin L., and Thomas M. Shapiro. 1995. *Black Wealth/White Wealth: A New Perspective on Racial Inequality*. New York: Routledge.

Outlaw, Lucius. 1996. " 'Conserve' Races? In Defense of W.E.B. Du Bois." In *W.E.B. Du Bois on Race and Culture*, edited by Bernard Bell, Emily Grosholz, and James Stewart, 15–37. New York: Routledge.

Patterson, Orlando. 1982. *Slavery and Social Death: A Comparative Study*. Cambridge, MA: Harvard University Press.

Porter, Jean. 1993. "The Unity of the Virtues and the Ambiguity of Goodness: A Reappraisal of Aquinas's Theory of the Virtues." *Journal of Religious Ethics* 21 (1): 137–63.

Randall, Vernellia R. 2006. *Dying While Black*. New York: Seven Principles Press.

Robb, Peter. 1997. *The Concept of Race in South Asia*. Oxford: Oxford University Press.

Roberts, Dorothy. 2011. *Fatal Invention*. New York: New Press.

Root, Michael. 2000. "How We Divide the World." *Philosophy of Science* 67 (Suppl): 628–39.

Sabia Jr., Daniel R. and Jerald T. Wallulis, eds. 1983. *Changing Social Science*. Albany: State University of New York Press.

Scheper-Hughes, Nancy. 1992. *Death Without Weeping: The Violence of Everyday Life in Brazil*. Berkeley University of California Press.

Scheper-Hughes, Nancy. 1996. "Small Wars and Invisible Genocides." *Social Science and Medicine* 43 (5): 889–900. http://dx.doi.org/10.1016/0277-9536(96)00152-9.

Scott, James C. 1985. *Weapons of the Weak*. New Haven, CT: Yale University Press.

Shelby, Tommie. 2002. "Is Racism in the 'Heart'?" *Journal of Social Philosophy* 33 (3): 411–20. http://dx.doi.org/10.1111/0047-2786.00150.

Shelby, Tommie. 2008. "Looking at Race, Racism through a Philosophical Lens." *Harvard Gazette*. November 6. https://news.harvard.edu/gazette/story/2008/11/looking-at-race-racism-through-a-philosophical-lens/.

Simon, Jonathan. 1988. "The Ideological Effects of Actuarial Practices." *Law and Society Review* 22 (4): 771–800. http://dx.doi.org/10.2307/3053709.

Smidley, Brian D., Adrienne Y. Stith, and Alan R. Nelson. 2001. *Unequal Treatment: Confronting Racial and Ethnic Disparities in Heath Care*. Washington, DC: National Academy Press.

Stone, John, and Dennis Routledge, eds. 2003. *Race and Ethnicity*. New York: Blackwell.

Sullivan, Shannon. 2013. "Inheriting Racist Disparities in Health: Epigenetics and the Transgenerational Effects of White Racism." *Critical Philosophy of Race* 1 (2): 190–218. http://dx.doi.Org/10.5325/critphilrace.1.2.0190.

Sundstrom, Ronald R. 2001. "Being and Being Mixed Race." *Social Theory and Practice* 27 (2): 285–307. http://dx.doi.org/10.5840/soctheorpract200127213.

Sundstrom, Ronald R. 2002. "Race as a Human Kind." *Philosophy and Social Criticism* 28 (1): 91–115. http://dx.doi.org/10.1177/0191453702028001592.

Taylor, Paul. 2000. "Appiah's Uncompleted Argument: W.E.B. Du Bois and the Reality of Race." *Social Theory and Practice* 26 (1): 103–28. http://dx.doi.org/10.5840/soctheorpract20002616.

Taylor, Paul. 2004. *Race: A Philosophical Introduction*. Cambridge: Polity Press.

Tilly, Charles. 1999. *Durable Inequality*. Berkeley: University of California Press.

Tilly, Charles. 2002. *Stories: Identities, and Political Change*. New York: Rowman & Littlefield.

Urquidez, Alberto G. 2016. *What Is Racism? A Wittgenstein Approach to Conceptual Analysis*. Doctoral dissertation. West Lafayette, IN: Purdue University.

Uvin, Peter. 1998. *Aiding Violence*. West Hartford, CT: Kumarian Press.

Washington, Harriet A. 2006. *Medical Apartheid*. New York: Doubleday.

Wilson, William J. 1996. *When Work Disappears*. New York: Random House.

Zimbardo, Philip. 2007. *The Lucifer Effect*. New York: Random House.

PART III
HONOR AND DIGNITY (REASON AND EFFICACIOUS AGENCY)

CHAPTER 5
AUTONOMY UNDER DURESS (1992)

In "Autonomy under Duress," Harris considers health and autonomy—the antithesis of life in necro-being. Harris argues that moral concepts (e.g., normalcy, dignity, and autonomy) are ensnared in tacit, context-bound webs of meaning, intervening background assumptions—what Foucault terms an *episteme*. Particular sets of intervening background assumptions tacitly encode particular groups, particular bodies to be singled out and valued differently. Based upon such assumptions, ethical reasoning from principle to action could easily countenance a well-ordered democratic society that features a population of innately, permanently subordinated persons. To illustrate the point, Harris turns to a figurative example— "eunuchization." If a doctor (and the healthcare profession) confronts particular racialized bodies assuming that dark-skinned people are invariably liars, ne'er-do-wells, and sexual predators, then that doctor (and the medical establishment) may very well find utilitarian, deontological, virtue-based, and religious justification for turning young dark-skinned boys into eunuchs. The reader is left to ponder the lot of racialized bodies in our present episteme. Harris affirms that the episteme must be challenged; our assumptions about personhood, bodily integrity, the moral community, and well-being must be challenged. Thus, critical traditions of struggle that compel the deconstruction and revaluation of background assumptions, are exceedingly important.

"What is the nature of health or wellness from an African American perspective?" "What are the roles of healers and patients in African and African American cultures?" These questions suggest certain answer types. The first question presupposes a phenomenon, "health," on which African Americans have a particular perspective. "Health" suggests at least one of the following answers: it is intended to either indicate a broad range of related phenomena or an essence of such phenomena. If an individual, or African people in general, hold ideas similar to the materialism of Hobbes, for example, they might believe that health means proper mechanistic or, in modern terms, neurological functioning of the body.

But there are other possibilities: Kantians, for example, may believe that health is the continuity of embodied transcendental consciousness; absolute idealists, that it is a congruence of a self-identified consciousness operating in an idealized domain. Among pragmatists, health may be construed as the existence of embodied experience in ways that allow for enriching instrumental manipulation of the environment; teleological determinists—Edward Wilmot Blyden, for example—may believe that health is the embodiment of "kind" or race purity living in accordance with its nature; and, lastly, Akan believers may conceive of health in terms of a peaceful embodied spirit.

The elements of this short list of possible beliefs from which to develop a detailed conception of health share an important feature: each recommends either a metaphysical or transcendental essence that is encoded in our being, of whose essence individuals can be instances. Thus, the existence of healthy persons is the instantiation of the ontological nature of humans as mediated by, or in congruence with, their metaphysical or transcendental essence. The relationship between patient and physician or healer would on these accounts be constructed or prescribed according to some modality that best promotes the realization of our ontological being.

The World Health Organization (WHO) avoids expressed commitment to metaphysical or transcendental beliefs. WHO's definition of health focuses on the ontological character of persons. And because it is a broad definition of health that is constantly debated and critiqued, it has progressively changed. It now incorporates conceptions of the patient as an autonomous agent and of health care professionals as equal rather than paternal agents of the mental and physical well-being of patients.

I will argue that concepts of autonomy do not escape entrapment in a web of meaning, that is, epistemological figures and intervening background assumptions that shape how subjects are constructed as agents. Concepts of autonomy allow for special criteria applicable to differentiated groups, for example, children or mentally impaired persons. Identical physiologies, however, as my examples will indicate, can be seen as categorically different depending on how subjects are constructed. Although a good deal of emphasis is usually placed on the existence of biological differences, comparatively little attention has focused on biological identities that are perceived as categorically different, depending on how the subject is constructed. Procedures for reasoning from principles or concepts to practice, inclusive of criteria for revising judgments to prevent prejudice, are, I argue, incomplete in ways that tend to ignore the importance of background assumptions. The idea I argue for is that there are limits for what we can expect a concept, even a theoretically rich concept, of autonomous persons to provide. I will suggest that at least one feature of African American history—the tradition that critiques and struggles against dominant authorities within the health care system— often compels revaluation of background assumptions.

By "autonomy" I will mean one of two views: (1) that autonomy is a form of independence and authenticity, that a person's preferences are to be honored if they accord with what he or she chooses or would choose under normal conditions; (2) that autonomy is a form of independence; it is also a side constraint such that a principle of respect for persons or bodily integrity may outweigh a person's preference, even if such preferences are in accord with their authenticity under normal conditions.[1] These views of autonomy are rule-governed. That is, they define autonomy (independence, authenticity), conditions for its effective expression (honor free choice, authenticity, respect for persons outweighing authenticity), and reasoning procedures for its appropriate application. There are certainly other views of autonomy besides these two and a wide range of reasoning procedures that can be applied. I believe, however, that these two views are strong, rule-governed approaches associated with theoretically rich reasoning procedures, and particularly well-developed Kantian deontological, contractarian, or utilitarian procedures.

The Patient Dr. Dick Did Not Fail To See

There once was a physician named Dr. Dick, a good doctor who was, by popular accounts, also a good person. That is, he was inclined to evaluate his cases strenuously and on rationally ethical principles, whether or not so doing was a requirement of his profession. He was an ardent admirer of Ralph Waldo Emerson, taking particular delight in Emerson's *Self Reliance, Nature,* and *Nominalist and Realist.* And, like most physicians, Dr. Dick was a realist. He usually considered deontological standpoints, utilitarian calculations, contractarian sensibilities, and his religious feelings in formulating ethical beliefs. He steadfastly tried to avoid logical errors in reasoning from beliefs to practices regardless of which standpoint he was testing prior to finally deciding. Since each standpoint was itself regarded as a rational mode of arriving at defensible actions, his survey approach offered a reasonable chance of acting justly.

Dr. Dick was concerned with the welfare of his community. He offered advice to patients on how to prevent illness. He studied diligently to remain abreast of new and well-tested cures. He treated patients as rational and autonomous agents, as best he understood what these terms entailed. He made sure that his patients were informed about available treatments, treatment options, and known and possible effects. In cases in which the best interest of a patient was not served by the patient's choice of therapy, he required extensive counseling, but in the end he tended to defer to a patient's will as long as it did not conflict with his view of respect for bodily integrity or authenticity. (He never confronted cases that involved a conflict between respect for integrity and authenticity, i.e., cases in which integrity demanded a cure that traditions of authenticity required rejecting.) In cases that seemed open to conflicting actions, he relied on other experts or the direction his good intentions recommended.

Dr. Dick believed that all persons regardless of race, religion, creed, gender, or nationality were equal members of the human family, endowed by their creator with inalienable rights. In this belief he differed radically from other members of his community, medical profession, religion, and social network; nonetheless, as a good person, he persevered in his belief. He charged Blacks and whites alike according to their ability to pay and services rendered, as well as, I might add, contributing his services once weekly, free of charge, to persons unable to pay.

Dr. Dick specialized in castration and abortion. As it happened one day, Dr. Dick made George Washington Carver a eunuch.

Dr. Dick had evaluated the practice of castration for the purpose of making eunuchs. He concluded that it was ethically justifiable according to several well-reasoned theories. On utilitarian grounds, his patients would become highly valued house servants and accountants. As house servants, they would likely receive some education and better treatment than field hands. They would avoid being lynched because they would be incapable of rape, given the type of castrations Dr. Dick performed. Although approximately 26 percent of lynchings in the United States had to do with accusations of rape, Dr. Dick was acutely aware of the popular practice of lynching. If a eunuch were accused of looking at a white woman the wrong way, at most he would probably receive a stout beating but not be lynched.[2]

Eunuchs normally held much higher status than slaves. They were natally alienated absolutely: they could not procreate or adopt; therefore, their kinship links were severed.[3] Their existence was strictly confined to being dedicated subordinates—a dedication enhanced by the impossibility of participating in creating progeny. Universally despised, unable to constitute a class to command power across kinship or generations, and bereft of the possibility of willing property to immediate biological family, eunuchs were prized possessions connoting a master's tremendous wealth.

By castration, therefore, George Washington Carver would become, to some degree, deracinated, that is, no longer a Negro capable of procreating and perpetuating the race but a titular-free surrogate, dedicated to service, and incapable of shaping a personally connected ascension of progeny. Dr. Dick reasoned that the young Carver would be fortunate to have the opportunity to express his genuine, or authentic, character under the improved conditions that "eunuchization" offered. Dr. Dick felt that he was constrained from making eunuchs of those for whom nature or circumstance was incongruous with the condition, and that he could not in good conscience refuse to act to offer a therapeutic benefit.

On deontological grounds, Dr. Dick felt that the integrity of a eunuch's body was preserved because informed consent was required prior to castration. Independent of consent, Dr. Dick reasoned, that if we were Carver with Carver's limited options, life chances, cultural specificity, and natural passions, it would not be unreasonable for us to choose castration. Moreover, the practice of castration for the purpose of making eunuchs was an ancient practice in nearly all systems of slavery. On Christian and Judaic grounds, the good doctor was apprised by received tradition that scripture did not strictly forbid making eunuchs of those destined for service, particularly if there were reasons to believe that their souls might thereby have a better chance of salvation.

Dr. Dick sold excised penises and testicles, or, as he preferred to call them, excised organs, to local stores for display or to wealthy white women as decorative ornaments and conversation pieces. He always sought permission from donors, shared the profit with the donors, and contributed to a local charity from his share of the profit. The historical record does not tell us what he did with Carver's penis, but it does tell us what procedures Dr. Dick followed before consenting to operate.

Dr. Dick discussed the operation extensively with Carver's master, his guardians (because he was an orphan), and with Carver himself. The master, it seems, needed a new house servant and companion for his daughter. Dr. Dick thought his reasons were too paternalistic. Carver's guardians, contrary to the normal practice of other physicians, were consulted. They consented on grounds that it would offer a better life for him. Although Dr. Dick knew that the consent was made under duress, he nonetheless considered the reason a strong one. Eleven-year-old Carver, again contrary to popular practices, was also consulted. The youth wanted to make everyone else happy and secure the opportunity for learning; he did not express a great interest in girls as future wives but seemed ambivalent or uncertain about the prospects of losing his penis. Dr. Dick felt that young Carver's penis might be a cause of future trouble, and since it seemed that all parties involved had reflected on what Dr. Dick perceived as a therapeutic operation, therapeutic in the same way as Dr. Dick perceived abortions, he proceeded judiciously.

One way to understand Dr. Dick's approach to castration as therapeutic is to consider his approach to abortion. A fetus in a Black woman's body, whether fertilized by a Black or white male, was considered in Dr. Dick's society as fundamentally different from a fetus in a white woman's body. The Black woman's fetus was potentially cheap labor, sex, and property. A white woman's fetus, if fertilized by a Black male, represented pollution, disease, infection, and corruption. The first required a special argument to justify abortion—an argument that had to show benefit to the welfare of a white male or his family. The second demanded, required, and obviously warranted a cure, that is, abortion on demand.

The privilege white women had to date rape Black men, like the privilege white men had to date, wife, or slave rape, was well known but rarely acknowledged. A Black male's refusal to be raped, or his participation in rape, meant the possibility of facing dreaded accusations: that he looked licentious, made lewd gestures, suggested sexual contact, approached aggressively, or even raped. Castration, lynching, and burning would be the probable reward reaped by a Black male, and in some cases, by his wife and children. The punishment of lynching always occurred after ritual beating, limb decapitation, and the nationally practiced use of plunging a corkscrew into the body of Blacks and reeling out flesh. Finally, parts of the corpse would be amputated as souvenirs for white men, women, and children. The removal of a fetus from a white woman thought to have been fertilized by a Black male was, for Dr. Dick, an unfortunate but necessary evil. He reasoned that neither the fetus nor the mother would live a flourishing life. The autonomy of the woman, as he constructed woman, was preserved. If the pregnancy was publicly known, the Black father was probably already dead or a fugitive; if not publicly known, abortion might help prevent the father from being harmed. On deontological grounds, Dr. Dick reasoned that women were equal persons and had a fundamental right to bodily autonomy. It was inherently justifiable and utilitarian to perform abortions, he believed, and particularly so because the women he served were all white. The fetuses they wanted to abort were going to be Negroes, "octoroons," "quadroons," or some other dreaded category.

For Dr. Dick, the interracial fetus of a white woman held a similar status to that of a Black male's penis—organs that could be justly excised after well-reasoned consent. Consent trumped utility, although such acts were further supported by utility; consent preserved freedom, independence, integrity, truthfulness, and the autonomy of agents as an inalienable good. Consent gained under duress was carefully weighed. Special attention was paid to whether the agent was well informed, to individual and social consequences, and to preserving authenticity, as these were understood and pertinent to the sort of agent involved.

I was told the following story by a poplar tree in Tuskegee, Alabama, on September 7, 1980, my first day as the Portia Washington Pittman Fellow at Tuskegee Institute.

In a brief moment before the castration of young Carver, his matured soul, then inhabiting the body of an executive for the National Medical Association, migrated into his eleven-year-old body, the time warp allowing only a brief second of presence. That soul, whispered the tree, realizing what was happening although not empowered to do anything about it, yelled with murderous anger to Dr. Dick, "Whose damn life is it anyway?" Dr. Dick's adult soul, then inhabiting the body of an executive of the American Medical Association, had returned simultaneously and with the same time warp and power limitations to Dr. Dick's body. Realizing what was about to happen and hearing Carver's voice, Dr. Dick's soul with genuine frustration and regard, yelled back into the expanse of paraspace, "Yours." A faint echo, like a voice mix, was heard in the paraspace of the transcendental as the souls immediately resumed their matured spatial-temporal slots—"Ours." The moment passed.

This was the story of Dr. Dick's attitude toward the subject.[4]

In principle, Dr. Dick may not have objected to the castration of white males for the purpose of making them eunuchs. The possibility, however, of castrating whites did not fit the epistemological figures or background conceptions of subjects, that is, castration was too obviously not a benefit for whites, obviously in no one's interest, and obviously contrary to their natures, authenticity, traditions, integrity, and codes of honor. The fact that white males were not made eunuchs reflected social meanings; they were not, as agents, constituted as innately, irreversibly, and permanently subordinate persons. They were not natally alienated in the sense of being constructed as agents unable to define descending generations or control the direction of ascending generations. Moreover, the meaning of their independence, rationality, or authenticity was a function of the levels and types of intrinsic ontological merit they were assumed to represent.

Using the historical reality of "eunuchization" as a figurative example suggests that relevant facts about the body are constituted by virtue of what the body is as an objective entity enmeshed with meaning. As genealogical isolates, eunuchs represent the preservation of separateness over time. The possibility of affection, kinship, or family ties between master and subordinate are absolutely negated in them. Analogously, the constraints applied determining what would not be done to whites and what could be done to Blacks was a function, not of the biological facts of identity, but of the way the body was constituted as different. The body of George Washington Carver, for example, belonged to Carver as agent, but the meaning of the agent's body was mediated by its social context. The bodily integrity of Blacks was not violated, in Dr. Dick's view, because their integrity entailed living lives as subordinates, that is, a fulfilling life for them was only possible as a life of happy or contented subordination. Their equality, in substance, meant a contentment that was equal in worth to the contentment of whites. The precondition for Dr. Dick to have arrived at a different view of person required a different set of intervening background assumptions about personhood, bodily integrity, the moral community, fulfilling lives, and utility.

The Patient Dr. Death Failed to See

When I received the program from the Center for the Advanced Study of Ethics and learned that there would be two distinguished respondents to my paper—a paper that I had not completed writing—I was very apprehensive and considered several drastic options. I first considered calling the Center, feigning illness, and informing them that I would be regrettably unable to present my paper. I realized, however, that I would still be required to write and submit my paper, having previously agreed to do so. The respondents would still have a chance to critique my views, only I might be left in the dark about their critique; worse still, they might ignore my views and present contrary perspectives before an audience that might be otherwise receptive. Taking the option of feigning illness also meant that my honor as a promise-keeper would be compromised. Moreover, my utilitarian calculation of the consequences of failing to present suggested that it would cost me emotionally in ways I found basically unacceptable.

I next considered calling the center and informing them that I was dead; but death normally includes the loss of the ability to communicate, at least over the telephone. Moreover, I would be lying if I were not dead. The option was rejected.

I then considered either presenting my paper and engaging in discussion and debate, or simply dying. I decided that it would be preferable to die rather than to live with any more apprehension, fail to be a promise-keeper when I was capable of keeping my promise, intentionally deceive, or risk having my views subjected to unanswered critique.

I called Dr. Death, who works at my HMO during the day and at the public hospital near my home on weekends. I spoke to Dr. Death's receptionist. Regardless of my urgent pleas, I was unable to get an appointment to see the good doctor in order to die until December. It was now August, and the program date was November 9. Dr. Death, it seems, had a long line of young African American males, abused mothers, and drug-addicted babies. Dr. Death had terror to inflict on the many African peoples whom Dr. Death's assistant, Dr. Misery, oppressed during their daily lives as powerless employees under the dominion of callous white males. Dr. Death stood at the hospital door, beckoning them in for treatment.

Dr. Death was overburdened as administrator for the maldistribution of public and private resources and too busy to ensure that attention was paid to the doctor–patient relationship, neonatal research, appropriate physical liability, and the value of continuing existence in an intensive care unit. In this way, in conjunction with the highly profitable business of heath care, comparatively few resources were spent on prevention, curing curable ailments, resolving conflicts of interest between business and the health care community, or the evaluation of research topics.

I expressed my deep empathy for Dr. Death's hectic schedule, but regardless of my efforts to be amicable, I was absolutely denied an earlier appointment.

I called Dr. Goodbody in desperation. Dr. Goodbody is well known for efficient and effective service. Analogous to three young African American males walking into a store to shop in Georgetown and expecting to be graciously received as potential customers but instead being received as probable thieves, it was not outside the sphere of possibility to expect death from Dr. Goodbody. But the receptionist who took and quickly evaluated my preappointment information, advised me, that the services of the good doctor, so well known for saving lives, would first require extensive tests. I simply left my name and telephone number, requesting that I be advised of the good doctor's next opening for an examination, prior to tests.

In truth, the receptionist did not actually tell me that I could not see or afford Dr. Goodbody's services. Rather, this conclusion was based on common sense and the *American Journal of Medicine*, which establishes correlations between whether a person has private insurance, Medicaid, or no insurance and the type of treatment he or she receives. Being Black in a racist society, I thought, could only aggravate the likelihood of maltreatment. I have private insurance and an HMO, so why should I give Dr. Goodbody a blank check to perform unneeded services and face the prospects of receiving from the same Dr. Goodbody a less than adequate diagnosis? Although I wanted the results of Dr. Goodbody's services, namely, death, I did not want to be exploited in the process.

Refusing to dethrone my honor by calling in sick, having the option of seeing Dr. Death foreclosed, and even my most readily available institutionalized source for death, Dr. Goodbody, excluded from my short list of possible harm providers, I resolved to live with my apprehension as *fait accompli*. Moreover, I counted myself fortunate because my apprehension was not a pancreatic cancer. This unusual way of constructing honor and the drastic effort to avoid completing and presenting my paper may seem unreasonable, particularly because other options were available. I could have written the center, explained my apprehension, and refused to submit my paper or to present it. I could have elected to go on a holiday with no thought of Dr. Death or an unfinished paper. I could have reevaluated the situation in the light of the fact that I really could not predict how my paper would be received. I could have completed my paper but submitted it for publication to a reputable journal, and if it were published, I would improve my chances for promotion in academia and simultaneously avoid the probability of needing to defend my views. I could have sought psychiatric help to overcome my apprehension, discovered its root or contributing factors, and acquired a greater sense of self-confidence—regardless of whether greater confidence, rather than less apprehension, would enhance my psychological stability.

What's rational requires taking into account variables that are not immediately on the surface of initial considerations. It is no small matter, for example, to have respondents from Georgetown University and Harvard University—particularly so as I am a professor at a small historically Black college, a philosopher in an era when philosophy has nearly lost its status, a radical author, and an African American promoting the idea of struggle against authority. The following were a few hidden concerns: Will I be perceived as representing the quality of professors at Morgan? Will I be perceived as representing all African Americans? Will my project of promoting the history and heritage of African American philosophic activity fare well before such distinguished respondents? Will they find my revaluations of the bioethical agenda totally afield of the way biomedical ethics is now constituted and in the future reject efforts by others to raise the same issues without due consideration because they were prejudiced by a poor paper from me? If my views are not defensible, will it be inferred that I am genetically inferior or defective? These questions and the meanings they convey dictate the fact that it is no small matter to have two distinguished respondents.

Taking hidden variables into account enriches but cannot dictate the outcome of considerations. What type of deference I am accorded, how important my presence is in the world, how significant my problem is to the corporate body of society, and what type of autonomy I am assumed to possess, are affected by what kind of rational agent I am considered to be. Considering my apprehension a substantive matter, and the above options drastic but not insane, for example, accords me regard as a reasoning agent, if not a rational agent. That is, outside the context of what presenting and presenting with two distinguished respondents means in a racist world, my reasoning arguably does not warrant regarding me as a rational agent. Instead, it warrants considering me less than fully rational because it is full of overgeneralizations and fallacies—precisely the kind of reasoning characteristic of actual well and poorly educated persons.[5]

The Body as Socially Enwebbed

My peculiar original reasoning, whether considered rational, misguided, or just peculiar does not affect perceiving me as an autonomous agent per se. The good that I have as an autonomous agent, however, is encased in a context that affects how beneficial my autonomy is to me. It is a dubious good, for example, in a social world in which my miseries are considered my responsibility in at least two senses: if they were preventable, then my choice-making activities were a major factor; if they were not preventable, then what is to be done is a function of my choices under duress. A functional argument can be made contending that the concept of autonomy readily allows health care professionals to blame victims, render less than adequate services, or withhold cures. To the extent that autonomy excuses society and health care professionals from responsibility and accountability to initiate life practices to prevent ailment, the benefit of being perceived as autonomous also carries harm. I do not, however, wish to offer a functional argument here.

The "body-as-object" is not, I believe, a physical phenomenon strictly separate from how it is socially constructed—and its construction involves relying on beliefs about the agent's rational being.[6] Assuming I gain entrance to Dr. Death, for example, the diagnosis and prognosis are affected by the status of my body in a web of beliefs about its merit. Whether, for example, I am constructed as "inferior, irrational, or hyperactive" prior to or independent of test results stands alongside concerns such as "Can I really afford the services or am I really a social pariah usurping taxpayer funds?" Assuming that I am accidentally, or because of moral luck, treated by a decent physician, that I am treated at all is conditioned by social factors and not the sheer objective existence of a physical ailment. Whether autonomy is considered an end state or an existential process of becoming, whether authenticity or a principle of bodily integrity and respect is considered of greater importance, the status of the agent affects their application. Autonomy, consequently, can be a dubious good for persons socially constructed as inferior.

The concept of the body as socially enwebbed may be controversial, and it is a concept that phenomenologists have argued for in far more detail than I will attempt. I rely on a weak form of the idea: that "objective" physical reality is necessarily mediated by subjective meanings. This view is fairly noncontroversial. However, when considered in connection to how the immiserated are treated, the idea suggests a departure from conceiving of the body as an object such that appropriate health care entails proper application of technology mediated by rational physicians. That is, a physical ailment would not simply be an object for pure science or medicine to observe but an object embedded in a myriad of perspectives that intrinsically and extrinsically encode it with meaning. Hypertension, diabetes, and AIDS, for example, are among the most common ailments afflicting the African American community (as if these conditions were ailments emanating from outside agents). If not totally preventable, at least the number of persons affected by these conditions could be reduced by alterations in social life. But to treat the social as the prime source of affliction (again, as if the ailments emanated from outside agents) is to conceive of the body in a social and phenomenological fashion (as a dialectical entwinement of object and subject).

What health is should be considered as an extension of a conception of the subject, that is, how the subject's being is to be perceived. Conceptions such as "autonomy" presuppose the existence of an essentially common humanity. How humanity is constructed is thus crucial to a defensible view of autonomy. Species membership, I believe, is adequate for encoding an undifferentiated quintessence of personhood to species' members. How functional, utilitarian, or capable we are of empathy with a given member of the species in actual or imagined contractual relations should be separate issues from whether agents are accorded peership as human persons.

Challenging the Episteme

It is arguable that if we have a sufficiently rich rule-governed conception of autonomy, well founded in ethical principles such that the autonomy of agents is given due respect, we should be able to apply conceptions and principles in ways that help limit socially demeaning characterizations of persons. An appropriate application would, as a consequence of a diagnostic reasoning procedure, render fair applications. It can be argued consequently that we could, with appropriate corrective procedures, require consideration of persons with equal regard as species' members.

Contrary to the Platonic ideal, injustice often pays because the unjust do not act alone but in a community that sanctions and makes injustice normal, restricting "greatest injustice to barbarians and outlanders."[7] Moreover, an intrinsically good person is not necessarily inclined either to know or to do good acts, particularly under duress. An absolutely congruent fit between principles and their application, such that the principle and an accompanying procedure necessarily tell us incontrovertibly what to do in all relevant cases, is not possible. Noting the impossibility of an absolute congruent fit between principles, procedures, and actions, I believe, is not controversial, but the recognition that the best possible fit could be foreshadowed by how the "other" is constructed suggests the need for considerations besides rule-governed procedures and correctives. The idea I am arguing for is that a conception of rule-governed principles constituting one singular rule or a lexical arrangement of rules from which we can inductively generate right actions is inadequate. Principles and practices, whether derived by uninterested rational agents or whether they are as justifiable as we can make them, do not escape the need for the existence of a critical standpoint toward social reality, that is, a critique that attacks how objects are categorized, constructed, constituted, and encoded with meaning.

It is not unusual for persons to arrange hierarchically the valuation of nonmoral goods. Societies, for example, characteristically value wealth, income, status, type of profession, power, and material possessions. The ill, poor, unemployed, and powerless are usually not as valued as persons with health, wealth, and power. Hauserman remarks that "the essence of the problem lies in the transference of such characteristic values to consideration of the human being as a whole. Society infers that the values associated with an individual's biological differences are indicative of the individual's overall personal values."[8] The sort of respect, deference, accord, regard, attention, and autonomy a person is assumed to warrant, at least in informal considerations, is affected by and affects the biological standing of persons. Background assumptions that shape how the body is formally or informally categorized constitute its meaning for the physician. Consequently, although a given physician may believe in a rule-governed principle of autonomy, and apply its rules judiciously, a sphere that configures prejudicial and demeaning practices may be left unaffected.

The primary markers determining a person's access to health care and their rank are social constructions, for example, class, race, religion, clan, nationality, or material accoutrements. They exist prior to a person's treatment by a physician. They affect how a person is ranked. Which markers are used depends on the society. Moreover, the traits of rationality, autonomy, independence, or authenticity are imputed in the sense that third parties are required to confirm, verify, grant, or award individuals such goods, and, on confirmation, determine what may or may not be done under normal conditions or conditions of duress. Whether, and in what form, an individual has such traits may be legitimately controversial; however, that persons are entitled to recognition as persons is not, and due regard should not, in an ideal world, be a matter of third-party evaluations.

Given the tendency to transfer valuations of nonmoral goods to valuations of persons, and assuming the continued existence of social markers, how subjects are primordially constituted is crucial to the possibility of equitable health care—the possibility of a health care system that is not complicit in immiseration. The minimally adequate level of autonomy that should be accorded persons across lines of social differentiation requires a conception of the subject that grants agents intrinsic good independent of and prior to ranking or countervailing considerations. A conception is needed that constructs agents as undifferentiated.

It is not, consequently, that the "principles to practice" mode of constructing reasoning is psychologically a mode of thinking that does not occur, or one that we should abandon, but that there are background assumptions and intervening considerations that procedural ethical reasoning cannot take into account because background assumptions surreptitiously legitimate or call into question procedures and the context of procedures. By calling the context of procedures into question I mean a revaluation of what is meant by normalcy, authenticity, respect, and independence.

Historically, African Americans and persons focused on ending the immiseration of Blacks have forced the positive consciousness of knowledge, its epistemological figures, its taken-for-grantedness, its "too-obviously-true-to-warrant-critiqueness," and its philosophy of life, into and onto the social, intellectual, literary, and medical state for critique.[9] We should certainly clarify principles, struggle for an invigorating ethos, and promote a covenant that inspires community. We should also continue to struggle over which conception of health, ethos, covenants, and methodological applications are defensible. The point is that this intellectual and practical struggle occurs on a background that must itself be continually revaluated and that the struggle includes how the subject is to be constituted.

The critiques offered by African Americans, acting from various perspectives and as agents of resistance, reshape the subject and challenge the episteme on which the health care system grounds itself. Contrary to the ideal of an all-seeing eye peering down on a static biological world of homo sapiens awaiting discovery of their finite and predefined categories, African American critiques often tender a critical judgment about the episteme, the intervening background assumptions and socially constituted configuration of subjects that precondition the object and the eye.

An arguable implication of this view is that a good deal more than promoting humanitarian beliefs and antiprejudicial attitudes is required to abate racism. The reason for this is that physicians are not understood as simply subjective agents peering out, hopefully through the spectrum of rational thinking, at an objective body. Rather, the body is a socially constructed and constituted subject entwined and configured by the physician and the physician's social context. If race-targeted advertising such as cigarette and alcohol advertising elicit less social consternation than we might hope, one reason may be that the target is not invested by physicians and society in general with ties of affection, compassion, kinship, merit, and value among those empowered to create change. This may be true whether those empowered are African Americans, reluctant to vie against their fellow health care professionals or whites, invested with a sense of class, but not race, superiority.

If we are not sufficiently aggressive in instituting cultural change to influence dietary habits as a way of curtailing diabetes, one reason may be that Africans and African

Americans shy away from being thoroughly self-critical since they are already subject to so many demeaning criticisms. Offering our own critique may seem only to add to the harm. Or empowered health care professionals may feel that authenticity demands allowing the least well off to immiserate themselves as a function of their independence (i.e., they are constituted as independent agents just in case self-immiseration occurs, or they are constituted as full persons deserving counseling just in case their actions or presence seriously influence others constituted as full persons). Moreover, what are considered public health matters of great importance, such as infant mortality or drug-addicted pregnant women, reflect the status of worth accorded different sectors of the population. Consequently, how we constitute the subject, as intrinsically worthy anterior to experience and due intransitive regard, are important grounds from which to fight racism.

Neither have I offered a sufficient view of health or the health care system, nor have I depicted a unique African American perspective on health or the role of healers and patients in the African or African American culture. There are certainly folk, religious, historical, and culturally popular beliefs about health among African people. There are certainly numerous African-based continuities helping to shape those beliefs. Moreover, the African American experience of the health care system is too often a demeaning experience, and this, on the background of centuries of suspicion. I have not covered the historical details that have informed suspicions that may, for example, account for the small number of Black organ donors, attitudes toward advice concerning sexual practices emanating from the health care system, or our reluctance to address race or ethnic-specific treatments, diseases, or cures.

The critical perspective I have presented may include features integral to the array of ways African American, and African people in general, view health and some concerns regarding patient–physician (as distinct from healer) relations. If it turns out, however, after a searching historical and sociological study of African American beliefs, that my critical perspective or the importance I place on the resistance tradition among African American health care professionals is not integral to that perspective, then it should be. Moreover, if an African American perspective does not exist, I would argue that there are strong grounds for creating one in the history and continued immiseration of African people by health care systems.

(I have completed my paper. I am now worried that Dr. Goodbody will actually see— and therefore construct—me.)

Notes

1. For the import of autonomy and authenticity, some examples include: Gerald Dworkin, "Moral Autonomy," in *Morals, Sciences and Sociality*, vol. 3 of *The Foundations of Ethics and Its Relationship to Science*, ed. H. Tristram Engelhardt Jr. and Daniel Callahan (New York: Hastings Center, 1978), 156–70; Gerald Dworkin, "Autonomy and Behavior Control," *Hastings Center Report* 6 (February 1976): 23; Bruce Miller, "Autonomy and the Refusal of Life-Saving Treatment," *Hastings Center Report* 11 (August 1981): 22–8. For the import of autonomy and self-respect, some examples include James Childress, *Who Should*

Decide?: Paternalism in Health Care (Oxford: Oxford University Press, 1982); John Rawls, *A Theory of Justice* (Cambridge, MA: Harvard University Press, 1971); Robert Nozick, *Anarchy, State, and Utopia* (New York: Basic Books, 1974), 28–35.

2. For the rituals of lynching and justifications of lynching and castration, see Trudier Harris, *Exorcising Blackness* (Bloomington: Indiana University Press, 1984); and Robert L. Zangrando, *The NAACP Crusade against Lynching* (Philadelphia, PA: Temple University Press, 1980).

3. For the concept of natal alienation, see Orlando Patterson, *Slavery and Social Death: A Comparative Study* (Cambridge, MA: Harvard University Press, 1982).

4. Nancy R. Hauserman, "Search for Equity on the Planet Difference" in *Biological Differences and Social Equality*, ed. Masako N. Darrough and Robert H. Blank (Westport, CT: Greenwood Press, 1983), 27.

5. For the concept of epistemological figures and episteme, see Michel Foucault, *The Order of Things: An Archaeology of the Human Sciences* (New York: Random House, 1970). For the concept of valuation and the integral way values help shape cultural imports, see Alain Locke, "Values and Imperatives," in *The Philosophy of Alain Locke: Harlem Renaissance and Beyond*, ed. Leonard Harris (Philadelphia, PA: Temple University Press, 1989), 34–50.

6. See Michel Feher, Ramona Nadaff, and Nadia Tazi (eds.), *Fragments for a History of the Body*, Part I, Part II (New York: Urzone, 1989).

7. Boxill, Bernard, "How Injustice Pays," *Philosophy & Public Affairs* 9 (4, Summer 1980): 369.

8. Nancy R. Hauserman, "Search for Equity on the Planet Difference," in *Biological Differences and Social Equality*, ed. Masako N. Darrough and Robert H. Blank (Westport, CT: Greenwood Press, 1983), 27.

9. See Foucault, *Order of Things*; and Locke, "Values and Imperatives," 34–50.

CHAPTER 6
HONOR: EMASCULATION AND
EMPOWERMENT (1992)

"Honor: Emasculation and Empowerment" was a contribution to an edited collection focused on rethinking masculinity in light of gender studies. Harris argues that honor—reverence, esteem, deference—is a social good. Individuals are afforded or denied honor based on their ability to stand as a representative member of a salient group or a moral community. When a particular group of people is excluded from the relevant group membership (based on phenotype, gender, religion, etc.), they are classified as improper recipients of honor. The plight of African American men is one such case, according to Harris. African American men have been excluded from the moral community and thus are systemically denied honor. They have been emasculated, barred from asserting their wills, from shaping their own futures, and from the possibility of empowerment across generations. Harris suggests that, when African American men (e.g., Martin L. King Jr.) are bequeathed honor in the American context, they are not honored as genuine members of the moral community; rather, they are given honor for exhibiting submissive, nonthreatening, or amusing traits that reinforce or service the hegemonic white patriarchal heteronormative order of things.

Honor is almost universally accorded men over women within social entities such as classes, ethnic groups, nations, or racial communities. Honor is a social good, that is, a form of reverence, esteem, and deference an individual receives from others. Persons excluded from a moral community, however, are also generally excluded from honor independent of gender. Exceptions to this generality of particular concern are well-established cases that an individual's will is subservient to the will of the dominant community. Conferring honor on groups excluded from a moral community is inimical to a core feature of honor—the possession of qualities that "relate existence to certain archetypal patterns of behavior."[1] Honor involves the imposition of wills, an imposition that often uses threats, demands, pressure, and aggressive behavior. The expression of such traits by members of subjugated communities is, however, normally considered a sign of insurrection or belligerence. Racism, I believe, helps account for why honor has been an elusive good for African American males despite occasional examples of individually honored African Americans. The honor accorded Martin L. King Jr., and the general subjugation of the African American community, is crucial for the possibility of an individual to be honored.

In the first section, "A Conception of Honor," I provide a working definition of honor. In "Honor and Emasculation," I explore the meaning of dishonor. I discuss eunuchs, lynching, and castration as exemplary of forms of emasculation and exclusion from the moral community. In "Honor and Masculinity," I consider the character of honor as a masculine good. In "Honor and Dr. King," I consider the traits that warrant honoring Dr. Martin L. King Jr. The honor accorded Dr. King, and the lack of honor accorded the African American community, does not defeat the idea I contend in "Dr. King as Counterexample" that membership in the moral community is essential for an individual to be socially honored. There is, I believe, an ambivalence in the American cultural fabric over what honor means. I suggest in "Honor and Empowerment" that the honor accorded Dr. King is different from the kind that we often rely on in normal social life as vicarious conduits representing archetypal behavior. The traits if love, care, compassion, and sacrifice are considered different from such traits as tenacity and aggressiveness but no less significant as features of social normality and sources of honor.[2]

A Conception of Honor

Parenting normally includes teaching children how to impose their wills—wiping their noses, deciding not to eat candy, exercising their preference for clothes, and discussing, arguing, and using body language in ways that help convince. Parents are authorities whether they use tyrannical means of domination or discourse as a form of coercing and shaping behavior. Analogously, children's play includes means for children to impose their wills on one another. It may be that the play of boys evinces a greater concern for competition, rules, and winning than that of girls; the play of girls may be more concerned with cooperation, sharing, and keeping a game enjoyable rather than determining who wins. Nevertheless, both forms of play share the project of will imposition, the first through verifiable results and the second through a cohesion that allows deciding who is included and who is excluded from the shared bonds. Threats, demands, pressure, and aggressive behavior are features integral to the imposition of wills in both parenting and play.

There are tremendously varied ways and purposes through which individuals seek to have their wills imposed on others. However, the fact of imposing one's will is cross-culturally important as a way of securing regard from others and developing a sense of self-worth. The personalization of politics is telling in attitudes of children toward race, war, and social identity.[3] Caring, loving, and nurturing children to become soldiers or to be supportive of soldiers has occurred generation after generation in American history.[4] The imposition of wills through a variety of techniques is a feature of the normal daily lives of children and parents, but it is hardly definitive or exhaustive of what is involved in either. The features of parenting and play that I have mentioned are also, however, important bases of honor.

Honor is a good often accorded because virtues and meritorious traits are assumed to be embodied by an agent. The willful obedience of children to their parents' most cherished expectations, for example, is a form of honoring one's parents. Honor reflects discrete and explicit social rankings and boundaries between agents. Failure to accord appropriate deferential behavior or appropriate regard for social rankings and boundaries, such as children cursing adults, bespeaks dishonor. Persons can be honored if they have no accomplishments, such as persons of noble birth, and honor can be bestowed on epic heroes as well as the dead. There are tremendously different forms of honor, different conceptions of what is required for a person to be honored, and different views about what counts as degradation. The above features of honor are certainly not exhaustive.

Peter Berger argues that honor in the modern world is no longer prevalent. He associates honor with socially imposed roles, chivalrous codes of behavior, and laws against insults to honor. However, for Berger, "A return to institutions will be *ipso facto* a return to honor" because institutions impose roles and establish hierarchies.[5] Contrary to Berger, normal social life has an array of hierarchies to support informal codes of honor. Moreover, the royal houses of Austria, England, Japan, and Saudi Arabia are faring well in modernity. A visit to nearly any multinational corporate headquarters, military barracks, or schoolyard might dispel academicians of the illusion that conceptions of honor are not prevalent in modernity. Nonetheless, I intend to mean by honor a variety of forms of exalted accord. One way to see that honor is a social good, and to present a sample of its many forms, is by considering what it is to be dishonored.

Honor and Emasculation

According to Orlando Patterson in *Slavery and Social Death*, slavery is the condition of being generally despised and natally alienated, incapable of defining descending generations or directing the course of ascending generations. "The dishonor the slave was compelled to experience sprang instead from that raw, human sense of debasement inherent in having no being except as an expression of another's being."[6] Contrary to Hegel and Marx on Patterson's account, slaves were not necessarily workers; they were never accorded the status of moral persons. Moreover, male and female slaves, no matter how rich, were always under the threat of harm from any member of the slaveholding class—child, homeless free person, woman, man, or even pets of the free. "The absolute ruler … requires the ultimate slave; and the ultimate slave is best represented in the anomalous person of the eunuch."[7]

Eunuchs were absolutely incapable of redemption—they could father no future generations and they were usually despised. They were emasculated, not only because as a group they could not function as normal biological parents, or hold the respect of their relatives if these were known, but because they lacked the possibility of empowerment over other men and dominance over women. As tax collectors, for example, they could shape the life chances of a tremendous range of wealthy as well as poor persons; but they could never participate in shaping the next generation as their surrogates, vassals of their values, or as testaments to their love; nor could they dictate the flow of wealth from one generation to the next. As a group, eunuchs could not stop the children of their masters from becoming adults that would despise eunuchs any more than African American "nannies" could stop the children they raised on behalf of their masters from selling them or their children, beating their husbands, raping their daughters, or castrating their sons. Eunuchs existed completely for the other—bodies for sport, sex, status, guards, servants, and administration—irredeemable physically, spiritually, and socially. The dishonor of eunuchs was conditioned on the exclusion of the eunuch community from the moral community, that is, the embodiment of virtues and meritorious traits by an individual eunuch was always tainted because individual eunuchs were members of, or perceived as members of, a generally despised community.

Thomas More's *Utopia* provides an excellent example of the importance performed by the boundary between membership in or exclusion from the moral community and the way that membership establishes which individual is potentially due deference. More considered slavery a substitute for death and an improvement in the life of the spiritually or virtue-dead person. In More's *Utopia*, there are no singular positions of exalted honor. Rather, the society of Utopia itself is an honorable social entity. Utopia is reached only by accident or luck. Almost no one ever leaves Utopia. Slaves and colonized aliens are voluntary subjects or ones subjugated for their own benefit. In either case, they are always pleased to have been saved from their previous state of decadence. Everyone that lived outside of Utopia could be ranked as more or less degraded in comparison to the life in Utopia. Persons were or became honored because they identified with, had the sentiments of, and conducted themselves in accordance with the norms of the social order in Utopia. That order is what More constructs as honorable. That is, social normality in *Utopia* is coterminous with nobility—everyone is in an exalted station and utopia itself is the highest earthly form of excellence.

The same is the case in *Ethiopia Unbound*, an idealized depiction of Africa by the noted Ghanaian nationalist J. E. Casely Hayford (1866–1930).[8] Hayford's *Ethiopia Unbound* has a hierarchical character that functions to promote egalitarianism; polygamy, chiefs, and provincial villages are grounded in Hayford's eyes on egalitarianism. The elite are exalted models of the best norms perceived as definitive of normality.

Utopias characteristically require the perfect ability of the utopianites to impose their wills—wills that are coterminous with perfect virtue. Normal social life is thereby coterminous with exalted character virtues.[9] A utopia is thus the best, or best possible, social world. That is, honor and normality are coterminous in conceptions of the best, or the best possible, world; the abnormal, inferior, and irredeemably lost souls exist outside of the honor of utopia's normality, that is, outside the moral community.

Social entities excluded from the moral community are also generally excluded from the social good of honor. Wealthy eunuchs, for example, were treated honorably although the poorest members of the caste enslaving eunuchs were empowered to demean them without reprimand. As a group, they could not be honored. Free American Blacks prior to 1865, regardless of their color, social graces, wealth, or stature in a military unit, for example, were always subject to the possibility of being enslaved and their progeny enslaved; a possibility that was not one any white person faced, regardless of class, status, or gender. The threat of being lynched is an example of the exclusion of African Americans from the moral community—a threat faced most often by African American males and a threat that existed independent of their virtues and merits.

Decapitation, torture, burning, and starvation were some of the common practices used in the process of forming and controlling slave communities in the Americas. The vast majority of persons treated as cargo, chattel, and fodder for plantations in the Americas were initially Black men. Moreover, it has been argued that "it was threat of honor lost, no less than slavery, that led them [southern American states] to secession and war."[10] Long after the formal end of American slavery in 1865, however, the project of exclusion of African Americans from the moral community continued. Trudier Harris, in *Exorcising Blackness*, describes an American mode of excluding Blacks from the moral community by its practice of lynching. Vicksburg, Mississippi, *Evening Post*, 1904:

> When the two Negroes were captured, they were tied to trees and while the funeral pyres were being prepared they were forced to suffer the most fiendish tortures. The blacks were forced to hold out their hands while one finger at a time was chopped off. The fingers were distributed as souvenirs. The ears of the murderers were cut off. Holbert was beaten severely, his skull was fractured, and one of his eyes, knocked out with a stick, hung by a shred from the socket … The most excruciating form of punishment consisted in the use of a large corkscrew in the hands of some of the mob. This instrument was bored into the flesh of the man and woman, in the arms, legs and body, and then pulled out, the spirals tearing out big pieces of raw, quivering flesh every time it was withdrawn.[11]

Quivering flesh, taken by avid corkscrewers, was thrown to the crowd for souvenirs. The bodies were burned, and after cooling, pieces of charred flesh were taken from the ashes by men, women, and children for souvenirs. Shopkeepers and women of class occasionally used severed hands as ornamentation. This ritual of violence was not isolated to Mississippi: in almost every case of lynching Blacks in America, a similar ritual was followed. With the increased accessibility of cameras, photographs of the crowd gloating over the body became a common feature of the ritual. ·

Approximately 25 percent of the lynchings studied by the National Association for the Advancement of Colored People in 1927 involved accusations of sexual harassment of white women as the justification for the lynching—the rest involved accusations of belligerence and property theft. When couples were lynched, the woman might be clubbed, hair cut and thrown to the crowd, fingers thrown to the crowd, corkscrewed through the breast and her flesh thrown to the crowd while the man was forced to watch what awaited him immediately upon completion of her torture. His genitals might be removed during his torturing and his "balls" later pickled as souvenirs. Lynching bespeaks the importance of the body as an object for degradation to substantiate the submission of persons excluded from a moral community; experiments on Black men are another example of the Black male body as a site for degradation.[12] In an excellent book, *Bad Blood: The Tuskegee Syphilis Experiment*, James Jones describes the "moral astigmatism" that allowed white government administrators, nurses, military personnel, entrepreneurs, doctors, news reporters, and poor Black and white workers to participate in a study for over forty years on the "effects of untreated syphilis on [399] Black men in Macon County, Alabama."[13] An experiment without procedures, an experiment predicated on the intentional withholding of known effective treatments, an experiment about which generation after generation of well-intentioned but astigmatic white physicians presented papers at professional conferences, is an experiment that suggests why there should be a basic distrust of professionals and unreflective workers. Both may be ready practitioners of moral astigmatism if for no other reason than that they performed their duties, following precedents, or pursued professional self-promotion in approved utilitarian fashions. Neither an unvirtuous character, an authoritarian personality, or evil intentions are necessary facets of persons deeply involved in perpetuating treatable pain and preventable misery. This is so because moral astigmatism often pervades relationships with persons excluded from the moral community. Consequently, individuals from social entities excluded from the moral community are burdened with raising the status of their community or finding some way to distance themselves absolutely from identification with their community in order to secure honor.

The above forms of terror most often confronted by African American males are not intended to suggest a well-designed conspiracy. They do suggest, however, a persistent pattern of immiseration and exclusion from the moral community. Honor is an elusive good for African American males in a world dominated by male codes of honor.

Honor and Masculinity

Honor has been most often a masculine good in the sense that the ability to kill, destroy, compel others to subordinate themselves, and control resources either necessary for survival or status has been most often a power held by men. Men, for example, are most often the symbols of a nation's warriors, regardless of the roles played by women. Neither the women warriors of North Vietnam nor the women guerrillas of Algeria and Zimbabwe are memorialized in nearly as vast an array of statues, street names, or government-sponsored ceremonies as are the men. Men have most often accorded the rewards and rituals of honor to other men within their communities.

Honor is not a masculine good when women accord women exalted regard independent of men or when the accord of exalted regard is not gender-specific. Queens, women warriors, free women in slaveholding societies, and women of upper classes and statuses, for example, may be honored for similar reasons as men—they are empowered in ways in which persons lower on the scale of membership in the moral community, or persons exiled from that community, are excluded. Even if exalted regard is itself considered a masculine trait, it is nonetheless a trait that has been held by women as women, for example, as goddesses and czarinas. The wife of any citizen of Athens held power over Aristotle because Aristotle, an outsider, a metic, could have become a slave but he could almost certainly never have ascended to a citizen. Any Athenian that might have married Aristotle, regardless of how rich or wise he might have become, would have lowered her status. Citizenship, as a family-based good, excludes persons outside of its network. Whether considered immoral, demented, irredeemably inferior, a witch, or a tramp, any white woman held power over every Black, whether the Black was a model mother, husband, father, mistress, Christian, servant, or entrepreneur. Race, class, status, gender, and citizenship can bifurcate who, and in what form, honor is accorded. Marriage is an example of a social institution that provides men honorable regard across these lines.

Honor through marriage is accorded to males in societies that practice patrilateral parallel cousin marriage (i.e., the marriage of one brother's son and another brother's daughter) as well as societies that practice exogamy.[14] Patrilateral parallel cousin marriage provides for a family and the male in these marriages a form of community respect for the family unit that can only be achieved through such marriages; their embodiment of spiritual, family, and communal leadership qualities are intoned by the marriage, not by any particular achievement otherwise. The poor as well as the rich gain status through such marriages. In Western societies, however, parallel cousin marriages are discouraged. Spiritual, family, and communal regard is frequently gained in Western societies by men through marriages with persons of the same or higher status as defined by wealth and education. Whether family solidarity is emphasized through affinal or agnate ties, honor is a good situated in social bonds. The family continues to be an important route by which men gain deference and regard from their affiliates. The status men gain by virtue of marriage, however, does not mean that all married men are held above all women: married men of Turkish heritage are not held above German women in Germany, married or single; married French Muslim men of Arabic heritage face prejudice in France although under less suspicion than single Muslim men of Arabic heritage; white American married men are not held in greater regard than Japanese women in Japan; married Muslim Palestinian men are not held above Jewish women in Israel. The increase of honor in marriage for men is tied to their community. There may be a greater respect for married men over single men within as well as outside of their communities. However, neither marital status nor gender defeats status designation by nationality, ethnicity, or race. Community membership and relationships between communities, I believe, are extremely important in situating the type of regard available to a person.

It would seem to follow that an individual from a generally subjugated community could not be honored by society in general because, as I have argued, honor is a good tied to perceptions of the moral community. Dr. Martin L. King Jr. is honored, however, although the African American community has not ascended to exalted regard. The honor accorded Dr. King, I suggest in the following, does not defeat the idea that honor is a social good tied to moral communities.

Honor and Dr. King

Dr. King followed a principle of communal love; that principle was central to a protest movement that permanently transformed the world.[15] He imposed his will, a will that was simultaneously associated with the will of a large community of immiserated persons. The Aristotelian concept of honor requires that an individual embody virtues. This embodiment affords them the right to demand deference from others. The Aquinian concept of honor requires that an agent temper claims to deference with the recognition that ultimately good virtues and good acts are made possible by God. Both concepts require that agents impose, or be capable of imposing, their will, and both require that agents to some degree embody virtues.[16] I suggest that a defensible depiction of the honor accorded Dr. King rests on an Aquinian conception of honor and an idea that was inconceivable in the Middle Ages: the idea that persons are nodally equal across lines of religion, nation, race, gender, and age.

The honor accorded Dr. King excludes the possibility of moral astigmatism because it is founded on an ideal that includes the necessity of moral reflection and commitment. We are enjoined in articles, sermons, and lectures to reflect on everyday moral concerns. An unjust law or practice, for Dr. King, is no law and not a practice we are compelled to follow. Rather, we are morally bound to evaluate social practices that define normality and required to pursue the change of unjust laws and immoral practices.

Dr. King embodies a crusade and a vision of a community, herculean struggle of the ostensibly weak overcoming the misguided strong; the fundamental transformation of the descendants of slaves—a dreadful heritage of humanity—to the status of free person; not a mystical, dialectical becoming through a Hegelian movement of spirit but a radical, this-worldly transformation. The song "We Shall Overcome," for example, has been sung by protesters in China, Russia, Germany, and South Africa. Its meaning has resonated with the dreams of millions. There are very few songs, dreams, or morally packed messages rooted in American history emulated by a greater diversity of peoples than the songs, dreams, and messages associated with Dr. King. Unlike the condition of president, soldier, entrepreneur, noble, or least well off, the honor accorded Dr. King is exalted because he represents ideals that are not expressed by granting accord to fairly circumscribed social roles.

Ironically, the honor accorded Dr. King is associated with his promotion of communal love: an ideal that is also associated with femininity, passivity, and emotional abandon. It is certainly arguable that Dr. King's life contributed to a redefinition of masculinity: commitment to *agape*, strength through compassion, caring even at the expense of self-harm. Dr. King's is not required to have lived some mystically perfect moral or normatively sanguine life—only that the life he did live was extraordinarily magnanimous. Dr. King is perceived as embodying virtues such as courage and tenacity, but these are subordinate to his image as a champion of non-violence and collective love. Arguments for a King memorial holiday, for example, do not rest on the family life of Dr. King as a model father or husband, a model minister, divine prophet, courageous savior of the polity, or fearless defender of the nation.

Even if after a thorough research of white attitudes it is found that whites accord Dr. King honor because they perceive his will as one totally subservient and nonthreatening to their will, it is still the case that the courage and magnanimous character required to love, care, be compassionate, and sacrifice should have an important place in the social fabric of Americans. The difficulty of according honor to such traits is considered below.

Dr. King as Counterexample

If honor is a social good accorded to members of a moral community, and the African American community is often excluded from membership, it would seem to follow that Dr. King could not be generally honored unless his will was clearly subservient to the will of the dominant community. It is arguable that Dr. King's pacifism (nonviolent direct action) helped make it possible for him to be honored in a way in which Malcolm X could not be honored. This is plausible if Dr. King's ideas and nonviolent methods are perceived as being or functioning in ways subservient to the will of the dominant community, for example, loving enemies, promoting the interests of the rich by nonviolent civil disobedience among the poor, promoting Black identity as "American" in the face of Black exclusion from equal treatment, and so on. If his ideas and methods are also perceived as "feminine" in the sense in which that which is feminine is considered somehow compliant, weak, and submissive to that which is masculine, then the view of Dr. King's pacifism as consonant with the will of the dominant community gains further warrant. However, I suggest that the above perception of Dr. King's ideas and methods fails to appreciate the specificity of race, the ambivalence in the American cultural fabric over the meaning of honor and the character of communal love.

A perception of Dr. King as submissive is simply misguided. Dr. King prevailed, for example, despite attacks by the US government's COINTELPRO (Counterintelligence Program) under J. Edgar Hoover's FBI orchestrated to blackmail Dr. King into committing suicide, and despite the attacks on this life by segregationists. Even if his ideas and methods functioned in ways subservient to the will of the dominant community, they were instrumental in bringing substantive change. The laws and institutional rules of segregation, as well as avowed prejudicial beliefs, have all declined in direct response to the civil rights movement in which Dr. King was a major actor.

A perception of Dr. King as feminine, when feminine is construed as compliant, weak, and submissive, expurgates Dr. King from being perceived as Black (already stereotyped inferior by race). Such a perception also requires erasure of the character of his proactive approach, that is, civil disobedience, nonviolent direct action, and courageous resistance to injustice.

The character of racial and gendered forms of oppression are not identical.[17] African American males, for example, do not face date rape or spouse abuse in anywhere near the proportion of women, Black or white. They are more likely to be the perpetrators of date rape and spouse abuse. They face, more than Black or white women, the likelihood of being unemployed. The minuscule group of middleclass Black males fares better than Black females, far worse than white males, and is far smaller in relation to their numbers than white females. Black males face the greatest likelihood of incarceration, regardless of guilt. For such reasons it is not intrinsically confusing to write about African American women and men facing multiple jeopardy (race, sex, gender, and class)—the character of the jeopardies is interlaced yet distinct.

If the specificity of the subject is not taken seriously, the victim is ignored. For example, if the abuse of children is simply subsumed under the abuse of spouses, children become effectually erased. Abused children are frequently under the care of abused mothers; however, an appropriate array of such abuses would allow for children as subjects with their own experiences—including experiences that warrant interests and rights against parents whether the parent is an abusing mother, father, relative, or stranger. The specificity of the subject does not reside outside of a social network—who are the abusers, who has remained silent about the abuse, who is empowered to aid the abused? A perception of Dr. King as submissive without remainder fails to take account of the specificity of his community, a community despised by the other.

In one sense, Dr. King is not a counterexample to the generality that honor is a social good accorded to members of a moral community—in the sense that his pacifism is perceived as completely in the service and interest of the dominant community. The federal government and most states have instituted a Martin L. King Jr. national holiday, for example, but they are under no pressure to disband their armies or militia thereby. The nonviolent message of Dr. King's pacifism is selectively applied according to the will of the agents intoning his message. However, his proactive method for imposing his will and his inclusion of African American people as full members of the moral community are sources of ambivalence for the larger community. One feature of the ambivalence involves honoring Dr. King as an agent that promoted love *and* change, when change is often accompanied by unkindly threats, pressure, and aggression.

If there is a difference between the way Dr. King and Malcolm X can be honored, the difference may rest on our evaluation of their different views of communal love. When Dr. King and Malcolm X intoned "I love my people," their views of how that love was best actualized differed. Love, in both cases, was a form of "empowerment" in a direct sense, that is, it was a good through which one engenders, among other things, the ability of others to impose their will. Parents, for example, help empower their children by caring, nurturing, and guiding; partners empower one another by support, dialogue, and aid; relatives empower one another by functioning as information networks, sites of belonging, and sources of encouragement. Loving is empowering, but its form and content may differ.

Dr. King's form of love allowed for an acquiescence to the culture of America as a combined entity and Malcolm X's did not. The *two nations* are for Dr. King at their best when conjoined in communal love; the two nations are at their best for Malcolm X when each is allowed its own cultural legitimacy and self-controlled empowerment.[18] Dr. King's form of love is empowerment in competition against the dominant order for the reformation of the society through the aegis of love, care, compassion, and sacrifice. Malcolm X's form involved empowerment in competition against the dominant order for the reformation of the society through aggression.

The ideals of communal love and nonviolent resistance have long histories in African American culture. Vincent Harding's *There Is a River* is a moving history of African American forms of resistance.[19] In addition, Harding's response to *Habits of the Heart* is an exploration into the difference between the norms defining the African American community and the white community.[20] Abolitionists, Reconstruction moral suasionists, civil rights activists, and various nationalist movements have promoted a notion of communal love and nonviolent resistance as moral imperatives. In the contemporary era, *Nation Conscious Rap*, for all of its aggressive, uncompromising, and sexually charged themes, has a major chord of communal love and nonviolent resistance.[21] The ideal of communal love and nonviolent resistance consequently reflects cultural ambivalence about the relationship of love and change and a similar ambivalence about the meaning of honor.

Honor and Empowerment

Honor, as one among many social goods, is a function of community. Analogously, power, in the way Jennifer L. Hochschild uses it to depict a variety of goods (economic, political, and internal motivation) affecting means and prospects regarding equal opportunity, is a function of community.[22] That is, the possibility of honor for an individual is integrally tied to the possibility of his or her community having, or potentially having, honorable status. The African American community gained because of the civil rights era symbolized by Dr. King in the sense that it gained status within the moral community of America. Its ability to protect its members from wanton attacks by the Ku Klux Klan or advance its members through legal redress, for example, is suggestive of its empowerment.

One difficulty with honoring Dr. King through the aegis of love, care, compassion, and sacrifice is that such traits do not readily bespeak other equally important sources of honor. Moreover, the imposition of wills through threats, demands, pressure, and aggressive behavior are not neatly separated from love, care, compassion, and sacrifice. (The parenting examples used earlier suggest the sort of intermeshing linkage that I mean.) Nor, it seems to me, are the traits of love, caring, compassion, or sacrificing reducible to a neat category of "affective." However, even if love and aggressiveness fit in separate trait categories, normal social life involves imposing wills through the aegis of both trait categories.

An inference from socially normal activity to the activity of an individual is an important inference because honor is a form of deference to individuals sustained by social groups—families, citizens, African Americans, Americans, peace-loving people, and so on—which sustain the bond between the individual and the existence that a social group perceives itself as embodying. Moreover, archetypal behavior is archetypal because it represents an inward nature only intimated by actual normal behavior. There is, in a sense, a two-way street between the individual and the social; between the socially normal and the exalted. If we honor, for example, a president, whether of the National Organization for Women (NOW) or of the United States, one reason is because he or she embodies, stands for, or represents some traits that we hold in regard. It is not required that we agree with everything representatives do, nor even that we like the organizations they head; what is required is that they embody traits that we hold in regard.

The moral community of America is most often conceived in ways that exclude the African American community. A perception of the African American community as capable of imposing its will, ranking above others, commanding deference—crucial features of normality—is contrary to America's perception of one of its least favored groups. Dr. King certainly imposed his will through tremendous labor, sacrificial love, and nonviolent resistance. A good deal of social normality is, however, the imposition of wills through threats, demands, pressure, and aggressiveness.

One reason parents, soldiers, entrepreneurs, the poor, teachers, and the elderly can be held in high regard is because they are perceived as persons who successfully manage exigencies against pressures to fail—exigencies that include, but are not restricted to, performances that have little or nothing to do with affective goods such as love, caring, compassion, or sacrificing. Parents, for example, clean, cook, wash, pay bills, and are often blamed for the atrocities that their children commit but are rarely applauded if their children perform laudable acts. There are no national holidays, however, dedicated to good parenting. Even if parenting in the modem world can be said to be in some sense "caused" by love, as distinct from the medieval view of parenting as a duty, the performances of generating income, paying bills, cleaning up, and spending time that directly takes away from other enriching adult activities require tenacity, diligence, thrift, aggressiveness, and discipline. There are, for example, more African American male single parents than white American male single parents in proportion to their numbers in society—but single fathering is hardly an image located in any social group's perception of African American males. Single parenting, for African American males, requires a willingness to do so despite the certainty that popular social media such as television, newspapers, novels, or church services will not offer much encouragement or recognition.

Parenting also requires tremendous aggressiveness and self-assurance for African Americans in general, and African American males in particular, to protect their children. Many grade school administrators, primarily male and white, and grade school teachers, primarily female and white, harbor and impose a daunting array of demeaning and destructive prejudices toward African Americans in general and especially African American males. The history of research on administrator and teacher attitudes, detailing their prejudicial practices toward African American males, is simply overwhelming: researchers may disagree on which array of prejudices and precisely how daunting, but they almost invariably portray a dismal picture of African American males receiving less attention, lower grades, harsher punishments, and fewer awards than white children with identical or similar performance.[23] Successful parenting requires diligence: persistently arguing, demanding accountability, and defending one's child against a barrage of prejudices against the very persons parents depend on for educating their children.

One of the most distressing features of aggressiveness and threatening behavior is that they are also implicated in the harms facing African American males. Black males receive harms in part because of the way they are socialized, not simply because of their sex.[24] Black on Black homicide, for example, is the cause of far more deaths than white on Black homicides. Black males physically inflict more harms on themselves than anyone else—it is improbable that this has nothing to do with their socialization and form of being nurtured. The imposition of wills through uncompromising or nearly uncompromising demands, mutually unpleasant encounters, aggressiveness, pressure, and threats may function well or horribly. Honor is often accorded the powerful—for example, presidents, entrepreneurs, nobles, and soldiers—through the conduits of their successful use of aggression and pressure for causes considered laudable. This, it seems to me, is true whether the honored are conceived as pure egalitarian pacifists ruled by affective emotions or absolute monarchical warlords ruled by meanness. Aggressiveness and threatening behaviors—traits that ruling groups tend to reserve as legitimate forms of behavior for themselves—may be tools in Malcolm X's sense, that is, traits that can help defend a person against an onslaught of social tyranny or help lift a person from the degradation of social death. Survival tools are invaluable in a chronically racist society that confronts obstacles from the improbability of prenatal care or fair treatment in grade school to the improbability of employment or income even nearly commensurate with others of similar endowment. Whether the traits of aggressiveness or threatening behavior are sources of harm or conduits for survival, they are features of social normality through which some forms of honor are obtained. Emasculation, however, is most assuredly not a basis for honor.

The attack on the African American male is arguably a sex-specific emasculating attack in the sense that African American men are the object, or at least African American men have received an undue array of harms, by virtue of their sexual socialization and race. It is a feminist issue in Ida B. Wells's sense—lynching for her was an issue for the nation and Africans as a people, yet it was particularly a feminist issue because Black men, sons and husbands, were its most frequent object. It is also fruitfully characterized as more than sex-specific: it can be characterized as a part of an attack on the body of a people—a people long excluded from the moral community and continually under duress. This is so not because Black men are breadwinners (except for a small sector of middle-class Black men, Black men have less income than Black women) or because Black men are leaders (the percentage of Black elected officials has radically improved, but it hardly corresponds to the percentage of the Black US population; civil rights leadership has been notoriously male-dominated and almost completely chauvinist—there are no reasons why this should continue).

It is an attack on the body of a people because in a certain sense "men" do not exist in social normality outside the context of associations, relations, networks, parents, and ascending and descending generations of persons. Men do not exist in the sense of their sharing identical material assets, powers to command deference from persons outside their communities, or ability to shape and execute life plans. Men of subjugated communities, for example, are characteristically emasculated. To be emasculated is to be disjoined from the possibility of empowerment across generations—a possibility that exists only in social connection.

The idea that in a certain way "men" do not exist as a social entity does not mean that "men" cannot be treated as an independent variable.[25] Without so doing it would be difficult to see chauvinist forms of gender oppression practiced by men across social entities of class, race, and ethnicity. It would also be difficult to see specifically gendered forms of male association. However, one of the limitations of treating "men" as an independent variable is the tremendous difference concerning what happens to men because of race, class, status, and culture. Native American men, for example, are hardly in the same position as American men of any ethnicity or race—the former are not a part of the American nation, and they do not have as a nation standing armies; it is not reasonable for Native American mothers and fathers to instill in their children an expectation of soldiering in an existing army as a possible future career. The disempowerment of African American men is, analogously, integrally tied to the status of the African American community.

There is little doubt that the African American community gained status as members of the moral community in the world because of Dr. King—it is debatable to what degree African Americans are accorded the status of full persons in America. That status, as Americans, conditions the possibility of empowerment and the negation of emasculation. It is certain that African American males are in multiple jeopardy—one part of which is the *elusive* good of honor of the kind that we can easily identify with through normal social life—a social life the character of which is due for substantive change.

Notes

1. John K. Campbell, *Honour, Family and Patronage* (Oxford: Oxford University Press, 1964), 271. Also, according to Julian Pitt-Rivers, "the claim to honor depends always in the last resort, upon the ability of the claimant to impose himself. Might is the basis of right to precedence, which goes to the man who is bold enough to enforce his claim, regardless of what may be thought of his merits": "Honor," in *Encyclopedia of the Social Sciences*, 2nd ed., vol. 6 (New York: Macmillan, 1968), 505. The general idea that honor is a social good is not particularly unique, although the way I argue for this view and its application is hopefully of interest.

2. An implication of my view of honor as a social good is that generally honoring an individual woman for virtues and merits associated with women as such is a function of whether "women" as a social group have status in the moral community and the sort of status that they have as a group. The analog for this is an African-American male (Dr. King) and the African-American community, i.e., social status in the moral community, is the crucial factor shaping the possibility of honor for an individual.

3. See, for example, Robert Cole, *The Political Life of Children* (Boston, MA: Atlantic Monthly Press, 1986); Janice E. Hale-Benson, *Black Children: Their Roots, Culture, and Learning Styles* (Baltimore, MD: Johns Hopkins University Press, 1986).

4. See Bertram Wyatt-Brown, *Southern Honor: Ethics and Behavior in the Old South* (Oxford: Oxford University Press, 1982). Honor was an important variable shaping the cohesion of Southerners; a cohesion sufficiently strong to compel tremendous sacrifice in defense of a segregated way of life. Also see Julian Pitt-Rivers, *Mediterranean Countrymen* (Paris: Mouton, 1963), 80. Also see Julian Pitt-Rivers and John George Peristiany, *Honor and Grace in Anthropology* (Cambridge: Cambridge University Press, 1992).

5. Peter Berger, "On the Obsolescence of the Concept of Honour," in *Liberalism and Its Critics*, ed. Michael Sandel (New York: New York University Press, 1984), 158.

6. Orlando Patterson, *Slavery and Social Death: A Comparative Study* (Cambridge, MA: Harvard University Press, 1982), 78. I am indebted to Patterson's work for comparing honor and degradation.

7. Ibid., 315.

8. J. E. Casely Hayford, *Ethiopia Unbound: Studies in Race Emancipation* (London: Frank Cass, [1911] 1969); J. E. Casely Hayford, *Gold Coast Native Institutions* (London: Sweet and Maxwell, 1903).

9. This is the case even if the utopia consists solely of women, imposing their wills on one another or imposing their wills on men, e.g., C. Gilman's *Herland* (New York: Pantheon Books, 1978), or S. S. Teppers's *The Gate to Women's Country* (New York: Foundation Books, 1988).

10. Wyatt-Brown, *Southern Honor*, 5.

11. Trudier Harris, *Exorcising Blackness: Historical and Literary Lynching and Burning Rituals* (Bloomington: Indiana University Press, 1984), 2. This quote has been used in the literature on lynching as a fairly standard example of the elements involved in the ritual.

12. See, for examples of honor accorded various body parts and expressions, Michel Feher, Ramona Nadaff, and Nadia Tazi (eds.), *Fragments for a History of the Human Body*, Part One, Part Two, Part Three (New York: Urzone, 1989). Also see Philomena Essed, *Everyday Racism: Reports from Women of Two Cultures* (Claremont, CA: Hunter House, 1990).

13. James Jones, *Bad Blood: The Tuskegee Syphilis Experiment* (New York: Free Press, 1981).

14. See Ladislav Holy, *Kingship, Honour and Solidarity* (Manchester: Manchester University Press, 1989), 125.

15. See John Ansbro, *Making of a Mind* (New York: Orbis Books, 1982); Carson Clayborne, David J. Garrow, Gerald Gill, Vincent Harding, and Darlene Clark Hine (eds.), *The Eyes on the Prize: Documents, Speeches, and Firsthand Accounts from the Black Freedom Struggle* (New York: Penguin Books, 1991); James M. Washington (ed.), *A Testament of Hope: The Essential Writings of Martin L. King, Jr.* (San Francisco, CA: Harper & Row, 1986).

16. For comparison and contrast of Aristotelian and Aquianian concepts of honor, see Maurice B. McNamee SJ, *Honor and the Epic Hero: A Study of the Shifting Concept of Magnanimity in Philosophy and Epic Poetry* (New York: Holt, Rinehart and Winston, 1960).

17. See Bill Lawson (ed.), *The Underclass Question* (Philadelphia, PA: Temple University Press, 1992); A. Zegeye, J. Maxted, and L. Harris (eds.), *Exploitation and Exclusion* (London: Hans Zell, 1991); Elizabeth Fox-Genovese, *Within the Plantation Household* (Chapel Hill: University of North Carolina Press, 1988); bell hooks, *Yearning: Race, Gender, and Cultural Politics* (Boston, MA: South End Press, 1990); David Goldberg, *Anatomy of Racism* (Minneapolis: University of Minnesota Press, 1990).

18. Andrew Hacker, *Two Nations: Black and White, Separate, Hostile, Unequal* (New York: Charles Scribner's Sons, 1991). Also see Haki R. Madhubuti, *Black Men: Obsolete, Single, Dangerous? The Afrikan American Family in Transitoin* (Chicago, IL: Third World Press, 1990).

19. Vincent Harding, *There Is a River: The Black Struggle for Freedom in America* (New York: Harcourt Brace Jovanovich, 1981); Vincent Harding, *The Other American Revolution* (Los Angeles, CA: Center for AfroAmerican Studies, 1980). Also see Donald Yacovone, "Abolitionists and the 'Language of Fraternal Love,'" in *Meanings for Manhood: Construction of Masculinity in Victorian America*, ed. Mark C. Carnes and Clyde Griffen (Chicago, IL: University of Chicago Press, 1990), 85–94.

20. Vincent Harding, "Toward a Darkly Radiant Vision of America's Truth: A Letter of Concern, An Invitation to Re-Creation," in *Community in America: The Challenge of Habits of the Heart*, ed. Charles H. Reynolds and Ralph V. Norman (Berkeley: University of California Press, 1988), 67–83; also see Robert Bellah, Richard Madsen, William M. Sullivan, Ann Swidler, and Steven M. Tipton, *Habits of the Heart: Individualism and Commitment in American Life* (Berkeley: University of California Press, 1985).

21. J. D. Eure and J. G. Spady (eds.), *Nation Conscious Rap* (New York: PC International Press, 1991).

22. Jennifer L. Hochschild, "Race, Class, Power, and Equal Opportunity," in *Equal Opportunity*, ed. Norman Bowie (Boulder, CO: Westview Press, 1988), 75–111.

23. See e.g. Jonathan Kozol, *Death at an Early Age: The Destruction of the Hearts and Minds of Negro Children in the Boston Public Schools* (Boston, MA: Houghton Mifflin, 1967); Jonathan Kozol, *Savage Inequalities* (New York: Crown, 1991).

24. I am indebted to Trudier Palmer, University of Pittsburgh, for the importance of noting the influence of socialization here.

25. For examples of the fruitfulness of so doing, despite problems of how much to weigh the variable as a cause, see Mark C. Carnes and Clyde Griffen (eds.), *Meanings for Manhood: Construction of Masculinity in Victorian America* (Chicago, IL: University of Chicago Press, 1990). See, for my ideas of community and agency, "Historical Subjects and Interests: Race, Class, and Conflict," in *The Year Left*, ed. Michael Sprinkler et al. (New York: Verso, 1986), 91–106; and "Columbus and the Identity of the Americas," *Annals of Scholarship* 8 (2, Spring 1991): 287–99.

CHAPTER 7
TOLERANCE, RECONCILIATION, AND GROUPS (2003)

In "Tolerance, Reconciliation, and Groups," Harris challenges absolutist conceptions of virtue and obligation. He argues that tolerance should be not taken as an intrinsic virtue, objectively true, or mandated by a supernatural authority. "Arguments that contend tolerance is a substantive virtue that individuals should possess because individual possession of the virtue will produce social beneficial results are misguided." First, human groupings are never composed of individuals with identical moral traits and behaviors. Individual traits taken collectively do not dictate social relations and institutions in a stable fashion. Second, tolerance as an intrinsic virtue does not, in fact, guarantee beneficial social results. In some cases, tolerance can pacify an immiserated people; it can reinscribe gross inequities. Harris argues that those who have suffered brutality or grave injustice should not be morally obligated to forgive or tolerate their victimizers. Victims are warranted in feeling indignation and may benefit from enmity toward their victimizers or the conditions that facilitated their victimization. In the end, Harris depicts both tolerance and indignation as pragmatic virtues—attenuated virtues that can be useful in context-specific deliberations as we struggle to create human liberation.

Moral pluralists consider tolerance a substantive virtue because they believe that it is compatible with reasonably appealing character traits such as serenity, forbearance, charity, patience, benevolence, and forgiveness. They also think that such traits are preferable, if not antithetical, to resentment, indignation, malevolence, antipathy, reproach, condemnation, and revenge. The forms of moral pluralism I will consider are those that contend that reasoned judgment should be the discourse method for use in selecting moral principles. In addition, such principles are not reducible, subjective individual proclivities.[1] Moral pluralists of this sort believe that there are no objectively moral truths independent of reasoned judgment. Despite the fact that there are no objective moral truths independent of reasoned judgment, some moral beliefs and actions can be considered preferable to others. A moral pluralist can argue, for example, that there are moral imperatives; however, such imperatives would be considered justified based on reasoned judgment, not objective truth.[2] Tolerance is associated with qualities of reasoning such as deliberative consideration and reflective reasoned judgment. Such qualities of thought are utilitarian in the sense that they are believed to help individuals appreciate that some questions are not, or not easily, decidable and that such reasoning traits are likely to prevent persons from becoming unduly judgmental, fanatical, or dictatorial. Consequently, for moral pluralists, tolerance is a good at least because it is a beneficial character and cognitive trait.

Moral absolutism is the view that there are objective moral truths independent of reasoned judgment. That is, by virtue of their intrinsic, natural or supernaturally determined character, some truths are objectively determined. Thus, a moral absolutist can contend "that there are some action types that ought never to be performed, irrespective of context or consequence."[3] Moral absolutists are not necessarily committed to believing that humans will ever possess a unified consciousness, single religion, political system, or uniform culture. Nor are they necessarily committed to the view that all persons should subscribe to an officially sanctioned and thereby orthodox set of beliefs. Absolutist, religious or otherwise, can support cultural and religious pluralism. The Ottoman Turks, for example, between 1456 and approximately 1918, officially recognized under a millet system Greek Orthodox, Armenian Orthodox, and Jewish religious communities. Each community controlled its own moral codes and customs. The system was far from perfect freedom, especially since each community forcibly imposed grotesque demands on its members to conform to their religiously defined moral codes. The millet system nonetheless proffered a form of self-governance within the context of a broader system.[4] Absolutists favor tolerance because they believe it is an intrinsic virtue, objectively true or mandated by a supernatural authority.

I

Dictatorial attitudes can be promoted by either moral pluralists or moral absolutists. That is, neither moral pluralism nor moral absolutism can claim an actual history of their followers exhibiting, more often than not, tolerance. Moral pluralists, as well as immoralists, can argue that necessity, force, power, coercion, and material conditions determine what persons should consider morally acceptable. A preference for, or expectation of, some form of dictatorship—whether class dominated as in the case of Marx or empowered authorities as in the case of Nietzsche—are proffered by these authors. There are also many examples of moral absolutists practicing dictatorial behavior. Christian missionaries in the eighteenth century, for example, were arguably the advance guards preparing and then sustaining colonialism throughout Asia, Africa, and South America. The terror perpetuated under South African apartheid, and the vicious murders sanctioned by the Belgium rulers of the Congo under Leopold I are only more contemporary cases of state-sanctioned moral absolutism. The only alternative religious and cultural practices tolerated were those considered beneficial to sustaining colonial rule because the colonized were considered inherently inferior and incapable or unworthy of civilization. Their cheap labor, arable land, and precious minerals were expropriated by religious and government authorities under the guise of sustaining objectively true moral beliefs. Government and religious authorities often claim that they are in possession of objective moral truth and that the subjugated participated in helping to arrive at such truths by their tacit consent (i.e., they would agree if they could arrive at an impartial judgment) or they do consent as witnessed by some coerced group of indigenous authorities collaborating with the colonizers.[5]

Societies that mandate tolerance are also noted for practicing some of the world's worst forms of terrorism. The authors of South African apartheid and American democracy promoted the idea that tolerance was a good; both enslaved and with varying degrees of success destroyed indigenous populations. The United States, for example, was successful in almost completely destroying its native population. Every major democracy in human history, whether Greek, Roman, Arabic, Chinese, or African, has also practiced slavery, colonial domination, and ethnocide of minorities.[6]

Moral pluralists and absolutists, for different reasons, often rely on at least one similar argument to help support their views, namely, that tolerance as an individual virtue can—under some set of conditions—coalesce in ways that produce virtuous social relations. Philosophies that are neither strictly pluralist nor absolutist also often rely on this view.

Utilitarianism, particularly John S. Mill's version, is arguably a form of moral absolutism at least for contending that tolerance is a good for objectively true utilitarian reasons. If human society is inherently inclined to eventually arrive at true moral principles, namely, the principles that maximize the greatest good for the great number of sentient beings, then tolerance is warranted for reasons associated with the objective good of maximizing pleasure. Pragmatism, particularly John Rawls's version, is arguably a form of moral pluralism for contending that tolerance is a good through reflective equilibrium reasoned judgment. If persons in an original position, representing impartial reasoning judges, would consent to consider tolerance a good, then tolerance gains the status of an entitlement or right as a function of reasoned judgment independent of claims about objectively true human nature, intuitions, or a moral social universe inclined toward achieving true moral principles. I consider these different approaches to tolerance below.

I will consider Mill's utilitarianism as a paradigmatic utilitarian approach to justifying tolerance as a virtue. Rather than Augustine of Hippo's argument that the persecution of heretics, the Donatists in particular, was a positive good, Mill argued that persecution of dissenters was ineffective for the purposes of either conversion of dissenters to state-sanctioned religious denominations or public stability. That is, tolerance was utilitarian for Mill because he believed that coercing persons to practice state-sanctioned religious faith caused undue social unrest and tended to fail. In addition, it has been argued that there is no way to create orthodoxy by coercion since coercion itself creates new sources of dissent. Tolerance is justified as a good because it is necessary for liberty to exist.[7] For Mill, error is an ineliminable part of the process of arriving at the truth. Thus, the state should tolerate peaceful dissent especially since preferable beliefs will eventually gain public acceptance through the process of overcoming error.[8] Mill also had epistemic reasons to encourage tolerance.

As a volitionist, Mill believed that individuals could be held responsible for beliefs freely chosen. Individuals exercising their free will voluntarily, for Mill, explained when principles were freely chosen. In this same tradition, moral absolutists have argued that refutation, conjecture, deliberative reflection, and disagreement are important features of discourse that enhance and make probable consensual voluntary agreement on true moral principles.[9] Moralists such as Mill contend that the reality of different ways of life, desires, preferences, and irreconcilable moral principles contribute to the possibility of arriving at peaceful solutions and defensible objectively true principles rather than spell an irreducible fact of human diversity. Utilitarians can favor a wide variety of tolerant relations between groups while consistently believing that individual exercise of free will can coalesce such that individuals and groups will sustain tolerant relations.

John Rawls's contract theory of justice as fairness argues for tolerance as a virtue for racially different reasons than Mill's utilitarian. Rawls relies on the tradition of contract theory to justify tolerance between individuals and groups. Rawls's approach to contract theory offers the following way to arrive at impartial and thereby objective as possible, justified principles: We are to imagine a situation in which individuals, not knowing or being committed to any particular society or social station, consider competing principles and consider what principles all such persons would consent to. The contract test is a test of impartiality, intended to be a reasonable basis on which reliable beliefs and actions could be based. The test is a thought experiment using rational and reasonable beliefs and actions as epistemic criteria. Its form of impartiality is intended to require judgments that are not influenced by partialities, preferences, and local prejudices. All persons, despite specific identities, would thus theoretically arrive at the same conclusions. This approach avoids requiring all persons to subscribe to the same substantive beliefs save those that promote fairness in a way that allows each person a way of life they prefer and a reasonable chance to accomplish their life plans. Numerous authors, such as Bayle, Locke, and Rawls, propose unique versions of contract tests; however, the above are central features of each test. Ideal conditions of reasoning impartially would arrive, on their accounts, at tolerance as a good.

According to Rawls, "the plurality of distinct persons with separate systems of ends is an essential feature of human societies,"[10] and, thus, for Rawls, justice as fairness sets limits but does not "try to evaluate the relative merits of different conceptions of the good."[11] Individual conceptions of the good, for Rawls, to the extent that they do not violate principles of fairness, are to be tolerated. He believes that justice demands tolerance because it is a reasonable and rational attitude that persons would select impartially for self-regarding and utilitarian reasons.

There are for Rawls, unlike Mill, inalienable rights not justifiably subject to utilitarian considerations such as how to maximized pleasure or public security for the greatest number if it means alienating the rights of some individuals. Even if tolerance in some societies would fail to generate public security or lead eventually to moral truth—and Mill certainly doubted that "inferior" societies would ever achieve the traits needed to warrant liberal tolerance—Rawls's *Theory of Justice* proffers tolerance as an individual virtue because of its cognitive association with traits beneficial to recognizing the dignity of other and associated rights. In his later works he argues for tolerance as a value of use for regulating relations between groups.[12]

Rawls, in his later works, offers a concept of "reasonable pluralism" to define the type of relationship between groups that tolerance warrants. Groups with "comprehensive doctrines reasonable on its own terms [internally coherent, rational, and reflective] and can recognize the reasonableness of other comprehensive doctrines, even if considered wrong" can be thought of as groups potentially sustaining fair relations.[13] Overlapping agreements between competing and conflicting comprehensive doctrines are the kinds of agreements making possible reasonable pluralism. Although there are no absolutely nonrelative ways of arriving at impartial principles or any way to completely escape provincialism to some degree in thinking, the idea of peaceful coexistence between groups is an intuitively valuable goal. Rawls contends, "The reasonable does, of course, express a reflective attitude to toleration, since it recognizes the burdens of judgment, and this in turn leads to liberty of conscience and freedom of thought."[14] Thus, reasonableness and overlapping agreements, given a contractual test, provides a basis for tolerance described as reasonable pluralism.[15]

II

Arguments that contend that tolerance is a substantive virtue that individuals should possess because individual possession of the virtue will produce socially beneficial results are misguided. Virtuous individuals, I contend, do not somehow form virtuous group relations of tolerance, let alone do disparate tolerant agents create freedom from vicious social institutions and structures. Thus, methodological individualist explanations fail to help justify tolerance between groups. The view that individual virtues become group behaviors is a form of methodological individualism. Methodological individualism is the view that social actions are adequately explained as the outcome of individual behaviors. Individual volitions are the ultimate causal force for methodological individualists.[16]

If every individual were endowed, or acquired the virtue of tolerance, it would be false that genocide, ethnocide, or colonial domination would be abated. It is false that every form of genocide, ethnocide, and colonial domination is a function of either individuals acting in unison or the accidental consequence of separate intentional actions. Groups are never composed of individuals with identical beliefs and behaviors. The consequences of group behavior, although occasionally the result of accident, are very often best explained in terms of the impact of institutions and structures. At the very least, integrative structures of some form, such as ownership of asset configurations and inheritance rules, class distinctions, boundaries defined by ethnicity and race shaping marital patterns, communities shaped by geographic location determining travel options, and separations by national sovereignty explain group behavior. More to the point, individual traits taken collectively do not form social institutions or dictate social relations between groups. The rules and procedures of institutions, followed almost always without prior individual intention, volition, or even awareness of their many intricacies, are not reducible to the thought and behavior of each individual. Nor are relations between groups, for example, nations or religions, reducible to the preferences, desires, or wills of each member. There are several excellent analogs in formal logic, I note below, that help us see the difference between individuals and groups.

The fallacy of composition occurs when attributes of the parts of a whole are assumed to have the property the whole. Thus, it is fallacious to assume that each part of an apple is identical to the whole apple. Analogously, it is fallacious think that each member of the working class is identical to the class itself.

The fallacy of division occurs when we assume that the whole has a property and its parts share in that same property. Thus, it is false that each part of a red apple is also red. Analogously, Aborigines of New Zealand are noted for believing that their indigenous homeland harbors mystical qualities, but it is false that each member has this belief.

Lastly, the fallacy of undistributed middle occurs when two separate categories are mistakenly connected because they share a common property. Round apples are not the same as round footballs. The assumption that roundness tells us the approximate weight or function of each is misguided. Analogously, if two populations are rural, it does not follow that both are pastoral.

Volitionists characteristically rely on a form of methodological individualism to explain individual, group, and institutional behavior. In particular, they rely on the view that individual beliefs and actions, taken collectively, cause institutional behavior. It is not just that they think that beliefs are causal of behavior but that beliefs and correlative actions cause each feature of institutional behavior. However, individual virtuous traits, taken cumulatively, never amount to socially practiced virtues between groups, *circa*, fallacy of composition. Groups, such as ethnicities, are not simply compounded collections of individuals with ethnic identities, *circa*, fallacy of division. In an antiblack racist society, each person of color is treated as if they possessed a Black identity; it is false that persons of color ubiquitously share a common racial identity, but even if they did, each identity would have its own unique features making any generalization about "Black people" a generalization that would not be identical to its members. Individuated virtues do not create group virtuous behavior because structures are not the cumulative result of individual traits, *circa*, fallacy of undistributed middle. That is, because separate individuals share a common property of virtuousness, it is false that we know anything about the groups and the group relations of which different individuals belong. The causal inference is spurious. Methodological individualism, which warrants that individual virtuous beliefs and behavior translate into group relations of tolerance, misguides because it offers a false account of the relationship of individual volitions to group behavior and, as I explore below, what it means to think of groups as "relating."

III

Tolerance as an intrinsic virtue is thought not just compatible but also causal of such traits as serenity, forbearance, charity, patience, and benevolence.[17] Tolerance as an intrinsic virtue is a good as a matter of something about the human spirit, conscience, or will. Tolerance as an intrinsic virtue is also associated with qualities of cognition such as reflection and reasoned judgment. Such traits are not just utilitarian in the sense that they help individuals appreciate that some questions are not, or not easily, decidable or that such traits are likely to prevent persons from becoming unduly judgmental, fanatic, or dictatorial. They are, rather, considered definitive of the way virtuous people think, and presumably the way they think would incline them to provide strong support for principles of fairness such as other regarding respect. Unfortunately, authors that often consider tolerance an intrinsic virtue also assume that tolerance will have salutary social results because they associate tolerance with cognitive traits they believe will provide salutary effects. The Truth and Justice Commission of South Africa will be used to explore why intrinsic individual virtue has little causally to do with social justice.

The Truth and Justice Commission of postapartheid South Africa was responsible for helping to create fairness between the victimized African population and their victimizers. The commission did so by providing a forum where primarily Africans could accuse and whites could admit guilt—but without a high likelihood of receiving punishment. Tolerance, rather than malevolence, resentment, indignation and antipathy, and forgiveness, rather than reproach and condemnation, were thought to be preferable. The forum provided by the commission could achieve the preferable result, it was thought. An important consequence would be more tolerant and understanding relations between Africans and whites. The commission, unfortunately, did not offer justice between groups—almost no substantive ownership of mines, precious metals, land, stocks, health insurances, real estate, or corporations were taken from whites and placed under the control of Africans, nor were any significant number of whites held to account for vast numbers of murders, rapes, expropriation of cheap labor, and theft. As of December 2003, 115 firms listed on the Johannesburg Stock Exchange; 23 were Black-owned, accounting for less than 10 percent of the exchanges value; the proportion of mining shares owned by Blacks is 7 percent; and Blacks hold 1 percent of real estate shares. No statistically significant amount of land or ownerships have been transferred from whites to Blacks through the commission, or any land or businesses acquired by virtue of the commission. Structures and institutions sustaining misery have been left too often unfettered. The asset ownership, inheritance structure, and conditions for acquiring land and other social structures between Africans and whites remained unaffected. Nonetheless, Africans were expected to forgive their victimizers.

Indignation, I contend, has proper moral functions, such as helping sustain just feelings of being wronged and sustaining the need to be vigilant against future wrongs. Victims may need encouragement to be self-confident, having been terrorized, exploited, abused, and made insecure in their hardworking pursuit of a life plan brutally disrupted by victimizers. Indignation, and not just forgiving, can be utilitarian and instrumental if not intrinsically valuable. That is, at least, for some victimized individuals, indignation, antipathy, reproach, and condemnation can have valuable moral functions even if they are not particularly intuitively enviable. Slaves, self-deprecators, and persons suffering from feelings of inferiority because of race, caste, or gender oppression, for example, are compelled to daily forgive their transgressors. Arguably, indignation toward their masters and victimizers is preferable to continued self-inflicted misery, self-hatred, and feelings of powerlessness.

Victims certainly have warrant to be self-regarding and work toward their own income and emotional well-being. They do not have a duty to be further harmed or a duty to accept feelings or actions that require them to sacrifice or burden themselves, especially in deference to the feelings, assets, or incomes of victimizers.

Humanity enjoys some common features of conscience. There is, for example, a normal tendency for everyone to feel guilty when they knowingly harm innocent children. It is just false, however, contrary to the belief of some moral absolutists such as Martin Luther King Jr., that humanity enjoys a common conscience about obvious injustices.[18] That is, obvious forms of injustice such as racial discrimination or the suffering of migrants and immigrants does not elicit, contrary to King's deep and abiding belief, a response of compassion from the common features of all human conscience. Victims of war crimes, for example, have no reason to believe that their suffering receives sympathy from their victimizers or that if the victims display compassion or forgiveness toward their victimizers, their victimizers will be persuaded—because they possess a conscience of the sort that invariably cares about the misery of innocent others—to compensate the victims or end their heinous behavior. Unfortunately, neither knowledge of the misery of others nor forgiveness by the victims of their victimizers is a pristine creator of a compassionate conscience. Just as there are diverse cultures and ways of life, there are diverse ways that the common features of human conscience may be related to particular events and circumstances.

One way to think about why indignation may be a valuable character trait is to think about why forgiveness is not a virtue.

I argue below that forgiveness is not a virtue. There are excellent reasons (instrumental and reasonable) not to forgive injustice and there are excellent reasons to be demanding of justice, respect, and due compensation for wrongs and transgressions as a function of feeling indignant.

Forgiveness necessarily entails forms of subservience and subordination of an inclination or preference. Forgiveness is supererogatory, not obligatory or an obligation. It is not a substantive virtue of the sort that we are warranted to consider as an obligation. That is, we can reasonably expect individuals and groups to be tolerant of competing ways of life, especially if those competing ways of life do not involve harms to individual. One reason that this is a reasonable expectation is that there should be a degree of credulity about the value of any particular way of life. However, victimizers have no reason to expect forgiveness from their victims. Rapists, for example, should not expect forgiveness from the raped: the raped do not have an obligation or duty to forgive the rapists. The raped should, however, tolerate the existence of rapists as well as individuals with related desires such as the desire to enjoy pornographic scenes of rape. The war crime of rape—when one group rapes the men or women of a population they deem as enemies, thereby demoralizing, debasing, and defiling their perceived enemies—is a crime of which the victims do not have an obligation to forgive. If it is emotionally healthy for some victims to feel indignation toward those who raped them, I see no reason why they should be obliged to forgive and thereby be deprived of emotions that encourage them to be resilient, stalwart, and attentive to prevent future rapes. If, however, forgiveness were an intrinsic virtue, then the raped would have an obligation, if not a duty, to forgive, and we would reasonably expect the raped to forgive the rapists. And if forgiveness were a substantive virtue, then the raped would have a strong instrumental reason to forgive because there would be predictable beneficial consequences. However, the consequences of indignation and contempt may be instrumental. The raped, for example, may well create institutions to fight such crimes because of feelings of indignation and contempt for their victimizers in conjunction with their desires to prevent future harms. Forgiveness, in addition, need not be considered a pragmatic virtue. It would be a pragmatic virtue if it worked well for individual or group flourishing. Individuals and groups, once subject to terrible forms of oppression, may very well flourish without forgiving their historical victimizers. Most countries in the world, for example, were once colonies; many currently flourish without a heritage of forgiving populations that previously exploited, raped, and victimized their nation.

Forgiveness, benevolence, and care as well as malevolence and distain are often exhibited by the same person. Contrary to Plato's ideal of virtuous persons exhibiting virtuous behavior and making right decisions because they are endowed with a virtue that determines their behavior and choices, most persons are far more complex. Methamphetamine and cocaine dealers are often loving mothers living in rural communities. A mercenary that flies a battle helicopter and is responsible for hundreds of civilian killings in Sierra Leone may also be a benevolent benefactor of hospitals and schools for children suffering from the ravages of war.[19]

Forgiveness, as McGary has argued, is more like the virtue of courage than honesty. We should expect people to be honest, and failing to be honest, we are justified in finding them lacking; we have no *prima facie* reason to expect people to be courageous, and they are not lacking as good persons if they lack courage. We can, for example, expect soldiers that volunteer for duty to exhibit courage; however, civilians are under no such expectation. Consequently, "overcoming resentment [and I suggest, indignation] is not a necessary condition of forgiveness."[20] Rather, indignation may serve for this purpose. Even so, such consequences as gaining dignity, overcoming the emotional terror caused by past wrong as well as gaining a sense of historical memory or feeling that one's wrongs will be remembered, are shy of what is required for justice.

If every guilty person who admitted guilt and every victim who was heard before the Truth and Justice Commission regained a sense of dignity, and if every victim forgave their former victimizers and gained a sense of tolerance toward their former object of hatred, it is false that social justice was served. No fundamental relations between Africans and whites changed as a function of the commission, for example, ownership of banks, home ownership, land control, copyright ownership, or institutions that determined the value of property. It is not just that little that was stolen was repaid, or few punishments for wrongdoing imposed, but that the boundaries between populations and the way assets are transferred from one generation to the next remained. The rules of ownership and inheritance, followed independent of any individual volition but requiring individual volition within an established regime, sustains inequities. Certainly, a good deal changed in terms of individual attitudes and the attitudes of numerous small groups, but the transformation from such transitions to just group relations could not, and did not, occur as a function of tolerance or forgiveness. Black Empowerment schemes of South Africa have been more effective in achieving parity than any activities having to do with tolerance between racial boundaries. If whites needed to acquire a sense of security and thereby willingness to remain in South Africa in order to create the possibility for government-sponsored Black Empowerment schemes to work, then tolerance was just functional rouge—not a functioning virtue.

Marx believed that a classless society would make other boundaries relatively superfluous. Differences in status, if there were no classes, Marx believed, would not result in substantive differences in working conditions, forms of personal authority, productivity, or asset control. Without private ownership of the modes and means of production, there would be for Marx no private control of wealth determining vast and unnecessary differences in life chances.

Marx was right in at least one way—class differences are not necessary. No singular form of boundary is necessary. I can find nothing in any reasonable account of human nature, even evolutionary accounts, that map invariable human traits such as the ability to think and speak in past and future tenses or the inclination to want more goods than less (of whatever is desired as supremely better, such as precious jewels or appreciation by close family members), to specific social boundaries such as ethnicity, race, tribe, feudal manner, nation, class, caste, clan, or aristocracy. However, some form of boundary is a necessary condition for the kinds of beings we are—sentient agents within the context of socially formed institutions.

Every form of "society" requires stringent boundaries between agnate communities. Inequalities of some form are sustained by the enforcement of differences, whether or not the difference is a consequence of accident, institutional rules, geographic advantages, class struggle, civil wars, or national histories.[21] Communities may be relatively isolated, speaking a language that is likely to disappear, or they may be international, such as the ruling classes of Britain or ethnically based ruling classes such as Mandarin Chinese speakers of Hun heritage. Boundaries are never absolutely permanent; of the ones that exist now almost none existed five hundred years ago. One way to think about social boundaries is in terms of how we are misguided when we think of groups as "relating."

IV

The pragmatist Alain Locke as well as John Rawls often presupposed that groups are stable, or relatively stable, ontological entities. At the very least, if Locke and Rawls in no way considered groups ontological kind, groups were considered internally governed well-formed bodies. Groups were thereby thought of as relating and interacting. Interactionalists commonly think of groups as having "relations."[22]

Groups, contrary to philosophies that consider them stable, or even relatively stable, are very often anabsolute. That is, they are often not well formed. Well-formed groups certainly exist, for example, stable breeding populations with unique internal institutions determining significant life chances. Well-formed groups sustain cohesive networks of friends, family, and business associates over time. These networks are the source of unmitigated trust. Such groups maintain boundaries, hoard assets, share advantages, and pass benefits on to their progeny. They are arguably stable ontological entities. The ontological status of groups is dependent on their historical character. The Bantus of southern Africa have often been described as a population, for example, when they are first and foremost a collection of languages. The Bantu languages form a subdivision of the Benue–Niger division of the Niger–Congo branch of the Niger-Kordofanian language family, inclusive of Swahili, Zulu, Xhosa, Sotho, Setswana, Makua, Thonga, Bemba, Shona, Kikuyu, Gonda, Ruanda, Rundi, Mbundu, Luba, Kongo, and Ungala. Consequently, the Bantus are certainly not a well-formed group or an ontological group; however, the Zulu is arguably at least a well-formed group. To think of "relations" between Bantus and Armenians or English speakers is to engage in a torturous way of construction nonexisting stable ontological populations. There simply are no contiguous institutions that link each of these language-based populations the way the geographic, religious, linguistic, and political history of Armenia can be seen to link Armenians together. African Americans, for example, did not exist as a race prior to the development of American race-based slavery that required nearly one hundred years of American history before solidification of racial boundaries—boundaries made stable by marital patterns, laws of inheritance, racially exclusionary practices of land ownership, and vicious physical suppression. To think of the Bantu relating to African Americans is to think of a relationship mediated by a white/Black racial construction; the "relation" does not exist between the integrative structures of two populations; the relation exists only as mediated through ideations of race such that a "Bantu" becomes a Negro in America and an African American becomes a "Negro" in Africa.

The boundaries separating populations are often bifurcated by institutions they share. The genocide in Rwanda did not destroy a single government institution such as banking, the use of paper currency, or military recruitment. The population shared governmental institutions such as the offices responsible for road construction or negotiating the value of the local currency, but boundaries were drawn across social/racial/ethnic lines, that is, language, race, marital heritage, social status, and job status.[23] African Americans are subject to vicious forms of discrimination, for example, high rates of being accused by police for violating civil laws. However, if there were no racism practiced by the police forces of the United States, it would still be the case that the institution of policing could exist. In addition, African Americans would still be subject to more violations of civil laws than whites because of their inherited lower-class status and behaviors as whites benefit from inherited class status, life insurance policies, bonds, and the behaviors required to sustain such assets. Interactionalism, in general, conceptually excludes conceiving of groups as anabsolute, emerging or fundamentally bifurcated by social institutions and structures in ways that make discourse about "relations" superfluous because boundaries are sustained in a myriad of ways.

V

We should think of tolerance as a pragmatic virtue, one that can be useful in deliberations as we struggle to create human liberation, rather than thinking of tolerance as a substantive moral virtue, one that if practiced by individuals would work well to regulate relationships between individuals and between groups. In this sense, tolerance is a feature of an interactive ethical sensibility. Utilitarian or pragmatist defenses of tolerance are not well served by reliance on methodological individualist justifications.

Tolerance, a pragmatic virtue, is arguably a moral imperative. As Alain Locke contended, in a more tolerant world, "Value assertion would thus be a tolerant assertion of preference, not an intolerant insistence on agreement or finality. Value disciplines would take on the tentative and revisionist procedure of natural science."[24] Although forgiveness is neither intrinsically nor substantively a virtue, it can be nonetheless a valuable quality of character and source of improved relations between persons.[25] Analogously, indignation has its moral uses. Without just institutions and structures, liberty of conscience and freedom of thought are impossible. In this sense, justice must exist institutionally and structurally prior to "relations" between groups being fair. Efforts to change social institutions and structures for the purpose of creating social justice across boundaries and categories include tolerance, not prior to justice, but along with institutional and structural change. Reasonable expectations of the causal power of tolerance and forgiveness to change social institutions and structures, however, requires considering it supererogatory, traits such as indignation accorded a proper place as morally beneficial rather than intrinsically harmful, groups as often anabsolute and emergent rather than ontologically stable, and justice as prior to fairness.

Notes

1. I am indebted to Klaus-Michael Kodalle, Jena University, Germany; Iris Young, University of Chicago; and Eduardo Mendieta, University of San Francisco for critical comments on an earlier version at the World Congress of Philosophy, Istanbul, Turkey, 2003, during the session "Reconciliation and Forgiveness." Their critical comments encouraged me to rethink the role of resentment as distinct from indignation. I exclude forms of subjectivism and expressivism from the way I will use 'moral pluralism' because these forms can consider human dignity as no more valuable than self-hatred, whereas all forms of favoring tolerance require a high regard for human dignity. See for example of moral pluralism that consider tolerance a good Ruth Benedict's "A Defense of Moral Relativism," *Journal of General Psychology* 10 (1934): 59–82; Richard A. Shweder, "Anthropology's The Origin Romantic Rebellion against the Enlightenment: Or There's More to Thinking than Reason and Evidence," in *Culture Theory: Essays on Mind. Self and Emotion*, ed. R. A. Shweder and R. A. Levine (Cambridge: Cambridge University Press, 1984), 27–66; Joshua Halberstam's "The Paradox of Tolerance," *Philosophical Forum* 14 (1982/83): 190–206; Geoffrey Harrison's "Relativism and Tolerance," *Ethics* 86 (1976): 122–35; Max Hocutt's "Must Relativists Tolerate Evil?," *The Philosophical Forum* 17 (Spring 1986): 188–200; Nicholas Unwin's "Relativism and Moral Complacency," *Philosophy* 60 (1985): 205–14: Jay Newman's "Ethical Relativism," *Laval*

Théologique et Philosophique 28 (1972): 63–74, and his "The Idea of Religious Tolerance," *American Philosophical Quarterly* 15 (1978): 187–95.

2. David Wong, *Moral Relativity* (Berkeley: University of California Press, 1984); Alain Locke, "Value and Imperatives," in *The Philosophy of Alain Locke: Harlem Renaissance and Beyond*, ed. Leonard Harris (Philadelphia, PA: Temple University Press, 1989), 31–50; Michael Walzer, *On Toleration* (New Haven, CT: Yale University Press, 1997); John L. Mackie, *Ethics: Inventing Right and Wrong* (Harmondsworth: Penguin Books, 1977).

3. Gordon Graham, "Tolerance, Pluralism, and Relativism," in *Tolerance*, ed., David Heyd (Princeton, NJ: Princeton University Press, 1996), 44.

4. W. J. Shields (ed.), *Persecution and Toleration*, vol. 21, Studies in Church History, published for the Ecclesiastical History Society (Oxford: Basil Blackwell, 1984); Benjamin Braude and Bernard Lewis, *Christians and Jews in the Ottoman Empire: The Functioning of a Plural Society* (New York: Holmes and Meier, 1982).

5. Adam Hochschild, *Leopold's Ghost: A Story of Greed, Terror, and Heroism in Colonial Africa* (New York: Houghton Mifflin, 1999).

6. Orlando Patterson, *Freedom: Volume 1: Freedom in the Making of Culture* (New York: Basic Books, 1991); Joseph C. Miller, *Way of Death: Merchant of Death and the Angolan Slave Trade, 1730-1830* (Madison: University of Wisconsin Press, 1988).

7. John S. Mill, *On Liberty and Other Essays* (Oxford: Oxford World Classics, 1998).

8. John Locke, "Letter Concerning Tolerance," in *Classics of Modern Political Theory*, ed. Steven M. Cahn (New York: Oxford University Press, 1997), 292–319.

9. Graham, "Tolerance, Pluralism, and Relativism," 44.

10. John Rawls, *A Theory of Justice* (Cambridge, MA: Harvard University Press, 1971), 29.

11. Ibid., 94.

12. Pierre Bayle, *Philosophical Commentary: A Modern Translation and Critical Interpretation*, trans. Amie Godman Tannenbaum (New York: Peter Lang, 1987); David A. J. Richards, *A Theory of Reasons for Action* (Oxford: Clarendon Press, 1971).

13. John Rawls, *Justice as Fairness: A Restatement* (Cambridge, MA: Harvard University Press, 2001), 3.

14. John Rawls, "Reply to Habermas," *Journal of Philosophy* 92 (3): 132–80, 150.

15. It is certainly the case that "principles of justice are themselves pluralistic in form," in the sense that even impartial thinkers are likely to have disagreements as argued by Michael Walzer in *Spheres of Justice: A Defense of Pluralism and Equality* (New York: Basic Books, 1983), 6.

16. Daniel Little, *Varieties of Social Explanation: An Introduction to the Philosophy of Social Science* (Boulder, CO: Westview Press, 1991); Barry Hindess, *Philosophy and Methodology in the Social Sciences* (Atlantic Highlands, NJ: Humanities Press, 1977); Rajeev Bhargava, *Individualism in Social Science: Forms and Limits of a Methodology* (Oxford: Clarendon Press, 1992).

17. Desmond Tutu, *No Future without Forgiveness* (New York: Doubleday, 1999).

18. Martin Luther King Jr., *The Trumpet of Conscience* (New York: Harper and Row, 1967).

19. Such stories as Daniel Bergner, *In the Land of Magic Soldiers* (New York: Farrar, Straus & Girous, 2003) are indicative of what I mean.

20. Howard McGary, "Forgiveness," *American Philosophical Quarterly* 26 (4, October 1989): 350.

21. Charles Tilly, *Durable Inequalities* (Berkeley, CA: University of Chicago Press, 1999); Leonard Harris (ed.), *Racism* (Amherst, NY: Humanities Press, 1999).

22. Alain Locke, Bernhard J. Stem (eds.), *When People Meet: A Study of Race and Culture Contacts* (New York: Committee on Workshops, Progressive Education Association, 1942); also Leonard Harris (ed.), *The Critical Pragmatism of Alain Locke: A Reader on Value Theory, Aesthetics, Community, Culture. Race, and Education* (Lanham. MD: Rowman & Littlefield, 1999).

23. Fergal Keane. *Season of Blood: A Rwandan Journey* (London: Penguin Books, 1995).

24. Alain Locke, "Pluralism and Intellectual Democracy," in *The Philosophy of Alain Locke: Harlem Renaissance and Beyond*, ed. Leonard Harris (Philadelphia, PA: Temple University Press, 1989), 57.

25. The International Day of Forgiveness, UNESCO, on November 6, and World Forgiveness Alliance, on the third week in August, are only two of the most important social events contributing to better human relations.

CHAPTER 8
DIGNITY AND SUBJECTION (2018)

In "Dignity and Subjection," Harris articulates a nuanced conception of dignity. Dignity is not taken to be an intrinsic property of persons *qua* sentient beings, rational autonomous agents, or organs of a purposive/teleological cosmos. Dignity is depicted as an inalienable sortal good, a common-denominator value. Dignity is understood as a pragmatic good for efficacious agency, which stands as a necessary condition for well-being and a resource to help defeat forms of collective degradation and demeaning stereotypes. Dignity manifests in various forms across differing cultures; there are various ways to be dignified. Thus, dignity is something that must always be created because there is no derivation manual leading us from universal principles, human nature, or right reason to particular ways of being dignified. Furthermore, Harris argues that dignity exists only if the necessary conditions are met, that is, when there are conditions that make possible feelings of self-worth, high aspirations, and viable expectations. Those conditions are antithetical the conditions of subjection. Hence, in creating dignity, we are attempting to create and maintain those the conditions that preclude likely forms of subjection and degradation.

Dignity is a sortal; it names a range of features that should be possessed by all beings of a kind. Dignity, as a sortal, is arguably inalienable and a type of "common denominator" value. A common denominator value is a feature that all cultures consider a good. The concept common denominator value is taken from the philosopher Alain Locke. It is analogous to the philosopher Kwasi Wiredu's meaning of universal traits endemic to the species. Such traits as seeing color, coyness, and language are common denominator values or universal traits according to Wiredu.[1] A desire for dignity may be such a constitutive trait. However, its expression by gestures and comportments are constantly shifting, and thereby dignity does not possess an essence to which all gestures and comportments of the sortal dignity are reducible. The Latin *intus* means the noncomparable; it is that which is *intestīnus*, meaning inside, hidden, and thereby that which is constitutive. Dignity is *intus*. There are, however, two substantive caveats to the above.

The UN "Declaration of Universal Human Rights" is anthropocentric. According to its preamble, "Whereas recognition of the inherent dignity and of the equal and inalienable rights of all members of the human family is the foundation of freedom, justice and peace in the world," and according to its articles, Article 1, "All human beings are born free and equal in dignity and rights"; Article 22, "cultural rights indispensable for his dignity and the free development of his personality"; and Article 23, "Everyone who works has the right to just and favourable remuneration ensuring for himself and his family an existence worthy of human dignity." "Rights" are a particular type of inalienable good for humans according to the declaration. If dignity is an inalienable good for "all sentient beings" and we use a Buddhist or Jainist conception of human, or *ahimsa* toward living beings, then all sentient beings are due the kind of status that warrants seeing them as possessors of inalienable goods. At the very least, dignity for humanity is a species of the larger genus that possess dignity, "all sentient beings." Whether beings besides humans can be said to have "rights" is not debatable on this view—they have and are due dignity. If there are forms of dignity that are not themselves a right, then a defensible conception of dignity should provide some guidance. That is, if animals have or are due dignity but not rights or not the same sort of rights as persons, a robust conception of dignity should indicate what type of sentient being is due juridical protection. The first caveat is that I will not consider dignity as a right in the sense that it is a warrant to be necessarily protected by juridical authority.

The second caveat is that dignity, I contend, is neither an intrinsic mysterious property of persons nor a thing-in-itself with an essence, sortal or otherwise. It is a desire that is too often treated as if it were an essence inhering within sentient beings or posited as a mysterious inherent thing-in-itself that all persons have. We do not need to posit a queer or categorically impossible intrinsic essence.[2] There are, I will argue, no gestures and comportments invariably conveying status nor conveying the idea of persons as worthy beings' independent of status. Dignity exists as a function of conditions that make possible well-being. It is a condition, I will argue, that makes what it is that is conceivably inalienable, that is, the possibility of a world without self-depreciation, self-loathing, collective degradation, subjection, delimiting boundaries between peoples; a world with self-confident persons and healthy agency.

Dignity: Property of Rational Beings or Existential Value?

The unity theory of virtues contends that virtues are intrinsic properties that map, correspond, or represent consistently expressed gestures and comportments. Expecting gestures and comportments to be neatly correlating to or representing intrinsic constitutive features of persons is, I contend, deeply misguided. There is no list of comportments or gestures invariably exemplar of someone being dignified or being treated with dignity. This is because dignity as a status is always conditional, contextual, and transient. There is no derivation manual from inherent qualities mapped to gestures. There can never be a derivation manual that takes the *intestinus*, inside, hidden, that which is constitutive of persons *qua* person and then linking that to some reasoning strategy that then tells us to express a particular gesture, comportment, or behavior.

I argue in support of the approach associated with sagacious and cultural pluralist traditions. The sagacious and cultural pluralist traditions promote the view that dignity is a substantive good that can be expressed by a plurality of gestures and treatments. This approach does not require conceiving of persons as rational agents in pursuit of a kingdom of ends, that is, a teleology, or that virtues are consistently expressed or mapped to a permanent set of behavior. That is, there is no single form of "dignity" of which a gesture or comportment is invariable a representation. Consequently, gestures and comportments convey dignity as defined by a given social context. Feeding a deceased person's body to vultures, thereby returning their body to nature and feeding other creatures; cremating a person's body and placing the ashes into a sacred river; or preserving a body with harsh chemicals to slow its inevitable decay may all be considered forms of undignified uses of the deceased. Common denominator values or universal traits of respect for the deceased have remained a constant species feature, although nearly all forms of burial rituals have changed.

I contend that the unity between base properties and their expression, if considered a stable relationship, requires orthodoxy, authoritarianism, and conformity.[3] I argue that we should reject the idea of dignity as an organ (i.e., an intrinsic trait that maps to expressions) and favor dignity as a pragmatic good (i.e., a condition that makes possible *prima facie* appealing results such as self-confidence). Gestures and comportments are like all juridical and governmental institutions, mere means to an elusive end—an intrinsic sense of worth, value, and dignity. That is why the lack of gainful work makes a person feel invaluable, depresses their aspirations, and engenders alienation. They lack the means to create self-fulfillment. And the existence of rape and racist stereotypes are effective ways to humiliate individuals and groups because individuals define themselves as representing a kind debased by rape and stereotypes—self-worth is harmed by the tools of race and stereotypes.

Common denominator values or universal traits can be expressed in a vast array of fashions. One way to see this is by simply considering the impact of new technologies. Technical innovations change what we eat and their cost: giant-scale purse seiners, ships that surround fish with a curtain of netting; lightweight polymer-based nets enable super trawlers to rake the ocean bottom for fish. Consequently, having caught fish by way of a single person with a net, spear, or a line with a single hook on the end are now passé. Catching fish in this fashion is no longer considered representative of the traits of guile, foresight, and excellence, except as sport.

The comportment of women during marriage ceremonies is another example of context-dependent meaning. In some Hindu ceremonies, the bride looks sanguine, demure, and glances askance but not at her husband; he is esteemed and she is prized. In some American Protestant ceremonies, the bride expresses adulation toward her spouse and she frequently looks at him with a demure expression. Brides are dignified in both ceremonies—that is, recognized by the audience as comporting themselves in ways that establish their inner quality of purity and control.

Expecting gestures to be forms of behavior representing intrinsic virtues and characters traits is the wish dream of the essentialist. This is because there is no static, stable, and unchanging virtues mapped to, expressed by or revealed by static and unchanging stable gestures and comportments. There is no reason to believe that existing social entities are permanent; *mutates mutandis*, no reason to believe that comportments and gestures representing dignity are permanent.

Collective degradation occurs when each and every individual of a group is treated as a representative of a social kind and all members of the kind are treated as defective, tainted, diseased, inferior, and always lacking virtues.[4] Given that nearly every form of subjection, whether colonial oppression or domination of one class or ethnic group by another, involves degrading the expressions of dignity by subjects, we have every reason to be suspicious of all forms of dignity. A vast array of behaviors may be an affront to a subjected population—like the parades of military guards dressed in uniforms of a foreign nation in front of a vanquished population or the existence of cemeteries featuring gods on tombstones located in neighborhoods that consider cemeteries a pagan practice that unduly sanctifies the dead rather than consider deceased persons' empty vessels of departed souls.

Collective degradation uses vicious stereotypes by categorizing persons as natural kinds with degrading traits. In seventeenth-century Mexico, Africans were routinely described in different ways. Some were described as Negro retinto (double-dyed Negro), Negro amulatado (mulatto-like Negro), and Megro amenbrillado (quince-like Negro). With the progressive rise of African slavery, the Wolof, Mandinga, Balanta, Kongo, and others were collapsed into the category "Negro." "Negro" became categorized as a singular kind and thereby capable of being collectively degraded. Whether retinto, amulatado, or amenbrillado, the possibility of collective degradation existed because persons are categorized as an undifferentiated kind with intrinsic base properties associated with submissive behavior. No matter what form of martial arts or wrestling were common among the Balanta or Wolof, for example, no form of their performance would receive recognition by the Spanish or the Portuguese as worthy. All gestures and comportments intended to express the intrinsic trait of courage were deemed expressions of cowardliness, insubordination, and the result of invariably irrational, emotive, and inane individuals. In 1994, Jean-Pau Akayesu at the Taba commune, Rwanda, promoted the rape of Tutsi women by Hutu men for the purpose of degrading the whole Tutsi population—rape was used as a weapon of civil war. The method involves trying to get each and every Tutsi woman pictured as a representative of an inferior population, made inferior by violated women. The use of collective degradation is a mode of subjection that is not owned by any particular population.

Individuals of populations that are or see themselves as empowered by technological sophistication, superior virtues, well-ordered governance, civic pride, and owners and controllers of enviable resources whether oil, forest, grand architecture, or ancient ruins are always in the position of possibly degrading and loathing others. That's why immigrants, former colonized nations, descendants of slaves, and populations in civic chaos or war often find themselves, independent of individual virtues or actual cultural traits, loathed, disrespected, and disdained. They do not receive the sort of privileges accorded persons considered due dignity. Stereotypes of some form are inevitable, and demeaning stereotypes are a subset of what happens when efficacious agency does not exist. Whether African, Baltic European, or the Dalit of India, individuals are always subject to be stereotyped as a function of their group membership.

Hacking to death someone of a targeted population is a way of humiliating that population; it is not only evidence of the vulnerability of a population but also denies dignified death by rendering the hacked body a mere carcass.

At Pimpri-Deshmukh in Maharashtra, following the hacking to death of the dalit kotwal (active mobiliser for the local Buddha Vihar) by upper caste men, the upper caste women came out in public complaining that the dalit man had harassed them and was sexually perverted. They claimed that they had incited their men to protect their honour, thus the agency of upper caste women was involved.[5]

Women in this case protected their honor by encouraging defilement of bodies perceived as threats to their status.

Lynching and bodily desecration is another way people promote collective degradation. Vicksburg, Mississippi, *Evening Post*, 1904:

When the two Negroes were captured, they were tied to trees and while the funeral pyres were being prepared they were forced to suffer the most fiendish tortures. The blacks were forced to hold out their hands while one finger at a time was chopped off. The fingers were distributed as souvenirs. The ears of the murderers were cut off. Holbert was beaten severely, his skull was fractured, and one of his eyes, knocked out with a stick, hung by a shred from the socket ... The most excruciating form of punishment consisted in the use of a large corkscrew in the hands of some of the mob. This instrument was bored into the flesh of the man and woman, in the arms, legs and body, and then pulled out, the spirals tearing out big pieces of raw, quivering flesh every time it was withdrawn.

This ritual, consistently practiced throughout the United States during the nineteenth century on African Americans, terrorized African American communities and simultaneously not just provided entertainment and souvenirs for whites but also was a way to both collectively degrade African Americans and elevate whites collectively as a population due high status as a function of their sheer existence.[6]

Both the possibility of collective degradation and dignity require a community of spoken languages. Ongota was spoken in southwest Ethiopia along the banks of the Weito River. Now the language is extinct, with many of the villagers in the area turning instead to Tsamai to speak. Qawasqar was used in southern Chile by the Kawesqar tribe. Qawasqar originally had a variety of different dialects within its structure, but that has since changed. Now the language is almost completely dead, with only twenty known speakers left, and the majority of them living at Wellington Island, just off the coast of Chile. The preservation of dying languages is arguably warranted in part because the ways of conveying dignity is contingent on the frames of meaning and modes of a language's expressions. Simultaneously, the death of such languages means that users facing its extinction must assimilate or, as is too often the case, struggle to avoid being depressed, traumatized, and subject to self-deprecating behavior such as alcoholism and drug use.

Contrary to the Roman Marcus Tullius Cicero (106–43 BC) and Immanuel Kant's linking of dignity to the human property of rationality, I argue for a critical pragmatist approach that does not require conceiving of persons as reasoning machines. Cicero and Kant considered human rationality as a property that makes possible excellence; the possession or potential possession of human reason is central to why persons are to be "raised above all price" and have "an inner worth, that is, dignity." According to Kant, "morality is the condition under which alone a rational being can be an end in itself, since only through this is it possible to be a lawgiving member in the kingdom of ends. Hence morality, and humanity insofar as it is capable of morality, is that which alone has dignity."[7] On Kant's anthropocentric account persons deserve to be treated with special regard, not because they are worth a price, occupy a revered social status, or perform useful work, but because they are members of the species, and a major reason that the species is special is because its normal members possess the property of rationality and pursue goals. On this view, dignity is not a quantitative trait for which we are due more or less of it from others, but constitutive, a feature consistently due all persons. I believe, however, that it is insufficient to claim that all persons are due dignity simply by having a membership in the species. Too often appropriate expressions of what rational persons should do as expressions of their virtues and dignity is attached to parochial expressions treated as if they were *sine qua non* with intrinsic good, thereby making possible cultural subjections.

The precondition for the possibility of dignity is, I contend, efficacious agency and viable aspirations. Given that persons invariably engage in transvaluation and transposition of values, proposing a permanent set of behaviors deemed exemplar of dignity is misguided. Gestures and comportments that are believed to represent intrinsic virtues are contingent and context-dependent. It is not a teleology or "kingdom of ends" that persons are capable of trying to create (often doing so by the aegis of genocide, colonialism, and slavery) that gives a warrant to dignity. Rather, it is the reality of our being as agents requiring reciprocity, mutual respect, recognition, and unmerited trust that creates the possibility of sociality that gives dignity its warrant. Sociality is maintained, not by the threat of punishment by policing authorities imposing concepts of rights that allow a parochial array of practices, but by substantive relations between persons in community.[8] Dignity, I contend, exists when there are conditions that make possible feelings of self-worth, high aspirations, and viable expectations; those conditions exclude the conditions of subjection.

Organistic Vitalism

Organistic vitalism is the view that there is an essential, vital, or intrinsic trait endemic to all normal persons and embedded in all cultures.[9] Each element of the organ, according to his view, is invested with essential traits of the organ, analogous to Aristotle's *Ousia*: "in all things which are composed out of several other things, and which come to be some single common thing ... in all of them there turns out to be a distinction between that which rules, and that which is ruled; and this holds for all souled things by virtue of the whole of nature." [10] The organ is the sort of emergent property of which the component parts share traits of the organ, that is, the organ is more than an epiphenomenon of its parts, not a heuristic theoretical entity, because each individual member is integrally defined by common traits. Bergson, Senghor, and Blyden each promoted a version of organistic vitalism. Each author considered the authentic expression of an individual best expressed when they expressed the authentic expression of their racial, culture, ethnic or national kind.

A problem with organistic vitalism is that the following individual traits are not identical to the traits of the organic entity. That is, there is a difference between individual traits of which the organic entity is composed of and the traits of the entity as a collective agent. The fallacy of composition is the failure to see the difference. No individual atom in a chair has the traits of the chair as an emerged entity. This is analogous to the same problem of essentialist concept of dignity, that is, when gestures and comportments of individuals are believed to supervene on the base or essential property of dignity as a species of a genus.

It is mistaken to think that individuals can express or be the embodiment of traits fully definitive of a kind. Riding a horse by maintaining a straight back and head held high is considered a comportment indicative of the intrinsic property of dignity by British equestrian riders—the behavior is the expressed ensoulment of the hidden property of dignity. If a British equestrian rider is thereby considered the embodiment of a unique British racial kind, therein would be an example of representative heuristics— an invariable feature of cognition. Representative heuristics, a rule governing feature of cognition used under conditions of uncertainty, is "the degree to which [an event] (i) is similar in essential characteristics to its parent population, and (ii) reflects the salient features of the process by which it is generated." [11] This guarantees almost always wrong judgments. But it is an easy computational method by which to make quick decisions— stereotyping consistently. Thus, the population of equestrian riders is mistakenly assumed possessors of the same degree and kind of self-control, earnestness, and worth as each equestrian rider. Collective degradation depends on this cognitive feature to be successful as well as granting honor and dignity to a collective population, for example, British equestrian riders are dignified when riding appropriately. We mistakenly think that each rider is identical to the kind and thereby ignore individual uniqueness. But this is normal. It is a mistake that helps make possible effective representations and stereotypes.

There are incongruities between values and behavior. Cognitive biases are common features of normal thought, for example, being overconfident because we use conflicting long-term and short-term preferences (believing that we will have a high future income if we have current disposable income), caring for others will be reciprocated (falsely assuming reciprocity because we are altruistic), avoiding losses versus possible gains (loss aversion activity erroneously convinces us that we are assured of future gain), exponential stereotypes (imagining a great number of feared events or social groups based on a small sample), and choice mismatches (the position of a food offering on a menu influences choices) and visual influence on individual preferences (pictures on a menu influence what meals are chosen). Incongruities and biases cannot be the source of consistent behavior. There is, consequently, no unity between virtues and consistent expressions—at best, we have inclinations, but normal incongruities and cognitive biases prevent the existence of a unity theory of virtue being warranted—no persons can have such a unity. This is another reason why the unity theory of virtue is misguided, that is, the idea that individuals invested with base properties of virtue will consistently behave virtuously is misguided because cognitive biases are endemic to consciousness and the influences of the environment shape behavior subtly. Thus, if there were a base property of dignity, it could not express itself in a consistent form. In addition, as Alain Locke argued, base properties can have unique associations: "the sustaining of an attitude, the satisfaction of a way of feeling, the corroboration of a value. To the poet, beauty is truth; to the religious devotee, God is truth; to the enthused moralist, what ought-to-be overtops factual reality."[12] More than one value mode can sustain a sense of awe, wonder, majesty, or sense of truth.

This is the Greek philosopher Zeno of Elea's (ca. 490–430 BC) paradox: Movement is not mathematically possible because the distance between any two points can be divided infinitely. Movement is impossible because reduction is perpetual. The analog between mathematically explained movement and actual movement pictures reality falsely. Movement happens because bodies are not a collection of infinitesimal points. Analogously, virtues are abstractions and are not reducible to infinitesimal points. This is another organic vitalist fallacy. "Immigrant women," "underclass," and so on are never reducible to each member of the respective category, whether we aggregate or do a summative collection of individual traits or see individuals as kinds of persons. Constant shifts in feelings renders the equation of sortals and their members at best limited. The analog between abstract defined traits, sortals, and particular gestures and comported expressions pictures reality falsely.

Reason

The rationalist tradition defines dignity as an intrinsic good due all persons because persons are uniquely rational. The tradition often associated with Immanuel Kant has a long and torturous history.[13] The following are several district features of the rationalist tradition I wish to highlight:

1. Persons inherently have worth best described as *dignitas* (abstract noun, Latin) or "worth" from the Sanskrit *vartate*.

2. Persons should have a sense of self-worth.

3. Persons are ends in themselves because the realization of their intrinsic nature requires expression of dignity or at least they should not be treated as tools.

Features 2 and 3 are prescriptions. And feature 1 is false because it postulates an intrinsic being as if there were a static sui generis species being. And this feature is normally associated with the unity theory of virtue. Sadly, populations are often bedeviled by persons who self-loath or are loathed by others. The prescriptions of features 2 and 3 have historically accompanied efforts to answer the following: (A) "who" counts as a rational person (e.g., Kant did not consider Africans full persons; women were only recently considered full moral agents by most European rationalists), (B) what degree of reasoning ability do different categories of persons intrinsically possess, and (C) what particular comportment bespeaks appropriate dignified behavior reflecting of character trait such as serenity, composure or self-control? All possible answers to A, B, and C require, if not racist, elitist, or colonialist formations, at least a hierarchical ranking of persons and cultures making some invariably inferior. Considering dignity a property of rational persons requires answering A, B, and C surreptitiously, if not openly, with a warrant for cultural subjection; the condition for knowing who counts as most worthy and what counts as appropriate representations of dignity makes subjection an invariable feature of defining dignity as a property of rational persons.

What counts as dignified behavior and expression requires, not a derivation from a mysterious transcendental or intrinsic nature by way of categorizing persons as naturally more or less rational according to whether they conform to a dictatorial regime of cultural codes usually established by a ruling class or dominant culture, but what the reasonable expressions are of our common regard for appropriate comportments making possible ascriptions of dignity and honor.

Incommensurability and Conflict

The discourse ethics approach of Karl-Otto Apel, Jürgen Habermas, as well as Seyla Benhabib contend that morals should be constituted by discursive criteria that allow competing values to be resolved.[14] Discourse ethics requires that all parties accept the idea that individuals have an entitlement to autonomy, that persons are right holders, and that collective groups as well as individuals are warranted to have their ideas apart of a consensus. The discourse approach to dignity thus requires that a "consensus" is formed. Discourse ethics fails when the kinds of gestures considered odious by one community is considered sacrosanct by another and compromise means a result that subjugates all parties.

Democracy does not provide a modus operandi for deciding what counts as appropriate forms of dignity. A population can consider honor killing, genital mutilation, child brides, or enslavement of orphans warranted as a function of democracy (understood as public and popular agreement, consenting adults, and considered conceptions of well-being). Liberal Americans' prison policy supported eugenic science, which routinely recommended imprisonment, castration, or killing especially persons considered insane or feebleminded. American popular opinion and legal practices until the late 1950s favored liberal eugenic approaches. There are different conceptions of what counts as human rights, egalitarianism, and liberation. It is always possible for any given population to reject any given conception of dignity because concepts of what counts as warranted communication, as well as rights, are controversial.

Dignity as an inalienable sortal good is variegated and therefore likely to be controversial even if democratically accorded warrant. One way to proceed is by accepting the following limitation: there is no derivation manual that will tell us what forms of dignity are warranted from the general framework of dignity as a sortal good. Given that no matter what requirements are suggested for appropriate criteria for how we might arrive at appropriated forms of dignity from abstractions are invariably entrapped in cultural pejorative preference, it is the conditions of possibility that should shape what is given particular warrant. What is warranted is open; what is closed are conditions that negate well-being.

The Greek historian Thucydides described transvaluation when he described the suffering from a plague as a part of "Pericles' Funeral Oration" from Thucydides' *History of the Peloponnesian War* (431–404 BC):

> All the burial rites before in use were entirely upset, and they buried the bodies as best they could. Many from want of the proper appliances, through so many of their friends having died already, had recourse to the most shameless sepultures: sometimes getting the start of those who had raised a pile, they threw their own dead body upon the stranger's pyre and ignited it; sometimes they tossed the corpse which they were carrying on the top of another that was burning, and so went off.
>
> … Perseverance in what men called honor was popular with none, it was so uncertain whether they would be spared to attain the object; but it was settled that present enjoyment, and all that contributed to it, was both honorable and useful.[15]

Preventing conditions that make likely forms of degradation, then, should be the goal, not looking for a formal criteria or list of appropriate behaviors to be imposed by juridical authorities.

Preconditions for the Possibility of Dignity

Honor is a good that is necessarily attributed to a representative of a kind; simultaneously, it allows the honored to ascend above their kind. Dignity is a species of honor, humiliation and insult its opposite. This is a form of representative heuristics—individual standing as a representative of a kind. Courage, for example, is a good that a Zimbabwean soldier can have as a Zimbabwean; the soldier has the good as a function of traits shared by all courageous persons. The soldier, however, can be honored as a function of being a soldier, independent of their national status. That is because being a "soldier" is a status associated with virtues of courage and sacrifice. Honor is a good that can be held just in case one is a member of a group that is susceptible to honor.[16] Consequently, antiblack racism renders every Black person a subject of humiliation. Honor, then, is possible for Black persons in an antiblack racist world just in case they hold a status (e.g., soldier, doctor, or lawyer) that is considered worthy; a world without antiblack racism would allow honor by respect without racist stereotypes. Jacobus Eliza Joannes Capitein (1714–1747) was born in West Africa and sold to the slave captain Arnold Steenhart, and was given by Steenhart to Jacobus van Goch, chief trader in Ghana at Elmina.[17] He was soon taken to Holland for formal education. Ordained by the laying on of hands on May 7, 1742, ten months later he gave a public Latin oration on March 10, 1743, entitled *Dissereatio politico-theologica de servitute libertati christianae non contraria*. Capitein argued that slavery was compatible with Christian doctrine because, given persons are ends in themselves, saving their souls was the highest good possible; utilities in route to that end were warranted.

Capitein faithfully pastored at Elmina. In Europe, laudatory poems were written about him, and as a man of great learning his reputation was highly regarded by the Asante king Opoku Ware. A portrait of Capitein bears the most telling description of the highest honor he could achieve: "Look at this Moor! His skin is black, but his soul is made white, since Jesus himself intercedes for him. He goes to teach the Moors in faith, hope and charity, so that they, made white, may honour the Lamb together with him."[18]

Capitein imagined a world of post-all indigenous African religions. All laudable character traits, for example, love, piety, sobriety, and grace were expressed in Dutch Christian terms by Capitein. His dress, the geography of slave castles, Latin, and so on were for him embodiments of Christian traits. His "post" world was, *ipso facto*, the end of all worlds whereby he could ascend to honor. Only in a world that included Africans, where Africans were not deemed inferior, could he achieve honor; but in his "post" world of Christianity where he would be invariably ranked low, honor would elude him.

Capitein could not achieve honor because the conditions he sustained excluded him from being honored: the conditions included an organistic view of persons (each person is a representative of a kind), each kind is embedded with a natural arrangement of virtues; racial and religious kinds exist; each race and religion can be ranked as higher or lower. African (Black) non-Christians were ranked lower and African Christians were always recipient of their religion from whites and thereby always beholden—thus endemically subordinate—to their benefactors. In Dante's *Inferno* (1317), persons that failed to appreciate their benefactors were relegated to the lowest level of hell. This is the culture in which Capitein is entrapped. A unity thesis of virtues requires that gestures and comportments supervene on base properties of virtues that are always determinant.

Capitein could express virtues of piety, benevolence, altruism, humility, obedience, compassion, and patience because these befit subservience and submission. However, he could not express the virtues of tenacity, enmity, indignation, resentment, guile, or audacity. These traits are rightly associated with power, dominance, and insurrection. Capitein's quiddity, a concept taken from Duns Scotus, which means that which is shared with others, is limited to what he can share with his racial kind. And that kind, in an antiblack racist world, is associated with taint and viewed as always lacking in virtues endemic to power and agency. Capitein was relegated to constantly trying to prove what he could never prove, namely, peership in the human family. Peership of species kind must be assumed as a condition of being, *simpliciter*; it does not admit of quantification or degrees.

Honor for Capitein would mean the death of his episteme. Capitein, like the image in the mind of physicians that made African men eunuchs because physicians believed that Africans were warranted to be eternal slaves, his authenticity, autonomy, and worth are entrapped in what his culture believed is due his kind. As a well-dressed and educated minister of the Dutch Reformed Church, he could be seen warranting the highest form of dignity befitting his kind. What is at best due his kind is entrapped—it is paternalistic and invariably a stunted form of social life lacking in conditions making possible appropriate aspirations and expectations of the sort that can allow a person to imagine a fundamentally different future.

An episteme that makes possible dignity allows for peership between populations with radically different histories. Historicism is wrong: we almost never have a defensibly true view of individual or group histories; yet, we grant respect to strangers relying on unmitigated trust and stereotypes. Histories of Western philosophy almost never mention the polytheism, bestiality, or pantheist beliefs of Socrates, Plato, and Aristotle. Instead, it is metaphysical fundamentalism that is compatible with monotheism, various forms of paideia that are compatible with theistic views of revelation and argument strategies that accept the limitations of inductive reasoning, making possible the realm of faith that gains favor. Historians of Western philosophy almost completely ignored transtheist views of "Jain," that is, rebirth, victory, a turning of the soul that not only is no longer concerned with the transient and impermanent sensual world but also is not concerned with the theist search for permanent truth and revelations of transcendental existence—let alone Christian pictures of a personal God or individual souls living in a transcendental world of bliss. Thus, historians and philosophers of Western iconography perpetuate a range of images about esteemed philosophers by shaping stereotypes of what was important in their philosophies. In so doing, despite the actual heritage of the Christian violent destruction of Greek and Roman religions, monuments, cemeteries, and documents as well as a heritage of massive histories of contrived interpretations and selective foregrounding of preferred ideas, contemporary Western philosophy is erroneously treated as worthy of high esteem as an unbroken heritage of coherent ideas and communities of convivial discourse, not the inheritors of deceit created by murderers and liars. The episteme of Western philosophy makes possible esteem for its followers not because the episteme and content are accurate, true, or rational but because it is possible to see its members as agents and authors, authentic, potent, and not, like Capitein, inherently self-subjugating, inauthentic, and essentially willfully subordinate. It is not knowledge, truth, communications, cultural sameness, or virtues of kindness or benevolence, let alone some notion that all persons are invested with a mysterious faculty of "reason," but rather pragmatic values, images, statuses, heritages of capable kinds, and effective agency of kinds in a world of goods that makes collective degradation unlikely and dignity possible.

Conclusion

A picture that accepts complexity, perpetual revisions, value transposition, complicated references, and a willingness to reject completely an episteme that is irredeemable is a preferable option to a picture of foundations and intuitions *sine qua non* with reason. Human dignity should be considered a good due all persons. There should be a hermetic, unsubstantiated, and unmitigated acceptance of persons as agents due dignity. This requires a fundamental change of reality; otherwise, forms of collective degradation will continue to abound.

The powerful are always advantaged in any arrangement intended to create a consensus. The rules may maximize the possibility of minority interest and contribution, but "maximizing" is not the same as having the greatest impact. What gestures are granted approval should not solely rest on discursive ethics. Conditions of possibility should, rather, be a central feature of what defines the basis of what gestures are capable of being warranted. If adequate conditions that promote health care is present, for example, gainful work, fair treatment, public safety, clean air, and water, then different enviable health outcomes occur.

We are not trapped in the current world where we can only imagine likely possibilities for the immediate future. We can imagine unlikely worlds that do not exist. It was at best an absolute fantasy for Mo Tzu (400s–300s BCE China, follower of Confucius) to believe in a world of impartial concern and universal love, in a world that had only known war and unquestioning dedication to nepotism. His attitude toward his existing world made him a philosopher engaged in promoting the fantastic. Nothing in the world made the ideas of abolishing slavery a defensible idea in a nineteenth-century United States by mostly illiterate abolitionists. The extremely rare availability of defensible histories of slavery made even the educated abolitionist fairly ignorant. Received knowledge by all the Abrahamic religions and every major school of history justified slavery. It would be, arguably, absolute insurrection to be a slave abolitionist in a world where social stability was often seen as made possible by slavery, and save for British imperialists trying to abolish slavery to secure for themselves a monopoly for their more efficiently produced goods and oversupply slave-produced goods, slavery was accepted by every major democracy. Arguing for the abolition of slavery in nineteenth-century United States only made sense by a philosophy that made possible worlds reasonably seen as impossible from the standpoint of an existing reality worthy of achieving, despite the odds. Dignity as a good commonly accorded persons requires the existence of efficacious agency and achievable aspirations; what aspirations exist and what gestures represent respect are forms of social existence that are invariably transient, always undergoing transvaluation and transposition. Relative and contingent contexts define what counts as appropriate gestures and comportments that convey presumed intrinsic virtues. The preconditions for the possibility of dignity are thus conditions that make possible agency. It is not the kingdom of ends—teleological goals that give warrant to the subjection of persons as a way of trying to create a future kingdom of ends—that give a warrant to dignity, but the reality of our being as agents requiring reciprocity, mutual respect, recognition, unmerited trust, and due regard for sociality. Preconditions for dignity are maintained, not by the threat of punishment or policing by authorities, but by substantive relations between persons in community.

Dignity can be conveyed in ways that are not captured by codified rules of law, and dignity can be denied in ways that are not punishable by rules of law. However, substantive goods can be created, recognized, and supported by practices of reciprocity, given the decidability of whether a given comportment is a violation or an acceptable comportment without using a formal algorithm, a simple set of principles with a derivation manual telling us that the principles justify or codified criteria. Locke's recommendation that we promote reciprocity, tolerance, and respect are the kinds of values that can help make possible dignity, not the stilted sort of which Capitein was entrapped, but the sort constantly created by a sense of conviviality, well-being, and real efficacious agency.[19]

Notes

1. See Jacoby Carter, "Alain Locke," *Stanford Encyclopedia of Philosophy*, http://plato.stanford. edu/entries/alain-locke/; Kwasi Wiredu and I. Karp, *Cultural Universals and Particulars: An African Perspective* (Bloomington: Indiana University Press, 1997).

2. See for a discussion of categorically impossible beings "The Horror of Tradition or How to Burn Babylon and Build Benin While Reading a *Preface to a Twenty Volume Suicide Note*," *Philosophical Forum* 24 (1–3, Fall–Spring 1992-3): 94–119. Republished: John P. Pittman (ed.), *African-American Perspectives and Philosophical Traditions* (New York: Routledge, 1997), 94–119. See for the relevant concept of "queerness" J. L. Mackie, *Ethics: Inventing Right and Wrong* (London: Penguin Group, 1977).

3. See Leonard Harris (ed.), *The Philosophy of Alain Locke: Harlem Renaissance and Beyond* (Philadelphia, PA: Temple University Press, 1989), 70. Also see "The Great Debate: Alain L. Locke vs. W.E.B. Du Bois," *Philosophia Africana* 7 (1, March 2004): 13–37; "Tolerance, reconciliation et groupes," *Guerre et Reconciliation, Jounee de la Philosophie al Unesco* 5 (2003): 59–94; "The Lacuna between Philosophy and History," *Journal of Social Philosophy* 20 (3, Winter 1989): 110–14; "Identity: Alain Locke's Atavism," *Transactions of the Charles S. Peirce Society: A Quarterly Journal in American Philosophy* 26 (1, Winter 1988): 65–84; Jacoby Carter, "Alain Locke," *Stanford Encyclopedia of Philosophy*, http://plato.stanford.edu/entries/alain-locke/.

4. Alanso deSandoval, *De Instauranda Aethiopum Salute: El Mundom de la Esclavitud Negra en America* (Bogata: Empresa Nacional de Publicaciones, 1956), 91; Colin A. Palmer, *Slaves of the White God: Black in Mexico, 1570–1650* (Cambridge, MA: Harvard University Press, 1976), 41–2; G. Aguirre Beltran, "Races in 17th Century Mexico," *Phylon* 6 (3): 213–15.

5. Sharmila Rege, "Dalit Women Talk Differently," *Economic and Political Weekly* 33 (44, October 31–November 6, 1998): WS39–WS46.

6. Trudier Harris, *Exorcising Blackness: Historical and Literary Lynching and Burning Rituals* (Bloomington: Indiana University Press, 1984), 2. This quote has been used in the literature on lynching as a standard example of the elements involved in the ritual.

7. Immanuel Kant, *Groundwork of the Metaphysics of Morals*, trans. Mary Gregor (New York: Cambridge University Press, 1998), 42.

8. Remy Debes, "Dignity's Gautlet," *Philosophical Perspectives* 23 (1): 45–78; George Kateb, *Human Dignity* (Cambridge, MA: Harvard University Press, 2001).

9. See Donna Jones, *Racial Discourse of Life Philosophy: Négritude, Vitalism, and Modernity* (New York: Columbia University Press, 2010).

10. Aristotle, *Politics*, I.4 1254a28-32, in *Complete Works*, ed. Jonathan Barnes. 2 vols. (Princeton, NJ: Princeton University Press, 1984).

11. See Daniel Kahneman and Amos Tversky, "Subjective Probability: A Judgment of Representativeness," *Cognitive Psychology* 3 (1972): 430–54.

12. Alain Locke, "Values and Imperatives," in *The Philosophy of Alain Locke: Harlem Renaissance and Beyond*, ed. Leonard Harris (Philadelphia, PA: Temple University Press, 1989), 37.

13. See Emmanuel Chukwudi Eze, *Race and the Enlightenment: A Reader* (Oxford: John Wiley and Sons, 1997); Robert Bernasconi, "True Colors: Kant's Distinction Between Nature and Artifice in Context," in *Klopffech-terein-Missverstandnisse-Widerspruche? Methodische und Methodolodische*, Perspektiven auf die Kant-Forster Kontroverse, ed. Rainer Godel and Gideon Stiening (Paderborn: Wilhelm Fink, 2012), 191–207.

14. See Thomas F. Murphy III, "Discourse Ethics: Moral Theory or Political End," *New German Critique* 62 (Summer 1994): 111–35; and works of Karl-Otto Apel, Jürgen Habermas, or Seyla Benhabib.

15. The translation of Thucydides 2.47.1-55.1 was made by Richard Crawley, *Thucydides, History of the Peloponnesian War* (Adelaide: University of Adelaide Library, 1903).

16. I argue for this conception of honor in "Honor: Empowerment and Emasculation," in *Rethinking Masculinity: Philosophical Explorations in Light of Feminism*, ed. Larry May and Robert A. Strinkwerda (New York: Rowman & Littlefield, 1992), 191–208. Also see Orlando Patterson, *Slavery and Social Death: A Comparative Study* (Boston, MA: Harvard University Press, 1982).

17. Hans Werner Debrunner, *Presence and Prestige: Africans in Europe* (Basel: Basler Afrika Bibliographien, 1979), 80–1. Also see Sander L. Gilman, *On Blackness without Blacks: Essays on the Image of the Black in Germany* (Boston, MA: G.K. Hall, 1982).

18. Portrait (1742): Jacobus Capitein (1717-1747). François van Bleyswijck—Rijksmuseum, Amsterdam (the Netherlands)

19. Publications by Leonard Harris regarding the nature of honor: "Walker: Naturalism and Liberation," *Transactions of the Charles S. Peirce Society: A Quarterly Journal in American Philosophy* 49 (1): 93–111, edition on Harrisian insurrectionist ethics; "Philosophy of Philosophy: Race, Nation and Religion," *Graduate Journal of Philosophy* 35 (1-2): 1–12; "Universal Human Liberation: Community and Multiculturalism," in *Theorizing Multiculturalism*, ed. Cynthia Willett (Oxford: Blackwell, 1998), 449–57; "Honor, Eunuchs, and the Postcolonial Subject," in *Postcolonial African Philosophy*, ed. Emmanuel C. Eze (Oxford: Blackwell, 1997), 252–9; "The Horror of Tradition or How to Burn Babylon and Build Benin While Reading a *Preface to a Twenty Volume Suicide Note*," 94–119; "Honor: Empowerment and Emasculation," 191–208; "Autonomy under Duress," in *African American Perspectives on Biomedical Ethics*, ed. Harley E. Flack and Edmund D. Pelligrino (Washington, DC: Georgetown University Press, 1992), 133–49. See, for Harrisian "insurrectionist ethics," Lee McBride, ed., *Transactions of the Charles S. Peirce Society: A Quarterly Journal in American Philosophy* 49 (1): 93–111.

PART IV
AN ETHICS OF INSURRECTION; OR, LEAVING THE ASYLUM (VIRTUES OF TENACITY)

CHAPTER 9
HONOR AND INSURRECTION OR A SHORT STORY ABOUT WHY JOHN BROWN (WITH DAVID WALKER'S SPIRIT) WAS RIGHT AND FREDERICK DOUGLASS (WITH BENJAMIN BANNEKER'S SPIRIT) WAS WRONG (1999)

In this piece, Harris tells a story about John Brown and Frederick Douglass, using poetic license, to argue that John Brown inherited the spirit of David Walker. The argument is best understood as a defense and valorization of David Walker and his distinctly insurrectionist character traits. Walkerian insurrectionist character traits (e.g., tenacity, irreverence, passion, and enmity) are contrasted with moral suasionist character traits (e.g., piety, restraint, serenity, and compassion). Walker understood collective entities as variegated and diffracted, more representative of national identity and material culture than ethnic or racial identity. Walker finds tenacity, irreverence, and enmity to be appropriate responses to the grave insult of chattel slavery (i.e., excluding a racialized group of human beings from the moral community, rendering them inherently irredeemable, incapable of receiving honor). Harris recognizes that Walker, given his theological stance and his belief that evil will be punished, evokes an *a priori*, apodictically knowable structure of personhood. And yet, Harris is an anabsolutist who posits an amoral universe. The story is dramaturgical—it is meant to conjure new possibilities, new porous and variegated groups of resistant agents bearing Walkerian virtues, authoritatively asserting themselves, tenaciously working to shape a future beyond the clutches of necro-being.

I argue for honoring the character traits that enlivened David Walker's *Appeal to the Coloured Citizens of the World, But in Particular, and Very Expressly, to Those of the United States of America* (1829).[1] Walker's pamphlet influenced insurrectionists in Virginia, South Carolina, North Carolina, and Maryland. He eloquently appealed for slaves to defend themselves, escape from slavery, and initiate insurrection. Supporting insurrection against race-based slavery was for Walker a Christian, and especially Protestant, morally compelling responsibility. The character traits exhibited by David Walker, such as tenacity, irreverence, passion, enmity—and the associated actions of insurrection—are due esteem. Insurrectionists, with their absolute belligerence and disdain for slavery's authorities, were magnanimous in ways different from abolitionists that relied on moral suasion to change civil and government behavior.

It is David Walker's spirit that, according to legend, inhabited John Brown, the famous insurrectionist that commandeered Harpers Ferry, West Virginia, in 1859.[2] That spirit, it is said, was inherited by Walker from slave insurrections in 1521 Hispaniola; from 1526 insurrectionists in the Spanish colony of South Carolina, under the explorer Ayllon; from the insurrectionists of Gloucester County, Virginia, in 1663; and from the 1712 Coromantee Indians, Paw Paw Negroes, Africans, whites, mestizos, Spanish, and Portuguese insurrections in New York—from stalwart souls engaged in killing the entrepreneurs of the vicious trade, sacking neighborhoods of slave supporters, and destroying ill-gotten assets. Imagine that! Blacks, marooning, just like slaves, serfs, and indentured servants leaving Europe for the United States; killing overseers and soldiers much like patriots breaking British law and killing supporters and soldiers of the British crown, then burying their bodies head down, their anuses pointing toward heaven so that their souls would go quickly to hell. But I am getting ahead of the story. Back to the dramaturgical potential of moral suasion.

Douglass was a moral suasion abolitionist. Moral suasionists believed that the power of moral argument, particularly arguments that emphasized Christian moral requirements, could persuade persons to radically change their behavior. Either directly, or through general social pressure, it was often believed that the profit, personal power over others, and privileges gained by whites from slavery might be relinquished with the aid of moral persuasion. In addition, suasionists believed that if they, or members of the enslaved racial/ethnic type, demonstrated enviable character traits the demonstration would help convince government and civil authorities of the humanity or potential humanity of the slave community. The demonstration would have such persuasive influence because it would be irrefutable evidence that there were esteemable contributions of which the slave type was capable. The demonstration would presumably then be useful in motivating authorities to end slavery. African American suasionists practiced a politics of "representation" by which they saw themselves as representing what slaves could become. The virtues of benevolence, piety, temperance, restraint, serenity, and compassion were usually considered commanded by Christianity, nature, or reason. Suasionists, if they were not absolute pacifists, often encouraged the use of government and direct military or economic force to end slavery. Neither the theology nor moral psychology of suasionists included a stringent responsibility to engage in highly risky insurrection against racial slavery. The evaluation of what strategies would be instrumentally successful to either end, or help end, slavery usually did not include insurrection as a wise or prudential option. Thus, suasionists did not believe that there were compelling moral grounds for insurrection and/or that insurrection as an instrumental or practical tool was likely to be successful or sufficiently valuable for ending slavery.

In an early version of the suasionist tradition, Francis Hutcheson's *A System of Moral Philosophy* argued against the idea that slavery was justified as the right of conquest, a reflection of unavoidable conquests resulting from the state of war between competing groups or an entitlement held by owners from just transactions.[3] Rational human beings should never, for Hutcheson, be made to suffer. Rather, for Hutcheson, we should be motivated by a natural sense of benevolence and pity to eradicate suffering. Moreover,

"All men have strong desires of liberty and property, have notions of right, and strong natural impulses to marriage, families, and offspring, and earnest desires for their safety ... We must therefore conclude, that no endowments, natural or acquired, can give a perfect right to assume powers over others, without their consent."[4] Slavery denies the inherent humanity of slaves and was therefore always unjust. There is presumably a vital, if hidden, "calm impulse of the soul to desire the gravest happiness and perfection."[5] In some versions of suasionism, a vitalist impulse is replaced by appeals to reason or nature as the font of such desires. In later versions of benevolent ethics, evolution is treated as inherently inclined to create or make manifest such desires. The character traits most often associated with suasionists were considered best instilled by abolitionists through mental discipline, moral education, and industrial training. Moral suasionists envisioned future communities as having a fair degree of equanimity of opinion, congenial associations, pastoral surroundings, and industrial cooperation. Morally suasive abolitionists, for example, William Lloyd Garrison and Frederick Douglass, greatly respected Walker but considered his works dangerous and incendiary.[6]

Walker was born in 1785 in North Carolina of a slave father and a free mother. He inherited the status of his mother. However, by the time he was a man, racial slavery was the norm. Free Blacks were considered inferior and as a class themselves always under danger of being enslaved. Walker, an owner of a secondhand clothing business, became a pamphleteer, distributing his *Appeal* throughout the United States beginning in September 1829 from Boston with the help of seamen and stewards. Walker published the third and last edition of the *Appeal* in June 1830; on June 28 of that year, Walker was found dead near his clothing shop.

Walker provided a Christian-inspired justification and legitimization for insurrection. He eloquently advocated slave insurrection and the rights of slaves to revolt, escape, and kill overseers, masters, and those that stood in the way of a slave's freedom. The character traits he considered admirable were not at all like the traits associated with Hegel's slaves—subservience, docility, or vicarious living through the will of the other. Nor were they the traits moral suasionists considered intrinsically admirable *and* instrumental for the purposes of ending slavery, for example, restraint, compassion, or "representing" an acceptable kind. The actual death of Jim and Jane Crow were not losses to be lamented for Walker; rather, the emphasis was on the entitlement of those seeking to end slavery and slaves seeking manumission. One of those entitlements included the use of deadly force to defend themselves and seminal principles of human worth, for example, that persons, regardless of race, creed, or color, are full human beings. The virtues of tenacity, irreverence, passion, and enmity were features of full human persons *and* they could be instrumental in ending slavery. These virtues were best instilled by independent entrepreneurship, moral living, and competition. The insurrectionist tradition envisioned future communities as primarily identical to the communities within which they lived—excluding slavery. There were very few slave insurrectionists that envision structural changes in future communities, even if they did envision special religious communities. Walker envisioned communities with a fair degree of contending beliefs, conflicting associations, chaotic intertwining, cross-fertilizing cultures, and competition over resources. That is, he envisioned a future world like the one he inhabited but without the degrading reality of slavery. Enviable traits such as frugality or self-confidence and hierarchically arranged social statuses such as farmer or wheelwright, for example, would be due deference in future communities envisioned by Walker.

Walker described the character of the slaves as degraded, wretched, servile, ignorant, deceitful, and abject. Blacks, according to Walker, were forced into a mean, low, and abject condition. The condition of forced servitude made the character traits of willed servility possible. Overseers, drivers, and slave-owners were considered by Walker as avaricious, greedy, usurpers, sordid, wicked, tyrannical, unmerciful wretches, and murderous. They practiced hellish cruelties, butcheries, debaucheries, and degradations. Walker argued that the system of racial slavery practiced in the United States was the worse form of slavery in human history. Barbarian, heathen, and uncivilized nations according to Walker were never so cruel as the white American Christians. Two reasons Walker provides for describing American race-based slavery in this way are particularly striking: first, no other nation so vast, advanced, and of importance made a whole class of people irredeemably, collectively, and individually condemned across generations to servitude. Second, race, as a criterion for the complete exclusion from any role of divine grace, spiritual embodiment, and membership in the human family was, if not completely unique to American race-based slavery, certainly historically a form involving more persons than any other. American slavery was thus preeminently sinful. It was sinful, on my reading of Walker, not because the United States practiced slavery. Walker seems to think that other slave systems were benevolent. As Walker puts it, "I call upon the professing Christians, I call upon the philanthropist, I call upon the very tyrant himself, to show me a page of history, either sacred or profane, on which a verse can be found, which maintains that the Egyptians heaped the *insupportable insult* upon the children of Israel, by telling them that they were not of the *human family*."[7] It is, for Walker, heaping insult upon injury "having reduced us to the deplorable condition of slaves under their feet" to then insult by exclusion.[8] It was sinful because it made slaves, their progeny, and every one of their kind spiritually irredeemable. They could never be full Christians and they could never be free. Individuals of the kind and the kind itself were condemned. American slavery was sinful also because it used race as a criterion of distinction:

> I ask you then, in the name of the Lord, of what kind can your religion be? Can it be that which was preached by our Lord Jesus Christ from Heaven? I believe you cannot be so wicked as to tell him that his Gospel was that of *distinction*. What can the American preachers and people take God to be? Did not God make us all, as it seemed best to himself? What right, then, has one of us, to despise another, and to treat him cruel, on account of his colour, which none, but the God who made it can alter? Can there be a greater absurdity in nature, and particularly in a free republican country? ... O Americans! Americans!!! I call God—I call angels—I call men, to witness, that your DESTRUCTION *is at hand*, and will be speedily consummated unless you REPENT.[9]

For Walker, destruction would be imminent if there were no general repentance, either through the hand of God or through the agency of the enslaved. He was not so romantic as to believe that Americans would change peaceably. Moreover, he entitled the slave to the same sort of worth as the free; thus, self-defense and pursuit of freedom were well worth the effort.

Even Henry D. Thoreau, in 1859, arguing against the romantic idea that humanitarian sentiments would soon be diffused in the Americas, thus leading to the rapid end of slavery through moral indignation, recognized that

> The slave ship is on her way crowded with its dying victims; new cargoes are being added in mid ocean; a small crew of slaveholders, countenanced by a large body of passengers, is smothering four millions under the hatches, and yet the politician asserts that the only proper way by which deliverance is to be obtained is by "the quickest diffusion of the sentiments of humanity without any outbreak." As if the sentiments of humanity were ever found unaccompanied by its deeds, and you could disperse them all finished to order, the pure article, as easily as water with a watering pot, and so lay the dust. What is that I hear cast overboard? The bodies of the dead that have found deliverance. This is the way we are "diffusing" humanity and its sentiments with it.[10]

It would take a civil war before slavery in the United States came to a progressive end.

Characteristic of most persons of his time, Walker understood the world in terms of collective entities. Walker's representative heuristics—the way individuals define themselves as representing collective entities—are the representative heuristics of complex identities. Walker argues against the plans of colonization societies—societies designed to encourage Blacks, particularly free Blacks, to return to Africa. Colonization societies tended to believe that Blacks and whites could never live together in the United States, and free Christian Blacks were needed in Africa to "uplift" the heathens and create a worthy civilization. Especially for Blacks in favor of colonization plans, however, a civilized and empowered Africa would stand as material evidence of Black equality.

It was perceptive of Walker to see that the variables of national identity and rootedness in material culture (i.e., how Blacks produced, what property they worked to own, what physical neighborhoods they felt a sense of historical continuity with, where their loved ones lived and died, etc.) were far more salient than ethnic and racial bonds. Explanations and programs dependent on Negroes or Africans bonding with one another by virtue of common racial oppression were explanations and programs with little hope of predicting the future or achieving civilization missions. Moreover, the African American for Walker had as much entitlement to the United States as any other ethnic group and as much entitlement to have an American identity. Blacks, as individuals and as racialized Africans, created the United States in cooperation with other individuals of various backgrounds—all, ultimately, subordinating their original ethnic identities to a broader American identity and republican governance. There is thus no expectation in Walker that each Black person represents, stands for, or functions as an individual leader for the creation of a civilization for all Africans when this meant rejecting their American entitlements. Moreover, the collective entity or social categories of "Negro" or "African" are not stable racial or ethnic essences. Rather, they are variegated, multiple, and transforming categories through which representative heuristics operate. This view of Walker's perception of identity, I believe, helps us understand why his commitments are for republican principles, equality, individual liberty, and religion.

Walker believed in providential determinism. Providence, for Walker, worked ultimately on behalf of the oppressed; oppression was motivated by wicked, vile, and immoral free-willed persons. God, for Walker, was on the side of the enslaved and thereby redemption and salvation from servitude for enslaved groups were assured. Slavery for Walker was a humanly created institution. In time, cruel, mean, wicked, and brutal persons would be punished in this life or the next; the abject, beaten, and innocent would be redeemed in this life or the next. For Walker, cruel nations would be punished, bad preachers condemned, and good Christians eventually rewarded. Responsibility for deviations from the Gospel rest with men and women, and the enslaved are required to take responsibility for their own redemption. For Walker, ancient civilizations consisted of the Greeks, Romans, and Egyptians; the ethnic geography consisted of Europeans, Africans, Jews, Indians, and numerous subgroups of the period. Walker, however, does not envision entitlements as group-based goods or the future as a world of alienated group identities. Walker does not envision persons as representatives of racial, national, or religious inalienable or natural kinds. Yet, he is deeply committed to representative heuristics; he sees himself as representative of Christianity, of humanity, and of the Negro. Moreover, these were for Walker ontological entities and categories, yet variegated, diffracted, and beset with internally conflicting subgroups.

The idea that injustice does not pay, that is, that the rewards of injustice are not forthcoming to its agents, was a myth deeply held by Walker. The emotionally comfortable romantic belief that those who are avaricious and greedy are, in this life, likely to face due hardships was also held by Walker. He was, in addition, committed to the myth that those who suffer will, at least in the afterlife, be especially accommodated.

Bernard Boxill is right and Socrates is most definitely wrong—injustice pays.[11] Similarly, Sissela Bok in *Lying* is right in arguing that lying, or at least withholding vital information in order to gain an advantage, can be very profitable.[12] Martha C. Nussbaum argues successfully in *The Fragility of Goodness* that accident and luck make goodness fundamentally a fragile goal even if it is earnestly sought, regardless of whether one believes that goodness exists.

There is abundant empirical evidence that injustice often pays. It is beneficial to quite a few individuals and many nation-states with long histories of slavery, indentured servitude, and serfdom. We also know that those who practiced well-directed butchery in the service of primitive or corporate capital accumulation in America's history of slavery more often than not lived longer, healthier, and happier lives than those they enslaved. Moreover, they died having received the services of modern medical care and with the good companionship of their thriving families, more often than those they oppressed did. In addition, persons that remained agnostic about slavery, or at least were not often engaged in contestation to end slavery, lived far more comfortably than those in the eye of the storm.

Walker's noble, but completely romantic notions of the instrumentality and wily ways of justice, avarice, and greed may not be neatly separated from his more realistic notions of honor and respect. Moreover, it is arguable that Walker did not have a defensible theory of oppression, because he was so deeply dependent on romantic notions of God's authority in the world on the behalf of good. Walker did have, however, a clear idea of what was unacceptable. As Walker put it:

> Yet those men tell us that we are the seed of Cain, and that God put a dark stain upon us, that we might be known as their slaves!!!! Now, I ask those avaricious and ignorant wretches, who act more like the seed of Cain, by murdering the whites or the blacks? How many vessel loads of human beings, have the blacks thrown into the seas? How many thousand souls have the blacks murdered in cold blood, to make them work in wretchedness and ignorance, to support them and their families? [How many millions souls of the human family have the blacks beat nearly to death, to keep them from learning to read the Word of God, and from writing. And telling lies about them, by holding them up to the world as a tribe of TALKING APES, void of INTELLECT!!!!!! *incapable* of LEARNING, &] However, let us be the seed of *Cain, Harry, Dick,* or *Tom!!!* God will show the whites what we are, yet.[13]

Representative heuristics are never, for Walker, of greater weight than entitlements a person has by being a member of the human family and therefore a member of a properly formed moral community. By a "moral community" I mean membership in a society in which persons grant, *prima facie*, trust, empathy, admiration, and obedience to persons that are otherwise strangers. Persons can imagine themselves as interchanged with others, feel a sense of sameness, and feel as if they can reasonably predict the behavior of others. Race-based slavery completely excluded a population from being understood as having the embedded character traits and moral psychology necessary for membership in vast spheres of social existence, for example, banking, trade in precious metals and jewels, production and sale of weapons, authors of medical technologies, and regard as physicians.

One way to see the importance of Walkerian character traits is to see why Walkerian traits are essential to honor and self-respect. Honor is a social good.[14] That is, the possibility of an individual or group being honored is always dependent on the "whole" social entity understood as worthy. Slaves, eunuchs, and the poor, for example, are never considered honorific social entities. Aristocrats, soldiers, or elected officials can be considered bearers of honor. "Honorableness—in the sense of being worthy of honor—*is* a true personal quality; what I have suggested is that you may have honor without being honorable, and that you may be honorable without having honor."[15] My examples of these seemingly paradoxical features of honor are the following: slave-owners had honor as a function of their status, but any given slave-owner need not be honorable.

A slave could be honorable, and recognized as such, but could never, by virtue of her status, attain honor, that is, attain the position of being understood as a representative and embodiment of honor. My concern is not with whether honor is a consequence of social relations, conscience, precedence, or power. What is crucial here is that honor is contingent on individuals having the possibility of representing a social entity considered worthy of being exalted. Put another way, honor for individuals is contingent on the subtle and nuanced ways that man, woman, daughter, soldier, scholar, worker, African, and European are necessarily perceived as embodiments of kinds due regard.

Far more than many of his contemporaries, Walker was clear on his disdain for the exclusion of slaves from the possibility of honor as a category of persons because they were considered inferior beings. This exclusion, as well as others, was among racial slavery's most damaging—it made redemption impossible and thereby made the possibility of honor, for individuals and for the group, impossible. *This is the insult that justifies enmity*, if not vengeance, as a natural response. It is natural responses that racial slavery systematically denies to slaves. The obviousness of the humanity of slaves is irrelevant in such systems. Slavery tries to hide, destroy, and prevent natural responses. It must, like any system that hopes to exclude whole categories, demean, insult, and exclude the group from membership in the moral community. *Prima facie* trust, empathy, admiration, and obedience are never granted to persons outside of a moral community.

Torture, burning, and starvation were some of the practices used in the process of creating and reinforcing the exclusion of slaves. The denial of agnate bonds of family, for example, were some of the most common. Slaves were denied control of their children and denied the authority to make decisions about the lives of themselves or their mates. Such forms of authority were always considered, not rights or entitlements by virtue of their sentiments and commitments, but goods granted by those to whom allegiance was due.

Possibly overstated, but nonetheless important, it has been argued that "It was threat of honor lost, no less than slavery that led them [southern American states] to secession and war."[16] A noted description of lynching, a practice customized in slavery and carried on long after its ending, is described in the Vicksburg, Mississippi, *Evening Post* (1904):

> When the two Negroes were captured, they were tied to trees and while the funeral pyres were being prepared they were forced to suffer the most fiendish tortures. The blacks were forced to hold out their hands while one finger at a time was chopped off. The fingers were distributed as souvenirs. The ears of the murderers were cut off. Holbert was beaten severely, his skull was fractured, and one of his eyes, knocked out with a stick, hung by a shred from the socket … The most excruciating form of punishment consisted in the use of a large corkscrew in the hands of some of the mob. This instrument was bored into the flesh of the man and woman, in the arms, legs and body, and then pulled out, the spirals tearing out big pieces of raw, quivering flesh every time it was withdrawn.[17]

The most reasonable and emotionally coherent response to insult is a tenacious, irreverent, passionate response of enmity. Such responses are one way that slaves, or agents understanding themselves as advocates for slaves, see themselves as authorial voices. Such responses take the slave to be full persons due membership in a moral community of persons. It is a response due praise and exalted regard, that is, honor.

At the National Hall in Philadelphia, Douglass lectured on "Self-Made Men," the same day that John Brown raided Harpers Ferry—October 17, 1859.

Douglass used Benjamin Banneker, the stalwart architect and almanac author praised by Thomas Jefferson as an example of a self-made man. Moreover, Banneker was seen as exemplar of the Negro race and Jefferson's opinion of him as a goal to be achieved, because Jefferson took Banneker's work as indicative of why doubts about the humanity of Negroes were misguided. "This was the impression upon the father of American Democracy, in the earlier and better years of the Republic. I wish that it were possible to make a similar impression upon the children of the American Democracy of this generation. Jefferson was not ashamed to call the black man his brother and to address him as a gentleman."[18]

Douglass, as we know, was wrong in his opinion of the slave-owning Jefferson. Jefferson was a paternalist toward Blacks, including his slave mistress and his interracial children that he maintained as slaves until they reached adulthood. Moreover, Jefferson never supported or engaged in warfare to end slavery, but he was most active as a commander in chief to protect whites and government institutions, all of which were supportive of the innocuous institution of brutal force.

Douglass discussed Brown's plans on more than one occasion. As early as 1847, Brown and Douglass discussed the feasibility of an insurrectionary force to maintain itself in the Allegheny Mountains at Douglass's home in Rochester, New York. Douglass rejected the plan because slave-owners might sell their slaves farther south rather than risk any contact with insurrectionists in the Allegheny Mountains of Virginia. In addition, it would be difficult to maintain supplies in the mountains and generate public sympathy for insurrectionists in such a remote area. On February 1, 1858, Brown visited Douglass's home again in Rochester, New York, and explained in detail his plans for a stronghold in the Allegheny Mountains. Shields Green, an escaped slave residing at the Douglass home, was recruited by Brown as a coconspirator. Douglass remained informed of, although not directly involved in, Brown's continued efforts to establish an insurrectionary force.[19]

On the night of August 20, 1859, in Chambersburg, Pennsylvania, in an old quarry, Douglass learned from Brown of his plan to seize Harpers Ferry. Brown tried to recruit Douglass but to no avail. Brown promised to defend Douglass with his life. After three days of discussions, Douglass declined to join Brown. Turning to Shields Green, Douglass asked Green about his intentions, and Green's famous reply was that he would go with the "old man."

Douglass believed that Brown's plan would not succeed. He thus did not feel warranted to risk his life and die in Virginia. Brown's plans were considered gallant but not wise. They were not wise for Douglass, I believe, given his important and well-deserved position as a moral suasionist leader. But was it wise from the standpoint of what counts as the most important form of action to free slaves, that is, end slavery and warrant respect and the possibility of honor?

Insurrection is never instrumentally wise. It is never certain that the insurrectionists will survive or that they will effect any substantive consequences. Neither uncertainty, however, is sufficient reason to refrain from insurrection. The women of the second Seminole War, for example, had every reason to support and fight against the colonizing and enslaving whites—nothing awaited them but rape, torture, loss of land, starvation, subordination of their agnates, and further erosion of their ability to increase their assets. They could not know for certain, any more than the women who supported the law-breaking militia of the American Revolution, that they would win or lose. If high probability of success were a precondition for insurrectionist actions, one would find it very difficult to justify the American revolution, nonviolent direct action protests, anti-lynching pamphlets by Black and white women, or membership in any of the insurrectionary forces that fought against colonialism, apartheid, or the Third Reich.

Walker's Christian theology, like Martin L. King's, held a stringent requirement for moral action against obvious evil.[20] Assured success for any given action, or type of action, was hardly sufficient reason to reject a type of action. Theologically defined responsibilities and conceptions of meritorious character traits justify radical risks. Unlike a phenomenologist, existentialist, nominalist, rationalist, empiricist, or utilitarian, a condition of being a person as well as a Christian for Walker was that persons necessarily had responsibilities to act in certain ways. That is, personal experiences, reasoned judgments, or instrumental calculations of how best to secure one's self-interest do not provide the rationale for compelling responsibilities. There is an *a priori*, apodictically knowable, structure of personhood that should be mirrored in each person's life. Self-ownership of one's labor, family bonds, and the ability to transfer assets across generations, for example, are definitive of full personhood for Walker whether a person is a Muslim or Christian. *Walker's ridged ahistorical standards of self-respect is what makes submissive slaves wretched and the conditions that maintain self-loathing persons, abject.* A Christian-inspired insurrectionist method, not a hermeneutic method, is foundational and offers timeless truth claims about the nature of persons. Actual revolutionaries and insurrectionists, rather than status-seeking pundits, academicians, popular intellectuals, or ministers without callings to radically liberate the poor, are driven by a sense of deep-seated responsibility to take unfathomable and unrewarded risks. Thus, Douglass in "The Heroic Slave" and Harriet B. Stowe's *Dred: A Tale of the Great Dismal Swamp* could support maroons and insurrectionists as literary gestures, but neither had any beliefs that required a responsibility to be a maroon or insurrectionist. The difference between observers and activists, like the difference between Douglass and Brown, is unbridgeable.

Douglass was fraternal with Brown and highly regarded his desire for slave insurrections. He placed himself in great peril by being associated with Brown. He allowed Brown to visit and reside at his home and supported Brown in small but important ways. Douglass did not lack in courage. After Brown's failed raid, Douglass was immediately suspected and was forced to flee the country. Nonetheless, Douglass applauded Brown. He recognized that Brown and his coconspirators demonstrated more courage (or more properly, a form of courage due high esteem) that he did not demonstrate. "To have been acquainted with John Brown, shared his counsels, enjoyed his confidence, and sympathized with the great objects of his life and death, I esteem as among the highest privileges of my life. We do but honor to ourselves in doing honor to him, for it implies the possession of qualities akin to his."[21] The difference between Douglass and Brown, however, does not turn on their different forms of magnanimous courage but on different conceptions of honorable character traits and warranted forms of representation.

Brown's plan to attack Harpers Ferry was not supported by Douglass for a reason of particular note not mentioned above—Harpers Ferry was a federal government installation. An attack on such an installation would occasion a response by the federal government. Moreover, the attack would be directed at the national government, not at an organ of civil society, that is, individual entrepreneurs or their agents involved in slavery, religious groups, auction houses that sold slaves, and proslavery apologists such as scholars or newspapers. The attack would directly seek destruction and usurpation of a storage facility and production site. The basic materials needed to sustain slavery were located at Harpers Ferry—weapons, a system of production, a system for the distribution of weapons, and a community of persons in which normal life meant sustaining the means to support cargo in persons. Harpers Ferry was such a community.

Douglass was right in his perception that an attack on Harpers Ferry would occasion a response by the federal government and right about the unlikelihood of its success. He was wrong if he thought that Brown should not attack the fundamental agent of slavery, its principal supporter, and a primary institution profiting from the taxes and largess of slavery; he was wrong if he thought that strategically Brown's raid, or raids of Brown's type, were any less capable of successfully hastening slavery's end than attacks on strictly civil or state-managed targets. Because there is no record that Douglass ever participated in, or supported, an insurrection any more directly than Brown's, there is no reason to suppose that Douglass would have participated in, or directly supported, insurrection as a normal feature of his protests.

But, again, I have moved far too afield of one of my objectives—to tell David Walker's story and consider the dramaturgical potential of insurrection. As Alice in *Alice in Wonderland* came to understand, it is the story that matters, especially so if the central character of the story is to be reincarnated, metaphorically or actually.

Once upon a time, not so long ago, not so very long ago at all, David Walker's spirit migrated, or so the story of this legendary figure goes. It is not known whether Walker's spirit ever migrated into the body of a moral suasionist. His soul, so they say, avoids bodies and webs of belief that would not be agents of insurrection, incendiary pamphlets, and persons who kill their masters and mistresses to get free.

Walker was himself the beneficiary of spirits from earlier generations: "In 1754, C. Croft, Esq., of Charleston, South Carolina, had his buildings burned by his female slaves, for which crime two of them were burned alive." Or again: "In 1755, Charleston, a Mr John Cadman had made provision for the liberation of his slaves, Mark and Phillis, at his death. The slaves learned of this and murdered their master hoping to hasten matters along. Mark was hanged and Phillis was burned alive."[22] Unsung heroes and sheroes.

Walker was in Richmond, Virginia, in January 1830 to meet with other insurrectionists and distribute his pamphlet; shortly thereafter, but not personally organized by Walker, Nat Turner's insurrection occurred. Journalists were writing in North Carolina in 1831 about the need to control distribution of the notorious "Walker Pamphlet." In Washington City, North Carolina, the incendiary pamphlet was freely distributed. By 1859, John Brown caught the fever. Shields Green's liberation, and his goal of liberating his wife, was the ideal goal and persona for emulation.

This is why legend has it that David Walker's spirit migrated into the body of John Brown. We know he directly influenced Maria W. Stewart, the first major Black woman political essayist for women's rights. Some say he lived in Pauli Murray, an insurrectionist.

There should be plaques, awards, statues, monuments, honoraria, schools, churches, and children named after insurrectionists.

Maroons in Florida, South Carolina, New Mexico, and Canada were successful insurrectionists, either in the sense of having achieved freedom through attacking civil supports of slavery or through organized resistance and escape. This is how Walker's spirit, inherited or not, lives.

Possibly modern insurrectionists and maroons will not hold the misguided belief that the virtues of benevolence, piety, temperance, restraint, serenity, and compassion are inimical to sustaining oppression, or that tenacity, irreverence, passion, and enmity are inimical to the cause of authoritarianism and oppression. Possibly they will pursue assets and take control of their lives, using the same means as every individual or group in human history, including subterfuge, guile, disdain, and belligerence toward maniacal and malicious authorities.

Maybe, with a few conjuring tricks, the insurrectionist spirit will more frequently find its way into the lives of those viciously abused by modern Christians, rapacious entrepreneurs, sex exploiters, and racists amassing ill-gotten wealth.

Notes

1. I am indebted to students Daphne Thompson and Daryl Scriven for interesting discussions in Independent Study courses that I taught, which included works on David Walker; to J. Everet Green for critical comments; and to discussions at my lecture "Revolutionary Pragmatism," Dotter Lecturer, Pennsylvania State University, March 1996. I use here the original title of Walker's book. However, all quotes from the book will be taken from David Walker, *Appeal to the Coloured Citizens of the World*, ed. Charles M. Wiltse (New York: Hill and Wang, 1969). See, for the history of David Walker and early insurrectionists, Peter P. Hicks, *To Awaken My Afflicted Brethren: David Walker and the Problem of Antebellum Slave Resistance* (University Park: Pennsylvania State University Press, 1997).

2. See Joseph C. Carroll, *Slave Insurrections in the United States, 1800–1865* (New York: Negro Universities Press, 1938).

3. Francis Hutcheson, *A System of Moral Philosophy* (reprint of 1755 edition; New York: A. M. Kelley, 1968). Also see Wylie Sypher, "Hutcheson and the 'Classical' Theory of Slavery," *Journal of Negro History* 24 (3, July 1939): 263–80. See, for interesting discussions of the

traits of patience, sympathy, sentiment, temperance, and belief in God the redeemer—despite the obvious fact that slaves lived miserable lives, were raped, beaten, worked without due compensation, robbed of their inheritance, stripped of assets, and died while their oppressors lived longer and happier lives—Robert S. Levine, *Martin Delany, Frederick Douglass, and the Politics of Representative Identity* (Chapel Hill: University of North Carolina Press, 1997).

4. Hutcheson, *System of Moral Philosophy*, 299.

5. Ibid., 10.

6. See Howard H. Bell, "National Negro Conventions of the Middle 1840s: Moral Suasion vs Political Action," *Journal of Negro History* 42 (4, October 1957): 247–60.

7. Walker, *Appeal*, 10.

8. Ibid., 10.

9. Ibid., 42–3 (italics in original).

10. Henry D. Thoreau, "A Plea for Captain John Brown (1859)," in *Civil Disobedience and Other Essays* (New York: Dover, 1993), 39.

11. See Bernard R. Boxill, "How Injustice Pays," *Philosophy & Public Affairs* 9 (4, Summer 1980): 359–71. Also see my arguments in "Honor, Eunuchs, and the Postcolonial Subject," in *Postcolonial African Philosophy*, ed. Emmanuel C. Eze (New York: Blackwell, 1997), 252–9; "Honor: Empowerment and Emasculation," in *Rethinking Masculinity: Philosophical Explorations in Light of Feminism*, ed. Larry May and Robert A. Strinkwerda (New York: Rowman & Littlefield, 1992), 191–208 (republished: second edition, 275–88); "Autonomy Under Duress," in *African American Perspectives on Biomedical Ethics*, ed. Harley E. Flack, Edmund D. Pelligrino (Washington, DC: Georgetown University Press, 1992), 133–49.

12. See Martha Nussbaum, *The Fragility of Goodness: Luck and Ethics in Greek Tragedy and Philosophy* (Cambridge: Cambridge University Press, 1986); Sissela Bok, *Lying: Moral Choice in Public and Private Life* (New York: Pantheon Books, 1978).

13. Walker, *Appeal*, 60–1.

14. I argue for this view in my "The Horror of Tradition or How to Burn Babylon and Build Benin While Reading a *Preface to a Twenty Volume Suicide Note*," *Philosophical Forum* 24 (1–3, Fall–Spring 1992–3): 94–119.

15. Frank H. Stewart, *Honor* (Chicago, IL: University of Chicago Press, 1994), 20–1.

16. Stewart, *Honor*, 10.

17. See Trudier Harris, *Exorcising Blackness: Historical and Literary Lynching and Burning Rituals* (Bloomington: Indiana University Press, 1984).

18. Thomas Jefferson's letter to Benjamin Banneker, August 30, 1790, cited in Philip S. Foner's "Introduction," in *Life and Writings of Frederick Douglass*, vol. 2, ed. Philip S. Foner (New York: International, 1950), 86.

19. Ibid., 88–92.

20. See Greg Moses, *Revolution of Conscience: Martin Luther King, Jr. and the Philosophy of Nonviolence* (New York: Guilford Press, 1987). The tenacity and stringent requirement of action exemplified by King's philosophy occasions the same sort of honor due insurrectionists.

21. Douglass to James Redpath, June 29, 1860, *Liberator*, July 27, 1860.

22. Carroll, *Slave Insurrections*, 30–1.

CHAPTER 10
INSURRECTIONIST ETHICS: ADVOCACY, MORAL PSYCHOLOGY, AND PRAGMATISM (2002)

In "Insurrectionist Ethics," Harris presents what has come to be known as the "insurrectionist challenge": that moral philosophies are defective if they fail to support or engage in slave insurrections or if they fail to make advocacy of the oppressed a fundamental, meritorious feature of moral agency. Given these criteria, Harris declares pragmatism morally defective. Pragmatism's deference to a method of intelligence, its experimental logic, its faith in democracy, offers no surety against patriarchy or racial imperialism. Harris notes that centuries passed in the United States where calm democratic inquiry and cooperative intelligence allowed the enslavement of Afrodescended people, the annihilation of indigenous populations, and the withholding of basic rights from women. Pragmatism seems committed to patient, accommodating, gradualist methods of social amelioration and thus lacks the resources that would motivate and encourage "the sort of advocacy and authoritarian voices that demand liberation of the enslaved." Harris suggests that this lack may be offset by an insurrectionist ethos, which (1) defies accepted norms and authority when they cause or maintain immiseration, (2) marshals the social and political force of porous and variegated social collectives on behalf of the subjugated, (3) recognizes all human beings as members of the moral community or potential bearers of honor, and (4) valorizes insurrectionist character traits (e.g., indignation, enmity, tenacity, or irreverence).

One might contrast Harris's *critical pragmatism* with Cornel West's prophetic pragmatism or Richard Rorty's bourgeois liberal neo-pragmatism.

A philosophy that offers moral intuitions, reasoning strategies, motivations, and examples of just moral actions but falls short of requiring that we have a moral duty to support or engage in slave insurrections is defective. Moreover, a philosophy that does not make advocacy—that is, representing, defending, or promoting morally just causes—a seminal, meritorious feature of moral agency is defective. I query whether pragmatism offers compelling intuitions, strategies, motivations, and examples for persons to be insurrectionists or to support slave insurrections.[1] I do so by first exploring the sort of morality practiced and advocated by model insurrectionists. In this way, I provide a sketch of the intuitions, strategies, and motivations common among insurrectionists. I then consider common features of pragmatic moral thinking. The argument is conjectural and incomplete; it is intended to raise vexing issues as much as it is intended as a more coherent inquiry.

David Walker, Maria Stewart, Henry D. Thoreau, and Lydia Child, I believe, practiced insurrectionist morality. I choose these authors as models because they lived during the formative years of classical pragmatism. The authors of classical pragmatism inherited a world shaped by racial slavery and lived in a completely racially segregated society. Insurrectionists fought to end both such worlds. My model insurrectionists lived during the US period of slavery and fought against a system that by any reasonable account was historically antiquated. Every Western and industrial nation, for example, had abolished slavery, racial as well as endogamous, prior to the US Civil War. If slavery was considered justified by appeal to some version of evolutionary ethics, racial slavery in the United States retarded evolution by stifling a valuable work force. If slavery was considered warranted because it was unknowingly used to enhance material production and thereby help secure longevity for a favored gene pool, or because it was a consequence of inevitable group conflict pitting a weaker group against a stronger one, then racial slavery in the United States lacked warrant. It was historically antiquated because the "white" gene pool became a hybrid, and it was hardly inevitable because the racial group categories of Black and white were historically constructed.

David Walker (1785–1830), born in North Carolina, published and distributed the *Appeal to the Coloured Citizens of the World* in September 1829. Walker, a free Black, owned a secondhand clothing shop near Brattle Street in Boston. Walker was the Boston agent for the distribution of the *Freedom's Journal*, a New York–based weekly abolitionist newspaper. Walker's *Appeal* provided a secular and theological basis for insurrection by arguing that racial slavery was morally the worst form of slavery in history: it made race a marker separating humanity and promoted perpetual servitude for a people as a way of transferring assets from one population to another, preventing the possibility of manumission save through purchase and promoting the enslavement by Christians of Christians. In addition, he argued that the fact that the majority of white Americans were proslavery indicated the morally deficient character of Americans. The unfortunate outcome of American democracy was not a warrant for those that suffered death, beating, rape, and dismemberment. Biding their time in hopes of some future salvation was no solace for slaves. Walker and his work were banned in several states, although Walker as well as his book was instrumental in initiating slave escapes and insurrections. On June 28, 1830, Walker was found dead near his shop, the most likely cause being assassination by proslavery forces. Walker used instrumental reasoning techniques as well as foundational principles to advance abolitionists' arguments and objectives.

Maria W. Stewart (1803–1879) promoted Walker's form of morality with particular emphasis on the liberation of women. As Stewart proclaimed in an 1832 Boston lecture, "Why sit ye here and die? If we say we will go to a foreign land, the famine and the pestilence are there, and there we shall die. If we sit here, we shall die. Come let us plead our cause before the whites; if they save us alive, we shall live and, if they kill us, we shall but die."[2] Stewart expresses a sense of tragic possibility: death with either action. And she expresses a sense of the possible: freedom if Blacks confront the very population that holds them in chains. Stewart also expresses righteous indignation not only at the condition of slavery but also at discrimination practiced for the benefit of white business women:

> I have asked several individuals of my sex, who transact business for themselves ... would they not be willing to grant them [Negro girls] an equal opportunity with others? Their reply has been, for their own part, they had no objection; but as it was not the custom, were they to take them into their employ, they would be in danger of losing the public patronage.

No matter the character, skill, taste, or ingenuity of Negro girls, they could scarce "rise above the condition of servants. Ah! Why this cruel and unfeeling distinction?" It is a lack, for Stewart, of moral character and religious conviction and the presence of greed that motivates persons to accept and to perpetrate prevailing heinous conventions. A sense of identity, the "we" that Stewart uses, entails herself and all persons subject to being enslaved or who were slaves. As a free Black, Stewart faced the possibility of being forced into slavery. She expressed righteous indignation and a refusal to accept instrumental calculations of individual benefits at the expense of the lives of others.

Henry D. Thoreau (1817–1862), in two important works, "Slavery in Massachusetts" (1854) and "A Plea for Captain John Brown" (1859), expressed deep sensibilities concerning the plight of Blacks.[3] His "Slavery in Massachusetts" argued against the fugitive slave acts. Numerous states, including Massachusetts, passed a series of laws that allowed whites to treat Blacks as chattel even if they were in a state that did not sanction slavery. Thus, if Black persons who had escaped slavery were found in a state that did not practice slavery, they could be captured and forcibly returned to their former owner. Blacks thus maintained the status of property even in free states; free Blacks could become property if they traveled to states that outlawed free Blacks and were deemed, through any number of contrivances, to be property. Moreover, in certain states, a child of a runaway slave might be deemed property of the parents' owner even if the child was born in a free state. Thoreau found such laws a violation of all good governance and human rights. "I would remind my countrymen, that they are to be men first, and Americans only at a late and convenient hour. No matter how valuable law may be to protect your property, even to keep soul and body together, if it do[es] not keep you and humanity together."[4] And in his support for the insurrection at Harper's Ferry led by John Brown, he praises Brown as "a man of rare common sense and directness of speech, as of action; a transcendentalist above all; a man of ideas and principles."[5]

Brown, a white abolitionist who attacked a federal arsenal, was considered notorious by much of white America for participating in the killing of white soldiers and attacking the principal supporter—the government—of slavery. Thoreau evinces a willingness to defy convention, popular preferences, and the instrumentality of law by sanctioning the use of civilian violence against reigning authority:

The slave-ship is on her way, crowded with its dying victims … a small crew of slaveholders, countenanced by a large body of passengers, is smothering four millions under the hatches, and yet the politicians assert that the only proper way by which deliverance is to be obtained, is by the "quiet diffusion of the sentiments of humanity," without any "outbreak." As if the sentiments of humanity were ever found unaccompanied by its deeds, and you could disperse them, all finished to order, the pure article, as easily as water with a watering-pot, and so lay the dust. What is that I hear cast overboard? The bodies of the dead that have found deliverance. That is the way we are "diffusing" humanity, and its sentiments with it.[6]

The absolutely murderous sentiments and acts of barbarity commonly practiced by American slavers to maximize profit and create subservience among Blacks were not the sort of character traits Thoreau believed were sufficiently condemned by discourse. Moreover, romantic notions of persons as subject to change without force would leave generations of victims to suffer.

Lydia Child (1802–1880), the noted abolitionist and suffragette, was hailed by the famous antislavery agitator William Lloyd Garrison as "the first woman in the republic."[7] The Radical Republican senator Charles Sumner credited her with inspiring his career as an advocate of racial equality; Samuel Jackson, an African American correspondent for the *Liberator*, proposed enshrining her alongside John Brown; suffragist Elizabeth Cady Stanton cited Child's encyclopedic *History of the Condition of Women* (1835) as an invaluable resource for feminists in their battle against patriarchy. Child's 1824 novel *Hobomok* included interracial marriage as a positive good. In so doing, she incensed liberal and conservative whites, despite her well-established reputation as an author and a journalist. In 1833, her literary reputation and her livelihood were sacrificed by publishing *An Appeal in Favor of That Class of Americans Called Africans*— continuing the approach to advocacy of Walker's *Appeal*—a sweeping indictment of slavery and racism that called for an end to all forms of discrimination, including anti-miscegenation laws. After the Civil War, Child crusaded for Black suffrage and land redistribution and designed a school reader for emancipated slaves; she campaigned against the dispossession and genocide of Native Americans, publicized the plight of the white urban poor, championed equal rights for women, and worked to promote religious tolerance and respect for non-Christian faiths. Child's life is indicative of what it is to engage in advocacy. Child knew that living by her principles would involve material losses, decline in social status, confrontation with established authority and opinion, and disadvantages to her family. When her sense of self-worth and respect as a principled person were measured and weighed against losses to others and to herself, surely there were reasons to avoid principles and actions for which there was little public support. Child, however, was dedicated to downtrodden and outcast groups that, like all the insurrectionists mentioned above, were groups understood as ontological entities and collectives of kinds (e.g., Negroes, slaves, whites, women, and Native Americans).

Representative heuristics "involves the application of relatively simple resemblance or 'goodness of fit' criteria to problems of categorization. In making a judgment, people assess the degree to which the salient features of the object are representative of, or similar to, the features presumed to be characteristic of the category."[8] The use of representative heuristics is replete with inferential problems. There is a tendency to view outcomes as if they represented their origins (if a Chinese American is found guilty of a crime, for example, it's not unusual for persons to suppose that China itself is implicated); or to judge each individual instance as if it represents a category (thinking that each rose, for example, is an exemplar of all roses); or to judge antecedents as representatives of consequences (for example, if the United States caused the action and is assumed to be a moral nation, then the consequence of the action is assumed to bear the marks of a moral outcome).[9]

There are also forms of stereotyping associated with representative heuristics. Some of the classical ways that representative heuristics is used in relation to racial and ethnic stereotyping include metonymic displacement, metaphysical condensation, fetishistic categorizing, and dehistoricizing allegories that strip the racial or ethnic category from being understood as a historically changing group. Representative heuristics is often a way of reifying the subject.

One fallacy and common feature of representative heuristics deserving special attention is that more often than not we believe that acts and beliefs are "dispersed" within the category. That is, we have a tendency to believe that individual bad moral acts are members of the class of bad moral acts, and that if such acts are performed by a group member, other members are highly likely to so perform; each act is not only added to the aggregate number of bad moral acts in the moral universe but also substantively influences that universe, that is, the universe is worse off, and each act influences that universe in a way that makes more such acts possible. Conversely, good acts add to the moral universe and will influence others (possibly because a good act adds to the aggregate and thus makes the good moral universe stronger, or in some amorphous world of consciousness, others will learn and be influenced by good acts).

We know that representative heuristics are faulty logical reasoning methods but that cognition is impossible without them, and they may not be, collectively, ineffective reasoning methods for the species. The naturalization of epistemology, at least the naturalization of this feature of how we understand reality, makes the idea of living "behind" reasoning impossible. In addition, the use of representative heuristic forms of cognition are not necessarily the source of ideations justifying or motivating oppression, although they can be major contributing factors. That is, it is not that the sheer existence of a necessary feature of what makes cognition possible is invariably a cause of oppression—a claim not even held by Derrida in *L'écriture et la différence*.[10] Rather, representative heuristics helps inform what sorts of categories we live through and how those categories inform our lived experience.

Insurrectionists were often against the imposition of conceptions of block universes, absolutes, and arid abstractions, and against treating abstract social entities as stable categories. This is possible—selfidentity as both transvaluing and representative of a kind—if the category that one understands oneself to be representing is a category that one is seeking to ultimately destroy. The deeply divided classes for Marx, the poor for Martin Luther King Jr., and the slaves for Walker are groups destined to go out of existence. For Alain Locke, limiting and provincial identities of segregated communities should, and would, succumb to a broader identity of humanity, a broader identity that would be mediated by local identities with much less meaning and stability than existed in human history. Walker, Marx, King, and Locke, however, saw themselves as representing groups that they hoped would go out of existence. Whether insurrectionists see themselves as representing a group that would eventually disappear, or whether they see themselves as representing the broad interest of humanity that should be used to end fractured or essentialized local groups, insurrectionists envision a world overcoming the very bounded local identities, categories, and kinds that they represent. In this sense, it is arguable that insurrectionists may very well stand against block universes, absolutes, arid abstractions, and stable categories. Yet, they promoted interests of narrowly defined categories, such as slaves, women, and natives. The world of limitation is replaced by a world with broader and more inclusive categories, for example, humanity, men and women, Blacks and whites, and so on. But these categories are not without the same sort of problems associated with any category invested with ontological status to some degree.

Pragmatists have frequently cautioned against the use of representative heuristics, particularly the use of general categories as if they were ontological entities, such as class or nation. Pragmatists contend that arid abstractions, treated as if they were real beings, are misleading. We should use categories as heuristic tools to help us think about problems and not about stable essences. What Alain Locke termed our "invariable tendency to make categories into entities," or what William James held was treating abstractions as a block universe, is to be viewed with suspicion. Pragmatist social psychology holds that "we" categories are suspect, even if a necessary or integral feature of cognition.

There are numerous ways that one might define oneself. Livingston, for example, might be right in believing that James's conception of the subject is extremely radical and revolutionary because it offers a way of seeing the subject as always in formation.[11] Moreover, for Livingston, James's view of the subject requires that we move beyond traditional Western conceptions of the subject as either "real"—having objectively defined and limited traits—or "natural"—having traits solely shaped by limited historical experience. Moreover, Livingston may have a strong defense for a Jamesian subject, because he argues that pragmatists are indebted to the ideals of proprietary capitalism—particularly ideals of small communities and self-motivated, experimenting entrepreneurs.

Would a Jamesian subject feel compelled, against popular sentiment, to promote, organize, or encourage slave revolts and insurrections? Would such a subject organize slave escapes, knowing that they would need to kill Jim and Jane Crow slave-catchers and sellers of children, as well as cause the unintentional death of innocent bystanders? These are not the same sort of questions as "should Americans have participated in World War I or II," because insurrectionist actions are against established community consent (quite possibly democratically formed) and against established authority. Nor are they the same sort of questions as "should workers have participated in or supported the Chicago Haymarket riots," which erupted in an effort to promote an eight-hour working day. Although James in 1888 considered the riots senseless and anarchist, the rioters were not attempting to destroy a system of governance. Moreover, riots, organized and spontaneous, are important and influential features helping to create social change.[12]

Are the normative resources so deeply ingrained in classical pragmatism adequate? Is the category of *humanity* understood in a way that would justify radical action on behalf of the downtrodden, even if the consequences were likely to be harmful to the actors and others? Contemporary forms of slavery, whether in Mauritania or southern Sudan, demand contemporary insurrectionists. In addition, they often require rejecting a commitment to one's own community and citizenship in favor of commitment to unknown persons. In racial slavery in the United States, slaves were seen as members of a separate human type and outside of the moral community established by whites. Commitment to such persons by whites was a commitment to people outside their community; so, too, for Blacks who, in the early days of American slavery, frequently saw one another not as "Black" but as strangers. It was not until the 1850s, for example, that Blacks held "Negro only" conventions, and this was only after years of debate concerning whether it was justifiable to hold conventions organized by Blacks for the purpose of establishing Black organizations to promote racial uplift. Such organizations or meetings were considered anathema to the objective of ending slavery, racial segregation, and a race-conscious society. What resources are available in pragmatism that compels individuals to reject their own community, citizenship, and national allegiance to risk their lives for the well-being of strangers?

It will do no good to point to the accomplishments of Jane Addams and the Hull House any more than it will be convincing to point to the Paris Commune or the First International as adequate examples of how pragmatist or communist practice can be enriching. Where, for example, are the pragmatist insurgents against contemporary slavery or the indentured servitude of Philippine nurses in California? I know where the monks, nuns, liberation theologists, Buddhist altruists, and communists are located on the world historical stage as agents of insurrection—but it is not clear that pragmatists are on the world historical stage as insurrectionists *as a function of their pragmatism*. There are certainly persons who cite pragmatism as one philosophy central to their philosophic orientation. Cornel West, for example, is a self-described prophetic pragmatist. However, his insurrectionist morality is clearly a function of his radical socialism, left-Christian sensibilities, and African American traditions of resistance against slavery, racism, and exploitation. Certainly, John Dewey, Alain Locke, and Jane Addams held deep commitments to uplifting the downtrodden. My query is whether there exist features of pragmatism that require, as necessary conditions to be a pragmatist, support for participation in insurrection.

Possibly, Theodore Draper is right in his story of the American Revolution—the revolutionaries never intended to create a democracy.[13] Their intentions, quite like those of most advocates seeking greater spheres of power, authority, and the imposition of their wills against prevailing traditional, religious, and political practices, were not realized. As agents in violation of prevailing customs and laws, they failed to shape social consequences to match their intentions. Voting, for example, involving the participation of the citizenry unfettered by exclusions according to station was hardly intended. Women, nonwhites, and men of low station, such as indentured servants, were normally considered persons who should not be allowed to vote because of some inherent defect. Possibly, Theda Skocpol has a defensible view: revolutionary theories purporting to predict outcomes based on scientific analysis of social conflict systemically fail in their predictions.[14] Her institutionalist, comparative historical approach—rather than a Marxist class analysis, a rational choice approach, an interactionalist sociology, or an interpretative narrative—may very well prove a more effective account of revolution. Institutionalist accounts look at how rules and regulations shape behavior independent of the reasoning actions and behaviors of agents. Institutional rules and practices often generate results that have more to do with expectations and disappointments than models of change usually allow.

One reason an institutional account may prove more effective than its rivals is because it insists on an incongruity between explanations and predictions, intentions and outcomes. Yet, Skocpol is not blind to the radical changes in ways of living shaped by strong advocates and actors. There is at least accord between many competing explanations of revolution to some degree on the singular point of importance to my argument: Concrete predictions of revolutionary outcomes are rarely in accord with the intentions of revolutionaries, yet fundamental alteration of social structures does not occur without the concerted effort of individuals who see themselves as representative of a group intentionally trying to create a new world. There simply are no modern revolutions that did not include, if not decisively, at least in terms of important discourses, class conflict, no modern revolutions without conflicts over what rules should be followed, and no modern revolutions in which intelligent plans and reasonable predictions were not nearly all wrong. Moreover, there are no revolutions or insurrections without representative heuristics, that is, without women who see themselves as representing "women" as an objective category, without persons who see themselves as representing the interests of the poor, without workers who see themselves as the embodiment of meritorious traits, and without environmentalists who see themselves as pressing for the best interests of all sentient beings by pressing for the interests of environmentalists.

What are the pragmatist sources for justifying insurrection, given that the outcomes of insurrectionist action or support for such actions are not predictable, that the vast majority of insurrectionist actions and movements fail to liberate, and that contributions to liberating a population by insurrection or support for insurrection range from useless to tremendous? Instrumental and functional reasoning can be of limited value for predicting future events.

Insurrectionists normally believe that the outcome of their actions will lead to eventual success. Walker held the romantic belief that individuals and groups responsible for unjust acts would eventually be punished—if not while they were alive, at least in the next life. Socialists normally believe that if not human nature then humanity's embedded sense of justice will incline people to favor greater income and ownership equity rather than less equity. Yet, income and ownership disparities have only increased over human history. Evolutionists and Marxists characteristically hold that antiquated forms of production will be replaced either because of a biologically driven tendency for populations to seek more effective and efficient control over reproduction or because conflicts tend to be resolved in favor of dialectically driven solutions. However, it is arguable that hope for ending the misery of existing generations is highly unlikely. If an individual has no duty, from a pragmatist standpoint, to alleviate the existing misery of strangers, will that absence of action negatively influence that individual's flourishing and moral development? Assuming we have duties that are not contingent on the successful outcome of action or on effective predictions of what will become successful, what duties are there from a pragmatist standpoint to overthrow slavery? No Americans had good reason to believe that their heroic acts to destroy slavery would, as an isolated set of acts, produce the desired results for themselves or for persons they loved. Nor had they any historical evidence to suggest that highly risky social acts would substantively encourage others to fight for abolition or result in successful outcomes.

The unpredictability of outcomes does not stand as a sufficient reason to defeat the justification that oppressed individuals or groups can offer for pursuing instrumentally useful paths. There is no human progress without the discord of social conflict, insurrections, and revolutions.[15] These are instrumental social actions. The outcomes are uncertain. Even if one is committed to an evolutionary view of change, there is no history of evolution without the history of insurrections, revolts, and revolutions. The uses of intelligence, dramatic rehearsal, dialogue, and discourse are hardly the sole modes through which institutions fundamentally change. As one author saw Dewey's views about revolution, "His theory could ride the crest of change but could not explain how such change might be initiated."[16] Moreover, even in Dewey's *Reconstruction in Philosophy*, there is no escaping the value of instrumental reasoning, although Dewey has numerous other reasoning techniques he promotes: "If ideas, meanings, conceptions, notions, theories, systems are instrumental to an active reorganization of the given environment, then the test of their validity and value lies in their accomplishing this work. If they succeed in this office, they are reliable, sound, valid, good, true …. Confirmation, corroboration, verification lie in works, consequences."[17] As I have argued, however, consequences and their predictions are not good criteria for justifying insurrection.

The range of sentiments that can work as means for defensible ends is hardly limited to the ones most appealing to Dewey, such as dialogue. Murder, pillage, and destroying the property of democratically supported governments have on occasion produced favorable consequences for some individuals and groups. The material and mental well-being of interested populations may also gain from such actions. To deny this would be like denying that evolution exists without conflict, parasites, or unanticipated consequences of intentional and unintentional action.

In Walkerian terms, what sort of slave, Christian, or republican is it that does not strike a blow for abolition? Slaves in nearly every society used a wide array of strategies to survive and resist. These strategies included, but were not limited to, infanticide, suicide, selfmutilation, poisonings of masters and their children, flight, marooning, arson, and revolt. What method is considered preferable is irrelevant to my argument. That the use of some methods of absolute destruction of slaveholders and the bonds of servitude, however, should be given meritorious ranking is a crucial feature of insurrectionist moral criteria. Moreover, advocacy representing, defending, or promoting in some form the liberation of self and other from bondage is a good that warrants special honorific status. Change may be best understood as irreversible, cumulative, and gradual. Change is not "one" phenomenon. It is a multitude of accidental, intentional, and unpredictable results. It does not happen, however, outside the context of insurrection—persons who want a different world and are willing to be insurrectionists of one form or another. Advocates and advocacy, regardless of the goal or method used, are necessarily authoritarian but not necessarily dictatorial—advocacy presupposes that the advocate or what is being advocated should determine reality and that the advocates have a fundamentally advantageous viewpoint. Advocating is always expressed in an authoritative voice; advocates want their ideals to shape or become reality. Moreover, character traits of aggressiveness, self-assurance, self-confidence, tenacity, irreverence, passion, and enmity are evinced and applauded by insurrectionists. Lydia Child and Maria Stewart were in no way passive in promoting women's suffrage, abolition, and racial equality. Nor did they believe that traits associated with aggressive behavior were traits best left to men. Such traits as benevolence, piety, temperance, compassion, self-assurance, and self-confidence were character virtues. That is, insurrectionists prescribed character traits that included traits associated with aggressive behavior for the downtrodden.[18]

John Diggins and Cornel West, for radically different reasons, recognize a serious lack in classical pragmatism: there seems no way to require advocacy and authoritarian moral voices.[19] West argues for a sense of the prophetic, particularly a Christian-inspired visionary leadership with an optimistic approach to the future as an authoritarian voice. It is the prophetic, rather than an evasion of philosophy as belief in that which cannot be established through the aegis of reason, that West considers important for our web of beliefs. Diggins, a critic of pragmatism in this regard, argues that pragmatism lacks the resources to justify the need for democratic institutional authority.

Is it the case that pragmatists see the self as necessarily lacking if it is bereft of such traits as aggression, self-assurance, self-confidence, tenacity, and irreverence? Are self-deprecators not just instrumentally and functionally disadvantaged but also in some sense morally lacking? It is certainly the case that self-deprecators could live more fulfilling lives if they had a greater sense of self-worth. But what principle or conception of fulfilling lives is there in pragmatism that says we are compelled to act in ways that prevent people from living self-deprecating lives? Walker describes the wretchedness of the slave in terms that make one feel that such a condition violates basic human nature. Normal life for Walker should include the possibility of accumulating assets, transferring assets to one's progeny, loving one's mate, and freely selling the product of one's labor. Are these endogenous to a pragmatist conception of the self such that if others lack such desires or the means to carry them out, pragmatists are duty bound to seek their liberation? If self-deprecators do use the method of intelligence and remain self-deprecators, are we duty bound to nonetheless change the conditions under which they labor, for example, change the conditions of poverty from which voluntary slaves do not seek to escape?

Evaluating processes, means, ends, and reflective considerations—the basic features of Dewey's method of intelligence—is no surety against someone's being a racist. Racism is not inherently a set of propositions that are internally contradictory.[20] It is arguable that the method of intelligence so frequently applauded by Dewey as a reasoning strategy, joined with the objective of socially engineering progress and increasing democratic participation, was useless during the era of racial slavery in the United States. The persons empowered to engage in social engineering favored slavery; persons invested with the education capable of appreciating the subtleties of Dewey's method were often proslavery; and Americans practiced one of the highest levels of democratic participation in human history, and the majority were in favor of slavery. As Orlando Paterson argues, societies that favor democratic freedom have been societies that characteristically practiced slavery.[21] Lives of millions were destroyed as abolitionists engaged in debates and protest. Abolitionists that promoted or helped persons escape the horrible trade could more often than not count actual lives saved—all such persons acted against extant law and popular authority. That is, the immediate lives of the enslaved were not changed by dialogue, debate, democratic voting, or petitions—such actions helped to eventually end slavery and certainly helped abate the misery that slaves might have suffered if not for the tempering norms influencing slaveholders and their friends. The point is that pregnant women, children, old men, and young men were lynched, beaten, raped, threatened, and coerced while the world of relatively civil abolitionist discourse and protest occurred.

In the advanced capitalist society of the United States, democracy works without centralized planning to effectively exclude and exploit while allowing open political participation. Corporations and rich families can accumulate vast sums of capital and enormous profits. Many personal life choices are open to them. Those who own little to nothing have their choices and employment options, by contrast, severely restricted. The city and the country, if Rabin's *Soft City* is at all near to being an appropriate picture, are spaces in which there are hundreds of overlapping locations of authority and no single entity capable of planning, implementing, or controlling social experiments or policies.[22]

Of what use is a "method of intelligence" in a postmodern society where very few persons are motivated by a desire to socially engineer society to enhance everyone's well-being? Of what use is the method of intelligence in a society where the misery of noncitizens is considered of little consequence, although the profit of citizens is contingent on expropriating the wealth of noncitizens? Without the self that James, Dewey, Locke, and Addams seem to presuppose—a self that is already motivated to desire the well-being of others—is there any reason to suppose that the method of intelligence would incline anyone to be motivated to seek the abolition of slavery through insurrection or seek the end of servitude, if it required a commitment to an ontological or an heuristic category (i.e., moral commitment to a group of strangers)?

Commitment to humanity is always a commitment to some group of humans first and always requires the use of representative heuristics. That is, it requires us to do just what good reasoning methods tell us to avoid—treat groups as if they were real ontological entities. Moreover, commitment to improving the condition of humanity requires that persons share meager resources with strangers and take personal risk they could well avoid. What, then, are the intuitive motivations, guidances, and criteria for pragmatists that require them, as pragmatists, to advocate insurrection, to help destroy realms of viciousness, the trade in land mines, proliferation of nuclear weapons, tremendous expropriation of wealth from less developed countries to wealthy Western nations, the sale and use of life-destroying drugs among adults and children, forced prostitution, and the selling of stolen babies and body parts?

If the advice a pragmatist would give to persons in a society of racial slavery did not include insurrection and honor for those engaged in insurrection—if no more than as a form of self-defense—then pragmatism's penchant for prudence and dialogue is sufficient to suggest that pragmatism is woefully inadequate. Moreover, if there are no resources in pragmatism to motivate and encourage persons to be insurrectionists, it is defective. The metaphorical reincarnation of Walkerian character traits are appealing— tenacity, irreverence, aggressiveness, self-assurance, self-confidence, tenacity, enmity, and passion—because they help make possible the sort of advocacy and authoritarian voices that demand liberation of the enslaved. The moral sensibilities of insurrectionists, including a willingness to lend support or act when consequences are likely to be unfavorable in the immediate future, disadvantageous for individual actors, and contrary to popular beliefs and practices, are important sources of motivation for insurrectionists. An insurrectionist would desire the destruction of oppression and would have a willingness to work through the enmity of irreconcilable differences. Advocates for change use authoritarian voices often representing abstract social entities, entities excluded from dominant moral communities.

Achieving the possibility of honor for communities or for members of communities is contingent on facing the reality of advocacy and authority enlivened by insurrectionist moral sensibilities and character traits. Moreover, the reality of representative heuristics should not be understood as inherently unfortunate features of cognition, always associated with misguided, arid abstractions. Rather, a philosophy such as Walker's that makes representing, defending, and promoting the well-being of a community because that community's human rights have been violated is preferable to one that makes such commitments suspect.

Notes

1. Portions of this paper were used in "Revolutionary Pragmatism," the Dotter Lecture, Pennsylvania State University, March 1996. For an example of the vast variety of slave revolts, see Joseph C. Carroll, *Slave Insurrections in the United States, 1800–1865* (New York: Negro University Press, 1938).

2. Maria Stewart, "Lecture Delivered at the Franklin Hall, Boston, September 21, 1832," in *Philosophy Born of Struggle: Anthology of Afro-American Philosophy from 1917*, ed. Leonard Harris (Dubuque, IA: Kendall Hunt, 2000), 34.

3. Henry D. Thoreau, *Civil Disobedience and Other Essays* (New York: Dover, 1993).

4. Ibid., 26.

5. Ibid., 33.

6. Ibid., 39.

7. Carolyn L. Karcher (ed.), *A Lydia Maria Child Reader* (Durham, NC: Duke University Press, 1997), 1. Also see Carolyn L. Karcher, *The First Woman in the Republic: A Cultural Biography of Lydia Maria Child* (Durham, NC: Duke University Press, 1994).

8. Richard Nisbett, Lee Ross, Daniel Kahneman, and Amos Tversky, "Judgmental Heuristics and Knowledge Structures," in *Naturalizing Epistemology*, ed. Hilary Kornblith (Cambridge: MIT Press, 1985), 195. Also see Richard E. Nisbett and Lee Ross, *Human Inference* (Englewood Cliffs, NJ: Prentice-Hall, 1980).

9. See the discussion of the judgments of the degree to which outcomes are representative of their origin, judgments of the degree to which instances are representative of categories, and judgments of the degree to which antecedents are representative of consequences, in Daniel Kahneman, Paul Slavic, and Amos Tversky (eds.), *Judgment under Uncertainty: Heuristics and Biases* (Cambridge: Cambridge University Press, 1982).

10. Jacques Derrida, *L'écriture et la différence* (Paris: Editions du Seuil, 1967).

11. James Livingston, *Pragmatism and the Political Economy of Cultural Revolution, 1850–1940* (Chapel Hill: University of North Carolina Press, 1994).

12. See John P. Diggins, "Pragmatism: A Philosophy for Adults Only," *Partisan Review* 66 (21, Spring 1999): 255–61.

13. See Theodore Draper, *The Struggle for Power: The American Revolution* (New York: Times Books, 1996).

14. See Theda Skocpol, *States and Social Revolution: A Comparative Analysi of France, Russia, and China* (Cambridge: Cambridge University Press, 1979); and Theda Skocpol, *Social Revolutions in the Modern World* (Cambridge: Cambridge University Press, 1994).

15. For an argument against the idea of evolutionary social change without revolution, see my "Response to a Conversation: Richard Rorty," *Sapina: A Bulletin of the Society for African Philosophy in North America* 8 (3): 14–15.

16. Richard Crockatt, "John Dewey and Modern Revolutions," in *Real*, vol. 7, ed. H. Grabes, H. Diller, and H. Isemhagen (Denmark: Gunter Narr Verlag Tubingen, 1990), 218.

17. John Dewey, *Reconstruction in Philosophy* (Boston, MA: Beacon Press, [1948] 1963), 128.

18. See Elizabeth Fox-Genovese, *Within the Plantation Household: Black and White Women of the Old South* (Chapel Hill: University of North Carolina Press, 1988).

19. John P. Diggins, *The Promise of Pragmatism: Modernism and the Crisis of Knowledge and Authority* (Chicago, IL: University of Chicago Press, 1994); Cornel West, *The American Evasion of Philosophy: A Genealogy of Pragmatism* (Madison: University of Wisconsin Press, 1989).

20. See David Goldberg, "Racism and Rationality: The Need for a New Critique," *Philosophy of Social Science* 20 (3, Summer 1990): 317–50, for an argument that racism need not violate the canons of formal logic and that it might rely on available facts as advocated by normal science. There are normative reasons to be against racism, but I doubt that any reasoning method invariably leads to such norms.

21. Orlando Paterson, *Freedom* (New York: Basic Books, 1991).

22. Jonathan Raban, *Soft City* (London: Hamilton, 1974); also see Leonard Harris, "Postmodernism and Racism: An Unholy Alliance," in *Racism, the City and the State*, ed. Michael Cross and Michael Keith (London: Routledge, 1993), 31–44.

CHAPTER 11
CAN A PRAGMATIST RECITE A *PREFACE TO A TWENTY VOLUME SUICIDE NOTE*? OR INSURRECTIONIST CHALLENGES TO PRAGMATISM—WALKER, CHILD, AND LOCKE (2018)

In "Can a Pragmatist Recite a *Preface to a Twenty Volume Suicide Note*? Or Insurrectionist Challenges to Pragmatism—Walker, Child, and Locke," Harris first argues that Alain Locke should be considered a classical pragmatist and that Locke's version, critical pragmatism, is a valuable orientation in the oeuvre of pragmatist philosophies. Yet, Harris queries whether the pragmatist can metaphorically recite a *Preface to a Twenty Volume Suicide Note*. That is, can a pragmatist offer a philosophy that acknowledges the perpetual insecurity, the cognitive dissonance, the impossible expectations of those under existential duress, and yet provide helpful terms, conceptual categories, depictions, explanations, and animus that facilitate the management of abjection, insecurity, and trauma, given impossible odds of relief? Can a pragmatist break free from genteel interceding background assumptions and *de rigueur* patterns of inquiry to offer a *philosophia nata ex conatu*—a philosophy that arises out of and works to escape abjection and necro-being? Harris suggests that those with an insurrectionist spirit (e.g., David Walker and Lydia Child) provide crucial resources and guidance—they can recite the *Note*. And Locke's critical pragmatism, read as a response to a world of paradoxes and dilemmas, helps Harris to intimate an insurrectionist disposition/spirit.

Alain Locke's version of pragmatism, critical pragmatism, provides a way to see how a philosophy contributes resources for the abused, subjugated, and humiliated facing existential crisis and impossible odds of relief. That is, it provides reasoning methods, terms, words, depictions, explanations, queries, dispositions, spirit, and conceptual categories as resources. I will argue that a viable philosophy should provide resources and reasoning methods that make the management of abjection and existential crisis viable, given impossible odds of relief; it should be encoded with, among other features, the sort of spirit needed to recite a *Preface to a Twenty Volume Suicide Note*,[1] that is, a philosophical orientation that gives credence to epideictic rhetoric, imagination, and insurrection. To this end, using Locke as a starting point, I argue against Socratic reasoning methods. I argue for an insurrectionist conception of philosophy, namely, a philosophy born of struggle. I leave open the question of whether a pragmatist can recite a *Preface to a Twenty Volume Suicide Note*.

Locke

I consider Locke a sojourning creator of American pragmatism, namely, critical pragmatism, although he has not been considered a founding member of pragmatism and thereby a "classical" pragmatist. I first suggest conceiving of classical pragmatism in a way that would include Locke, and then explore the reasoning methods and conceptual resources of special value provided by Locke's critical pragmatism.

Locke was a resident of Hertford College, Oxford University, as the first African American Rhodes Scholar from Harvard, 1907–10. One of his tutors was F. C. S. Schiller. Schiller's *Studies in Humanism* (1907) had established him as a follower of William James's approach to knowledge. The Hibbert Lectures by James, titled "On the Present Situation in Philosophy," at Manchester College, Oxford, from May 4 to May 26, 1908, were the basis of James's 1909 work *Pluralistic Universe: Hibbert Lectures at Manchester College on the Present Situation in Philosophy*.

Locke and Schiller attended at least one of James's lectures together; Locke was admonished by Horace Kallen to organize an audience of American students at Oxford to attend James's lectures. From his notes, we know Locke was in the audience at the third of the lectures, on May 18. That lecture heard James reject Hegelian absolutes.

Between 1910 and 1911, Locke left Oxford and enrolled at the Universität zu Berlin, Friedrichstraße, to pursue his interest in the Austrian school of value theory, a school of value theory that was not considered a worthy philosophical approach at Oxford, and to get away from the racially pejorative academic culture of Oxford. Locke took a class under Georg Simmel; he was at the university with Hugo Munsterberg (director of the Amerika-Institut), having been among Munsterberg's coterie of students at Harvard. Locke's address in 1910 was c/o Thomas Cook and Son, Unter den Liden, 5; in November, c/o Frau Haupt, Grossbeerenstraße 5 III, Berlin S.W. German; and in January 1911, Karlsdad 22 II. Taking a class with Simmel and working with Munsterberg while managing dwindling funds and constantly changing addresses may have made the sojourn in Germany a bit too arduous. He joined Howard University in 1912.

Under the auspices of the National Association for the Advancement of Colored People, Locke delivered a series of lectures at Howard University, Washington, DC—*Race Contacts*, 1915–16—prior to completing his dissertation at Harvard in 1917.[2] Franz Boas had offered one of the most radical views about race of his time, namely, that the existence of races could not be established by scientific methods. However, Boas tended to remain committed to the existence of races as biological kinds. Locke, however, contended that neither are races biological kinds nor are cultures caused by race; rather, races are social, historical civilization types and transitory cultural categories. Returning to Harvard University to complete his doctoral degree, Locke was a student in Alfred Hoernle's Logical Theory class in 1916, a class focused on logic and value theory.[3] One of

Locke's papers was "Logical and Epistemological Theories," which focused primarily on Bradley, Bosanquet, Russell, Husserl, and Meinong.[4]

Ralph B. Perry was Locke's dissertation advisor. Locke's dissertation, "The Problem of Classification in the Theory of Value: or an Outline of a Genetic System of Values," was submitted in 1917. He graduated with the class of 1918. His dissertation distinguished his version of value theory. The dissertation begins with a critique of Dewey's and Perry's value theories. Locke moved away from the Jamesian idea that values came from an expression of interest that thereby shaped modes of good and evil as well as the idea that values formed a logical arrangement of preferences or passions. Rather, taking cues from Christian von Ehrenfels, Alexius Meinong, Wilbur Urban, and Franz Brentano, Locke argued that values were fundamentally relative categories and thereby irreducible to stable categories since they are always modes subject to transvaluation and transposition. Given that values are not transcendental categories of the good, they can nonetheless inform or be shaped as universal traits such as symmetry, balance, or common denominator values (i.e., kinds of values or traits endemic to humanity) such as repose that are arguably normatively universal but uniquely expressed.[5]

By "valuation," the Austrian value theorists such as Christian von Ehrenfels and Alexius Meinong and the American Wilbur Urban meant objects created by being valued. In 1930, Urban wrote,

> It is the development or realization of selves that constitutes the "good" ... and the theory of ethics which makes this the locus of value is called the ethics of self-realization. By this is meant that the locus of the good is not found in pleasure, nor in organic survival or welfare, but in the complete energizing of our capacities as selves or persons.[6]

Urban locates the "good" in self-development the way Locke locates the good, a location that often found him criticized as elitist. It is, nonetheless, the expression of a melioristic hope in a world that offers no guarantee that beauty and goodness will occur together. The ethics of realization and a relativism toward beauty and goodness finds a compatible seat in Locke's philosophy:

> Art must first of all give beauty,—and somehow, too, a sincerely truthful version of life, if it is to last ... The Negro artist must still continually be on the lookout for the ditches of rhetoric and pitfalls of propaganda. To repair the damaged morale; to clarify the social vision and stimulate the social will is not the Negro artist's prime mission, but when he succeeds all the greater is the effect and the credit.[7]

The meaning of "classical pragmatism" changes when the requirement of a linear line of communication between authors is dropped.[8] Every university employing the usual authors who are considered classical pragmatists, whether Harvard or Columbia, had a written or tacit rule that excluded Negroes, Jews, and women. Despite formal exclusion, forms of communication occurred between Locke and other pragmatists, sometimes directly, but often in tandem. In Locke's case, Horace Kallen, Albert C. Barnes, Josiah Royce, and Sidney Hook, philosophers closer to Locke's age and more directly communicating with Dewey, were his associates. Kallen, for example, consistently credited Locke with the authorship of the concept "cultural pluralism" since their collegiality at Oxford. At least on one occasion, Barnes (Dewey's associate and coauthor of two books) praised to his employees about Locke's achievements as a Negro who rose from humble beginnings to become educated (although he knew Locke came from a middle-class background); the first article in Locke's first major publication, *The New Negro* (1925), was authored by Barnes. Barnes, however, ceased communicating with Locke after the publication of *The New Negro* because Locke's aesthetic conceptions and views of African art in "Legacy of Ancestral Arts" (1925) differed from his; Locke's most significant treatise in philosophy, "Values and Imperatives" (1935), was recruited and published by Kallen and Hook in *American Philosophy* (1935).[9]

Locke found common cause with the Baha'i faith of Baha'u'llah and its avid stance favoring race-blindness and openness toward unlimited sources of cultural and spiritual inspiration. Bernard Stern and Locke's edited volume, *When Peoples Meet: Race and Culture Contact* (1942), embodies the sort of cultural pluralism Locke considered crucial for a viable democracy.[10] Rejecting race as a biological kind causing cultural behavior, Locke promoted African American culture as a source of universal aesthetic values. Universal values for Locke are always born of local, albeit ethnic, racial, national, or gendered realities, not colorless abstractions. Contrary to aesthetic realism, Locke's aesthetics presents the beautiful as evincing value categories through, and in conjunction with, attributes such as symmetry, balance, and rhythm, for example, Duke Ellington's riffs, William Grant Still's symphonies, or the poetry of Robert Frost and sonatas of Frédéric Chopin.

Locke, like other pragmatists of his era, was critical of cultural intolerance, provincialism, dogmatism, absolutism, foundationalism, and "either-or" dualism. Locke supported the first and second world wars and gave credence to various socialist revolutions. Unlike other pragmatists, however, Locke was particularly critical of "uniformitarian universalism" and cultural uniformity, stereotypes, proprietary culture, experimentalism, scientism, racism, missionaries, paternalism, and the brutality of colonialism. Locke promoted advocacy aesthetics, group self-expression, anti-colonialism, self-fidelity, cultural ascendency, and self-confidence.[11] Locke's array of sources from the African American adversarial tradition, such as Frederick Douglass and W. E. B. Du Bois, provide a substantive array of approaches and concerns, such as the role of Haiti in the historical formation of democracy in the Americas.[12] These distinguishing features of Locke's philosophy shape its "critical" edge. These features make his version of pragmatism "critical" in the *oeuvre* of classical pragmatism.

Taking account of tandem associations and communications gestures toward a vast array of neglected themes that can be developed, not as a mimic of past voices, but as sounds of new and different voices that call and recall different historical figures. The meaning of "classical pragmatism" is, I believe, far richer with this approach than historians such as Schneider and Elizabeth Flower allowed.

One way to read Locke's critical pragmatism is to read him as if he is confronting a world of paradoxes and dilemmas. Locke's response to that world helps us see his contribution to the value of imagination and the insurrectionist spirit.

Locke's views regarding moral imperatives, stereotypes, and the conflicting dynamics of racial chauvinism and racial identity are examples of his management of seemingly intractable paradoxes and dilemmas. He uses epideictic rhetoric to negate, praise, condemn, and declare choices in a world beset with moral dilemmas.[13] Locke contended,

> All philosophies, it seems to me, are in ultimate derivation philosophies of life and not of abstract, disembodied "objective" reality; products of time, place and situation, and thus systems of timed history rather than timeless eternity ... But no conception of philosophy, however relativist, however opposed to absolutism, can afford to ignore the question of ultimates or abandon what has been so aptly though skeptically termed the "quest for certainty."[14]

A tension between the reality of relativism and the need in some situations for certainty and moral imperatives is encoded in how Locke views "philosophy."

Locke believed that we should accept moral imperatives. He recognized that the promotion of moral imperatives was often occasioned or warranted dogmatism and absolutism. We should certainly try to avoid uncritical attitudes associated with dogmatism and absolutism, as well as intolerance. However, I interpret Locke as warranting a degree of self-certainty, uncompromising attitudes, and belief in otherwise unwanted behavior that accompany actualizing moral imperatives. "Moral Imperatives for World Order"[15] (1944), for example, are just that: imperatives.

> Realism and idealism should be combined in striking for a world order ... Nationality now means irresponsible national sovereignty ... Confraternity of culture[s] will have to be put forward ... The idea that there is only one true way of salvation with all other ways leading to damnation is a tragic limitation ... The moral imperatives of a new world order are an internationally limited idea of national sovereignty, a non-monopolistic and culturally tolerant concept of race and religious loyalties freed of sectarian bigotry.[16]

No credulity or admitting fallibility saves the supporters of an imperative from being responsible for being as self-certain as dogmatists. Pretentions of innocence, willful ignorance, an attitude of being irresponsible for known unintentional consequences of willful action or our fallibility notwithstanding.

Locke's approach to stereotypes is another way to take account of dilemmas that require making a choice.[17] Very often, the least offensive choice is not without moral trepidations or quandaries. Efforts to abate racial stereotypes and end the existence of essentialized racial identities, for example, require the use of the folk concept of race, itself a concept that is fraught with morally heinous associations. As we attempt to dislodge pejorative racial stereotypes, we use the very term that sustains what Dorothy Roberts has termed the "Fatal Invention" (race as a biological kind).[18]

Locke's 1925 *The New Negro* imagines a future of racial amity. Locke had no practical way of bringing racial amity into existence. An anthology was hardly substantively causal for changing who owned material and cultural assets. *The New Negro* was an eclectic anthology of prose, poetry, religious songs, pictures of book covers, cartoons, and sculptures. It was intended by Locke as "an attempt to repair a damaged group psychology and reshape a warped social perspective." Given the vicious history of stereotypes, exploitation, and self-loathing, "little true social or self-understanding has or could come from such a situation."[19] (Hoernlé's copy of *The New Negro* has a dedication on its front page, Wartenweiler Library, University of Witwatersrand, South Africa, Hoernlé's adopted homeland.) Locke had no way of knowing that *The New Negro* would help shape aesthetic attitudes in the African world.

Stereotypes are, for Locke, inescapable cognitive heuristic devices. As such, it is not stereotypes as such that are invariably harmful, since we use them as tools to navigate the world (i.e., an impossibly massive degree of information is managed by shortcut devices like overgeneralizations and stereotypes). It is the kind of stereotype that can be draconian.

By 1939, Locke recognized that he had been a bit too enamored with the Harlem Renaissance artistic community. He had expected it to be both a conduit for racial upliftment and a mediator between African Americans and whites that would achieve a decline in racial discord and help create an ascendency of cultural democracy and mutually rewarding cultural exchange. The Harlem Renaissance had a major influence on creating a sense of self-respect among African Americans, general rejection of minstrelsy stereotypes, and greater appreciation of African American creativity, but it was not a causal elixir creating equal opportunities, incomes, assets, or cultural capital, let alone the death of racism or creation of democracy.

It would be nice to believe with Dewey that "all art is a process of making the world a different place in which to live, and involves a phase of protest and of compensatory response," or with W. E. B. Du Bois that art is at its best when in the service of liberation.[20] Would either be so. They were both wrong. On my account, creativity is a slave to many masters: autocrats, pedophiles, corporate executives, dictators, conservatives, libertarians, and social justice advocates alike. Artistic creativity was not, and is not, an epistemic basis leading to transcendental enlightenment, a pure vision of reality greater than one offered by other methods of production, or a font of beneficial creations and processes subject to rewarding self-critical reformations. Nor is there any reason to believe that artistic communities are privileged sites of creativity inclined to be causative agents, ushering in a new humane world.

The creative power of art should also be credited for some of its most powerful capacities: creating new effective forms of racism embedded in subliminal media messages, religious symbols intended to defame, pornography directed at children, photographs that glorify war, designs for prisons, and stores designed to help create spendthrift consumers. Art and misery are in an unholy alliance.

Art does not have queer power. That is, products of creativity are not automatically inclined to be morally laudable nor cause the artist or audience to be, know, or appreciate morally beneficial realities. There are no properties causing insightfulness embedded in art nor do humans have a cognitive faculty or intuitive power that could identify such properties.[21] Religious, commercial, and pornographic art, for example, are hardly arenas of artistic creation that promote a singular set of moral preferences. Possibly, the Apostolic Christians who favor child brides and the producers of child pornography have more in common than is apparent, but I just do not think that their art is to be credited with partaking in the imagined queer power of art to be supremely laudatory. Such powers do not exist in any event. Valorizing and stereotyping the "New Negro," consequently, was arguably a provisional stereotype useful to combat the degrading stereotypes of minstrelsy, and it helped repair a fractured social consciousness.

The existence and use of the concept of race for Locke, another example of a dilemma, embroils us in a "grave dilemma." "The proposition that race is an essential factor in the growth and development of culture ... faces a pacifist and an internationalist with a terrific dilemma, and a consequently difficult choice." The dilemma: "Would you today deliberately help perpetuate its [race] idioms at the cost of so much more inevitable sectarianism, chauvinistic prejudice, schism and strife?" For Locke, this is a "grave dilemma." It is unavoidable, and there is a risk of being "impaled on either of its horns." Cultural, albeit racial, differences have historically been "roots of the engendered feelings of proprietorship and pride."[22] Locke faces the cornucopia of dilemmas associated with cultural differences, which can be ethnic, racial, or national.

Locke contends that if we "do away with the idea of proprietorship and vested interest,—and face the natural fact of the limitless interchangeableness of culture goods ... we have a solution reconciling nationalism with internationalism, racialism with universalism."[23] The solution, even if far from perfect, makes possible living with diversity without essentialism. Locke's idea of a "free-trade in culture" may be arguably fantastic, shifting the meaning of "race" and "nation" to a position where they have no referent other than "culture," and requiring the death of proprietorship with no real way for creating its negation is arguably phantasmagoric, but he faced the dilemma and provided an exit that involved absolute negation.

Locke uses race to help subvert race; he recognized that arguments for simple race eliminativism fail because people in healthy race-based communities use it to help sustain networks needed for survival and to fight prejudice. Its elimination would accompany the demise of networks of institutional supports and thereby leave them even more vulnerable.

Simultaneously, he vies for cosmopolitanism and the eventual elimination of race. There is no reason to believe that races, let alone existing racial categories, are necessary forms of classifying persons and treating them as bearers of moral and social traits associated with those classifications. Locke employs radical imagination by envisioning a new world, given seemingly intractable dilemmas and quandaries.

Locke, especially in relationship to stereotypes, provides resources and guidance; Marx, especially in relationship to the bourgeoisie, provides resources and guidance.

I know why it is just fine to act on affective inclinations against an ill with no means/ends analysis, deliberation, method of intelligence, meliorism, or community approval for Locke: Reprehensible stereotypes are categorically impossible pictures of persons. Racist stereotypes fail because there are no kinds of beings for which they could be viable depictions, that is, there are no persons with never-changing value categories for whom neither value transvaluation nor transposition exists.

Locke, arguably, was not an insurrectionist. I draw from the issues that distinguish him from other pragmatists to help picture my account; it is his critical stance that helps me intimate an insurrectionist disposition, attitude, spirit—for example, critique of "uniformitarian universalism" and cultural uniformity—stereotypes, proprietary culture and promotion of advocacy aesthetics, group self-expression, anti-colonialism, self-fidelity, and self-confidence.

Nothing in John S. Mill's view of utility prevents a utilitarian from being a Hindu, but nothing gives impetus to be a Hindu. Nothing in Dewey's view of pragmatism prevents a pragmatist from supporting slave insurrections, but what gives impetus, requirements, duties, and imperatives?[24]

Locke embraces moral imperatives, utility of stereotypes, and the dilemma of race, facing without pretention the quandaries that attended each. In doing so, he imagines a world that was reasonably seen as impossible from the standpoint of existing reality: a "New Negro" and an imagined new world. Locke's critical pragmatism and Walker and Child's spirit and disposition help provide resources and guidance. I leave open the question of whether Locke's meliorism lends weight to a radical, if not critical, pragmatism in the sense that there may be no reason in principle to restrict possible ways to improve life through human effort or limits to modes of valuable forms of cognition and reasoning methods.

Imagination and Incommensurability

Imagination requires leaving categories given to us by experience. Fail we will. Try we should. I will never live in a world without that world seeing me as Black. No matter where I go on the planet, it is almost certain that I will be seen as African, Black. Male, five feet six, gray hair, and wearing glasses will also be a part of what others see in their gaze. But it is the racial gaze that shapes the meaning of all other traits. To imagine a world without race, I must leave behind experience and common social reality. Imagination allows new categories that may arise in tandem with new corporeal, technical, and geographic realities. What a world without race and its pantheon of racial identities would constitute is at best wild speculation. Octavia Butler's novel *Adulthood Rites* created an imagined world. A human-Oankali (alien) child is torn between two species but finds a way to surmount the limitations of each and help create a different world. Butler's *Adulthood Rites* series imagines a world beyond entrapment in established racial and sexual identities, yet the use of race and sexual identities are themselves conceptual features drawn from the existing world.[25]

We are not completely trapped in the current world. Emergence is a real phenomenon; sometimes large patterns generate unanticipated results; sometimes chaos and accident emerge. Emergence sometimes requires leaving experience. Discord. Negation. Separation. Emergence is sometimes a violent rupture, sometimes ruthlessly, morally unwanted, ferocious, and cruel. Given that we are invariably entrapped in the limitations of existing language, cognitive reasoning strategies, viable categories, and well-researched "best" empirical facts, explanations, and predictions, there will be trailing vestiges of some feature of the past extended into new emerged realities. The norms that I emphasize are those that emerge from the abolitionist spirit of agents such as David Walker and Lydia Child.[26]

Imagine this: what you can say is too often limited to linguistic paralysis, limitation of available words, grammars, morphologies, and categories in common use. Imagine that complete escape is impossible. Escape is not easily achieved pragmatically, rationally, intelligently, or by following a scientific, experimental, self-known perspectival, self-known contextual, instrumental, consequential, or reasoned judgment method. Facing indeterminate situations may mean not appealing to traditional or codified modes of inquiry nor relying on presumed pithy, valorized virtues.

All reasoning methods of inquiry are entrapped in the same world as all language. Entrapment is sometimes total. Leaving is what Veena Das calls "wakening"—the difficulty of reality, choosing between equally horrible options. "Something other than rational argumentation is called for in the face of this condition, not simply emotion or empathy as opposed to reason, but wakefulness," seeing or simply accepting a duty to others.[27] Letting die. Whether in Delhi, India, Johannesburg, South Africa, or Gary, Indiana, the least well-off too often face excruciating choices between whom to let live and whom to let die, choices of whether to care for an elderly parent or a new baby, whether to sell a kidney or watch a child suffer malnutrition, accepting what obligations I can fulfill and walking away from others. There is no algorithm for this. There is no escape from the dilemmas that make whatever choice is taken a moral quandary accompanied by irrational conditions. When do you stop expecting that your child, once diagnosed with stage 5 cancer and predicted to die in three months, will not die? Even after death, very often we still hope.

When there is no reasonable hope that the raping of persons will end anytime in my lifetime or that of anyone living, it may be vain to expect that no rapes ever occur. But that is what I hope. There is no reason to believe that thousands of young persons who are abused regularly will ever live lives without undue trauma outside of prison walls, but I nonetheless hope for prison abolition now.

David Walker (1796–1830) and Lydia Child (1802–1880), two stalwart slave abolitionists, knew full well that millions of people would lose their ill-gotten wealth and that innocent workers who relied on trade within the abominable institution would suffer. "Gradualists" distinguished themselves from "abolitionists." Gradualists wanted to either reform slavery to make it a benevolent practice or slowly abolish it in ways where slaves would continue to suffer but the free could slowly adjust to gradual losses and thereby limit their disadvantages. Slave abolition for Walker and Child meant the immediate end of slavery. Nothing in the world made the ideas of abolishing slavery viable in nineteenth-century America. It would be, arguably, absolute insurrection to be a slave abolitionist in a world where social stability and solidarity were often seen as being made possible by slavery. Nearly every democracy before 1900 included legal slavery.[28] Slavery in America was gradually abolished. I am an abolitionist. Keep vain hope.

What, Then, Is Insurrection?

Or How to Do Philosophy without Really Trying

"Socratic philosophy" means, at the very least, dialogic discourse about foundational issues in metaphysics, epistemology, and aesthetics. Those issues are usually categorized as either emerging from or concerned with *phronesis* and *theoria*. "Philosophy born of struggle" means, at the very least, engaging issues that have their origin in struggles to destroy boundaries.[29] This kind of philosophical orientation is well pictured neither as *phronesis* nor as *theoria* but bespeaks emergent discourses inclusive of poetry, testimonials, and discordant arguments concerned with or from realms of imagination, ignored realities, and oddly formed questions that may not neatly fit categories of metaphysics, epistemology, or aesthetics. The very distinction between *phronesis* and *theoria* can be abandoned.[30]

"Struggle" philosophy is intended to start from the voices of those loathed, humiliated, and stripped of honor and assets. It is false that that voice is ubiquitous. Contrary to what is written in the *Manifesto of the Communist Party*, the "communist" cannot simply be the voice of the working class, having no interest but the interests of the working class, any more than any particular social formation of abolitionists can be the voice of slaves. Aaron Swartz, in his "Guerilla Open Access Manifesto" (2008), defends hacking in ways that expose authoritarian rule and secrets. The hacker's creed is that "you have a duty to share it [information] with the world … But all of this action goes on in the dark, hidden underground. It's called stealing or piracy, as if sharing a wealth of knowledge were the moral equivalent of plundering a ship and murdering its crew. But sharing isn't immoral—it's a moral imperative."[31] Exposure, however, consists of casting secrets into a world that has no corresponding manifesto of assured progress; it is a casting of information into an abyss. Doing philosophy born of struggle always involves questions, assumptions, and visceral emotions that treat extant categories of reality as tangential: not something to live within its boundaries but something to be ignored as a source of sufficient meaning.

A philosophy that fails at speaking to miseries such as necro-being, that is, that which makes living a kind of death—life that is simultaneously being robbed of its sheer potential physical being as well as nonbeing, the unborn (e.g., nonexisting children of forcibly castrated men and women)—is a failed philosophy.[32] The Socratic method of looking for the form, nature, or essence of normative traits such as piety or justice misguides; it is not just that no meaning of merit is there to be discovered but that the method requires distinguishing between individual or particular properties and the general category within which they fit, types and tokens, instances and kinds. There is no world that is so neat, made of distinct normative and social categories filled with correlative appropriate particulars, instances, types, tokens, and kinds. The search is a gaze of stasis. It is entrapped in linguistic tools of distinction, definition, and categorization that do not sufficiently match the real world.

In order to condemn misery, I do not need a grand theory to tell me the role of a particular misery in relationship to all other social activity, nor do I need a theory that tells me the nature or form of misery. Nor do I need a grand theory to require that a philosophy has, among an array of considerations, resources and guidance of direct benefit to the immiserated. A philosophy should speak not tangentially or as a matter of conjuncture but as a matter of its words, depictions, explanations, queries, categories, demands, requirements, duties, and terms constitutive of its traits—what it is that makes it what it is and distinguishes it from other orientations. Its speaking should give voice to the slaves of the world. If this is a form of foundationalism or an *a priori* grounding, fine. If it is a Lockean type of moral imperative, fine. It is a better imperative than an unspoken one, silence in the face of an abysmal existential void, willful blindness, or what Walker meant by willful ignorance—seeing obvious misery but proceeding bereft of taking responsibility for choosing (insurrection?) in a world unfree of dilemmas and value-neutral standpoints.

Let me begin here: abolish all prisons, violence work, slavery, child soldiers, nation-states, minstrelsy artistry, and racism. By "abolish," I mean the absolute negation—all rules, behaviors, buildings, and performances that constitute the array of human sociality that forms their primal existence. I do not favor prison reform. I favor abolition.[33] I favor moderate cosmopolitanism. I do not favor the perpetual existence of nation-states. I favor their abolition. Cosmopolitanism provides an example of an orientation encoded with dilemmas.

Cosmopolitans favor the existence of human well-being in a way that cuts across lines of race, ethnicity, gender, nation, and class. A radical cosmopolitan is "one who refrains from fixating on tribal (racial/ethnic/national) loyalties and is especially suspicious of employing such loyalties as criteria in moral deliberations ... A radical cosmopolitan feels no compulsion to be loyal to his roots, origin, or heritage."[34] A radical cosmopolitan rejects the need for individuals or groups to define themselves in terms of authentic cultural moorings.

A moderate cosmopolitan is one who favors "cultivating cultural resources associated with specific ethnic groups, not on cultural, ethnic, or nationalist grounds, but on the premise that such measures are provisionally necessary."[35] Moderates, at the very least, believe in some form of social transformation through dialogue and consider authenticity as a continually created phenomenon.

Valuation in Locke's value theory necessarily involves transvaluation and transposition. Such features of valuation create new categories. Universally appreciated aesthetic forms of the beautiful for Locke, for example, are often created from local folk culture. The local, provincial, and parochial are the source of the universal. In so doing, populations that are the source of such creations enhance popular perceptions of them as worthy of respect. Langston Hughes's vernacular poetry, with a blues-based rhythm and Southern colloquialism, can be read for its underlying forms and become appreciated by a wide audience. Conviviality between the local and the cosmopolitan is created in such cases. Minorities, parochial communities' partisans of the ethnic and racial groups that suffer discrimination of various kinds, can, consequently, achieve dignity in such cases—a recognition of worth. The end goal for Locke is the elimination of race and self-realization. Locke can be classified as a moderate cosmopolitan with a caveat, namely, that his position is intended to be strategic because he hopes for a reality without racial identity and expects cultural identities to exist without pejorative proprietorship.

A nativist cosmopolitanism emphasizes cultivating and maintaining separate ethnic, racial, national, or cultural communities because a nativist believes that groups are substantive natural or social kinds. Individuals are seen as group members. Nativists also believe that some form of group separation allows groups to protect and transmit their cultural values. A nativist believes that cosmopolitanism is a negotiated set of relations between coequal groups and considers authenticity as a function of traditions.[36]

"Sophisticated cruelty" is the kind of cruelty that helps sustain effective forms of subjugation and simultaneously produces increased efficiencies such as standardized weights, currencies, languages, and religious practices.[37] Cosmopolitanism, whether radical, moderate, or nativist, is compatible with sophisticated cruelty. Historians of numerous persuasions, for example, Cheikh Anta Diop, *Precolonial Black Africa*; Orlando Patterson, *Freedom*; Fernand Braudel, *The Mediterranean and the Mediterranean World in the Age of Philip II*; Adam Hochschild, *King Leopold's Ghost*; and Jared Diamond, *Guns, Germs, and Steel* have presented the seemingly always concurrent presence of increased efficiencies that enhance human well-being concomitant with sophisticated subjugations.[38]

Cosmopolitanism, as a practice of promoting common forms of communication, entails undue pain and suffering, sometimes intentionally, sometimes unintentionally. A cosmopolitan reality requires that some dying-language community, fringe religion, peculiar sexual orientation, or commitment to a culture or homeland will be destroyed and subjugated—populations are faced with assimilation into a *lingua franca* the imposition of the material culture such as guns, cell phones, and television. Failure to have one's nonmajor language, for example, Hausa or Yoruba, translated into a major world language means that it will likely die a local death.[39] That death is always embodied. Fetal alcoholism, domestic violence, self-mutilations, self-loathing, high rates of suicide, ill-health, and depression are all embodied suffering that we know to commonly accompany language-losing communities.[40]

New technologies introduced to populations that in no way can produce the goods that are controlling their lives is an introduction of the conditions that invariably promote feelings of utter impotency. We know it will happen. Our experiments and our best efforts to avoid harming others are no longer purely the sources of unintentional consequences; they are willful, and, even if excusable, we are not absolved of being responsible and at fault. It is not unusual that an immigrant Zimbabwean waiter in Cape Town, South Africa, receives less in his monthly salary than an ecotourist spends on his eco-friendly shoes—shoes that made a profit for a nefarious owner of an eco-friendly company. There is no redemption. There is no escape from such paradoxes. All choices entail some degree of quandary.

Only a few archives are dedicated to preserving the historical record of dying-language communities. Desperately trying to hold on to languages that face death, such communities are sadly isolated with little to no hope of survival. This is cosmopolitan cruelty: we know we promote pain and suffering, albeit, unintentionally, sorrowfully, and at best with every effort to avoid undue harm by showing and supporting institutions that aid helpful assimilation. But there is no pure escape from responsibility. Archives are foreign institutions using technologies foreign to the home of dying languages. We kill as we try to save.

I fully accept responsibility for favoring a philosophy that I know, in advance, will entail undue pain and suffering. No pretentions. No world free of paradoxes and dilemmas.

I argue that if a philosophy tells us of a viable mode of inquiry, valuation, living, and relating to others, as well as providing guidance and suggestions of how to conceive reality, it should be of service to a slave, serf, and proletariat, and a resource for the abused, subjugated, or humiliated, and the object of abjection. A philosophy should help us escape concrete experience, keep vain hope, go beyond art, negate *a priori* commitments that require stable value congruity, and leap into an abyss. If it cannot, something about that philosophy is lacking.

A philosophy should provide some resources to help consider what counts as unacceptable. If a philosophy says "rely on deliberative democracy" to tell us what should be unacceptable, for example, such a philosophy may be indefensible for this purpose. Girl children in Assam, India, betrothed to elderly men, may be approved by Apostolic Christians; child prostitution in Taiwan may be tacitly approved by a community of law enforcement agents; misogyny may be tolerated by well-educated women. Deliberation may yield, as it often has, justification for torture, genocide, and child slavery. Cannibalism of children for culinary satisfaction, not hunger, has been socially acceptable and publicly known in numerous European societies.[41] In less than two decades, between 1907 and 1925, California authorized the performance of 4,636 sterilizations and castrations: "Mental patients were sterilized before discharge, and any criminal found guilty of any crime three times [especially Blacks] could be asexualized [castrated without consent] upon the discretion of a consulting physician."[42] There is only evidence that the physicians, lawyers, and parents involved were more often than not sympathetic, compassionate, and empathetic. Cruelty, empathy, and piety are bedfellows.

If a philosophy says "rely on warranted contracts," such a philosophy faces some of the same problems as those that rely on deliberative democracy—immigrants, undocumented aliens, acephalous societies, and shifting groups without a stable state or civil institutions (e.g., Somalia, civil war zones) do not form a group with self-directed agency. That is, they may not be networked by intermarriage, sharing the same language, geographic location, religion, or ethnic identity. That is one reason why a philosophy should provide some resources, not an algorithm, foundation, necessary eternal principles, or Kantian duties. Conceptual resources that help define what counts as acceptable are beneficial for creating a personal sense of stability given constantly changing, radically shifting, and incongruous conditions. Recommending community discussions, deliberating with others, open public forums, and written rules that are publicly available, for example, as democratic resources and bulwarks against injustice are deeply limited resources. The Azande of South Sudan, for example, rarely speak the languages of their neighbors, paper is not readily available, written rules stored online or in a government office are not easily available, and open public forums enhance the chances of attacks from conflicting ethnic groups or marauding government forces. Populations of well-ordered societies that are not located in a singular state cannot be seen; their well-being or suffering should not be treated as a sort of subtext, to be inferred or calculated from what counts as well-being or suffering within a model of a well-ordered nation-state. Suffering is not derivative, that is, what kinds of miseries, discrimination, and exploitations for which one population is subject are not identical to those of populations living under very different rules and authorities.

Let's face it: *Weapons of the Weak* fail in the *War against the Weak* to defeat the strong in the lifetime of most agents courageously wielding weapons to end suffering.[43] Worker strikes, self-mutilation, and publishing well-researched facts about undue misery and suicide fail to terminate, for the agents, the successful use of eugenics, underemployment, or misleading advertisement creating overmedication for suffering agents. The weapons of the weak have tremendous effect, over time, on institutions, rules, and behavior. But agents of change very often do not benefit from their own agency; they may suffer without relief. Generations of African Americans who protested and demanded the right to vote, for example, never had the chance to vote; the contemporary voting agency of African Americans in no way replaces the inability of past generations to express themselves through voting. If a philosophy cannot tell us to abolish social formations such as prisons or slavery that are arguably irredeemable—no meliorism, compromise, or tolerance— then something is wrong.

Insurrection is the negation of a world. It is an attempt to create a new world hopefully with no remainder from the old. There simply may be no permanent revolution, eternal return, nor pithy progress through the method of intelligence by way of concrete experience. Like all organic nouns, whether democracy, philosophy, pacifism, or revolution, there are different types, shapes, forms, and warrants. Thomas Hobbes's *Leviathan* (1651) favored democracy under conditions that citizens first relinquish their rights of autonomy and the Sovereign impose his rule; democracy will be a fact of life for Marx after the working class ascends and is the only existing class. Some insurrectionists are terrorists, and others are absolute pacifists and hermits abstaining from sensual pleasures as much as possible. Some are poets, taxicab drivers, hairdressers, owners of publishing companies, or novelists.

The justification of insurrection of any kind begins with a concept of, or one like, oppression, subjection, abjection, impurity, pain, temporality, or boundaries. I begin with the negation of abjection and boundaries.[44] There is no algorithm that provides a way to match the word to a limited array of ways to pursue change, but all insurrectionists imagine, engage, recommend, or practice something that entails a difference from the present and, at best, gestures toward a new convivial world.

I believe that it is imperative to be a slave abolitionist, given that there are abolitionists of different kinds. All slave abolitionists share an interest in radical newness. This newness is like LeRoi Jones's (Amiri Baraka's) *Preface to a Twenty Volume Suicide Note* ....: a long, fragmented, introspective voice where he critiques both bohemians and the Black bourgeoisie; lampoons a Black man for gawking at a white woman and enjoying European artists, when he is bohemian, bourgeois, married to a white woman and well educated about European poets. The book does this through calm lyric, parody, and sarcasm while foregrounding cultural rebellion and suffering, moving away from racial self-loathing and recommending radical praxis as a precursor to a suicide that may never come. The poem "Hymn for Lanie Poo" in *Preface to a Twenty Volume Suicide Note* .... expresses the author's incongruous emotions, rapid transformations of identity, transvaluations, and struggles with sadness, discouragement, and discordance with his relation to his ancestors. We need to be able to metaphorically read such a poem, that is, have a philosophy that warrants the process of searching and making difficult decisions under condition of trauma, insecurity, and fear, especially for the subjugated.

FROM HYMN FOR LANIE POO

> *Vous êtes de faux Nègres*
> —Rimbaud

Each morning
I go down
to Gansevoort St.
and stand on the docks.
I stare out
at the horizon
until it gets up
and comes to embrace
me. I
make believe
it is my father.
This is known
as genealogy.[45]

Swartz committed suicide while under duress; Baraka stayed alive while under duress. The *Note* is living with perpetual insecurity and imagining termination of a concrete existence: abandon neat methods of reasoning, transvalue using epideictic rhetoric and simultaneously analyze.

David Walker and Lydia Child provide resources and guidance. Walker describes the misery of slavery in *Appeal to the Coloured Citizens of the World* (1829) using the following terms: slavery supporters are avaricious usurpers, political usurpers, and tyrants; their character is that of sordid avarice, cruelty, bloodthirsty, unmerciful, deceitful, seekers of power; the misery, pain, and traumas suffered by slaves is viewed by slavery supporters through the lens of willful ignorance.[46] The slave suffered shame, humiliation, was generally loathed and, according to Walker, became wretched (self-loathing, voluntarily aiding the continuation of slavery). Walker was absolutely indignant in the face of unmitigated cruelty. W. E. B. Du Bois was right: Walker's *Appeal* was outrageous.

The abolition of American slavery only made sense in hindsight, that is, past time. Slavery existed in every major democracy; similar cultural and religious communities practiced racial slavery. American abolitionists had too few examples of movements that were successful in ending slavery to suggest the possibility of success, and almost none used insurrection. From the standpoint of the nineteenth century, the abolition of slavery was sheer imagination. Imagination also requires making sense, not of past time entrapped in linear sequences of known patched-together events, but of no time, a make-believe future being. There should be resources to imagine a new social world, radically different from this one. Openness, reevaluating, reexpressing, which a pejorative dogmatism would codify as categorically unneeded, would allow for a leap into the abyss.

Walker and Child lived within 5 miles of each other in Boston, although there is no evidence they ever met. Child, in addition to letting her home be a site for the underground railroad, authored *Appeal for That Class of Americans Called Africans* (1833), which argued for the abolition of slavery and intermarriage between races as a way to eventually end racial differences. She promoted women's rights, freedom for Native Americans, and a different orientation for the education of children. Roundly ostracized by nearly all women's rights advocates and abolitionists who favored the preservation of separate races, Child continued to use Walkerite terms to describe human misery and encourage some form of a new world. Walker's and Child's spirit are the sort needed to recite a *Preface to a Twenty Volume Suicide Note*.

I have no hope that I will ever live in a world without reprehensible racial stereotypes, but I still want to stand against reprehensible stereotypes. If this is just visceral, fine. But invariably, all warrants rely on some form of visceral (i.e., affective, experiential) foundation. Maybe embrace futility rather than stopping, dying, and giving up in the face of futility. Imagine the impossible. Locke was right: valuation is total, all-encompassing, complete. There is no end. We are always trapped in having background assumptions and valuations that cannot be revealed. Locke's relativism was right. There is no standpoint that is not also a value standpoint: no methods, reasoning approaches, or pragmatic considerations that exist beyond the pale of valuation. The best explanation, discussion, evaluation, judgment, risk analysis, probabilistic account, or prediction is just that, "best." To simply recognize the ever-present possibility of fallibility is inadequate. Sexual slaves can gain no solace by others claiming that the abolition of sexual slavery may be replaced by other forms of servitude or that any definition of sexual slavery is controversial. At what point is the demand for ending sexual slavery an unmitigated moral imperative, given the impossibility of a definition without reasonable cases of exemption? Refusal to decide on a definition simultaneously entails the impossibility of deciding what counts as, and what should be, its absolute abolition. Absolute fallibilism is simultaneously absolute unintended acceptance of an inability to decide, picture, imagine, and define an abolition of rape, brutality, and cruelty. Absolute abolition is making all experiences of it, as victims or perpetuators, impossible. Even if racism, for example, cannot be well defined because it is a sort of essentially contested concept, that is not a sufficient reason for defeating the need to settle on a definition.[47] The misery suffered by conditions commonly associated with race-based subjection can hardly be abated by nominalism. Imagining its abolition requires, among other actions, deciding what is absolutely to be ended, named, or unnamed.

In Plato's *Republic* "Allegory of the Cave" dialogue between Glaucon and Socrates, Socrates explains that philosophers are like prisoners once confined to looking at their shadows on the walls of a cave but, having turned toward the sun, perceive reality.[48]

Imagine Socrates as a citizen of a nation that represents about 4.4 percent of the world's population but with a prison population that constitutes around 22 percent of the world's prisoners, citizens who own more weapons than any other nation, its soldiers having killed more "enemies" in various wars than any other nation, its citizens using more opiates than any nation its size and eating meat voraciously. Then imagine Socrates describing this population as only caring about good jobs, cheap health care, and discovering piety's essential form through pure and practical reason.

Violence workers are persons trained to kill and confine; torturing, maiming, raping, and wounding are occasional ancillary activities considered as benefits of the job by employed workers. Soldiers, police, prison guards, and supporting staff are highly prized occupations. They are well versed in imposing, and watching, suffering. Status and employment, as well as feelings of empowerment, are some of the rewards. Americans are commonly proud of their ability to kill, constrain, watch, and confine. They have successfully killed and imprisoned more citizens than most if not all nations of a similar kind, let alone those killed and maimed in conflicts abroad. "Mistresses's violence against slave women in the plantation household [during American slavery] ran along a continuum: Bible-thumping threats of hell for disobedience, verbal abuse, pinches and slaps, severe beatings, burnings, and murder." Frederick Douglass described one victim as "pinched, kicked, cut and pecked to pieces," with "scars and blotches on her neck, head and shoulders."[49] Weapons wielded by female and male violent workers included cowhide whips, brooms, tongs, irons, and shovels.

Violence workers, their practices of killing and confining, and traits esteemed by them do not appear in such works as Owen J. Flanagan's *Varieties of Moral Personality: Ethics and Psychological Realism* or John M. Doris's *Lack of Character*.[50] Analogously, the description that I imagine Socrates gives of Greek citizens is like a shadow because it pictures, if not fictional features, fractured images—it is full of gaping omissions and a selection of special features used to define what concrete reality counts as concrete reality.

Maybe Socrates was blinded by the light. Maybe when he returned to his fellow citizens in the cave no one listened to him because he failed to admit that he, too, was bound by assumed valuations while condemning them for being embedded in unexamined valuations.

This is what Socrates saw when he turned from looking at his shadow on a cave wall and faced the sun: his fellow warmongering, misogynist, avaricious, well-educated slave-owning citizens professing, in a self-effacing manner, like him, their enlightened placid virtues.

Maybe this is why Socrates, in his dialogue with Euthyphro (399 BCE) wanted to know not particular temporal instantiations, subjective experiences, or examples of piety but its form: indignation, guile, self-confidence, and aggression by the subjugated needed to be neatly attached to forms of chaos, temporal reality, rashness, and vile incongruity. Magic. The piety, sanctity, and holiness of Greek violence workers was a reflection, instantiation, or a corresponding refraction of transcendental or universal unchanging essences, the cruelty of violence workers a cauldron of base chaotic, temporal, and rash forms upon which higher forms stand, unassociated, because cruelty, empathy, and piety are never bedfellows.

We never simply observe and analyze experience, using tools of understanding, distinction, exegesis, and clarification. Observation certainly is beneficial. However, observations always occur within background assumptions. What experiences matter at first situate what is observed. The observing author, having selected what is in the field of view, then has power over the reader. The author makes no moral commitment to the people that have experiences but are not in the field of view. The author acts like a Nietzschean priest of piety—garnishes praise from the reader because he is purely a neutral self-effacing (if not holy) revealer of our tortured being to our tortured being. The tools of the observer are the sorts of tools Plato (the author of Socratic dialogues) preferred—structured forms of inference, techniques of analogy—neatly transferable and presumably perfect instruments never needing revisions. These are tools unlike the horrible tools of the poet—inspiration, revelation, testimony—none of which are transferable, never reliable, and always producing different results from one poet to the next. The observer surreptitiously stands in the position of the holy. Of course, what he reveals is enlightened, especially because he admits his fallibility. Experience is not a playing field full of appealing moral emotions or a self-referential playground upon which we can escape. We are faced with deciding what experiences are to count as sources of catharsis and inspiration.

Imagine that we are all in an Asylum, something like the one described by Erving Goffman in *Asylums* (1961).[51] The managers abuse us, and we look to the managers for counseling help; we protest by not eating or throwing our dinner plates on the floor weekly in a ritual of complaint; managers respond to our protests by beating patients randomly, plate thrower or not. Monthly, we and the managers have family night, and we are kind to one another. We ask for more potatoes for dinner, and they give us more rice, increase the cost of dinner, and decorate the walls with pictures of potatoes. The next day, abuse and protest rituals return. We—Black, white, and brown—like watching *COPS* on TV, especially the episodes where Black and brown people are humiliated, beaten while drunk, pushed into police cars, crying in jail cells and bleeding from head to toe from being abused by a husband or wife. Liberals in my wing of the Asylum watch TV shows that have happy endings; conservatives know better. They are not desperate for cosmopolitan friendship. Their wing is closed after dark. No Asylums ever closed because the psychiatrists cured all the patients. Meanwhile, in the front office, neuroscience ethicists justify the dispensing of opiates (proof that science has progressed since frontal lobes were cut to cure madness).

Scientific research has proven that opiates are safe for pharmaceutical companies to advertise (with a few desiderata), and by abductive reasoning, we can infer that opiates will create rational beings who believe God assures that Americans have a right to own guns and kill something sentient. Polling companies have corroborated these results.

Thinking that the mad are smart and would otherwise act in their own best interest if they were just not being abused and the managers are really kind and would be helpful if they were just not being paid to terrorize and control the mad so the mad would stay mad and the owners of the Asylum could continually reap profit from the Asylum may itself be a bit mad.

Possibly escaping the Asylum is like, if not committing suicide, escaping meliorism and valorized methods of inquiry while reciting a *Preface to a Twenty Volume Suicide Note* written by someone who is loathed, humiliated, and depressed.[52] The *Note* is a saying why, saying that, sadness, screaming, self-mutilation, ranting, pleading, condemning; it is filled with bad analogies, impossible expectations, hopelessness, defeat, admission of failing personally set goals, ecstasy, rage, loss of faith—like expecting a social movement to create universal human liberation—otherwise known as the Socratic *God That Failed*, inane—faith that at once is the height of freedom from corporal existence and enslavement to transcendental nothingness. The *Note* is creating alternative categories, models, cosmologies, and images of possible futures like the abolition of slavery.[53]

Existential crises are rarely faced. The vast majority of humanity is not incarcerated, raped, humiliated, or loathed. Nor are their homes summarily pillaged, bombed, robbed, or burned. They are not stateless, nationless, or encamped in squalid refugee camps. They are not, even for the least well-off, constantly confronting the enmity of violence workers. The life expectancy for nearly every population has improved over the last one hundred years; so, too, incomes and education levels. In addition, there are fewer sufferings from predictable natural disasters such as annual river floods from the Nile, Yangzi, or Mississippi Rivers. Yet a philosophy gains some appeal if it has resources for life under existential duress—helping to make it possible for us to see conditions that make misery possible and help promote abolition.

Reason makes no sense in the face of existential crisis. Suicide solves nothing for the dead. The movement toward suicide is not a route we want to recommend as a good method of inquiry. It only stops at "wakening." Then it starts again. For twenty volumes.

It is a reciting because the author may not be the reader. The best recitations convince the audience that the reader is the author. Subterfuge. Suicide notes may be written in the third-person, twice removed. The reader joined the insurrection. Left the Asylum. Can a pragmatist recite a *Preface to a Twenty Volume Suicide Note*?[54]

Notes

1. I am indebted to critical comments on an early draft to Lee McBride, The College of Wooster; Jacoby A. Carter, John Jay College of Criminal Justice, New York; Mindy Tan, Purdue University; Corey Barnes, University of San Diego; and Alberto Urquidez, Gustavus Adolphus College. LeRoi Jones, *Preface to a Twenty Volume Suicide Note* ... (New York: Corinth Books, 1961).

2. Alain Locke, *Race Contacts and Interracial Relations: Lectures on the Theory and Practice of Race* (Washington, DC: Howard University Press, 1992), 187.

3. For Hoernle's history, see Robert Bernasconi, "The Paradox of Liberal Politics in the South African Context: Alfred Hoernle's Critique of Liberalisms Pact with White Domination," *Critical Philosophy of Race* 4 (2): 163–81.

4. See Leonard Harris and Charles Molesworth, *Alain L. Locke: Biography of a Philosopher* (Chicago, IL: University of Chicago Press, 2009).

5. I am indebted to Jacoby Carter for taking note that "universal" in Locke is not meant as a claim about traits supposedly encoded in all persons.

6. Wilbur M. Urban, *Fundamentals of Ethics: An Introduction to Moral Philosophy* (New York: Henry Holt, 1930), 77.

7. Alain Locke, "The Negro in Art," *Bulletin of the Association of American Colleges* 18 (November 1931): 363–4.

8. Cheryl Misak, *The American Pragmatists* (Oxford: Oxford University Press, 2015); Elizabeth Flower and Murray G. Murphey, *A History of Philosophy in America* (New York: Capricorn Books, 1977); Bruce Kuklick, *The Rise of American Philosophy: Cambridge, Massachusetts 1860-1930* (New Haven, CT: Yale University Press, 1977); Herbert Schneider, *A History of American Philosophy* (New York: Columbia University Press, 1946); Max H. Fisch (ed.), *Classic American Philosophers* (New York: Fordham University Press, 1996). See as an example of complex, nonlinear picture: Charlene Haddock Seigfried, *Pragmatism and Feminism: Reweaving the Social Fabric* (Chicago, IL: University of Chicago Press, 1996).

9. Alain Locke, "Values and Imperatives," in *American Philosophy, Today and Tomorrow*, ed. Horace M. Kallen and Sidney Hook (New York: Lee Furman, 1935), 312–33.

10. Bernard J. Stern and Alain Locke (eds.), *When Peoples Meet: Race and Culture Contact* (New York: Progressive Education Association, 1942); also see, for Locke on democracy and freedom, Jacoby Adeshei Carter and Leonard Harris (eds.), *Philosophic Values and World Citizenship: Locke to Obama and Beyond* (Lanham, MD: Rowman & Littlefield, 2010); Christopher Buck, *Alain Locke: Faith and Philosophy* (Los Angeles, CA: Kalimat Press, 2005).

11. See for "advocacy aesthetics," Richard Schusterman, *Surface and Depth: Dialetics of Criticism and Culture* (Ithaca, NY: Cornell University Press, 2002), 123–38.

12. See Jacoby A. Carter, *African American Contributions to the Americas' Cultures: A Critical Edition of Lectures by Alain Locke* (New York: Palgrave Macmillan, 2016); Louis Menard, *The Metaphysical Club: A Story of Ideas in America* (New York: Farrar, Straus & Giroux, 2001).

13. Robert Danisch, "Cosmopolitanism and Epideictic Rhetoric," in *Philosophic Values and World Citizenship: Locke to Obama and Beyond*, ed. Jacoby Adeshei Carter and Leonard Harris (Lanham, MD: Rowman & Littlefield, 2010), 147–64.

14. Locke, "Values and Imperatives," 321.

15. Alain Locke, "The Moral Imperatives for World Order," *Summary of Proceedings, Institute of International Relations*, Mills College, Oakland, CA (June 18–28, 1944), 19–20; Leonard Harris (ed.), *The Philosophy of Alain Locke: Harlem Renaissance and Beyond* (Philadelphia, PA: Temple University Press, 1989), 143.

16. Ibid., 19.

17. See Astrid Franke, "Struggling with Stereotypes: The Problems of Representing a Collective Identity," in *The Critical Pragmatism of Alain Locke: A Reader on Value Theory, Aesthetics, Community, Culture, Race, and Education*, ed. Leonard Harris (Lanham, MD: Rowman & Littlefield, 1999), 21–38; Chielozona Eze, "Ethnocentric Representations and Being Human in a Multiethnic Global World: Alain Locke Critique," in *Philosophic Values and World Citizenship: From Locke to Obama and Beyond*, ed. Jacoby Adeshei Carter and Leonard Harris (Lanham, MD: Rowman & Littlefield, 2010), 189–202.

18. See Dorothy Roberts, *Fatal Invention: How Science, Politics, and Big Business Re-Create Race in the Twenty-First Century* (New York: New Press, 2011).

19. Alain Locke, *The New Negro: An Interpretation* (New York: Albert and Charles Boni, 1925), 10.

20. John Dewey, *The Collected Works, vol. 1, 1925: Experience and Nature*, ed. Jo Ann Boydston (Carbondale: Southern Illinois University Press, 2008), 272; W. E. B. Du Bois, "Negro Art," *The Crisis* 22 (1921): 55–6.

21. See J. L. Mackie, "The Subjectivity of Values," in *Ethics: Inventing Right and Wrong* (Hammondsworth: Penguin Books, 1977), 15–49.

22. Alain Locke, "The Contribution of Race to Culture," in *The Philosophy of Alain Locke: Harlem Renaissance and Beyond*, ed. Leonard Harris (Philadelphia, PA: Temple University Press, 1989), 202; Alain Locke, "The Problem of Race Classification," in *The Philosophy of Alain Locke: Harlem Renaissance and Beyond*, ed. Leonard Harris (Philadelphia, PA: Temple University Press, 1989), 168; also see Jacoby A. Carter, "Does Race Have a Future?," *Transactions of the Charles S. Peirce Society: A Quarterly Journal in American Philosophy* 50 (1): 29–47.

23. Locke, "Contribution of Race to Culture," 203.

24. See Alex Sager, "Liberation Pragmatism: Dussel and Dewey in Dialogue," *Contemporary Pragmatism* 13 (2016): 1–22.

25. Octavia E. Butler, *Adulthood Rites* (New York: Aspect, 1997).

26. See David Walker, *David Walker's Appeal to the Coloured Citizens of the World* (New York: Farrar, Straus and Giroux, [1829] 1995); Lydia Child, *Appeal for That Class of Americans Called Africans* (Amherst: University of Massachusetts Press, [1833] 1996).

27. Veena Das, *Affliction: Health, Disease, Poverty* (New York: Fordham University Press, 2015), 131.

28. See Orlando Patterson, *Freedom: Volume 1: Freedom in the Making of Culture* (New York: Basic Books, 1991).

29. "Philosophy Born of Struggle," Conference records, Purdue University, Archives record: http://earchives.lib.purdue.edu/cdm/search/collection/msp194; Philosophy Born of Struggle discussions: University of KwaZulu Natal, Centre for Critical Research on Race and Identity, June 2016/'Philosophy Born of Struggle: A Philosophy Born of

Massacres—UKZN'"; "Meaning of 'Philosophy That Is Born of Struggle,'" www.youtube. com/watch?v=GGFpFzqr3aY; "Ethics of Insurrection," Texas State University, February 24, 2016, https://www.youtube.com/watch?list=PL00HLQPCtXjFa6XFb6aOltBEA_2LTYTXH& v=FWCcC00VQq4; Interview with Leonard Harris, Purdue University, 2009, earchives.lib. purdue.edu/cdm/singleitem/collection/msp194/id/72/rec/1; Philosophy Born of Struggle interview with Cornel West, 2013, www.youtube.com/watch?v=cVSdZDh3Pig&list=PL00 HLQPCtXjFsmpaFSbktzacGQreiiAkC; "Lewis Gordon: Living Thought, Living Freedom through Three Portraits of Philosophy Born of Struggle," Purdue University, May 27, 2014, www.truth-out.org/news/item/23971-living-thought-living-freedom-through-three-portraits-of-philosophy-born-of-struggle; Interview with Angela Davis, February 25, 2015, www.youtube.com/watch?v=q6Mfgl-5dd4.

30. I am indebted to Corey Barnes, University of San Diego, for raising this issue. I am indebted to Tommy Curry, Texas A&M University, for emphasizing the complexity of the relationship between philosophy and social practice.

31. Aaron Swartz, "Guerilla Open Access Manifesto," July 2008, https://archive.org/stream/ GuerillaOpenAccessManifesto/Goamjuly2008_djvu.txt.

32. See Leonard Harris, "Necro-Being: An Actuarial Account of Racism," *Res Philosophica* 95 (2): 273–302; also see Leonard Harris, "Insurrectionist Ethics: Advocacy, Moral Psychology, and Pragmatism," *Ethical Issues for a New Millennium: The Wayne Leys Memorial Lectures*, ed. John Howie (Carbondale: Southern Illinois University Press, 2002), 192–210.

33. See Angela Davis, *Are Prisons Obsolete?* (New York: Seven Stories Press, 2003); Dylan Rodriguez, *Forced Passages: Imprisoned Radical Intellectuals and the U.S. Prison Regime* (Minneapolis: University of Minnesota Press, 2006).

34. Jason D. Hill, *Becoming a Cosmopolitan* (Lanham, MD: Rowman & Littlefield, 2000), 121.

35. Ibid., 131. Arguably, Locke, Anthony Appiah, and Martha Nussbaum can be considered moderate cosmopolitans.

36. Arguably, Edward W. Blyden, J. G. Herder, and Pixley I. Seme were nativist; see Leonard Harris, "Cosmopolitanism and the African Renaissance: Pixley I. Seme and Alain L. Locke," *International Journal of African Renaissance Studies* 4 (2): 181–92.

37. Previous use of "cosmopolitan cruelty" in Harris, "Cosmopolitanism and the African Renaissance."

38. Cheikh Anta Diop, *Precolonial Black Africa* (Chicago, IL: Chicago Review Press, 1988); Fernand Braudel, *The Mediterranean and the Mediterranean World in the Age of Philip II* (Berkeley: University of California Press, 1996); Adam Hochschild, *King Leopold's Ghost: A Story of Greed, Terror, and Heroism in Colonial Africa* (New York: Houghton Mifflin Harcourt, 1999); Patterson, *Freedom*; Jared Diamond, *Guns, Germs, and Steel: The Fates of Human Societies* (New York: Norton, 1997).

39. Ngugi Wa Thiong'o, *Decolonizing the Mind: The Politics of Language in African Literature* (Chicago, IL: Chicago Review Press, 1998).

40. I am indebted to Tommy Curry, Texas A&M University, and Gretchen Curry, Alabama State University, for calling my attention to suicide rates and Black male rape.

41. Bill Schutt, *Cannibalism: A Perfectly Natural History* (Chapel Hill, NC: Algonquin Books, 2017).

42. Edwin Black, *War against the Weak: Eugenics and America's Campaign to Create a Master Race* (Washington, DC: Dialogue Press, 2003), 122.

43. James Scott, *Weapons of the Weak: Everday Forms of Peasant Resistanct* (New Haven, CT: Yale University Press, 1985); Black, *War against the Weak*.

44. See Leonard Harris, "What, Then, Is Racism?," in *Racism*, ed. Leonard Harris (Amherst, NY: Humanity Books), 437–51.

45. Jones, *Preface to a Twenty Volume Suicide Note ...*, 9 (section 4 of "Hymn for Lanie Poo").

46. Walker, *David Walker's Appeal to the Coloured Citizens*. This is a list of common terms used by Walker to describe misery.

47. See Leonard Harris, "The Concept of Racism: An Essentially Contested Concept?," *Centennial Review* 42 (2): 217–32.

48. Plato, *Republic*, 514a–520a.

49. Qtd. in Thavolia Glymph, *Out of the House of Bondage: The Transformation of the Plantation Household* (Cambridge: Cambridge University Press, 2008), 35.

50. Owen J. Flanagan, *Varieties of Moral Personality: Ethics and Psychological Realism* (Cambridge, MA: Harvard University Press, 1991); or John M. Doris, *Lack of Character: Personality and Moral Behavior* (Cambridge, MA: Harvard University Press, 2002).

51. Erving Goffman, *Asylums: Essays on the Social Situation of Mental Patients and Other Inmates* (Garden City, NY: Anchor Books, 1961).

52. Jones, *Preface to a Twenty Volume Suicide Note ...*

53. Richard H. Crossman (ed.), *The God That Failed* (New York: Harper & Brothers, 1949).

54. I leave it as an open question whether historically classical pragmatism could recite the *Note*.

PART V
BRIDGES TO FUTURE TRADITIONS

CHAPTER 12
UNIVERSAL HUMAN
LIBERATION: COMMUNITY AND
MULTICULTURALISM (1998)

In "Universal Human Liberation: Community and Multiculturalism," Harris considers a seemingly intractable issue—should those committed to the negation of misery and necro-being favor (1) universal human liberation or (2) the interests of particular social entities? Universal human liberation includes freedom from various boundaries, including boundaries of national and racial ideation that separate and rank communities hierarchically, boundaries that exclude the poor and subjugated groups from the basic dignities afforded to recognized members of the human family, and boundaries that mark stigmatized groups as the appropriate recipients of distrust, humiliation, and terror. Harris argues that "the pursuit of universal human liberation always occurs through the struggles of particular communities." But it is not necessary to embrace a doxastic picture of social entities within which social entities invariably embody stable interests and essences. Through representative heuristics, social entities can form as socially constructed coalitions and adversarial groups (e.g., workers, feminists, and racialized ethnic groups). These adversarial groups can strive for universal human liberation, all the while fully anticipating the disbanding of these socially constructed adversarial groups. The formation and subsequent liberation of the proletariat anticipates a classless society—the negation of both the proletariat and the bourgeoisie. Liberation from race-based oppression will require the negation of the racial identity of the oppressor and the oppressed. It is here, in these adversarial particularities, in these resistance struggles, that we are most likely to find the social agency for universal human liberation.

I consider a seemingly intractable conflict—the conflict between favoring universal human liberation and favoring the interests of particular social entities. I consider alternatives to the view that a particularity should be favored for instrumental reasons, for example, that we should support the working class because its interest will help destroy capitalism, or that we should support existing races or ethnic group proto-nationalisms to protect their cultural integrity.

A doxastic conception of thought takes the following form: ideas, beliefs, attitudes, virtues, and morals are coterminous with actions, behaviors, policies, and institutions. *The Closing of the American Mind* argues that the American mind, as a sort of collective thinking entity with definitive traits—traits directly associated with behaviors—has become intolerant, invirtuous, and conceptually misguided in part, because education is not encouraging the pursuit of certitude, knowledge, and the good.[1] This approach considers relativist commitment to ethnicities not only contrary to the spirit of democracy but also an approach that fails to acknowledge that cultures are not all equal. *The Opening of the American Mind* argues that America has been historically plural.[2] The "American mind" has different traits on this view; and cultural diversity and particularity offers beneficial contributions. Both approaches, however, presuppose a doxastic picture of thought and action. Significant disjunction between thought and action would suggest that actions, behaviors, policies, and institutions considered odious may be associated with ideas considered laudable. Disjunctions of this sort must be treated as less than significant for an argument presupposing a "mind" in some substantive way encoded in a social entity.

A doxastic picture of social entities takes the following form. Social entities embody interests or essences coterminous with their agency. Such entities as nation-states, working classes, native populations, women, and so like can be thought to have interests and essences. The doxastic picture of social entities has been criticized by numerous philosophers.[3] Characteristically, for example, Marx is criticized for believing that the working class would be a cohesive group, pursuing ownership, control, communal management, and fair distribution of wealth.[4] Marx is also criticized for treating social entities as if they were ontologically real, that is, undifferentiated groups. However, numerous philosophers share a desire for universal human liberation.

Universal human liberation includes freedom from the very boundaries of the names through which freedom is sought—the deafening boundaries of national and racial ideation separating communities; boundaries excluding the poor, workers, proletariat, and the wretched from peership in the human family; and boundaries subordinating the powerless from participation, ownership, and control of material resources.

The above view of universal human liberation hardly includes all of the features associated with the concept. Marx, for example, would certainly include the realization of humanity's species being, for example, transformation of nature, negation of alienation, and self-realization through participatory control of the means of production. Humanity, or rather, liberated workers would be empowered to exercise their distinctly human capacities without the fetters of alienating mythologies that fail to reasonably conform to reasoned scientific judgment. Edward W. Blyden, for example, would include the realization of ethnic empowerment. Empowerment of ethnic kinds, that is, Africans, Asians, Europeans, Hispanics, and so like, would allow the possibility of equality between natural kinds; authentic cultures could flourish, and modernity would be enhanced because each kind would feel sufficiently motivated to improve their material conditions and make their unique contributions to universal civilization. Deweyan pragmatists would reject the idea of an end state. When universal human interest was achieved, however, the Deweyan pragmatist would focus on the importance of scientific reasoning as a way of maximizing changes for enhanced flourishing. This is why the Deweyan pragmatist avoids the conflict between deontological as well as teleological conceptions of justice.[5] The Deweyan pragmatist also avoids conceiving persons as genuine if and only if they are either encoded in communities or are perceived as isolated individuals.[6]

I believe that the above depiction of universal human liberation is defensible, although insufficiently developed. A good deal of the argument here is, moreover, admittedly speculative, tentative, and suggestive.

The pursuit of universal human liberation always occurs through the struggles of particular communities. Yet critics of the ontological status of social entities often deny that social entities (1) pursue interests that would liberate themselves and the whole of humanity, and (2) deny that social entities have the agency, power, or capacity to cause or create universal human liberation through the empowerment of any particular community. Moreover, warranting "empowerment" of a particularity, namely, the authority to decide what persons have preferred treatment in receiving jobs, homes, business opportunities, healthcare services, and expenses for schools is, on some accounts, warranting authoritarianism.

The condition of liberation for a particularity is either its own negation or its universalization.

The liberation of a population subjugated by race is an example of a particularity in which liberation includes, but is not limited to, liberation from identification by race. Peoples and cultures can exist and flourish quite well without confinement to racial identities. It is fallacious to identify race and culture as if they were inextricably mutually causal and invariably and eternally tied. I have argued elsewhere that the primary interest of any social race is the negation of all identity by race and empowerment through control of assets.[7] There is nothing redeeming about entrapment in debilitating stereotypes of race. Liberation requires the negation of the racial identity of the oppressor and the oppressed. Moreover, the negation of the links between biology and culture, biology and character, biology and potential, and biology and rights should be negated. However, the death of racial identity does not mean that racism is dead. Rather, the negation of all institutions, interests, and benefits that sustain oppression by race is required.

In a nonracist world, social races would not exist. No one would be born into a race or have a nonmoral duty to be the representative of a race. Internal unity of the raciated is a necessary instrumental condition for the possibility of independence from the terror of race-based oppression: the unspeakable holocausts ravaging Gypsies, Kurds, or Black South Africans, as well as race-based working-class exploitation.[8] The social instruments of racial identity, however, are hardly transhistorical. The enriching and vibrant reality of African culture, on the other hand, has transhistorical warrant as a constantly evolving source of universalizable cultural good and local cultural sustenance.

The liberation of woman is an example of a particularity in which a condition of liberation includes, but is not limited to, engagement in universality. Stereotyping women as incapable of exercising authority as soldiers, corporate executives, or athletes is arguably extinguished when such roles are no longer seen as the provinces reserved for men. If they are considered provinces in which persons are engaged, the stereotype is no longer operative. Multiple identities and trait ascriptions may be common in a world that has achieved universal human liberation, that is, a world that does not restrict persons to roles assumed inherently and inalterably encoded in their gender, race, ethnicity, class, or nation.

The warrant for the universalization of well-being cuts across lines of race, ethnicity, gender, nation, and class. The negation of starvation, communicable diseases, debilitating but curable illnesses, preventable premature deaths, torture, rape, unjust incarceration, degrading insults, and demeaning treatment require the imposition of values across lines of particularity. The universalization of these interests is, in effect, the universalization of interest intrinsic to particularities.

One way to see the importance of the universalizing of values and the realization of universal human interest is to consider the following: it is time someone said it—multiculturalism is dead. Monoculturalism has already won. Discourse about multiculturalism is just that—discourse. It does not pick out or point to a reality in much of the world nor does it pick out or point to any substantive trends. If the history of America, for example, is the history of cultural exchanges between historically and contemporary evolving social entities, those entities are now far more similar than ever before—there is one currency, banking system, common sources and forms of energy, near-standardized forms of medical care, and even common rules regulating garbage disposal. There are fewer language differences, religious differences, loyalties to tribes, clans, lords, chiefs, kings, queens, city-states, and nations; fewer races, ethnic groups, and peoples generating loyalty; fewer wars of attrition than the earth has known since the decline of the iron age.

Pragmatists such as John Dewey favored using scientific principles to explain human behavior and the use of the experimental method to engineer social improvements. However, Dewey believed that the future was always open; accident, a change in views or opinions, chance, or new discoveries might easily alter the course of future events. Alain Locke, a radical pragmatist, criticized persons that relied on the scientific method in hopes that they would not forget the importance of imperatives, that is, moral or value imperatives.[9] Such imperatives included, for Locke, the need to avoid the imposition of absolutes and the need to promote cultural reciprocity and tolerance. And one of Locke's close working associates, especially in the 1940s, Ruth Benedict, argued for a form of cultural relativism in her early anthropological work. This version held that cultures were incommensurable, that is, meanings were endogenous to a culture and are not translatable to persons not sharing the mores and ways of a culture. Cultures, for Benedict, sustained values at best relevant to their own environment.

None of the assumed consequences of a world that one might expect, if the above perspectives of Dewey, Locke, or Benedict prevailed, have occurred. We might assume, for example, that accident, chance, uncertainty, and incommensurability between cultures would continue to assure a world of substantive differences. Such variables have failed to generate difference. The future is not open—diversities of the past cannot happen, authentic racial kinds cannot continue, ethnicities segregated from the influence of world cultures are no longer a possibility, and substantively independent nation-states are a relic. Everywhere, cultures that fail to offer some form of commensurability with modernity die; everywhere, tolerance exists if and only if the monoculture of the world flourishes and within it discourse and exchange occurs. The tourist trade is one of the most common forms of cultural commonality. Cultural reciprocity is too often a matter of the native, as an object of our gaze, functioning as a living relic. Simultaneously, the very world of modernity, whether it is Broadway in New York or Carnival in Bahia, makes itself an object for its own agents as well as an object of a gaze—tourists visit these sites while these sites are filled with self-conscious agents actively creating.

The monocultural world Marx, Adam Smith, Ibn Khaldun, and Edward W. Blyden imagined has turned out to exist. The monocultural world may be the result of imposed values; if so, those imposed values are often normalized.

There is no "natural" social world in any event, which is analogous to the myth that nature exists on earth outside the context of being under the control of humanity or substantively effected by humanity. There simply are no significant unmapped spaces on the planet. For Marx, capitalism would universalize the world. Capitalism would destroy all feudal models of production, all antiquated forms of barter in deference to a money economy, all languages that were not coterminous with the language of commerce. Marx was right in these regards. Even if capitalism has not destroyed, in its wake, all religions, pagan rituals, or nation-states, it has substantively helped universalize—make common—standard ways of doing business, using money, and creating wealth. Even if capitalism has not created clear class divisions that stand in clear opposition to one another, it has helped to create fairly common sorts of classes. Socialist, communist, and capitalist alike use surprisingly similar standards; at the least, there are agreed conversion tables for exchanging the currencies of every nation and more world treaties regulating the rules of war, employment, and citizenship than ever before. It is at least arguable that the class struggle is being waged between enemies far more similar than ever before, despite the romanticization of postmodern difference.

Khaldun was right—law would prove among the most powerful tools for making common the Koran. It would prove to be the most powerful tool for making common world religions as well.

And Blyden was right—the world is divided between geographic ethnic kinds—Africans, Europeans, Asians, and Hispanics. These are hardly racial kinds of the sort Blyden believed were the representative stock of pure blood types. They are, however, dominant identities through which people often identify their cultural and geographic loyalties.

Multiculturalism points to, given the reality of monoculturalism, the inescapable reality of ontological entities. Social entities can be the conduits for, and sites of, universal human liberation. That is, the transhistorical interest and traits (if not essences) encoded in particularities, equally as important as impermanent, transient, elliptical, and illusory interests and traits, are both embedded in particularities.

Changes in structures would signal a change in the reality of racism, not the disappearance of temporal ideations that may or may not spell change in the material realities, social entities, or social formations of populations—contrary to a doxastic picture of ideas and behaviors in which ideas are nearly invariably associated with, if not considered directly causal of, behavior. Race, for example, is a temporal social construction: what counts as a social race in America is hardly what counts as a social race in Sri Lanka. There are constantly shifting identities.

> As a culture, we call ourselves Spanish when referring to ourselves as a linguistic group and when copping out. It is then that we forget our predominant Indian genes ... We call ourselves Hispanic or SpanishAmerican or Latin American or Latin when linking ourselves to other Spanish-speaking peoples of the Western hemisphere and when copping out. We call ourselves Mexican-American to signify we are neither Mexican nor American, but more the noun "American" than the adjective "Mexican" (and when copping out).[10]

Mestizo may affirm both Indian and Spanish heritage, raza may refer to Chicanos' racial identity. "Copping out" is an invariable feature of positively identifying with a race or ethnic group. Authenticity is not achieved by either identifying or copping out. Multiple and shifting ethnic as well as raciated identities are rather common. However, the negation of race as a temporal illusion, or recognition that ethnicity is an unstable category, is hardly identical to the negation of racism or ethnocentrism.

The egregious joys and power acquired through the monetary profit secured by racists and the advantages enjoyed by dominant populations in racist societies is not negated by ideation changes. The social entities and social formations are already arranged to generate wealth, jobs, and opportunities for dominant populations. That is, changed ownership, control, participation, and access to material reality will have a far greater impact on creating a deraciated and socially viable world.

The possibility of human liberation is contingent on the agencies and interests of social entities. Communitarians are right to think that special obligations to families, relatives, friends, and neighborhoods, as well as broader identities such as nation, ethnicity, or gender, are obligations we have that we never choose. Moreover, we must attach intrinsic, noninstrumental value to social entities and formations that sustain special obligations. Communitarians and pluralists are wrong, however, in assuming that social entities and formations are stable and should never be the object of destruction. I see no reason, for example, to warrant the existence of slavocracies such as pre–Civil War America.

Social groups are the decisive forces shaping human history, present realities, and future situations. Reasoning through social entities is not an unfortunate form of self-delusion—acting as if one is, represents, stands for, means, is obligated to, bonded to, and is the conduit for a social entity or social formation. Representative heuristics—the way individuals define themselves as representing collective entities—is a normal feature of cognition. The utilization of representative heuristics is simply not inherently oppressive. Erroneous strategies, inferences, and implications can bedevil representative heuristics as well as reasoning, as if one in no way represented, stood for, or was bonded to others. However, there is no reason to believe that existing social entities are permanent driving forces of human history; no reason to assume that universal human liberation equates each entity gaining authenticity according to its Aristotelian essence.

There are strong reasons to earnestly consider what entities we warrant, what particular and universal goods they offer, and what counts as the mode of liberation associated with their endogenous traits.

Contrary to a doxastic picture of social entities—a picture in which social entities invariably embody stable interests and essences—it is the adversarial features of social entities that may be the most important arguable sources for liberation. It may not be the "working class" as an undifferentiated entity with an array of definitive interests and modes of agency, which is the engine of universal human liberation. However, it may be the adversarial sector that warrants special regard for its intrinsic worth. One way to see what I mean by this is by considering the reality of radical traditions. Adversarial traditions, that is, traditions of resistance that emanate from oppressed social entities, are voices that often perceive community as becoming. That is, the immiserated members of social entities—women, African Americans, Hispanics, workers, and so on—can only pursue liberation by engaging in resistance struggles intended to create new traditions and alternative communities.[11] That is, new bonds. If our imagined communities are the communities of the downtrodden, wretched, degraded, raped, victims of cruelty, the objects of viciousness, then they are subjects integral to a conceptualized community that is to become. When the least well-off are agents in the moral community, the future is a becoming in a way that counts the immiserated.

The disjunction between ideas and actions, as well as the disjunction between social entities and agency, do not render irrelevant the import of ideas or entities. The agency of particularities are necessarily the agencies, conduits, and forces that create the reality of universality.

A radical transformation of misery, exploitation, starvation, the hopelessness of immigrants, racial stereotyping, and ethnocentrism may well depend on our achieving, through the aegis of our multiple locations, conditions for the possibility of liberation. Moreover, it may be especially the agency of the excluded, downtrodden, wretched, and immiserated of particularities and their transhistorical interests that hold the key to future realities. That is, the adversarial, insurrectional, and revolutionary struggle to materially and institutionally create communities fundamentally different from the horribly confining and destructive boundaries currently constricting freedom.[12]

Notes

1. See Allan D. Bloom, *The Closing of the American Mind: How Higher Education Has Failed Democracy and Impoverished the Souls of Today's Students* (New York: Simon and Schuster, 1987). Similar social psychology approaches are evident in such works as Carter G. Woodson, *The Mind of the Negro as Reflected in Letters Written during the Crisis, 1800–1860* (Washington, DC: Association for the Study of Negro Life and History, 1926); Earl E. Thorpe, *The Mind of the Negro: An Intellectual History of Afro-Americans* (Baton Rouge, LA: Ortlieb Press, 1970).

2. Lawrence W. Levine, *The Opening of the American Mind: Canons, Culture, and History* (Boston, MA: Beacon Press, 1996).

3. See Dwight Furrow, *Against Theory: Continental and Analytic Changes in Moral Philosophy* (New York: Routledge, 1995).

4. See for an interpretation of Marx that considers his historical materialism and the role of classes as central to Marx's philosophy, Allen W. Wood, *Karl Marx* (Boston, MA: Routledge and Kegan Paul, 1981).

5. See Henry S. Richardson, "Beyond Good and Right: Toward a Constructive Ethical Pragmatism," *Philosophy & Public Affairs* 24 (2, Spring 1995): 108–41.

6. I am indebted to Judith Green, Fordham University, for suggesting this article: Sandra B. Rosenthal, "The Individual, the Community, and the Reconstruction of Values," in *Philosophy and the Reconstruction of Culture: A Pragmatic Essay after Dewey*, ed. John J. Stuhr (Albany: SUNY Press, 1993), 59–77.

7. See Leonard Harris, "What, Then, Is Racism?," in *Racism*, ed. Leonard Harris (Amherst, NY: Humanity Books, 1999), 437–50; also see Leonard Harris, "Rendering the Subtext: Subterranean Deconstruction Project," in *The Philosophy of Alain Locke: Harlem Renaissance and Beyond*, ed. Leonard Harris (Philadelphia, PA: Temple University Press, 1989), 279–89; and Leonard Harris, "Historical Subjects and Interests: Race, Class, and Conflict," in *The Year Left*, ed. Michael Sprinkler et al. (New York: Verso, 1986), 91–106.

8. See Robin D. G. Kelley, *Race Rebels: Culture, Politics, and the Black Working Class* (New York: The Free Press, 1994).

9. See Alain Locke, "Values and Imperatives," in *The Philosophy of Alain Locke: Harlem Renaissance and Beyond*, ed. Leonard Harris (Philadelphia, PA: Temple University Press, 1989), 31–50. Also see, for the unavoidability of metaphysical commitments or imperatives, Sidney Hook, *The Metaphysics of Pragmatism* (Chicago: Open Press, 1927).

10. G. Anzaldua, *Borderlands/La Frontera: The New Mestiza* (San Francisco, CA: Spinsters/Aunt Lute, 1987), 63.

11. I argue this in "The Horror of Tradition or How to Burn Babylon and Build Benin While Reading a *Preface to a Twenty Volume Suicide Note*," *Philosophical Forum* 24 (1–3, Fall–Spring, reprinted in 1992–3): 94–119, reprinted in John P. Pittman (ed.), *African-American Perspectives and Philosophical Traditions* (New York: Routledge, 1997), 94–119.

12. See Henry A. Giroux, "Insurgent Multiculturalism and the Promise of Pedagogy," in *Multiculturalism: A Critical Reader*, ed. David T. Goldberg (Oxford: Blackwell), 328–43.

CHAPTER 13
COMMUNITY: WHAT TYPE OF ENTITY AND WHAT TYPE OF MORAL COMMITMENT? (2001)

In "Community: What Type of Entity and What Type of Moral Commitment," Harris argues that "conceiving of communities as complicated, interlaced populations and dropping the language of the absolute 'Other' recommends defensible moral commitments and explanations." This helps us to discern which moral commitment is more compelling: fighting for the liberation of a raciated ethnicity (race/ethnic enclave communities) or fighting for the liberation of the working class? The answer to such a question will depend on the context, particularly which type of social entity and what type of moral commitments we have to that entity. As argued in "What, Then, Is Racism?" Harris maintains that races are not stable ontological entities. Rather, African American (or Black) social entities are best described as complex variegated, raciated ethnicities. The Black community is not explained well by a singular set "authentically Black or African" values; rather Black communities are best explained as complicated interlaced associations. This allows us to recognize that racial ethnicities are bifurcated by rich and poor—that is, there are working class and managerial class Black communities. This means that one's moral commitment to the abolition of capitalist commodification may affect particular enclaves of the Black community differently. Black and white may find a common cause, common moral commitments that cut across race distinctions. Moreover, conceiving of Black communities and white communities as absolute Others, conceals the various commitments Black American Protestant Christian communities hold in common with white American Protestants. Harris suggests that the Black community is well-explained by multiple strategies to secure income, assets, dignity, and control over labor and labor time. On this view, "Identities are platforms we negotiate, use, create, and maintain to help form social locations to extend prima facie trust, shared experiences, and information." Communities are groups whose future is contingent on variables that shape their character—"there are ties that bind, but not invariably." Harris, thus, offers a way to conceive raciated communities avoiding both the absolutism of romantic racial ontology and color-blind ideology. Harris hopes to provoke motivation to sustain and create the sort of communities needed to help destroy the terror, exploitation, and humiliation of antiblack racism.

Communities are forms of association. Thinking of communities as disconnected aggregates or ontological entities, I venture, is misleading. Conceiving of communities as complicated, interlaced populations and dropping the language of the absolute

"Other" recommends defensible moral commitments and explanations. I discuss how moral commitments are influenced by the way we explain and conceive communities.

Which moral commitment is more compelling: fighting for the liberation of a raciated ethnicity (race/ethnic enclave communities) or fighting for the liberation of the working class? If the liberation of the working class will end racism and racial liberation is the highest priority, then fighting for the liberation of the working class has a strong moral appeal. On this view, the exploiting classes, including Black members of such classes, would not be considered a group for which liberation is designed. However, if class liberation will not end racism across lines of class as predicted, then the moral appeal to fight for the liberation of the working class is less compelling.

If racism will end with the success of race or ethnic enclave economies, then a moral commitment to a raciated ethnic group uplift outweighs appeals to class liberation: the ending of racism on this view means that Black members of exploiting classes can sustain their class status but would no longer suffer racial discrimination or insults. In addition, if racial or ethnic identities are considered an abiding source of pride, self-worth, and self-confidence, then high moral commitment to a racial group is quite reasonable. Under the condition of racial slavery, for example, every Black person had a good reason to only focus on Black abolition. However, if a prediction of racism ending with the success of racial enclave economies in a modern capitalist world is false and the highest priority is racial liberation, then the moral appeal of romantic racialism is less than compelling.

The moral commitments we should accept for the purpose of class or racial/ethnic liberation are heavily influenced by the efficacy of our predictions—predictions that depend on the saliency placed on race and class as causal variables. The usual way of thinking about moral commitments, I believe, is often confused because the crucial role of explanatory prediction is undervalued and because conceiving of communities as ontological entities, entities in a world of Manichaean "Others," lends itself to untenable moral positions.

Raciated ethnicities and classes are, I suggest, fundamentally two different kinds of entities and merit certain important distinct considerations when deciding on appropriate moral commitments—especially commitments to communities that entail strata of both race and class divisions.

The term "raciated ethnicity," which best describes African Americans, collapses the distinction between race and ethnicity.[1] A raciated ethnicity is to be understood as a social construction. "The term 'social race' is used because these groups or categories [e.g., Negroes in America, mulattos in Brazil, and mestizos in Mexico] are socially, not biologically, defined in all of our American societies, although the terms by which they are labeled may have originally referred to biological characteristics."[2] Actual biological categories have little to do with the way social races are defined. Actual ancestry and appearance are normally manipulated, for example, one drop of sub-Saharan African blood makes someone Black in the United States rather than 51 percent; white women almost never announce they are related to Black women by virtue of often sharing the same paternal great-grandfather. Even if there are no integrative structures between Blacks in the United States and Blacks in Brazil, the world of racial identity is imposed. Race can refer to a category of individuals with socially ascribed properties. The integrative structures of family, business, religion, language, class, or geographical ties help shape ethnic traits; categorization as a race forms one such trait. A raciated ethnicity, however, is not the same kind of entity as a class.

Classes always share types of assets, skills, income, and ownership patterns as integrative structures. Classes invariably divide societies and may be conceived as divided into upper, lower, and middle; divided in terms of proletariat, working, petty bourgeois, bourgeoisie, ruling, and capitalist classes; or divided in status definitive terms such as managerial, service, wage-earning, salaried, property-owning, and business class. Each of these modes of describing a "class" rests on background assumptions about the nature of humans, explicitly or implicitly. A few of these ways will be discussed later in this chapter.

Liberals tend to think of persons as individual actors, subject to the whims of fate or evolution and likely to fall into one of three rather arbitrary divisions of upper, middle, or lower class. Liberals are likely to describe relations in terms of "interactions" between individuals or loose-fitting groups and view development as flowing in tendentious progress or mysteriously ordained development. The existence of classes tends to be considered relatively stable with, at best, changes in the future world where the least well-off may improve their lowly condition, while class divisions remain. Class membership is usually considered achieved by the force of character, luck, heritage, or some set of personal traits. Aristotle, Thorstein Veblen, and Robert K. Merton, for example, thought in terms similar to the description of the upper, middle, and lower classes.

For Karl Marx, it is the arrangement of competing economic interests, labor, and the means of production that are the primary sources of value. Persons are driven by material condition, and as producers within defined circumstances, those circumstances shape what they tend to think and how they tend to act. The existence and ownership of private property determines, more than any other variable, inequalities of income, status, and privilege. Class conflicts tend toward teleology of universal human liberation. Classes are objectively defined; independent of how individuals define themselves, they fit into a class according to their relationship to production. For Marxists, such as E. O. Wright or David Harvey, liberation is a matter of the ending of class conflict, thereby making possible the existence of freely producing agents unfettered by harmful and unnecessary national, racial, ethnic, and gender divisions.

For Max Weber and Émile Durkheim, persons are driven by a psychosocial desire for status, for a sense of being worthy, and to be owners of the symbols and sources of power. The hoarding of opportunities and transferring of privileges to a select group are some of the main causes of inequalities such as income and ownership. Class membership is defined by social perceptions and market positions (e.g., occupation and the degree of deference or privilege enjoyed). Status is the source of privilege. Thus, a eunuch may be rich but he is always without the status of an aristocrat, even if the aristocrat is poor, destitute, and stupid. At best, the least well-off may gain status markers or status markers associated with the least well-off may become less offensive. The probable course of life is shaped by a variety of structures, for example, rules, formalized behaviors, laws, and methods of controlling life choices. The classes that exist might change for Weber, but classes as such are endemic to our being. Managerial, industrial worker, peasant, or some other form of segmented market descriptions may be used. However, no one class is driven to ensure universal human liberation. Whether character traits, modes of production, or structures conjoined with sociopsychological natures, classes in the previous examples are understood in terms of market segments corresponding to kinds, more or less permanently segregated and causing behavior across lines of national origin, ethnic identity, racial composition, or geographic location.

Raciated ethnicities share properties like skin color, language, and tastes (aggregated traits) as integrative structures. They also share, in a very uneven fashion, common experiences and status that help form group behaviors and allegiances. The core culture of African Americans, for example, includes Christian churches of the Protestant or Baptist sort, deep race consciousness especially of vicious exclusion, family structures ravaged by slavery, limited asset inheritances, and expressive cultural forms of dance or songs and Africa, especially Anglophone West Africa, which is seen as the ancestral home. There are institutions that enliven and sustain these relationships. But it is false that Blacks not bound to the core culture or not sharing its traits are inauthentic and necessarily lacking in self-respect.

A raciated ethnicity is composed of relational variables. Members of a raciated ethnicity, for example, biologically reproduce one another. That is, they intermarry, with the parents passing their assets on to their progeny. Approximately 93 percent of all Black and white Americans marry within their race; Asians, especially Japanese American women, are highly likely to marry outside their ethnicity. "Hispanic American," for example, is a census category that includes any number of races; it is a language formation that binds and is a marker or other binding trait such as religion and heritage. In another example, the majority of Blacks outside of Africa are bound together by Portuguese and a South American experience (Black Americans are not representative, linguistically or culturally, of Blacks outside of sub-Saharan Africa, although they are collectively the wealthiest and thereby dominate media presentations internationally). Thus, some populations are relatively stable breeding groups and others are in radical transition, but all are highly likely to change marital patterns. What sanctions and rewards incline persons to form long-term commitments and parental habits?

Heritage is a proxy for ethnicity and, in a racist society, a proxy for race. Raciated ethnicities have a stake in maintaining their ethnicity, if not their race.[3] Persons of the same social kind tend to trust one another. Every survey on trust tells us that whites distrust Blacks more than they distrust other whites or Asians. Blacks, given a history of suffering from racist stereotypes, do not trust one another as much as whites trust other whites. Blacks, however, receive far greater respect and recognition from other Blacks, while whites tend to deny Blacks high regard and privileges.

The most important ties we have are those that bind wife and husband, father and mother, siblings, cousins, aunts, uncles, lovers, and friends; that bind us to sources of sustenance; including jobs, retirement benefits, and health care resources; that bind us to the physical neighborhoods wherein we feel comfortable and to the people who share, even if imagined, similar experiences; that bind us to the people we share our vacation time with and, when depressed, our deepest fears. All of these ties shape communities. Such relations are often discussed in terms of "community." Our first responsibilities and thereby moral commitments are to those that constitute this day-to-day world. Yet, status, class, and race markers complicate these very real day-to-day relations. One way to understand the distinction I am describing is to think that a raciated ethnicity is a category like male/female, Christian/Muslim, or citizen/foreigner, and continua such as rich/poor, ruling class/working class, and so on bifurcate this category.[4] We often gain a sense of self-worth from embedded identities and feel deeply humiliated or insulted when the group or one of its members is treated with disdain. Yet, I believe, it is the complexity of categories and continua that shape outcomes. However, believing in the universal salience of race as a categorical or continua variable is deeply misguided.[5]

Racism, I believe, is a way of killing by viciously robbing the assets of one population for the benefit of another. Differential accumulation of assets and opportunities are compounded, recurring exponentially over generations and thereby perpetuating radical categorical differences. However, contrary to Derrick A. Bell, I do not believe that raciated entities are permanently constructed in their current form. Even if they are, they do not, contrary to romantic racialists, constitute stable ontologies reflective of human natures or historically causing, invariably, arrangements of human life across stratifications, classes, categories, and status.[6]

One way to see why races are not stable ontological entities with the type of forceful integrative structures as classes is by considering moral conflicts that entail competing conceptions of the Black community. The goal of the following example is to suggest that it is possible to have a moral commitment to the Black community (as a collection of core associations)—which is a commitment of a certain kind—and a commitment to the working class. The latter commitment conflicts with a community commitment in cases where there is a conflict between "workers" (inclusive of white workers) and Blacks who are not members of the working class. Although the Black bourgeoisie or managerial class has never been large enough to matter much, it has been large enough to generate conflicts with those that have a commitment to the working class or to a romantic racialist definition of the "Black community" (i.e., biological or socially defined races forming closed historical kinds within which emotional and material goods should be developed). I limit the discussion to romantic racialist and socialist, bourgeoisie or not, in the following discussion.

Edward W. Blyden understands the world in terms of ethnic kinds (African, European, and Asian) coterminous with racial kinds (Negroid, Caucasian, and Asiatic) and numerous subgroups of races.[7] He, however, has a singularly similar understanding of human nature as his fellow romantic racialists: all persons are fundamentally driven to constitute separate racial kinds and form civilizations corresponding to those kinds. "Communities" for Blyden are always raciated. Analogously, Johannes G. Herder as well as Herbert Spencer cut up the world in similar ways—biology, nature, and consciousness cause behaviors according to racial and ethnic kinds.

Blyden uses a sort of interactionalist account (races need their own nations so they can have equitable interactions with each other). He is dedicated to a raciated ethnicity (African Negroes in his case) and is simultaneously a socialist (dedication to the uplift of the working class and equitable distributions of social goods). The reason that he can hold dual commitments is that the two entities are fundamentally different kinds. However, he also believes that an authentic Negro would be motivated by unique African traits (such as communal, deeply religious, expressive, and so on), that Blacks formed an ontological entity, and that anyone who does not agree with him is existentially inauthentic. Such general traits, however, provide no certain direction about whether to support workers against capitalism, whether to believe that class differences are inevitable, or whether managerial classes have the best interest of the least well-off at heart. Blyden has no way of neatly deciding about class conflicts within each racial or national kind, nor does he have a way of arguing for class unity across lines of national kinds. Thus, to the extent that he believes in the universal salience of race, his moral commitments are so tied and there is no way for him to be committed to a socialism that crosses ethnic and racial boundaries.

Marcus Garvey's Universal Negro Improvement Association (UNIA), the largest nationalist movement in the history of African Americans; W. E. B. Du Bois's National Association for the Advancement of Colored People, the nascent organization that promoted legal changes to segregation as well as nonviolent direct action protests and directed boycotts; and Hubert Henry Harrison's Socialist Party, a party that exemplified the largest allegiance of African Americans to socialism—all vied for the loyalty of African Americans. The road to liberation from racism, they believed, was dependent on their approach. Moral commitment was demanded by each group and opposing approaches were decried as fundamentally harmful and indicative of approaches that created self-deprecation or inclined persons to be self-deprecators.

The tremendous migration of African Americans from declining agricultural and rural locations to the growing industrial and urban centers in the early twentieth century provided a new material situation. Increased incomes and effective mass communications enhanced the process of ethnogenesis. Progressively, African Americans saw themselves as a race and an ethnic group distinct from and oppressed by other groups. Kansas City, Chicago, Cleveland, Philadelphia, and New York became not only important industrial centers employing African Americans but also cultural centers where previously itinerant musicians, artists, and journalists could find regular employment and maintain stable families. American slavery had already accomplished the destruction of nearly all native African religions and, thus, African Americans were a homogenous religious population. At most, there were competing denominations and subpractices that were African survivals or new adaptations but no specific gods or coherent faiths of the Mende, Fulani, or Asante. Even voodoo, surviving especially in the Caribbean and South America, survived in America as only a practice within Christianized communities. Civil religious orientations were divided in the same way that humanist traditions were divided, that is, along competing conceptions of moral commitment, self-conceptions, justifiable methods of change, visions of possible futures, explanations, predictions, and conceptions of instrumental strategies to effect change.

By the early twentieth century, tremendous numbers of nearly every ethnic and racial population in the world became urbanized, compelled to join the industrial working class, and watch folk cultures transformed by commercialism and commodification. Black soldiers returned to the United States after the First World War as victors, having participated in segregated units, paid far less than white soldiers, never promoted on merit, and denied any substantive leadership roles in combat or in ordering white soldiers. They were American soldiers and victors nonetheless. "What is liberation?" had to be answered in terms of what it is to be liberated for a race, an ethnic group, and every class and status shared with all other Americans. Approaches to this question were thus peppered with numerous background assumptions about moral commitments to community and visions of the future. These background assumptions were foregrounded when irreconcilable competing commitments had to be faced.

The "Garvey Must Go" campaign was an example of irreconcilable moral commitments. Socialist parties and numerous liberals such as Du Bois contributed to destroying the UNIA by cooperating with various government investigations of mail fraud charges against Garvey. The nuances of how "community" should be defined and what moral and nonmoral commitments were due were foregrounded—whether, for example, community entailed a nodal commitment to racial/ethnic kind, class, or nation; whether the goal of social action should be a conscious effort to create a civilization of separate kinds or a radical cosmopolitanism; and whether the destruction of self-deprecation required romantic racialism, the negation of racial categories, or the embedding of racial identity within a notion of multicultural diversity.

The working class for socialists and communists, whether it is Richard Wright's, Hubert Henry Harrison's, or A. Philip Randolph's version, is the instrument for universal human liberation. The possibility of the negation of racism is contingent for socialists and communists on the ascendancy of the working class to power. The "African American community" is not, *mutatis mutandis*, the source of its own liberation. Rather, the empowerment of the working class, of which African Americans were a central component (but only a component) within its historical course, holds the key to the liberation of all African Americans. Liberation is not as a separate community but as a community of workers in pursuit of the destruction of substantive class, status, racial, and ethnic distinctions. What counts as liberation is not equity in the sense that African Americans would have similar incomes, rights, powers, and privileges as whites per their class and status position but in the destruction of significant class and status distinctions as well as the destruction of divisive racial and ethnic distinctions.

If class is universally salient, then there are good reasons to be morally committed to working-class liberation even if it does not automatically ensure the end of racism. There is a choice to be made between the uplift of the least well-off (decreasing their exposure to illness, premature death, unjust long-term incarceration, risks of homicide, and increasing control of their labor, income, ability to transfer assets, and availability of mates) and the demise of insults and equalizing of income and wealth between races. If a raciated ethnicity is liberated from the scourge of racism, the working class of the raciated ethnicity remains oppressed as a class. This is so unless one believes something like one of the following: that people are essentially racial kinds and liberation is a matter of realizing racial authenticity, or that racial parity is adequate to make class and status differences irrelevant to appropriate moral commitments.

Discussions of community are always parasitic on suspending what we know about the social position of people in terms of class and status. That is, we must suspend discussion of such distinctions and treat "communities" as ubiquitous.

The brutality suffered by Blacks from the criminal justice system is one way to think about the distinction between community, raciated ethnicities, and classes that I am trying to capture. At least one in four Blacks are involved in the criminal justice system on any given day. They are on trial, imprisoned, or on probation, and may or may not receive fair representation by Black police officials, judges, and juries. When Black people find themselves in prison, which may be located in cities headed by a Black mayor, they are likely goaded by Black and white prison guards, they may be raped by Black, white, or Hispanic gang members operating with relative impunity, and they will eat food sold to the prison by white-owned companies and probably prepared by underpaid, single, Black women. Prisoners are housed in concrete and steel buildings built by Black and white construction workers under contracts that include minority-owned construction and supply companies. To think that the "Black community" exists outside of deep class and status differences is to miss the multiple forms of brutalization suffered by the least well-off and avoid substantive distinctions that might recommend different types and degrees of moral commitment.

When we think of the "Black community," we must suspend everything we know about how Blacks are linked to everyone else, for example, that Black Americans have a commitment to promoting Protestant or Baptist forms of Christianity that far outweighs commitment to the "African world" that is predominately non-Christian, at least, and anti-Christian implicitly. We are likely to focus on variables that reveal how excluded Blacks are from the ownership and control of massive capital assets, for example, ownership of patents on computer products and of precious metal mines, hotels, restaurant chains, shipbuilding companies, and airplane parts contractors. The variables tell us that white-owned assets dominate Black life even until death—funeral home products, cemeteries, and Black churches mortgaged by white-owned financial institutions. They also tell us that whites do not trust Blacks—Blacks are constantly overpoliced each time they enter a store or drive down the street or take an exam in school. No matter what African traits exist in the Black American community, and no matter what role Blacks have played in creating modernity, as a people, the world of Blacks is a world subjugated under the yoke of white supremacy. For example, the real wages of American Blacks in the 1990s averaged three-quarters of what whites made at all educational levels. Black men's wages declined by 5.7 percent between 1989 and 1997. In 1997, 37.2 percent of all Black children lived in poverty; more specifically, 8.4 percent of white-headed households lived in poverty, as opposed to 23.6 percent of Black-headed households. The vast majority of Black children are raised by single mothers. Out of all ethnic/racial groups in the United States, Blacks have the least amount in retirement assets and trust funds and transfer the least real wealth growth across generations.

Simultaneously, Black Americans are culturally, religiously, and materially members of the modern capitalist world. Black Americans, for example, are the wealthiest Black population in the world. The first language of Black Americans is English. Black Americans produce within Western capitalism—rap music is exported and missionaries carry evangelical emotivism to orthodox African Christian communities and traditional faiths. Black spies, Agents P-138 and P-800, helped the Federal Bureau of Investigation destroy the UNIA. Even many of the ideals, such as the Afrocentric belief in a common African set of character or cultural traits, is a modernist conception of Africa such that all internal African conflicts, differences, and influences are treated as less than significant causal variables in deference to common character or cultural traits. Moreover, ethnic enclave economies and cultural traits, whether African continuities, Chinese religious practices, or Irish dances, have always been features of American society. The Black community is thus a curious patchwork quilt.

A fallacy occurs when we abstract from the existence of the Black community as an association that is divided in numerous ways and suppose that common salient causes that influence the behavior of all persons do not influence Blacks: supposing, for example, that class interests motivate whites but not Blacks, that religious faith motivates whites to be authoritarian imperialists but not Black missionaries, or that dedication to military protocol motivates whites but is an irrelevant variable for Blacks.

Imagine that Palo Mayombe, Santeria, Candomble, and voodoo religious faiths are all explained as African adaptations satisfying needs of displaced, enslaved, and exploited Africans in the New World. Such an explanation would not tell us the obvious—that these people believe their religious views are actually true; that they are motivated, at least in part, by the same motivation of European Christians, including those Blacks who are Quakers, Puritans, Protestants, or Episcopalians; and that persons of common faith share information, grant loans, trust one another, and raise their children to hold beliefs that conflict with opposing faiths and pursue common missionary projects. Thinking of "Blacks" and "whites" as absolute "Others" arguably has no way of seeing the deeply common projects of Christians of which, at best, ethnic or racial forms of faith expressions legitimately occur under the institutional and religious rubric of the faith.

Imagine that the Black American community is described as culturally African and motivated by deep senses of faith in the spirituality of the cosmos, define wealth in terms of personal relationships rather than material goods, and are communal. If these are considered general cultural traits that motivate Black cultural behavior—that is, *if the descriptions are used to explain*—the described cultural traits reflect an extremely Western definition of "African." As such, nearly all of Islamic Africa must be excluded; almost all of East Africa is influenced by North Africa and the Middle East; the Black world of the Middle East does not share the precepts of Western evangelical or racialized Christianity; and all orthodox Christian Africans and everyone that has a deep sense of national or tribal identity such that others are considered immigrants, enemies, or infidels must be excluded. Magically, a massively complex people—bound together by geography, family heritages, religious conflicts, and victimization by racist stereotypes; entrapped in lower classes because of the recurring asset accumulated by inheritors of past generations of upper/ruling-class oppressors; and survivors of diverse forms of colonial histories and the use of terror of evolving into and through modernity—is reduced to explanatory stereotypical traits. (Any manager of Caterpillar International knows better, especially if he or she wants to sell a single earthmover to diverse populations with local currencies, interests, and needs.)

In addition, it is necessarily true that one, if not all, of the previously mentioned religious faiths hold false beliefs. To think of the Black community without thinking of what people believe as true—given vast differences in beliefs—is to think of the Black community as peopled by stereotypical kinds rather than dynamic, empowered, struggling, exploited, excluded, and yet conquering people. However, if these descriptive traits are seen not as overly explanatory or causal but as descriptive generalizations to be adjudicated for locations, then they can be very useful.

The Black community is simply not well explained by a singular set of "authentically Black or African" values; rather, it at least evinces, if it is not best explained by, multiple strategies to secure income, assets, dignity, and control over labor and labor time.

What if Marx was right: What and how we produce shapes who and what we are, independent of any romantic ideal of ethnic, racial, or national ideals. Who and what we are now, in late capitalist postmodern global villages and African diasporic communities, must be different from who and what we were two hundred years ago. Thus, it can be true that Blacks are a hybrid people, as in Paul Gilroy's sense in *Black Atlantic*, and also an African people, as in Cedric J. Robinson's sense in *Black Marxism* or Alain Locke's in *The New Negro*. Code shifting and identity sliding are hardly unique, dangerous, or indicative of an inauthentic character or bad faith of any sort. Embedded identities are platforms that we negotiate, use, create, and maintain to help form social locations to extend prima facie trust, shared experiences, and information. It is these platforms of identity wherein our deepest moral commitments to mates, children, relatives, lovers, friends, coworkers, and physical surroundings are constituted. What moral commitments we make, especially in cases of conflict between loyalty to class or racial liberation and their accompanying competing definitions of liberation, should take into serious account the importance of predictions that rely on causal variables.

Communities, rather than simple ubiquitous ontological entities, are groups whose future is contingent on variables that shape their character. Rather than disjointed aggregates, there are ties that bind but not invariably. Admittedly, the ways I offer of categorizing and seeing communities and classes is speculative. However, the approach is offered in hopes of finding ways of seeing and discussing topics that avoid the absolutism of romantic racial ontology and also color-blind images.

African Americans are a raciated ethnicity, and liberation, I venture, will depend on freedom from forces that prevent African Americans, as a raciated ethnic group, from amassing assets and transferring wealth across generations, from the racism that creates systemic humiliation and denial of trust and honor, from the lowly status of human worth attributed to Blacks, and from the terror of massive class exploitation and vicious class differences between the wealthy and the poor. It will require that Blacks trust themselves and that others trust Blacks in the multiple ways that formal and informal contracts are constituted and insider information shared. Such perspectives are difficult to arrive at if communities in general and the Black community in particular are conceived in a Manichaean fashion—"us" and "the others"—rather than complicated and interlaced associations.

It is hoped that we will find motivation to sustain and create the sort of commitments needed to help destroy the terror of super exploitation and racial humiliation ravaging Black lives—the sort of commitments that are coterminous with explanations that allow us to see the structures that need to be changed and the forces likely to influence hoped-for realities.

Notes

1. Alain Locke (ed.), *The New Negro* (1925; reprint, New York: Maxwell Macmillan, 1992); Leonard Harris, "Prolegomenon to Race and Economics," in *A Different Vision: African American Economic Thought*, ed. Thomas Boston (New York: Routledge, 1997); and Leonard Harris (ed.), *Racism* (Amherst, NY: Humanity Books, 1999).

2. Charles Wagley, "On the Concept of Social Race in the Americas," in *Contemporary Cultures and Societies of Latin America: A Reader in the Social Anthropology in Middle and South America*, ed. Dwight B. Heath and Richard N. Adams (New York: Random House, 1965), 531–45.

3. See Leonard Harris, "Historical Subjects and Interests: Race, Class and Conflict," in *The Year Left*, ed. Michael Sprinkler et al. (New York: Verso, 1986), 91–106. I have argued elsewhere that no one has a legitimate interest in perpetually sustaining racial categories.

4. Charles Tilly, *Durable Inequality* (Berkeley: University of California Press, 1999).

5. Harris, "Historical Subjects and Interests."

6. Harris, "Historical Subjects and Interests"; Harris, *Racism*; and Victor Anderson, *Beyond Ontological Blackness* (New York: Continuum, 1999).

7. V. Y. Mudimbe, *Africa: Gnosis, Philosophy and the Order of Knowledge* (Bloomington: Indiana University Press, 1988).

References

Adeleke, Tunde. 1993. *Un-African Americans*. Cambridge, MA: Harvard University Press.

Anderson, Victor. 1999. *Beyond Ontological Blackness*. New York: Continuum.

Bell, Derrick A. 1992. *Faces at the Bottom of the Well*. New York: Basic.

Blyden, Edward W. 1967. *Islam, Christianity and the Negro Race*. Edinburgh: Edinburgh University Press.

Chaudhuri, Nupur. 1998. *Western Women and Imperialism*. Lexington: University Press of Kentucky.

Dilthey, Wilhelm. 1883. *W. Dilthey: Selected Writings*. Edited by H. P. Rickman. Reprint, Cambridge: Cambridge University Press, 1976.

Du Bois, W. E. B. 2000. *Biography of a Race*. New York: Henry Holt.

Durkheim, Emile. 1933. *The Division of Labor in Society*. Translated by George Simpson. Reprint, New York: The Free Press, 1964.

Foner, Philip S. 1977. *American Socialism and Black Americans*. Westport, CT: Greenwood.

Garvey, Marcus. 1987. *The Marcus Garvey and Universal Negro Improvement Association Papers.* Edited by Robert A. Hill and Barbara Bair. Berkeley: University of California Press.

Gilroy, Paul. 1992. *The Black Atlantic: Modernity and Double Consciousness.* Bloomington: Indiana University Press.

Harris, Leonard, ed. 1983. *Philosophy Born of Struggle: Anthology of Afro-American Philosophy from 1917.* Dubuque, IA: Kendall-Hunt.

Harris, Leonard. 1986. "Historical Subjects and Interests: Race, Class and Conflict." In *The Year Left*, edited by Michael Sprinkler et al. New York: Verso.

Harris, Leonard. 1997. "Prolegomenon to Race and Economics." In *A Different Vision: African American Economic Thought*, edited by Thomas Boston. New York: Routledge.

Harris, Leonard, ed.. 1999. *Racism.* Amherst, NY: Humanities Press.

Harvey, David. 1989. *The Condition of Postmodernity.* Cambridge: Blackwell.

Herder, Johannes G. 1968. *Reflections on the Philosophy of the History of Mankind.* Chicago, IL: University of Chicago Press.

Hutchinson, George. 1995. *The Harlem Renaissance in Black and White.* Cambridge, MA: Belknap.

Lewis, David Levering. 1981. *When Harlem Was in Vogue.* New York: Knopf.

Locke, Alain, ed. 1925. *The New Negro.* Reprint, New York: Maxwell Macmillan, 1992.

Locke, Alain. 1992. *Race Contacts and Interracial Relations.* Washington, DC: Howard University Press.

Mannheim, Karl. 1940. *Man and Society in an Age of Reconstruction.* New York: Harcourt, Brace.

Mannheim, Karl. 1953. *Ideology and Utopia.* New York: Harcourt, Brace.

Martin, Tony. 1976. *Race First.* Westport, CT: Greenwood.

Merton, Robert K. 1968. *Social Theory and Social Structure.* New York: The Free Press.

Mishel, Lawrence, J. Bernstein, and J. Schmit. 1993. *The State of Working America.* Armonk, NY: Sharpe.

Mudimbe, V. Y. 1988. *Africa: Gnosis, Philosophy and the Order of Knowledge.* Bloomington: Indiana University Press.

Robinson, Cedric J. 1997. *Black Marxism.* New York: Routledge.

Smith, Adam. 1994. *The Wealth of Nations.* New York: Modem Library.

Spencer, Herbert. 1897. *The Principles of Ethics.* 2 vols. New York: D. Appleton.

Stewart, Jeffrey C. 1992. *Race Contacts and Interracial Relations.* Washington, DC: Howard University Press.

Tilly, Charles. 1999. *Durable Inequality.* Berkeley: University of California Press.

Veblen, Thorstein. 1965. *Theory of the Leisure Class.* Reprint, New York: A. M. Kelley, 1965.

Wagley, Charles. 1965. "On the Concept of Social Race in the Americas." In *Contemporary Cultures and Societies of Latin America: A Reader in the Social Anthropology in Middle and South America*, edited by Dwight B. Heath and Richard N. Adams. New York: Random House.

Weber, Max. 1994. *Sociological Writing.* Edited by Wold Heyderbrand. New York: Continuum.

CHAPTER 14
TRADITION AND MODERNITY: PANOPTICONS AND BARRICADOS

In "Tradition and Modernity," Harris is critical of conceptions of modernity and their correlative forms of reasoning. Modern European traditions and Enlightenment rationality, for example, have been a source of licentiousness and barbarism. The panopticon has been used as a paradigm for modern carceral state. Harris suggests, however, that the barricado is a paradigm for modernity and slavery. Both modernity and slavery exhibit ways in which scientific reasoning was wielded to facilitate both the carceral state and the slave trade. Harris rejects the notion that "Reason," as it is portrayed in the European Enlightenment, should be taken as the supracultural standard by which to judge the sophistication or maturity of disparate human populations. To the contrary, Harris recognizes modern forms of reasoning as one set among many; he advocates for polyvalent populations bearing unique cultural traditions and corresponding reasoning strategies. To facilitate genuine cross-cultural communication between disparate, polyvalent populations, Harris suggests a morality of cultural reciprocity. Reciprocity requires that "all persons, independent of group membership, should be considered members of the moral community and thus due dignity." Honor and dignity will not be awarded from the gaze of those on the other side of the barricado. "Honor and dignity can be achieved from within the world of those that accord one another full personhood."

Introduction

Modernity is a battleground where traditional and Enlightenment "scientific" reasoning methods are locked in cruel conflict. I will suggest a morality of reciprocity to help regulate the conflicts between traditions and modernity. Although my argument is narrowly focused on reasoning methods, it is intended to contribute to works critical of valorizing "scientific" reasoning. It also seeks to augment works that promote a high regard for new visions of rationality that include populations historically subjected to racial and ethnic exclusion.[1]

"Modernité" originally referred to fleeting, ephemeral, transitory life in an urban metropolis and the way that art can, or should, capture the motion of that experience.[2] It also came to mean the process of secularization, industrialization, juridical institutions, and social surveillance by government authorities—all of which involve subjugation of traditional rituals that rely on unsubstantiated intuitions and inefficient forms of labor.

Traditions and their associated reasoning methods are presumed retrograde and thereby in a battle against modernization. Modernity has become synonymous with forms of reason, such as enumerative reason (natural ordering), evidentialism (rules of evidence determining objective certainty), and material causal explanations. Individuals using these forms of reasoning are often considered the causal basis for modern society—that is, individual, rational persons create rational groups and communities. I consider the merits of the above reasoning methods and the view that self-legislative reasoning by individuals is the causal basis of rational group behavior (methodological individualism and interactionalism support this view of the link between individuals and groups).[3]

Enlightenment as Darkness (Panopticons and Barricados)

Modernity, under the aegis of the Enlightenment or the "Age of Reason," was characterized by slavery, colonialism, and imperialism. Nearly all of the European philosophers of the Enlightenment used categories of racial and ethnic types they considered confirmed by science, ranking types and ascribing such traits as superior, inferior, heathen, or uncivilized.[4] There are certainly important distinctions between different regions and traditions of European philosophy. Using racial rankings and treating populations as inferior is not unique to Europeans. My examples, primarily from England and Germany, are intended to be paradigmatic and focus on the peculiar ways racial and ethnic cauterization and reason are expressed in the modern West.

Categorizing the natural world using enumerative reason included classifying humanity into racial and ethnic kinds. The kind designations involve ranking and assigning them irrevocable natures of inferiority and superiority, which were proclaimed established by following the rules of evidence based on objective matters of fact. Each kind assumed fossilize into a permanent essence; a species kind correlative to a divinely sanctioned hierarchy. Accountants, lawyers, soldiers, compradors, slave catchers, producers of guns, knives, poisons, and rapists used scientific knowledge and saw themselves as self-legislative authors. A few random examples may help illustrate what I mean by the categorizing, ranking, and use of enumerative reason and evidence inherited from the Enlightenment that supported slavery, colonialism, and imperialism.

There was only one racial category consistently used by the American census between 1865 and 2010: "white male." The classification of "colored," designated a generally defective and inferior population. In the United States Compendium of the Eleventh Census, 1890, racial classifications included: "The colored Population Classified as Blacks, Mulattoes, Quadroons, Octoroons, Chinese, Japanese, and Civilized Indians." The term "colored" was used to classify all nonwhites. The racial category of "Asian" collapsed all differences, save geographic location. The 1890 "Report on Populations," for example, noted that members of the nation's "colored element included Chinese, Japanese, and Indians."[5] These categories were correlated to those commonly used in France, England, and Germany at that time. However, the United States created its own form of legal racialism, namely, the one-drop rule. This rule defined a Negro as a person with any heritage from sub-Saharan Africa, thereby classifying all Negroes as hypo-descendent.[6] A person could become Negro, but none could become white. For Americans, "white" was understood to be unmixed descendants from a mythical, racially undifferentiated, all-white Europe.

During the First Opium War (1839–42) and the Second Opium War (1856–60), the British sold opium as well as defective goods to Chinese that they knew would kill children and adults alike. They managed brothels and camps of enslaved workers, knowingly calculating the death rates of Chinese workers the same way that they calculated those of slaves on ships crossing from Africa to the Americas. In these two scenarios, slavery and imperialism, the populations were not only treated as commodities but were also loathed. And as such, they merited disdain to the extent that even their dead bodies received no sanctuary.[7]

Winston Churchill revealed his racial elitism and contempt for populations considered uncivilized when discussing the fighting between the British and Sudanese forces at Omdurman in 1898: "These extraordinary foreign (Sudanese) figures march up one by one from the darkness of Barbarism to the footlights of civilization and their conquerors, taking their possessions, forget even their names. Nor will history record such trash." According to another, more sober English observer, "It was not a battle but an execution. The bodies were not in heaps … but they spread evenly over acres and acres."[8] Churchill saw himself and was seen by his moral community as acting in good faith and with good reason. Politicians, soldiers, census statisticians, industrialists, and torturers used the same effective reasoning methods of enumeration and evidence for their own nefarious purposes and professions.[9]

In 1791, Jeremy Bentham designed an institutional building, a Panopticon, for observing inmates without them knowing whether or when they were being watched, "a mill for grinding rogues honest."[10] The Panopticon (optic=visible; pan=all) consisted of a tower, which overlooked an open courtyard and housed the "watchers" above the courtyard. Michel Foucault considered the Panopticon a paradigm for modern society: "He who is subjected to a field of visibility, and who knows it, assumes responsibility for the constraints of power; he makes them play spontaneously upon himself; he inscribes in himself the power relation in which he simultaneously plays both roles; he becomes the principle of his own subjection."[11] The "watched," however, come to discipline themselves in ways benefiting the watchers. Prisons are a paradigm for modernity, particularly modern factories, schools, families, hospitals, and the military. Modern society is thus carceral—the ruled and the rulers are entrapped by institutions that regulate their behavior and dictate their lack of self-formation.[12]

The barricado, I believe, is a fitting paradigm for slavery.[13] It is also a paradigm for modernity because it allows us to talk about modernity with particular attention to a world beset with racial and ethnic stereotypes. A barricado is a spring-loaded pike fence or wooden board that could be dropped across the middle of a slave ship's deck. The barricado separated slaves from the crew. The crew could then fire their muskets down from the stern deck directly through holes in the barricado or use half-pikes or pokers to stab revolting and non-revolting slaves alike. The barricado was designed to suppress rebellions and sustain an atmosphere of helplessness among slaves. The crew became seemingly omnipotent overlords because they controlled all instruments of death and all resources for life. The slave ship *Parr*, built in 1797, was a 566-tonne ship fitted to carry 700 slaves and 100 crew members and made ten voyages. Like the slaveships *Marie Seraphique*, *Brook*, *Brownlow*, *Hesketh*, and *Diligent*, it used either a barricado or a method consonant with the *Parr*'s efficiency to sustain control of its cargo. Using the barricado as a paradigm for modernity especially helps capture what it means to be modern yet seen as exotic, racial, or ethnic "other."

If a crew member became trapped on the wrong side of the barricado during an uprising, and between one-fifth and two-third of all voyages experienced an uprising, he was abandoned. The protected crew wantonly shot anyone on the slave side of the ship. If a rebel leader was identified among the slaves, his body was normally left on board to rot before throwing his body into the ocean—the same way that mutilated body parts from slaves were routinely, an unceremoniously, tossed overboard.[14] No sanctuary. The death of slaves was calculated as an acceptable loss, given, according to the most well-educated accountants of the day, that it was more profitable to carry more slaves than fewer.

Female slaves housed on the crew's side were routinely raped and beaten during the voyage. Their shame, made public because of the exceedingly close quarters on slave ships, assured their humiliation. Humiliating women provided a sadistic joy for the crew, an ancillary, unpaid benefit made all the more rewarding by witnessing the emasculation of male captives while well-educated captains stood watching.

Cruelty is not tangential to a slave system; there is no system without cruelty. The barricado made management of the collective possible because it allowed all members of the crew to receive undue privilege, and each enslaved individual could be treated as a racial kind. Each individual slave was identical to any other and inscribed with the essence of all; the enslaved learned not only to watch passively but also to discipline themselves. Witnessing or learning about the torture of members of the slave's racial kind was sufficient to traumatize all members of the subjugated population, slave or free. Subjection and self-subjection became in popular imagination synonymous with their kind, that is, the class of persons known as colored, barbaric, uncivilized, Black, Negro, African, slave, former slave, possible slave, or descendent of slaves.

Banality toward the suffering of others is a hallmark of the objectivity of reason; it separates itself from its object of utility. The "other" is a thing to be expropriated, used, and bartered in the sex-trade industry, the body parts of the "other" harvested and sold to the highest bidders. What counts as evidence, appropriate categories, and rankings are treated as sacrosanct, scientifically and objectively verifiable social kinds. Social kinds such as races are seen as empirically confirmed social facts evidenced and confirmed by science.

Science, in particular the biological sciences, creates social kinds and then makes them social facts that affirm what "science" created. Slave ledgers and manuals on breeding slaves through rape and the prevention of marriage used the same accounting techniques as manuals for breeding horses and ledgers for recording their worth.[15] When slaves remained unmarried, this was taken as evidence that slaves did not want to marry. When African Americans were forced to live in segregated communities, this was taken as evidence that they wanted to be segregated. "Evidence" does not exist in a vacuum of pure cognition, structure, abstraction, and knowledge. It exists only within a network of meanings that give the content, as evidence, warrant.

Modernity includes regimes of externality, exclusion, prejudice, and disdain for a whole population; the xenophobia, racism, ethnocentrism, and arrogance of the modern West is not tangential to Enlightenment. There is no history of Enlightenment reason without its history of categorizing and ranking people into ethnic and racial kinds. There is no modernity (or postmodernity, although I will not argue it here), without population displacement, migrations and new group formations because of interethnic and racial marital relations. In addition, constant changes in needed skills, technologies, and products assure groups are constantly emerging and forming new ceremonies and practices. The constant creation of racial and ethnic categories of kinds stands starkly against heinous stereotypes and persistently maintained illusions of racial and ethnic categories associated with demeaning stereotypes.

The barricado is a paradigm for modernity because modern society is beset with racial and ethnic prejudice that separates peoples and nations into racial kinds correlative to heinous stereotypes. Gazing through xenophobic eyes from the standpoint of the contemporary West, Europe, and the United States, everyone is exterior, an object, instrument, toy, or spectacle, exotic, foreign, bizarre, mysterious, atypical, abnormal, barely civilized, alien. That xenophobic gaze is inherited from the Enlightenment.

Incommensurability: Tradition and Modernity

Persons who are logical can practice racism and ethnocentricity. It is not their logic as a matter of the structure of their reasoning that fails. It is the array of beliefs trapped in categories considered objectively confirmed. Such persons may also exhibit the moral traits of care, compassion and empathy, but it is how such traits are expressed and to whom they are directed that constitutes whether ethnocentric persons as prejudiced. It is false that all forms of racism and ethnocentricity fail to be rational. By "rational" I mean arguments that do not commit formal logical fallacies.[16] Arguments in favor of racism and ethnocentricity may avoid formal fallacies, although the content of their propositions and conclusions are entirely false. In addition, such arguments rely on heinous views of humans, for example, they categorize and rank populations as superior, inferior, civilized, or barbaric. Such arguments are unreasonable, as distinct from rational.

Being self-critical and versed in formal reasoning skills is in no way an assurance that ethnocentric or racists views will not prevail. Learned men have been complicit in every form of heinous attitude and behavior such as genocide, slavery, colonial domination, and banal attitudes about torture. I will use Plato and Kant as examples of what I mean by the use of methodological individualism or interactionalism within modernity's regime of reason—a use quite compatible with heinous attitudes and behaviors.

Contrary to the popular account of Plato's visits to Sicily, I contend that Plato was misguided by his own expectation that the power of individual right reasoning results in true answers—an expectation that, I believe, engenders tremendous arrogance in the person who believes that he has infallible reasoning ability. The usual story is that Plato's three visits to Sicily to educate a philosopher king met with failure because he was disappointed with Dionysius I as a student. Plato became a victim of the selfish and irrational behavior of Sicilian tyrants and was forced to abandon his educational project. There is evidence to suggest that Dionysius I was instrumental in selling Plato into slavery upon his return from his first of three visits to Sicily (early 390 BC to the summer of 388 BC). Plato was sold into slavery in Aegina, a city-state at war with Athens. A Cyrenian admirer, Annikeris, provided enough resources for Plato to pay for his freedom. Plato was able to secure his freedom using fewer resources than what was provided by Annikeris. Plato purchased the land where he founded the Academy in 386 BC, a garden near the shrine of the hero Hekadêmus, with resources from Annikeris that were intended to pay for his freedom. Plato never considered his subterfuge—using resources given to him for one purpose for something entirely different without the donor's permission—to be an instance of his lack of integrity.

Despite his experience as a slave, Plato, nonetheless, returned to Sicily twice. On his second trip, he secured a position with Dionysius II. And although Dionysius II likely was aware of Plato's proven penchant for betrayal, he allowed Plato to remain and become his teacher.

On his third and final trip to Sicily, Plato refrained from helping his close associate and student, Dion, when Dion fought against Dionysius II. Some of Plato's students were eventually instrumental in Dion's demise. Plato never successfully fulfilled his desire to educate a philosopher king, nor did he ever ascend to such a lofty position. When Plato died, he owned five slaves.

The dates, locations, and major events regarding Plato's visits are fairly well established facts. I simply do not take Plato's self-report of his virtuous motivations or his account of his situation as warranted, namely, that his virtuously motivated failure was due to Sicilian tyrannical irrationality. This well-known story relies on Plato's own descriptions and anecdotal comments by other authors, such as Plutarch. I assume, for the sake of argument, that Plutarch is to be believed and that the letter attributed to Plato is, if not his, a reasonable depiction of his experiences.[17] However, I suggest the following contrary story: Plato's arrogance is motivated by his misguided sense of certainty—the use of reason as if it were sacrosanct and the association of individual traits with group behavior. Plato considers "reason" to be enmeshed in the structure of reality. He treats his own motivations as invariable derivations from "reason" itself. Hence, for Plato, his arrogance and self-serving account are beyond repute. He is confident that he knows what "reason" dictates for his own situation in Syracuse. His disparaging judgment of nearly every person and group he mentions is given sanctimonious warrant because it is not really Plato who presents the facts; his presentation is simply the expression of the pure truth derived from reason itself. No matter what Plato did in Sicily, he contends that he was only following the dictates of reason. Because Plato sufficiently won the disfavor of his student and benefactor, Dionysius I, I speculate that it was due to the good graces of Dionysius I that Plato was allowed to return to Athens even as a slave rather than be killed. And it was the benevolence of Dionysius II that prevented Plato's re-enslavement or death during his second and third visits. When individuals or groups do not behave the way that Plato assumes that they should, it is their lack of reason, virtue, wisdom, or knowledge of the good, the beautiful, or the just that is at fault, never Plato's misguided, feigned asceticism, pretentions of aristocratic status, deceitful approach to relationships, self-serving behavior, or myopic cultural elitism. Plato considers his cultural traits as *sin qua non* with high civilization. This is Plato's incipient methodological individualism and interactionalism, that is, individual character traits explaining group traits.

Immanuel Kant's 1784 response to *Was ist Aufklärung?* ("What is Enlightenment?") depicts modernity as entrapped in a "slumber of self-induced immaturity."[18] The solution for this deficiency was Enlightenment through "scientific knowledge and self-legislation." Enlightenment is understood by Kant as a social condition that has overcome "self-induced immaturity." Modernity is the world that comes into being as a function of overcoming immaturity. "Immaturity" can be read as the world of the uncivilized and barbaric. By 1784, Christians had decimated nearly all endogenous ethnic tribal entities in Europe and their accompanying religions as well as residual invading populations such as Huns, Turks, and Moors. In "On the Different Races of Man" (*Über die verschiedenen Rassen der Menschen* [1775]), Kant described ostensibly inferior, primitive, savage races and argued that a transcendental basis was needed to properly justify racial rankings.[19] The next phase of European maturation, with Christianity having achieved the death, subjugation, and vanquishing of local uncivilized barbarians, was for Christians to ascend further through the use of science, including the application of its racial categories. This, I speculate, is what Kant imagines as the triumph of reason.

Kant describes the solution to immaturity in terms of reasoning traits that exist only in social formations: scientific knowledge is created by a broad range of persons using reasoning methods morphed, or congealed, through the agency of self-legislation. Kant paints an image of the collective phenomenon of scientific knowledge as it exists through the agency, taken collectively, of self-legislative persons. There should be very little incommensurability between rational persons, let alone groups, if Kant were right, because reason lends itself to objective truth and corrective right behavior. This is Kant's incipient methodological individualism or interactionalism.

Societies do not "slumber," contrary to Kant's metaphor describing the condition of society as "slumbering." And "scientific knowledge" can hardly be the cause of a new social world, as if a form of reasoning is isomorphic with a set of prescribed behaviors or its categories are bereft of its own prejudices.

Kant's idea of a "metaphor," I contend, serves as an example of why "reason" can be systematically misleading. Kant's belief that "the source of all error is metaphor" is itself a metaphor. His assertion requires imagining the existence of a "source" that is the font of secondary and transitional "consequences"; the contrast to "error" is "correctness." Kant uses a metaphor to claim that metaphors are the source of errors. The structure of what is considered to be reasoning excludes the possibility of dialogue between persons of equal status because the users of metaphors are systematically misguided. The users of metaphors would only be expressing views sourced in error—in this case, Kant.

Reasonable people, using Kant as an example, are not bereft of self-refutation, internal conflict, heinous proclivities, and misguided views of metaphors that shape what they consider to be reasonable. It is systematically misleading to think that an argument can be bereft of presumptions, images, and metaphors, thereby making it pure analytic. There is no distortion-free communication between individuals or, metaphorically, between groups.

Group behavior is what matters in discussions of cross-cultural communication. Reasoning traits of individuals are certainly important, but collective behavior is best described in holistic terms, for example, institutions and structures, such as family, assets, and group preferences, rather than individualist terms, such as a self-critical attitude or empathy toward others. The traits associated with individual reasonableness (e.g., coherency and logical form) and attitudes (self-critical, consensus seeking, and accepting self-fallibility) are not identical to the kinds of traits associated with cultural relations between groups (e.g., ownership patterns, land rights, laws covering inheritance and assets, class structures, and symbols of status and authority).

If individual members of two separate groups with incommensurable values exhibit the traits of communicative competency, it does not follow that there will be effective cross-cultural communication between their groups.[20] To think that a group of individuals (who are self-critical, self-regulated, and masters of enumerative and evidential rules of reason) will form a group that is itself a rational agent is to commit a fallacy of composition—assuming that the whole exhibits the traits of its parts. There is an asymmetrical relationship: a population is composed of individuals, but a population, as a collective, is not identical or best described in terms of traits of its individual members—assuming that the traits of individuals are synonymous with or explain the traits of the whole. When this is considered a symmetrical relationship, it is what I term the fallacy of compositionality reason. Plato and Kant commit this fallacy.

Groups do not "reason" with one another. Certainly, the British and the Sudanese at Omdurman in 1898 did not. Blacks and whites in the United States, for example, do not engage in reasoning across lines of dissimilar cultures. To talk about groups as communicating, as if that communication occurs between two groups each with a mind that reasons, creates an image of cognition that does not exist. The structure of methodological individualism and the interactionalist approach to the impact of reasonable individuals on group behavior is misguided.

Situations free from unequal positions of power between groups is unlikely because emergent populations are necessarily unstable and less in control of the instruments of power than more established populations. In addition, all individuals use representative heuristics (broad generalizations and stereotypes) to communicate, which makes the possibility of self-criticism necessarily circumscribed.[21] There is no history of human social orders without generations distinguishing themselves from previous generations. These facts of cognition and population emergence suggest that individuals cannot be the source of undistorted communication: distortion is a necessary feature of normal communication, made worse by communication fettered by prejudice. However, there is no reason to believe that subjugation, racial stereotypes, and markers depicting persons as abject or uncivilized will invariably be a feature of future societies.

A hegemonic culture is antithetical to a viable future. In addition, a hegemonic culture is not a condition necessary for the ending of racism and ethnocentricity. One way to see this is to consider language emergence and disappearance. It is empirically true that languages are constantly being lost; it is also empirically true that new identities are constantly being formed. Language communities are relatively stable at best. If we imagine communities as emerging, then norms regulating relationships of constantly shifting community formations are important. A singular, well-defined reasoning procedure is hardly sufficiently efficacious to make communication competency possible. Any successful formal mode of association between two or more changing communities requires constant revision in the modes of effective association in order for communities to be convivial. Shifting parameters and forms of communities can conceivably aid viable exchange, given unstable social categories. The reason for this is that the instability of what things mean, including what is deemed consensus and who counts as a member of a moral community, makes communication possible. New meanings are what communities make. Incommensurability is an inescapable variable. If, however, reciprocity and dignity are present as social goods, cross-cultural dialogue that preserves these goods is possible. An individual may fail to show others respect and lack good reasoning skills, but the group *qua* group must always be seen as the kinds of persons capable of being honored. Although this may seem counterintuitive, it is institutions and social instruments that shape relations between groups (i.e., ownership patterns, land rights, laws covering inheritance and assets, class structures, and symbols of status and authority).

The Morality of Cultural Reciprocity: Honor among Equals

A morality of cultural reciprocity, I suggest, is preferable to a morality that posits the need for a singular form of reasoning, which is seen as indicative of maturity or civility. I suggest that the possibility for genuine cross-cultural communication should include "reciprocity" as a normative principle. Reciprocity could make possible the exclusion of cruelty as an integral part of the conflict between modernity and tradition.[22]

Arguably, a *lingua franca* makes the arduous task of understanding incongruous language and cultural meanings easier than translating languages and trying to grasp different cultural meanings. It is, nonetheless, the case that common cultural or linguistic mooring is no surety of communal conviviality. Reciprocity enables "free-trade in culture." "Culture-goods, once evolved, are no longer the exclusive property of the race or people that originated them. They belong to all."[23] If we think of cultures as simultaneously stable, shifting, emerging, and producing goods that belong to humanity, then reciprocity between groups will be seen as a process. Groups will also be seen as constantly changing and consisting not of demeaning stereotypes but complex social formations. Reciprocity is not an algorithm for all forms of effective cultural dialogue; it is a value orientation.

Reciprocity, assuming incommensurability and tensions between cultural groups, requires a form of humanism: all persons, independent of group membership, should be considered members of the moral community and thus due dignity. Dignity is a social good that helps make freedom possible, and paradoxically, it also helps make servitude impossible. The reason for this is because no one can be treated as a commodity on a slave ledger.

Communities should be empowered with the institutional instruments that help make servitude impossible. It is not some array of "scientific" reasoning methods that bolsters the possibility of honoring a group or individuals; it is the existence of viable institutions within which cultural populations participate and are treated fairly. That is, servitude and the imposition of heinous stereotypes are less likely when cultural groups are not segregated or entrapped by unfair ownership patterns, laws covering inheritance and assets, class structures, and symbols of status and authority.

A morality of reciprocity drops the expectation that honor and dignity will be awarded from the gaze of those on the other side of the barricado. Honor and dignity can be achieved from within the world of those that accord one another full personhood, that is, from everyone sharing the same side of the ship. I posit that it is necessary for persons historically described as "other," alien, exotic, colored, or oriental to show honor to themselves and their fellow compatriots before it is possible to be honored by persons entrapped in the xenophobia of an Enlightenment gaze. African Americans, for example, must first show honor to themselves before it is possible to receive it from others. There can be, I believe, conciliation of traditions and modernity within a conviviality of creative tension in the future.[24]

Traditions are not necessarily dead weights on modernity or confining remembrances of past achievements; they are created, invented, and shaped for new purposes.[25] They also provide sites of pride for ancestral struggles against heinous obstacles. Traditions may be constituted by practices and reasoning strategies that are outdated and sustain indefensible beliefs. Such traditions should remind us to reexamine the imprisoning practices, strategies, and ceremonies that modernity imposed to replace the past. Given the reality of a world full of ranking human groups, the struggle to end racist and ethnocentric group stereotypes and accompanying discrimination, whether against Chinese, South Africans, or minority groups within a nation such as African Americans, may require reciprocity.

Reciprocity makes possible cultural respect between populations without the misguided idea that populations are stable racial and ethnic kinds. The Enlightenment model of modernity is rooted in considering traditions necessarily retrograde. A morality of reciprocity encourages a rejection of this approach and instead recommends cultural conviviality between polyvalent populations. Given that there are unique cultural traditions buoyed by correlative reasoning strategies, a morality of reciprocity encourages granting *prima facia* respect to persons *qua* persons, not as representations of racial and ethnic stereotypical kinds.

Unlike the architecture of the Panopticon and, analogically, a society that is structured to control privacy and create stifling routines, future architecture and social life should allow open spaces and freedom to remember the past yet explore alternative lifestyles. Unlike the architecture of the barricado and, analogically, a society that divides populations into permanent ethnic and racial groups, future architecture and society should allow safe spaces for communal sociality that flows openly to other spaces, which in turn makes reciprocity, tradition, and exchanges between populations possible.

Notes

1. The first version of "Tradition and Modernity" was presented at Shanghai Jiao Tong University, Shanghai Jiao Tong University, Minghang campus, Shanghai, China, April 19, 2013. It is a continuation of the argument initially developed in "Telos and Tradition: Making the Future, Brides to Future Traditions," *Philosophia Africana* 16 (2, Winter 2014): 59–71.
   See Paulin Hountondji, *La rationalité une ou plurielle?* (Oxford: African Books Collective Limited, 2007).

2. Charles Baudelaire, 1821–1867, Christine Buci-Glucksmann, *Baroque Reason: The Aesthetics of Modernity* (Thousand Oaks, CA: Sage, 1994); Anthony Giddens, *The Consequences of Modernity* (Stanford, CA: Stanford University Press, 1990).

3. Evidentialism is the view that the justification of a belief depends solely on the evidence for that belief; see as an example Allen Wood, "The Duty to Believe According to Evidence," *International Journal for Philosophy of Religion* 1 (3, February 2008): 7–24; interactionalism is the view that social processes are to be explained by relationships between groups; see as an example Mitchell Aboulafia, *The Cosmopolitan Self: George Herbert Mead and Continental Philosophy* (Urbana: University of Illinois Press, 2001); methodological individualism is the view that social phenomena can be explained by how they result from the motivations and actions of individual agents, see for examples Lars Udehn, *Methodological Individualism* (London: Routledge, 2001); Max Weber, *Economy and Society*, ed. Guenther Roth and Claus Wittich (Berkeley: University of California Press, 1968).

4. See Emmanuel Chukwudi Eze, *Race and the Enlightenment: A Reader* (New York: John Wiley, 2008); Emmanuel Chukwudi Eze, *On Reason: Rationality in a World of Cultural Conflict and Racism* (Durham, NC: Duke University Press, 2008); Robert Bernasconi, *Race* (New York: John Wiley & Sons, 2001); Robert Bernasconi and Sybol Cook (eds.), *Race & Racism in Continental Philosophy* (Bloomington: Indiana University Press, 2003).
   Philosophers relied on normal science by popular physicians, botanists, and zoologists such as Georges Cuvier (1769-1832), Christopher Meiners (1747-1810), or Carl Linnaeus (1707-1778) to warrant their racial rankings. Also see Stephen Jay Gould, *The Mismeasure of Man* (New York: Norton, 1981).

5. See Martha Hodes, "Fractions and Fictions in the United States Census of 1890," in *Haunted by Empire*, ed. Ann Laura Stoler (Durham, NC: Duke University Press, 2006), 259, 258–66.

6. See for examples of racial categories and the role of biological and medical sciences in creating racial categories, Dorothy Roberts, *Fatal Invention: How Science, Politics, and Big Business Re-Create Race in the Twenty-First Century* (New York: New Press, 2011).

7. See James Allen, *Without Sanctuary: Lynching Photography in America* (Santa Fe, NM: Twin Palms, 2000).

8. John McKay, Bennett Hill, John Buckler et al. *A History of World Societies, Volume C*, seventh edition (New York: Houghton Mifflin, 2007), 791.

9. See, for examples of slave ledgers and manuals, brutality, training of violence workers, and the maintenance of terror in slave systems, Joseph C. Miller, *Way of Death: Merchant of Death and the Angolan Slave Trade, 1730–1830* (Madison: University of Wisconsin Press, 1988); Marcus Rediker, *The Slave Ship: A Human History* (New York: Viking, 2007); David B. Davis, *Inhuman Bondage: The Rise and Fall of Slavery in the New World* (Oxford: Oxford University Press, 2006); and Lisa Yum, *The Coolie Speaks: Chinese Indentured Laborers and African Slaves in Cuba* (New York: Temple University Press, 2009).

10. Janet Semple, *Bentham's Prison: A Study of the Panopticon Penitentiary* (Oxford: Clarendon Press, 1993), 152.

11. Michel Foucault, *Discipline and Punish: The Birth of the Prison* (New York: Vintage Books, 1995), 202–3 (*Surveiller et punir: Naissance de la prison* [Paris: Gallimard, 1975]).

12. Ibid.

13. See, for the first use of this concept, Leonard Harris, "Walker: Naturalism and Liberation," *Transactions of the C. S. Peirce Society* 49 (1, Winter 2013): 93–111. The concept of slavery as a form of parasitism has a long conceptual history; see Orlando Patterson, "Slavery as Human Parasitism," in *Slavery and Social Death: A Comparative Study* (Cambridge, MA: Harvard University Press, 1982), 334–42.

14. Rediker, *The Slave Ship*, 339. Also see Robert Harms, *The Diligent: A Voyage through the Worlds of the Slave Trade* (New York: Basic Books, 2002).

15. Edward Donoghue, *Black Breeding Machines: The Breeding of Negro Slaves in the Diaspora* (Bloomington, IN: Author House, 2008), 134–6; also see Richard Sutch, "The Breeding of Slaves for Sale and the Westward of Slavery, 1850–1860," in *Race and Slavery in the Western Hemisphere: Q Studies*, ed. Stanley L. Engerman and Eugene Genovese (Princeton, NJ: Princeton University Press, 1975), 173–210.

16. See David Goldberg, "Racism and Rationality: The Need for a New Critique," in *Racism*, ed. Leonard Harris (Amherst, NY: Humanity Books, 1999), 369–97.

17. See Gertrude R. Levy, *Plato in Sicily* (London: Faber and Faber, 1956); Plato's "Seventh Letter," 360, "Plato to the Relatives and Friends of Dion, Welfare." Plato explains why he abandoned Dion and his experiences while sold into slavery, http://classics.mit.edu/Plato/seventh_letter.html.

18. Immanuel Kant, "What Is Enlightenment?" ("Was ist Aufklärung?" [1784], http://www.columbia.edu/acis/ets/CCREAD/etscc/kant.html); Allen W. Wood, *Kant* (New York: Blackwell, 2005).

19. Immanuel Kant, "Of the Different Human Races," in *The Idea of Race*, ed. Robert Bernasconi and Tommy Lott (Indianapolis, IN: Hackett, 2000), 8–22.

20. An example of communicative competency is presented by Jürgen Habermas, *The Theory of Communicative Action*, trans. Thomas McCarthy (Cambridge: Polity, 1984).

21. See Hilary Kornblith, *Naturalizing Epistemology* (London: Bradford Books, 1981); Daniel Kahneman, P. Slovic, and A. Tversky, *Judgment Under Uncertainty: Heuristics and Biases* (Cambridge: Cambridge University Press, 1982).

22. See as an example Alain Locke and B. J. Stern (eds.), *When Peoples Meet, A Study in Race and Culture Contacts* (New York: Committee on Workshops, Progressive Education Association, 1942); Linda Benson and I. Swanberg, *China's Last Nomads: The History and Culture of China's Kazaks* (Armonk, NY: M.E. Sharpe, 1998).

23. Alain Locke, "The Contribution of Race to Culture," in *The Philosophy of Alain Locke: Harlem Renaissance and Beyond*, ed. Leonard Harris (Philadelphia, PA: Temple University Press, 1989), 206; also see Leonard Harris, "Tolerance, réconciliation et groupes," *Guerre et Réconciliation, Jounée de la Philosophie àl Unesco* 5 (2003): 59–94.

24. Leonard Harris, "The Horror of Tradition or How to Burn Babylon and Build Benin While Reading a *Preface to a Twenty Volume Suicide Note*," *Philosophical Forum* 24 (1–3, Fall–Spring 1992–3): 94–119.

25. See, for the concept of tradition as an on-going invention, ibid.

CHAPTER 15
THE HORROR OF TRADITION OR HOW TO BURN BABYLON AND BUILD BENIN WHILE READING A *PREFACE TO A TWENTY VOLUME SUICIDE NOTE* (1997)

In "The Horror of Tradition or How to Burn Babylon and Build Benin While Reading a *Preface to a Twenty Volume Suicide Note*," Harris describes traditions as human inventions that evince a social entity's shared values, questions, vocabulary, methodologies, and ideals. Traditions establish norms, draw boundaries, set the stage, and assign the scripts. As such, they are intrinsically conservative. Harris sees no escaping of tradition and thus aims to articulate a defensible conception of tradition. Harris advocates progressive traditions—traditions that recognize their own formation and ongoing invention. On this account, living transvaluing social agents are involved in the shaping of consensus and the building of bonds through tradition. Traditions are depicted as dead (unrevivable) bodies that we inhabit and live through; they are horrors incarnate—"the categorically impossible past that shapes the present." Existing identities are always being shaped and reshaped by active agents living through an unrevivable past. The African American philosophical tradition—philosophy born of struggle—is one such example. The creation of this tradition serves various functions for its adherents, including fostering analyses of the experiences of immiserated populations, calling into question the intervening background assumptions of the Western philosophical tradition, and conjuring imaginative scenarios of emancipation (i.e., "reading a *Preface to a Twenty Volume Suicide Note*"). And transvaluation, the reinvention of a tradition, the shaping of a new future (for a progressive tradition) will require the abandoning of lifeless traditional confines (i.e., "burning Babylon to build Benin").

What if traditions in philosophy are analogous to traditions in the theatrics of horror? What if traditions in American philosophy since the influence of modern science are analogous to traditions in the theatrics of horror since the advent of movies? If the texts of philosophy perform, and theatrics can be read as text, we can draw an analogy between the traditions in each arena. I first explore what is meant by a "tradition." I then consider the import of the analogy between the traditions of philosophy and the theatrics of horror.

A Philosophy of Struggle

Aphorism I

In a narrow sense, tradition means institutional interactions that are or result in fairly well-defined, repeated communicative events.[1] "Tradition" will be capitalized when I mean it in a narrow sense. Traditions consist of attentiongetting activities, as distinct from pedestrian acts or normalized communicative events. Traditions include intrinsically ambiguous categories, extreme salience of meaning, and standardized protocols. Traditional "objects or practices are liberated for full symbolic and ritual use when no longer fettered by practical use."[2] Well-defined Traditions, such as that of the shape of sailor hats, perform no practical function. Sailor hats certainly make reference to their own symbolic meaning, but unlike baseball helmets, they perform no nature-transforming or protective function. This feature of Traditions has long been recognized by investigators of the phenomenon.

Who has an authorial voice to speak the truth is different from what they speak and claim as true. It has been argued, for example, that "what makes certain types of discourse 'traditional' [akin to my narrow sense of Tradition] can be described as a *specific organisation of the claims to truth*."[3] Traditions of philosophy and science determine "who has the right to speak."[4] The presence of Traditions in science and philosophy does not mean that professionals in these fields all share a world view. Traditions help form institutionalized sources for claims to truth in the sense that they provide rites of passage, language, and situations that define authorial voices that can claim to be asserting a truth, especially a truth that is the unspoken existing, or legitimately possible future, consensus.

One important mark of a Tradition, which also helps distinguish it from other forms of historically repeated behavior, is that a Tradition is marked by welldefined revered symbols and archetypal figures. A horror movie that does not begin with eerie music would seem out of character. A horror movie without a manifestly impossible but frightening monster or event is hard-pressed to qualify as a horror movie. Traditions of horror movies will have archetypal figures, particularly monsters, associated with them. Similarly, a Tradition in philosophy will have archetypal figures, texts, and communicative events that are to be repeated as a part of enacting the protocol of the Tradition. The honored seating of philosophers at annual King's College don gatherings or annual presidential lectures at the American Philosophical Association Eastern Division meeting are Traditions in the narrow sense.

Although I have described Traditions by means of traits commonly found in anthropological studies, the intent has been to describe traits that are central to, but not exhaustive of, well-defined Traditions. There is also a broad sense of "tradition," integrally connected to but distinct from both the narrow sense of Tradition and from a totalized sense.

A web of consensus, shared values, vocabularies, rhetorical devices, institutional recognitions, rules and rituals of protocol, methods, questions, and criteria of evaluation refined generation after generation help define traditions in a broad sense. George Allan captures the broad sense in which "tradition" has been used by him as well as such authors as Foucault and Auerbach:

> Tradition is to be understood as a vast Bible, a system of written and therefore objective assertions, a structure of truth serving as the guide and governor for all human activity. This one book of cultural articulation, to which all individual "books" contribute, is precisely what I have meant by the totality of linked importances. It is an objective order of things, functioning to separate meaning from meaninglessness, rationality from madness, truth from error. Under the tutelage of this enduring value system, I learn how to think and act and feel in a civilized way, which is to say in a way that makes me confident that what I do is worthwhile and satisfying.[5]

In this broad sense, intellectuals discuss what they mean by "the Western tradition," the "German tradition of sociology," "the discursive tradition," the "Aristotelian tradition," and so on.[6] On Allan's account, the Western tradition is exemplified by "universality arising from particularity as its child and redeemer. A strange idea, although an ever-present seam running through the fabric of those enduring importances that characterize the Western peoples, its light fading now in these times of cultural forgetfulness and breakdown."[7] The concerns of Derrida in *Writing and Difference*, for example, include the existence and efficacy of centered structures and the search for an *arche* between essence and appearance, content and form, representation and the thing itself.[8] These have formed a misguided array of concerns important to Western intellectual traditions on Derrida's account. For Richard Rorty, the search for epistemological foundations, particularly rational forms that could dictate what the content of our beliefs should be, has been an important, but misguided, thread in the Western tradition of philosophy.[9] These authors rely on a broad sense of tradition for such depictions, although they may use other senses as well.

A broad sense of tradition is also used to depict the activities of fairly well-circumscribed social groups, such as professional philosophers. David Hollinger's "communities of discourse," for example, consist of professionals who share a community by virtue of shared values, questions, importances, affinities, vocabulary, methodologies, ideals, and rhetorical devices.[10] They may share common procedures for credentializing new professionals and types of evidence for establishing rank. This application of "tradition" has become common in studies of professionalism.

When tradition is used broadly, its content is especially empty, save what an author supplies, and the already entailed reverence for Tradition. It is the substantive meaning of Tradition that significantly defines the import, and thereby an important boundary, of tradition. The import of tradition is, I believe, always parasitic on that of Tradition. If, for example, an author believes that an Aristotelian tradition of virtue ethics should be redeemed, the author normally does not mean that all of the beliefs and arcane practices of Aristotle or Periclean Athens should be everyone's guide. Rather, the author means that some set of principles, concerns, or attitudes associated with the history of Aristotelian virtue ethics should be redeemed and given broader acceptance. What may be entailed, if not stated, is that the author would like for this tradition (as a set of beliefs or principles embodied in a discourse) to become normalized, that is, repeated, reiterated, and for it to become a standard through which persons must pass as a condition of their having a claim to other independent or derived truths. This entailment is a distinguishing mark of Traditions.

Traditions and traditions are conservative repositories of claims and possible claims that are enrolled in the project of perpetuating or creating a given consensus, one that is or should become normalized. Traditions and traditions certainly change; the point is that they provide the stage on which legitimate claims can be made, including claims about how or why the Tradition or tradition should change.

They also exclude; exclusion is a necessary function of tradition. The "West," for example, can only conceive of itself by constructing others as at least external, alien, and separate, if not primitive and exotic.[11] "Western" is sometimes identified with "European," but "Europe" doesn't come into existence as an imagined community until the late eighteenth century.[12] It is a nonnatural array of associated states that has come to be considered a culture, continent, and people. To the extent that "Europe" is a social entity, it is not unreasonable to consider what entitlements or rights persons have that maintain their identity as European. Such entitlement or rights would be goods held by Europeans, exclusive of persons that are not members of its cultural/continental community. Who has a *prima facie* stake in speaking, and the status for speaking, about what entitlements or rights are warranted is conditioned on who counts as European. Traditions and traditions identified as European, consequently, have an implied warrant for existence if considered endemic to the social entity of Europe. European history is replete with civil strife over what traditions count as alien, demeaning, not genuine, and bastardizations of an imagined pristine past.

Another sense of tradition is the totalized sense, not always clearly distinct from the broad sense. The totalized sense (hereafter trad) has two always-present ideas—that *all* ideas, practices, and symbols involve or include repetition, and that all persons are normally contextualized or situated in a society engined by prejudgments, a world view, life world, or form of life. The broad sense of "tradition" considers the past as a vast bible; the totalized sense considers every facet of life interwoven into a contextualized, repeated, interlinked well of cognition. The broad sense can be applied to a limited range of practices, for example, language-use or the practices and ideas of anthropologists; the totalized sense necessarily includes all practices.[13] The totalized sense considers all forms of social life as implicated in privileged communicative or cognitive inheritances. For example, agents can be completely unfamiliar with the Bible and thereby excluded from persons said to practice religion in ways associated with its traditions in a broad sense; in the totalized sense, these agents fit in a world inhabited by the Bible and its associated traditions, familiar to them or not. A totalized conception purports to tell us about the world as a whole.

Impartiality of judgment is, on accounts that rely on a totalized sense, as impossible as having a starting point of analysis that is not distorted by uncritical attitudes, beliefs, habits, customs, prejudgments, and prejudices. A metaphysics, ontology, epistemology, or aesthetics is necessarily distorted by communicative practices that invariably include inherited and privileged structures, forms, assumptions, and codes that remained unstated. The subject, on such accounts, may be considered problematic because the subject may inappropriately present its ideas as ones that surmount the limitations of what it is to be a subject—contextually bounded. A method of reasoning, or at least considering various methods of reasoning, for such authors as Gadamer and Rorty is important as a way of approaching the facticity of trad and the need for critical reflection; neither "facticity" nor "critical reflection" escapes contextuality into a pure realm of the impartial, but both can have more or less defensible characteristics.

From the broad sense of tradition, we can infer claims about the nature of life. The totalized sense, however, can be used to directly depict a conception of life. Tempels's *Bantu Philosophy*, for example, depicts an alleged worldview that totally defines the practices and ideas of the Bantu, actually a dubious language grouping, such that any unanticipated event or new idea is necessarily locked into, interpreted by, and explained in terms of preconstituted ideas.[14] Tempels holds that the "being" of the Bantu is defined by its world view and its traditions/Traditions immediately determined by that worldview. Humanity is for Tempels the collection of different beings, equal in their entrenchment in inescapable but mutually valuable world views. The deduction from Bantu worldviews to Bantu practices is reductive, that is, the practices provide insight into the worldview and the worldview provides insight into the practices. In effect, the idea that people can build airplanes corresponds to, fits, is inferentially reasonable or deducible from world views just as the idea that people should have reverence for the forest can be read from social practices.

Trads are the manifestation of the totality of "the truth," at least "the truth" of persons engaged in the trads. Comte Joseph de Maistre and Felicite Robert de Lamennais considered trads the manifestation of common, racial reason lodged in a group's practices. Failure to submit to trad (the Roman Catholic tradition in their case) meant, just as it meant for Tempels, that a "raciated" agent was violating their true being and risking the evil of destroying "the truth": for Tempels, the truth of the relativity of logic; for de Maistre and de Lamennais, the truth of the Holy Roman Church.

Aphorism II

I resonate with the politicized side of the invention approach to the history of traditions; it holds, in general, that traditions are historical constructions.[15] "Invented traditions" is taken to mean a set of practices, normally governed by overtly or tacitly accepted rules of a ritual or symbolic nature, which seek to inculcate certain values and norms of behavior by repetition, which automatically implies continuity with the past. In fact, where possible, they normally attempt to establish continuity with a suitable historic past.[16] Inventions are not necessarily fabrications, falsehoods, or outright lies. Inventions are imagined, created, discovered; they are contrivances, gadgets, and doohickeys; they are the Alchemy of Finance, the Alchemy of Race, as well as the Alchemy of Community.[17] King Arthur was neither a king nor an important warrior (an intentional lie told by British historians and repeated year after year); the Pilgrims did not land on Plymouth Rock, Paul Revere was a nobody during his lifetime, and Americans did not lavish sentiment, toys, or education on their children until the mid-nineteenth century.[18] "Invention" is intended to include lies and fabrications, but the facets of central importance are imagined ways in which links are conceived. Benedict Anderson described the way the past is marshalled to establish an imagined link and legitimacy:

> Even the most determinedly radical revolutionaries always, to some degree, inherit the state from the fallen regime. Some of these legacies are symbolic, but not the less important for that. Despite Trotsky's unease, the capital of the USSR was moved back to the old Czarist capital of Moscow ... the PRC [People's Republic of China]'s capital is that of the Manchus (while Chiang Kai-shek had moved it to Nanking), and the CCP leaders congregate in the Forbidden City of the Sons of Heaven.[19]

Similarly, Washington, DC, was a slave-trading capital and bastion of displaced mercantile aristocrats—no haven for democratic anything. The "ancien régimes" of Europe did not see themselves as forming a body of "aristocrats" until aristocracy as such was nearly extinct: we see them as a body.

Conceiving traditions as inventions entails accepting the view that the content and form of traditions are historical developments, that is, there is nothing natural about any particular tradition; they are normative formations, constructed in a myriad of ways. There may be biologically compelling reasons for the existence of mating, for example, but there are no such reasons for mating traditions that favor either patrilateral parallel cousin marriage or exogamy.[20] Similarly, conceiving communities as imagined requires that the content and form of the bonds that define links to persons outside one's immediacy are imagined bonds that make communication, trade, peace, and war possible. There may be geographically and biologically compelling reasons necessitating community cohesion and bonds of trust, care, and compassion among kin and commune; there are no such reasons necessitating the character of existing nation states.

What is occasionally termed discourse analysis—the works of Nietzsche, Foucault, and Said are examples—is closely associated with the invention approach to traditions.[21] They hold in common that discourse does not represent social reality but rather constructs that social reality through an array of linguistic techniques. "Discourse analysis" as I use it is intended to emphasize the scholarship on the way discourse is implied in the construction and deformity of what we count as normal and abnormal reality. My argument does not require that the numerous authors associated with the generalization "discourse analysis" hold identical philosophies, for example, they may be more or less Marxist or more or less Husserlian phenomenologists. Discourse is hardly a neutral picturing of reality, on the discourse analysis account, but a social and political mode of presenting and re-presenting the subject and deforming the other. Discourse analysis "cannot safely be founded on redefined 'traditions.'"[22] The reason is that discourse analysis uses the tools of detailed history, ethnography, genealogy, sociology, and linguistics to evaluate discourses that purport to represent a tradition and has found that they rely on salient notions that surreptitiously repeat favored dichotomies, stereotypes, and assumptions about authenticity. Traditions are understood as dichotomizing, totalizing, and violent ventures that too often falsely pretend to be expressive of universal, objective, and rational principles rather than actually entrapped provincialisms. Discourse analysts who consider totalities and surreptitious dichotomies to be unappealing seek to avoid granting traditions significant appeal. However, depending on the author, some form of tradition may be considered important for social cohesion and political struggle. Discourse analysis, I believe, has provided additional weight to the invention approach to traditions.

Philosophers often use the "Western tradition of philosophy" to mean a line of conversation extending from Athens through primarily Western Europe (and not including Egypt, the Ottoman and Byzantine Empires, Huns, Moors, and Islam; the United States and Canada may be thrown in as addenda to the "Western tradition," depending on the author). Economists, by contrast, often mean by "Western" industrialized nations such as Japan, Brazil, Europe, United States, Canada, and Mexico. Sociologists may mean by "Western" North and South America. The use of "the Western tradition of philosophy" can refer to a broad range of beliefs, acts, dominant themes, and the like; it is, however, at once inventing itself and simultaneously relying on content that is arguably present, given appropriate erasures and silent voices.

Aphorism III

It is false that people who watch horror movies normally go away and perform acts of terror; just as it is false that people who read philosophy normally go away and perform the acts philosophers take delight in applauding. It is equally false that people replicate, in mirror fashion, the ideas replete in philosophy or the ideas replete in horror movies.

Assume that history is not driven toward an end-state such that the reality of human history is rationally structured and sequenced to achieve that end-state teleologically. Further assume that practical reason, reasonableness, or rationality neither saturates nor is even dominant in the actual cognitive practices of normal persons. Rather, suppose that the sorts of incongruent, heuristic, and fallacious cognitive practices described by numerous naturalizers of epistemology are characteristic of human cognition.[23] Given these assumptions, it is arguable that traditions (broad sense) in philosophy are as contingent on the nature of human imagination as traditions of horror, if such traditions are contingent on how people actually think. The reason this is so is that traditions require us to imagine that the consensus which they embody is, or should be, identified with normality, such that normality is coterminous with a general or particular nature of being. That "nature of being" can be conceived as an ontological essence or intended as a benign nativism depicting our species character. In either case, we can be confident—in watching a horror movie or living our lives—that we are securely moored in normality.

One reason philosophies are not like horror movies, although both can be understood as performances enlivened by texts, is that philosophies have been coconspirators in, or help make possible, genuine terrors. Roughly, terror is distinguished from horror by the extent to which the acts depicted are or can be considered real; acts that are considered unreal or at best a singular aberration of normal possibility can be considered horror. A horror, such as the instant death and maiming of millions, once considered an impossible feat except by divine intervention, can become an actual terror (Nagasaki and Hiroshima), but not the other way around.

Horror movies have yet to be substantively implicated as a cause of or deep contributor to reigns of terror; no horror movie has ever been used as the definitive text to legitimate domination into perpetuity; nor have any horror movies helped form the theoretical basis for revolutions to overthrow exploitation, exclusion, and tyranny. Horror movies have played roles in each of the above situations but as bit actors within a play; the play, stage, plot, meaning, and characters were deeply entwined with philosophies. This is so not because philosophies are mirrored in practice but because the type of imaginative scenarios they offer are intended to be, and have been "traditional" sources for, helping people select right thinking to guide practice (e.g., rational, reasonable, dialectic, postmodern, African, or scientific). Imagination plays a role in shaping what fascinates us about philosophies just as imaginative possibilities play a role in shaping what fascinates us about horror movies, although horror movies bear no mirroring in shaping what we do in practice.

The thought theory of emotional responses to fiction "maintains that audiences know horrific beings are not in their presence, and indeed, that they do not exist, and therefore, their description or depiction in horror fictions may be a cause for interest rather than either flight or any other prophylactic enterprise."[24] On this account, the categorically impossible beings that inhabit horror movies command curiosity and fascination. The interest and enjoyment we gain from horror movies outweighs the distress. The distress, in fact, may be an integral feature of the enjoyment; the distress is enwebbed in what forms the fascination, if not a particular person's enjoyment. Horror movies remain entertaining in spite of and because of the distress.

The "beings" that often inhabit works of philosophy, for example, the virtuous pagan Athenian, the workers that have as their interests universal human interest, the citizen engaged in communicative inquiry, or the sage in the African village who carries the wisdom of ancient Egyptians, are presented as real beings for our emulation. If the practices and reasoning of such beings are believed manifestations of their traditions, their traditions stand for the collective being of those with right dispositions, right thinking, and practices that make possible right choices. Not even Frankenstein was so bold.

There is a difference between "acting as if," such that our acts make the "as if" real, and "acting as though," such that our acts do *not* make the "as though" real. Acting *as if* there really is a community of philosophers makes, *mutatis mutandis*, the community of philosophers; acting *as if* the virtues of Aristotle were the sort we should follow makes, *mutatis mutandis*, the agents followers of the virtues of Aristotle, if they are earnest believers. Imitating a model, for example, provides us in a sense with an initiation into what it is to live like the model. We improvise, imagine, and add our own unique variations until our lives feel comfortable with the model or models woven together to help form our character. However, acting *as though* the virtues of Aristotle were the sort we should follow makes the action the type well designed for theater. One who acts this way is not necessarily insincere or a disbeliever but an actor, not just an agent. However, if the actor makes the fatal mistake of treating the virtues of every character played as definitive of their being, then the actor is making their characters' virtues real at least in the sense that the actor is living their experience under the aegis of those virtues. The actor ceases acting and ceases having a distinguishable character apart from the various parts played and the process of performing those parts. Acting *as though* a monster in a horror movie is real at best makes us scared—otherwise we would not be in the theater very long. [25]

Consequently, imagination in acting *as if* entails a form of reality that differs from acting *as though*. The first is concretized, that is, I am the concrete agent, I need a passport to get into the imagined community of France. The second makes a community of genuinely lived experience impossible.

In the next three sections, I consider several built-in tendencies of conservatism in philosophy that render support for the belief that traditions (all three forms) are intrinsically conservative inventions, inventions that mitigate against lived experiences. I also consider a defensible approach, given the inescapability of traditions, using American and African American philosophy as examples.

Aphorism IV

One reason competitiveness and critique are not as radical a feature of the Western tradition in philosophy as might be believed is because traditions, Western or otherwise, are highly regarded as sites of hidden truth. The same authors, repeatedly noted as important, are often noted not because they are authors with right answers in Western philosophy, but because they are authors whose works pose the right questions, make interesting distinctions, use appropriate prose forms, and provide controversial answers within an accepted range of conceivable answers. By immersion in their works, as one didactically, argumentatively, critically, and competitively cajoles an ancestral spirit, one will be empowered with the potential to speak the truth. Having acquired the potential, the easiest way to maintain the newly acquired power is to speak through the agents who are the conduits of one's authority. That is, to interpret or reinterpret the canonical figures, to critique and revalue the canonical figures, to speak one's own truth as a clearer version of the truth only intimated, implied, or suggested by the canonical figures, is to proclaim that one's truth is the hidden truth long submerged inside the intricacies of the authorities already canonized as being closest to the truth. No one is born Kantian,

Marxist, or pragmatist; and who counts as a legitimate one of these is a continual subject of debate (e.g., Is Derrida really appealing to Kant? Was Trotsky or Stalin the genuine Marxist? Is Rorty really promoting the spirit of Dewey's pragmatism or was Emerson really a pragmatist?). Moreover, what the features of a tradition are, are very often, if not contrived, constructed in one of many possible ways. Meanings always differ from person to person; no matter how slightly, weight placed on different knowledge claims shifts, sometimes ever so slightly. The actors invent, over time, the same play that is of necessity a different version. However, in order to maintain authority within a tradition, its authorial voices must be interpreted or shown to provide witting or unwitting support. In this fashion, the critical theorist remains Marxist, having advanced or surmounted Marxism; the neopragmatist remains pragmatist, having focused on experience and rejected either-or dichotomies; MacIntyre remains true to Aristotle although he holds hardly any views of Aristotle; Mudimbe remains an Africanist although he deconstructs "Africa"; Wiredu remains an African philosopher although his views on rationality are Kantian in inspiration.[26]

The Egyptian mystery system is not paradigmatic of Pharaonic Egypt without a myopic focus on death, life after death, eternal servants for royalty, and the possibility of obliteration for persons improperly buried. Traditional African philosophy is not paradigmatically African without the moral community defined in kinship and kind terms. Periclean Athens, without practices of infanticide, animalism, human sacrifice, polytheism, and predestination, is not Athenian. Thomas Aquinas, without any form of Christianity, conception of the natural subordination of women to men, or God-dependency as the ultimate source of right action, is not the same Thomas Aquinas that he aspired to being. Tradition construction invariably involves, to some degree, erasures. A selection of principles, structures, styles, attitudes, or questions that were important to an author are excised, promoted, or erased. The contexts of claims are ignored or emphasized according to whether they are in some way enlightening in relation to the general ideas the construction wishes to promote. The tremendous range of possible routes makes the notion of a rational tradition, understood as an unvaried, unbroken, communicated line of behavior, and beliefs worse than superstition. An argument to reinstate Franz Fanon's sense of moral indignation without the regenerative role of violence, an argument to reinstate an Aristotelian sense of virtue without wealthy citizens standing as exemplars of the most virtuous, or an argument to reinstate a Thomistic traditional sense of morals without noblemen as important characters is analogous to arguing for the mass production of Model-T Fords in a Toyota plant. The appearance as form can be exactly duplicated, but the content and character of its producers would, in almost no respect, match the original Model-T Ford.

The search for necessary and sufficient conditions of truth, for example, has one of the longest histories in philosophy; or rather, with the way "philosophy" has come to be delineated, the history of the search for necessary and sufficient conditions of truth has been constructed as central. The impact of science, in particular, significantly influenced the importance of this issue in the history of American philosophy. It is not that authors addressing this issue were conversant with one another. Cases in which they were are given special importance. In retrospect, the defenses, responses, and lines of reasoning that authors offered are constantly reconstructed as if they were in conversation with one another. The reconstructions, compiled year after year, layer upon layer, makes it easy to imagine that there is a continuous history within this narrow range of literature. As conversations between persons regarding necessary and sufficient conditions of truth increase, imagination comes to instantiate itself and makes itself concrete with more and more real examples of communication. The feat of imagination, even after a multiplicity of real communicative events, is an important feature of tradition as a perpetual construction—each successive wave of commentators looks back to revise and reenvision a debate; each abandons what it considers irrelevant, tacky, indefensible, embarrassing, or simply unimportant to their projects; each appeals to the past for support and legitimation—as if Pharaonic Egyptians, Ogottemeli, Fanon, Periclean Athenians, Aristotle, or Thomas Aquinas would in some form concur with their reformation.

As an aside, Dr. Frankenstein was not at all pleased when his monster did not obey orders.

Aphorism V

I sometimes believe, contrary to popular interpretations, that Frankenstein movies, and quite a few other classics as well, are not horror movies. If an agent, say Dr. Frankenstein, steps beyond the pale of extant knowledge, applies that knowledge, and creates a being that according to extant knowledge is impossible, then the movie appears less classically horrific. If a person is clinically dead, their revival is possible only by accident, divine intervention, or knowledge that exists beyond the pale of extant knowledge. Ruling out accident, Dr. Frankenstein has similar effectual powers as a divine interventionist. Sometimes, upon reflection, however, I believe Frankenstein movies are classical horror movies. Frankenstein rejoins the ranks of the classical horror genre if a dead person (unrevivable) is not revivable because "death" outside of accident or divine intervention is exclusive of life and potential sentient life. As long as death and life are absolute contraries, Frankenstein is a classical horror movie. Frankenstein is a third, categorically impossible, being. If I treat Frankenstein's "categorical impossibility" as an actual, potential, or even a possible option, however, Frankenstein ceases to be horror. The cessation of Frankenstein as horror is paradoxically parasitic on Frankenstein as horror. Like all forms of parasitism, the relationship between the possible and the impossible is unstable and elastic.[27] Whether Frankenstein is horror or not depends on how I treat extant knowledge of reality.

Traditions (the narrow sense) and lived experiences are mutually exclusive in the sense that lived experiences occur through inherited symbols of the normal in which we, like chaotic floating signifiers, continually constitute unique meanings necessarily different from what has been inherited. Traditions are dead (unrevivable) bodies that we inhabit and live through. They are horrors incarnate—the categorically impossible past that shapes the actual present.

Fanon, in "On National Culture," had it right when he argued that the colonized often usurp the demeaning stereotypes of the colonizer and reshape them into the stereotypes that define their self-images.[28] The new images, particularly the ones in the service of the bourgeoisie, are used to make traditions that have little to do with the real redistribution of power. The native is vitalistic, sensual, and emotive, and the colonizer logocentric, scientific, and calculating—all praise to vitalism while the population starves and the colonizer produces and owns the products of modernity! The categorically impossible past can give cause for self-esteem; simultaneously, it can be used to shroud the lived experience of misery borne by the populace in the name of the nation—but in the material benefit of the ruling elite that in practice care nothing for such trifles. However, without a link to the past—without reclaiming the Forbidden City of the Sons of Heaven, the Islands of the Kings, or the Benin Empire as seats and sources of legitimation—it's not clear that social transformational ideals can sufficiently regenerate a people's sense of having a coherent social nexus and responsibility.

The impossibility of absolute impartiality—because we all have a starting point, a background of inherited, developed, family-influenced unreflective habits, beliefs, and customs—is the other side of the impossibility of absolute contextuality, particularly in the modem world. Traditions, in a broad sense, symbolize a peoples' immediacy and ascendancy. Fanon is noted for having failed to appreciate the influence of the past— as a remembering, reliving, source of meaning and guide for future practice. Muslim women, for example, returned to the veil, Islam did not fade, and autocratic forms of association did not disappear as a result of the Algerian National Liberation Front's (FLN) participatory form of organization and struggle against the French—any more than the critical Marxism of Serbian intellectuals replaced or prevented deep-seated parochial ethnocentricity. Moreover, Fanon tended to neglect the importance of inherited beliefs about commitment to family, friends, siblings, and future generations; these often form an array of intuitions that motivate people to place their living existence at tremendous risk in order to remain faithful to beliefs that define their person. How social entities are constructed, inclusive of what traditions are taken to be central grounds for bonding, is crucial to the kind of consensus that shapes social entities. Living agents are involved in shaping that consensus, not dead bodies or a mysterious historical consciousness of remembrances. That's why it is better for a people to write and rewrite their own dictionaries—several university editions of the *Webster Dictionary*, for example, include "Aryan" but not "Akan"; and if one relies on the *Encyclopedia Britannica*, African people hardly exist. The *Encyclopedia of Philosophy* should be renamed the *Encyclopedia of Eurocentric Nationalism*.

Living persons in a multiplicity of associations and networks participate in shaping and reshaping their being, individual and social; that being provides social agency. Persons share a common nature as transvaluing social agents bonding through fluid forms of social identity. The livingness of identity is why E. W. Blyden's *Christianity, Islam and the Negro Race* has an appeal that V. Y. Mudimbe's *The Invention of Africa* does not; Blyden provides a sense of the past and a telos for a collective entity that gives cause to a willingness to sacrifice for future generations and defend African people against the actual murderous and exploiting Europeans.[29] The coherent social nexus Blyden provides is primordial and providential; the nexus Mudimbe provides is accidental, contrived, alien, and the consequence of adaptations to force. Mudimbe has no way of providing a reason to be concerned with future generations because the collective entity of Africa for Mudimbe is invented in the sense that its historicity is not tied to a telos. Its collectivity forms a being through which people can see themselves as instantiations but not instantiations tied to their nature, character, or even their own imaginative creation. Invention approaches do not provide providential, historical, material, or anthropological natures and inherent personality traits as causes and reasons for behavior. At best, politicized invention approaches are associated with transformational ideals. Experiences are nonetheless mediated through some categorically impossible features of the past; some causally associated or naturally connected links of coherency legitimating current risks.

If what has been termed the Sartre/Roquentin picture of the self is appropriate—a picture that contends persons are disjointed agents without coherent lives as narratives— it is certainly the case that lived experiences are mutually exclusive of traditions.[30] This is so because imagining the past entails constructing causal links between events that are not causally connected. Also, lived experiences can usurp traditions in the service of either progressive transformation or empty platitudes about revising ancient norms to salvage modem insecurities. Moreover, if MacIntyre's picture of the self as a coherent agent is true, that is, a coherent agent with narrative stories that may include falsifications (in part, because it's not clear what a narrative would be without falsifications, because agents are also authors of their own stories, and coherent life plans tend to have a telos), it is still the case that traditions and lived experiences are mutually exclusive.[31] This is so because lived experiences include, but are not reducible to, causal connections. Having pain is not reducible to an imagined narrative; needing to defecate is not identical to participating in a tradition that dictates the protocol for so doing; killing a colonizer who has spent her life raising sons to rape and exploit the colonized is not identical to saluting a rebel flag—somebody kills and somebody dies.

Personal necessities, choices, accidents, and moments of individuated feelings exist. The having and making of such experiences are not *prima facie* necessarily instantiated in what existing or imagined repeated performance define. Even if what is meant by tradition is trad (the totality of human existence), the actual having of feelings and dispositions by an individual cannot be substituted for the actual having of feelings and dispositions by another individual. The repeated practices of others are not identical to my repeated practices. They can be conjoined, mutually influential, similar, and common, but the having is always individuated. Such individuation does not deny the presence of historical, contextual, or situational influences, only that they are not substitutes for individual experience. This view of lived experiences does not deny the existence of viable communities, imagined as they are; but it does deny that existing communities are substitutes for past communities. Given the importance that the past plays in defining identities, existing identities are always themselves being shaped and reshaped by active agents—living through a categorically impossible past.

Traditions are not horrors in the sense that we can step beyond the limitations of extant knowledge through imagination. We can revise, rewrite, and define the past differently. We can include the historically excluded, consider the strengths of persons that were perceived as self-deprecators, and offer new ways for persons to have a sense of belonging and self-respect. Conversations between traditions, conflicts of traditions, new formations, and the death of previous points of reference contribute to imaginative possibilities. The categorically impossible is not expressed by the noun contraries of death and life but by the instability of their disjunction. Imagination and symbolic meanings are among the goods we use to help define the world of possibility; they are unstable and elastic, thereby allowing inventions, creations, and new forms of authenticity.

If presentation of the structure of the universe in symbol form occurred, generation after generation, it might be considered a custom. Such a custom could be repeated with reverence and generate attention when discussed. In addition, it could be reasonable to revere the knowledge of inherited, repeated symbol systems that present the structure of the universe. That is, repetition and reverence for this symbolic language could become a well-defined Tradition if and only if the symbolic language were useless. If persons who mastered or contributed to the symbol system that presented the structure of the universe were considered claimants to other truths, the symbol system would have additional grounds as a Tradition. The more useless the symbols presenting the structure of the universe, that is, logical positivism's *philosophia perenia*'s truth, the more they shade toward Tradition; the more useful, the more they face the degradation of immediacy without the shroud of reverence. The more useless cowboys became to the cattle industry, the more cowboys could become symbolic of America's spirit of independence—real cowboys and real people familiar with the experiences knew better.

The symbolic language presenting the structure of the universe could be useful as a recursive, self-referential language. That is, symbolic language that concerned symbol systems, how well they presented the universe or how we might continually improve the minimal ways their presentation was inaccurate, could be useful. Traditions, however, require an inability to be other directed, for example, no practiced ethical systems could be actually justified because of a symbolic language.

It is impossible for a tradition to be rational and supply other-directed knowledge if rational means, minimally, the lack of some set of fallacies and the presence of some rules of inference subject to presentation in symbol form. If rational means reasonable, for example, considering alternatives, evaluating particular instances in relation to general principles, and offering justification for beliefs, traditions cannot be reasonable.

A tradition cannot move as if moving from one premise to the next because change within a tradition occurs cognitively in the realm of symbolic or imaginative behavior. Traditions change as if chaotic floating signifiers determine inferences, not track inferences associating particulars to general principles or codify comparative evaluations. That is, no historical array of discourses can match an array of argument designs or proceed from one set of practices to another as if each practice represented a premise in a reasonable argument. Traditions are at their best when they do not match a strictly preformed model of inferencing within the boundaries of what the tradition symbolizes and do not substantively inform other-directed practices and beliefs.

One tradition can be based on more reasonable principles and sustain more reasonable practices than another; the boundaries of one tradition can afford a more useful array of imaginative options or restrictions than another. However, to treat "traditions" as entities such that they change in ways that parallel reasonable inferencing is to treat traditions as Hegelian modes of consciousness. There is certainly a distinction between conversation that can occur between two reasonable traditions and picturing a conversation between two reasonable traditions as the flow of an argument. The latter erroneously treats "traditions" *as if* they were real entities whereas the former treats "traditions" *as though* they were real entities. Inventions, treated as real, like nations supposing they are really the embodiment of an absolute spirit and like performances in which the actor allows the part played to define how the actor shall live after the play is over, are imaginative scenarios that do not require treatment as substances, even if they have properties.[32] This is so because the content of traditions are extremely variable, that is, what an array of symbols means or warrants can shift radically. American judges, for example, wear robes but are not servants of the queen; kente cloth symbolizes royalty but more often the regality of African people than the royalty of the Asanteheny. The properties of traditions, consequently, are always inadequate to form boundaries the way the boundaries of France can be neatly drawn and concretely maintained without change. (Imagine saluting the US flag as a sacred symbol of the country in 1776 and saluting the US flag in 1992—the "country" includes children as citizens with rights, women as rights holders identical to men, Blacks as full moral persons—scandalous ideals that were not shared by writers of the Constitution.) The more a discourse is actually involved in shaping lived experience, the more it shades away from being a tradition and may be more properly described as custom, popular practice, contested guidelines, or possibly societal rules of conversation. So doing, of course, involves a loss of the description's surreptitious legitimation or defamation by parasitism on Tradition.

When a collection of philosophies is constituted as a national tradition, it is very difficult for such a tradition to incorporate authors and ideas that mitigate against the very foundation of repetitions intended to be the embodiment of the community or the community that's coming. "American Philosophy," for example, is confronted with just such a challenge in relation to that grain of African American philosophical activity that most involves a sense of struggle. That history and heritage challenge who counts, what issues are important, what life experiences are exemplary, what "America" and "philosophy" means, and what ideas and practices should be repeated. The character of the invention or staging is, in effect, challenged, not what play is to be performed. As indicated in what follows, African American philosophers such as Equiano, Crummell, Walker, and Locke were all staunch believers in fairly popular theologies or philosophies.[33] They challenged traditional views about who had the right to claims of truth, what styles actors should present, and the weight to be placed on different lines in the play—and about what the play means.

Aphorism VI

The Society for the Advancement of American Philosophy's (SAAP) *Newsletter* is adorned with the pictures of eleven archetypal American philosophers: Emerson, Thoreau, Peirce, James, Dewey, Royce, Whitehead, Santayana, Suckiel, and Dooley. Olaudah Equiano (Gustavus Vasa, the African), author of a slave-narrative form of ethical and social critique; David Walker, author of the impassioned call to arms by the enslaved; Alexander Crummell, Cambridgeeducated Platonist and a moral suasionist; and Alain Locke, critical relativist and radical pragmatist do not adorn its cover. The latter group is absent, I believe, not because of a malicious intent on the part of SAAP but because the texts of Equiano, Walker, Crummell, and Locke are rarely considered to be philosophy. They arise out of a history of personal and intellectual struggle which is neither university-bound nor confined to the central issues in the history of philosophy or reflective of an accepted American grain. The American grain of doing philosophy, as John McDermott aptly describes, does not include righteous indignation to the point of killing or self-sacrifice.[34] To be nostalgic about the lives of Equiano, Walker, Crummell, or Locke is to be nostalgic about a struggle to create a different reality or a reality that includes those despised by both the gentry and radicals of the dominant culture, a struggle that applauds extremes in its name.

Equiano, Walker, Crummell, and Locke are Western intellectuals. That is, the way they did philosophy was creatively their own but through prisms of prose and ideas fairly common in Western culture. They were, after all, Christians, Platonists, or pragmatists. The history and heritage of Christianity and of the Greco-Roman-Egyptian world involved their invented ancestors in a way similar to that in which it involved the invented ancestors of white Europeans and Americans. The *subjects* of their world, however, included the enslaved and the segregated as real agents—not phantoms whose rights would eventually be insured by the fiat of evolution, the rational application of the scientific method, social experiments guided by the dialogue of a community from which they were excluded, or the spiritually inspired principles of the progeny and kin of prevailing authorities.

David Walker's *Appeal to the Coloured Citizens of the World* (1848) advocated the violent overthrow of slavery by killing slave masters, running away from plantations, and disregarding claims of property rights when made by slave owners or their accomplices. Walker advocated maroonage, death blows, the rupture of stability, normalcy, and dispassionate rational dialogue. Walker favored the principles of Christianity, democracy, capitalism, and the popular virtues of thrift, frugality, and chastity; he wanted them actualized without regard to race. The future that Walker envisioned did not differ in structural character from popular visions except for the, existence of racial slavery— which required a radical break with the rules of civility. Walker offered, in a sense, a negative dialectic.

Walker distanced himself from being "American" so long as "American" meant the legitimation, as it did, of slavery. An "American" was either a slave owner or one empowered to potentially become a slave owner. Walker belonged to a group that at best could only be peripheral slave owners, for example, Black owners of slaves could conceivably become slaves; but the worst possible fate white owners faced was indentured servitude. Analogous to the difference between indentured servitude and slavery is the difference between a slave and serf—the realms of personal freedom from harm and potential realizable life plans substantively differ.[35] Walker is an example of what I mean by righteous indignation—right thinking, right making, and right choices for radical change are explicit and intended as derivations from general principles.

If American philosophers are pictured as a motley crew of curious intellectuals, what do we do with those Americans whose very life and intellectual project suggests the sheltered, segregated, and insulated conundrum of the motley crew? What do we do with the ideas of American philosophers regarding race relations when those ideas were not always savory? We can, as has been the case, construct a tradition that remains blind to diversity—particularly to that sector of the American philosophical scene that compels a revaluation of the scene itself—while simultaneously applauding pluralism, difference, and community. The tradition I have decided to promote cannot afford this deceit.

I consciously participate in the tradition of American philosophy. The tip of the iceberg, however, is that I consciously participate in the creation of a tradition that did not exist as such before. It would be bad faith to contend that the tradition of African American philosophy existed prior to its formation and discussion as such, not because discourse defines existence or is fairly analogous to it, but because the texts that form its canon were not texts that "debated" one another. Some authors were in direct conversation, such as W. E. B. Du Bois and Booker T. Washington; but the Du Bois/Washington debate hardly forms a "tradition" in philosophy.[36] It can be constructed as one feature of a tradition but only after a "tradition" is conceptualized. Neither Du Bois nor Washington saw themselves as philosophers, or offered an array of arguments around the kinds of issues definitive of professional philosophy. Alain Locke, I believe, is the sentinel historical figure in the history of African American professional philosophers because he conjoins an interest in the historically important issues of social well-being crucial to the African American intellectual agenda with central issues in the modem history of philosophy.

I participate in the creation of the tradition of African American philosophy because the definition of philosophy has been so restrictive that it excludes the possibility of insights from intellectuals that spoke to those disenfranchised, stereotyped, stigmatized as parasites, raciated as inferior, and immiserated. There are, I believe, a fair number of nascent and potentially compelling issues addressed by intellectuals that were themselves excluded from the moral and intellectual community of formal philosophy. I remain convinced that the imaginative scenarios encoded in the created tradition of African American philosophy offer the possibility of ideas of moment for human liberation—not because I expect these philosophies as a collective entity or the ideas of anyone in particular to be neatly mirrored in reality—but because their presence helps form imaginative scenarios of emancipation, that is, their scenarios are, and are about, struggle for liberation. (Moreover, and independent of these concerns, I needed an intellectual community and the community of American philosophy was peculiarly alien.) It is, however, as inappropriate to look for an Emerson within Black history as it is to look for a Walker within Native American history. It is also inappropriate to assume that every phase of philosophy is replicated, in some mirror-type fashion, among each racial or ethnic group. The idea that the presence of philosophy is evidence of humanity, proof of intellectual potential, or justification for a sense of pride is misguided.

Philosophy Born of Struggle constructed a tradition in the sense that the tradition it portrayed involved unconnected individuals, working through diverse institutions, but individuals with experiences of similar ilk and addressing similar issues.[37] The tradition is formed, not by repletion of a body of codified ideas that individuals intentionally or unintentionally repeated with unique variations, but by showing the sense in which they participated in addressing situations similar to those of their predecessors of the same discipline. It is a construction. It is an adversarial construction, that is, it is intended to give voice to concerns that have been, within the Western tradition of philosophy, considered illegitimate sources of truth because they referenced individuals and situations that call into question the legitimacy, universality, and meaning of the Western tradition.

The Philosophy of Alain Locke is an anthology intended to give voice to Alain Locke's philosophy of critical relativism, a form of radical pragmatism.[38] It is first rooted in debates about race in a racist society, and, second, debates about the merits of science, the importance of individuality, or the value of experience as a reference point for a coherentist view of truth. Race gives voice to an area of concern that helps shape the special features of Locke's radical pragmatism just as the importance of provincialism and nationalism help shape the special features of Dewey's ethical arguments. An appeal to authors that form the African American tradition is an appeal to authors that in many respects confront and reshape the meaning of Western, and in particular, American philosophy.

If the picture of the archetypal American philosophers on the front of SAAP's *Newsletter* included Equiano, Crummell, Walker, or Locke, it would no longer be a picture of fairly gentle, contemplative, raucous, cantankerous intellectuals and public activists. It would include the embattled, excluded, protesting, and the image of those still too often considered less than human. There would be something peculiar about a picture of the archetypes enjoying themselves on a beach. It is not only that if they were all alive at the same time some of them would not be caught dead on a beach with others because of sexism and genuine philosophical or personal differences, but also that the Blacks would not have been allowed on the beach with white women and men. It is this terribly wrenching facet of the national history of the United States that makes the collective identity of "America" lose some of its luster, some of its myth-making and symbolic power. Alienation from, and redefinition of, the United States is captured by works that address the continual redefinition of the moral community.[39] A rapprochement or a new moment of the tradition would require a different way of perceiving the United States.

The African American tradition, however, does not escape a tendency toward conservatism, valorization, and canonization. The character of racism confronted by

Equiano and Locke, for example, differs from the character of racism confronted by Broadus Butler and Angela Davis. Locke's arguments, decontextualized, can be well designed. There are certainly strong reasons for believing that Locke has the most warrantable claims. If he does not, then his works lose appeal, regardless of how well they might function as foils. If Locke's authorial voice, as a subtext, is honestly treated and works well to help reshape the Western and American tradition, destroy its hegemonic control over who and what count as important, and force consideration of the racism that infests Western philosophy, it is an authorial voice that should be a text and a subtext. If, in the future, the hegemonies of American philosophy are defeated, and it turns out that Locke's ideas have received regard, the functional utility of Locke should cease; the consensus should be lived as new musicians mount the stage in their own names. Newly invented traditions are, like all traditions, reformations of previous authorial voices. Traditions whose loyalties are with the least well-off are intended as praise songs for the widow—rituals of moment for adversarial struggles to overcome immiseration and domination. This view of adversarial traditions does not require essentializing the least well-off, as if they were invested with some purity of vision or as if persons who see themselves as promoting the interest of the least well-off were invested with some special truths. Rather, it requires believing that traditions emanating from adversary voices are likely to perceive community as a becoming that includes the least well-off as subjects. If the imagined community that is the home of one's loyalty is the community of the downtrodden, wretched, degraded, raped, victims of cruelty, the object of viciousness, they are subjects integral to the conceptualized community that is to become. Present traditions may be considered corruptions of a previously existing pristine state of affairs or demeaning practices of a chronically racist society; in either case, if the least well-off are considered agents in the moral community, the future is a becoming in a way that counts the immiserated—any future consensus takes their voices as meaningful in defining what counts as consensus.

A progressive tradition should include conditions for self-reformation, given the impossibility of self-destruction. Traditions are intrinsically conservative; as a tradition becomes a Tradition, it loses its substance. A progressive tradition, I suggest, should entail recognition of its own formation and continuation as an ongoing invention; an ongoing process of remaking theatrics that should abandon its representatives and valorized forms of consensus in the service of vitalization. Metaphorically, the living actors should clearly stand apart from the characters they portray and take a bow as agents. Failure to do so perpetuates the facade that the living are only embodiments of the past; that the current consensus is given in the nature of being.

A progressive tradition should be metaphorically a jazz tradition. Traditions in jazz are moments to relive the past, moments to pass through, instantiate, overcome, and moments of creation. The being expressed by the agent and the truth that is hidden is a truth that must, as a condition of crucial importance to the definition of jazz, be a truth either uniquely expressed by the agent or itself a function of unique expressions. The uniqueness or newness of an expression is not an intransitive good. Rather, it is a good within the arrangement of goods that make for a jazz tradition. That arrangement includes appreciation of the past but not its valorization; the being of the jazz agent is not constricted by a particular medium (e.g., Miles Davis is not an inauthentic jazzman on Tutu nor inauthentic for integrating Jimi Hendrix's sound). Jazz evolves, transforms, transfigures, transvalues, and decenters; it constructs, builds, molds, and creates new anew. Designs and content should be continually reformed, that is, jazzed, neither fantastic nor sheerly relative.[40]

Burn Babylon, otherwise known as Athens. The burning is the building of Benin.

Aphorism VII

Can the discursive formations of nihilists form a tradition? Nihilism, as I mean it here, is a philosophy that mitigates against the idea that there are unchanging or revisable universal principles and supports the idea of sheer relativized principles and a perception of the past as completely invented.

The object of a philosophy is usually to become repeated, orated, performed, acknowledged, and accepted (inclusive of earnest or fortuitous nods to rationality, critique, and continual self-reflection). Value-relativists that are not nihilists, for example, can participate in and form traditions if they want others to accept their position and form a consensus communicated across generations. It is counterintuitive for a nihilist, paganist, Marxist, pragmatist, critical theorist, or rationalist to deny that as many people as possible should, over time, hold their position. The possibility of a plurality of radically divergent paganists in proximity to one another, for example, requires that each does not (or does not succeed if they try) destroy others different from themselves. If a paganist community holds what it considers a preferable philosophy, it would seem preferable that as many people as possible hold and practice its philosophy. For that to be the case, each successive generation would engage in tradition-formation and maintenance with the intent of having its values survive in practice across generations, even if the community did not engage in proselytizing.

It is not unusual for nihilists with various approaches to refer to the works of other nihilists as commendable; it is also not unusual for postmodernists to analyze the same authors as exemplars of modernity or the emergence of postmodernity. For nihilism to be intrinsically self-critical, it would be necessary for it to include a claim that its archetypes and reference sources are used in the process of making and remaking; a process that cannot combat its own conservatism. An argument for nihilism can be offered that does not rely on references to earlier texts, even if it gave credence to earlier authors and argument forms that provide support. However, the form of legitimation that characterizes tradition—symbols that function at their best when they are useless—would continue to be the subtext by which the argument for nihilism surreptitiously gained unintentional warrant—the stage is already set because a sense of continuity is easily imagined by virtue of an admittedly disjointed history. Nihilists, unable to combat their own conservatism or live in a world that has not already set the stage, cannot act toward themselves the way they want persons to act toward the world—as agents of sheer relativity living through sheer relativity. The discursive formations of nihilism form a tradition even if, counterintuitively, nihilists are not interested in perpetuating their philosophy. That is, the discursive formations of nihilism, if understood as forming a tradition, do not escape the conservatism its content vies against.[41]

Tradition and its derivations should be a *Preface to a Twenty Volume Suicide Note*.[42] At least we would know whether we were about to witness the performance of a good horror movie or another philosophy of terror—inhabited by categorically impossible beings—possibly good models for vicarious identity but scary beings otherwise. If they were a *Preface to a Twenty Volume Suicide Note*, this might be of some small aid in deciding to live as if, rather than as though, we were agents, acting as if, rather than as though, the totality of possible conscious life were already manifest in existing or historically pristine contrivances, gadgets, and doohickeys.

Notes

1. Pascal Boyer, *Tradition as Truth and Communication* (Cambridge: Cambridge University Press, 1990), 3.

2. Eric Hobsbawm and Terence Ranger (eds.), *The Invention of Tradition* (Cambridge: Cambridge University Press, 1983), 4; also see George Allan, *The Importances of the Past: A Meditation on the Authority of Tradition* (Albany: State University of New York Press, 1986), 156.

3. Boyer, *Tradition as Truth and Communication*, 117.

4. Magill S. Larson, *The Rise of Professionalism* (Berkeley: University Press of California, 1977), 9.

5. Allan, *The Importances of the Past*, 200.

6. See, e.g., Wolf Lepenies, "'Interesting Questions' in the History of Philosophy and Elsewhere," in *Philosophy in History*, ed. R. Rorty, J. B. Schneewind, and Q. Skinner (Cambridge: Cambridge University Press, 1986), 141–72.

7. Allan, *The Importances of the Past*, 242.

8. See Jacques Derrida, *Writing and Difference* (Chicago, IL: University of Chicago Press, 1978).

9. Richard Rorty, *Philosophy and the Mirror of Nature* (Princeton, NJ: Princeton University Press, 1979).

10. See David Hollinger, *The American Intellectual Tradition* (New York: Oxford University Press, 1989).

11. See Edward W. Said, *Orientalism* (New York: Pantheon Books, 1978); and Stanley Diamond, *Culture in History* (New York: Columbia University Press, 1960).

12. See Marshall Hodgson, *The Venture of Islam* (Chicago, IL: University of Chicago Press, 1974); see also Clifford James, *The Predicament of Culture: Twentieth-Century Ethnography, Literature, and Art* (Cambridge, MA: Harvard University Press, 1988).

13. See Paulin Hountondji, *African Philosophy: Myth and Reality* (Bloomington: Indiana University Press, 1983), particularly his critique of ethnophilosophy, and Claude Levi-Strauss, *The Savage Mind* (Chicago, IL: University of Chicago Press, 1966); also see Boyer, *Tradition as Truth and Communication*. For arguments that rely on trad but are concerned with starting

points and communication between trads, see H. J. Gadamer, *Philosophical Hermeneutics*, trans. David E. Linge (Berkeley: University of California Press, 1976).

14. Placide Tempels, *Bantu Philosophy* (Paris: Presence Africaine, 1959); also see Deusdedit Nkurunziza, *Bantu Philosophy* (New York: Lang, 1989).

15. By the "invention" approach to tradition I mean the approach taken by the following: Hobsbawm & Ranger, *The Invention of Tradition*; V. Y. Mudimbe, *The Invention of Africa* (Bloomington: Indiana University Press, 1988); Christian Delacampagne, *L'Invention de Racisme: Antiquité et Moyen Age* (Paris: Fayard, 1983); Roy Wagner, *The Invention of Culture* (Chicago, IL: University of Chicago Press, 1975); Werner Sollors (ed.), *The Invention of Ethnicity* (Oxford: Oxford University Press, 1989); Denys Hay, *Europe: Emergence of an Idea* (Edinburgh: Edinburgh University Press, 1968); and Allan, *The Importances of the Past*. For the importance of reiteration, repetition, causal criteria of truth, and rituals as the conveyors of tradition, see Boyer, *Tradition as Truth and Communication*.

16. Hobsbawn and Ranger, *The Invention of Tradition*, l.

17. See Patricia Williams, *The Alchemy of Race and Rights* (Cambridge, MA: Harvard University Press, 1991); and George Soros, *The Alchemy of Finance* (New York: Simon & Schuster, 1987).

18. See Richard Shenkman, *Legends, Lies and Cherished Myths of American History* (New York: Harper & Row, 1989).

19. Benedict Anderson, *Imagined Communities* (London: Verso, 1983), 145. For ideas of community and agency, see Leonard Harris, "Historical Subjects and Interests: Race, Class, and Conflict," in *The Year Left*, ed. Michael Sprinkler et al. (New York: Verso, 1986), 91–106; and "Columbus and the Identity of the Americas," *Annals of Scholarship* 8 (2, Spring 1991): 287–99.

20. Ladislav Holy, *Kinship, Honour and Solidarity: Cousin Marriage in the Middle East* (Manchester: Manchester University Press, 1989), 125.

21. I borrow this term from James's *Predicament of Culture*.

22. James, *The Predicament of Culture*, 268.

23. See Richard Nisbett and Lee Ross, "Judgmental Heuristics and Knowledge Structures," in *Naturalizing Epistemology*, ed. Hilary Kornblith (Cambridge, MA: MIT Press, 1985), 195; Richard Nisbett and Lee Ross, *Human Inference: Strategies and Shortcomings of Social Judgment* (Englewood Cliffs, NJ: Prentice-Hall, 1985), 17–42; Daniel Kahneman, Paul Slovic, and Amos Tversky, *Judgment Under Uncertainty: Heuristics and Biases* (Cambridge: Cambridge University Press, 1982).

24. Noel Carroll, *The Philosophy of Horror or Paradoxes of the Heart* (New York: Routledge, 1990), 206.

25. This distinction does not deny the existence of akratic action. Someone can genuinely believe in the existence of a monster in a movie, believe that the monster in the movie is immediately before them, be genuinely scared, and sit through the movie although their fear has not made them immobile. Akratic actions do not, however, generally characterize people confronted with terror or the immanent likelihood that it will be directed at them.

26. Kwasi Wiredu, *Philosophy and an African Culture* (Cambridge: Cambridge University Press, 1980).

27. The analogy with parasitism is intended to suggest that parasites can be more or less harmful, and more or less dependent, on a host; conversely, a host can more or less benefit from a parasite. The relation is unstable and elastic, depending on the nature of the host and the parasite.

28. Franz Fanon, *Wretched of the Earth* (New York: Grove Press, 1963). For an interesting counterpoint to Fanon as well as a good deal of invention literature, see Edward W. Blyden, *Christianity, Islam and the Negro Race* (Edinburgh: Edinburgh University Press, [1887] 1967).

29. Blyden, *Christianity, Islam, and the Negro Race*; Mudimbe, *Invention of Africa*.

30. Alasdair C. MacIntyre, *After Virtue: A Study in Moral Theory* (Notre Dame, IN: University of Notre Dame Press, 1981), 214–18.

31. My conception of lived experience is closer to Dewey's and its importance is informed by Alain Locke; it is not intended as a paraphrase of MacIntyre's view of a living tradition.

32. See David-Hillen Ruben, "The Existence of Social Entities," *Philosophical Quarterly* 34 (129, October 1982): 295–310.

33. Gustavus Vassa, *Equiano's Travels* (London: Heinemann, 1967); David Walker and Henry H. Garnet, *Walker's Appeal & Garnet's Address to the Slaves of the United States of America* (Salem, NH: Ayer, 1969); Alexander Crummell, *Africa and America: Addresses and Discourses* (Miami, FL: Mnemosyne, 1969).

34. John J. McDermott, *Culture of Experience: Reflections on the History and Phiosophy of American Culture* (New York: New York University Press, 1976).

35. For an example of the distinction between serf and slave, see Peter Kolchin, *Unfree Labor: American Slavery and Russian Serfdom* (Cambridge, MA: Harvard University Press, 1987).

36. See Lucius Outlaw, "African American Philosophy," *Social Science Information* 26 (1): 75–97; and William R. Jones, "The Legitimacy and Necessity of Black Philosophy," *Philosophical Forum* 9 (2–3, Winter–Spring 1977–8): 149–60. For a discussion of my conception of the history of Black philosophy, see Leonard Harris, "The Lacuna between Philosophy and History," *Journal of Social Philosophy* 20 (3, Winter 1989): 109–14; for a critique of my view, see Paul Jefferson, "The Question of Black Philosophy," *Journal of Social Philosophy* 20 (3, Winter 1989): 99–109. For an interesting discussion of identity, see David B. Wong, "On Flourishing and Ending One's Identity in Community," *Midwest Studies in Philosophy* 13 (1988): 324–41.

37. Leonard Harris, *Philosophy Born of Struggle: Anthology of Afro-American Philosophy from 1917* (Dubuque, IA: Kendall Hunt, 1983).

38. Leonard Harris, *The Philosophy of Alain Locke: Harlem Renaissance and Beyond* (Philadelphia, PA: Temple University Press, 1989).

39. For examples of the way African Americans have been, in practice and conception, excluded from the moral community, see Trudier Harris, *Exorcising Blackness: Historical and Literary Lynching and Burning Rituals* (Bloomington: Indiana University Press, 1984), and Orlando Patterson, *Slavery and Social Death: A Comparative Study* (Cambridge, MA: Harvard University Press, 1982).

40. This view of jazz traditions is analogous to traditions of particle physics, i.e., traditions of transitivity in search of the primordial such that the primordial is a subject for continual revaluation.

41. For a view of nihilism as banal, dogmatic, and a philosophy that makes serious ethical questions a matter of aesthetic taste, see Karen L. Carr, *The Banalization of Nihilism* (Albany: SUNY Press, 1992).

42. See Amiri Baraka [LeRoi Jones], *Preface to a Twenty Volume Suicide Note ...* (New York: Totem Press, 1987).

CHAPTER 16

TELOS AND TRADITION: MAKING THE FUTURE—BRIDGES TO FUTURE TRADITIONS (2014)

In "Telos and Tradition," Harris discusses the building of traditions aimed at the seeking of ascendency beyond abjection within a material pluralverse and a pluralist view of epistemology. First, Harris articulates the theocratic determinism of Edward W. Blyden. Blyden presupposes a teleological, moral universe, which gives purpose to the plunder and expropriation of Africa. Blyden argues that Africa's ascendancy to modernity with dignity, its return to intrinsic virtuous traits, its regaining of sovereignty, and surpassing past glory is (teleologically) destined. Harris argues that "such visions, images, and illusions should be abandoned." In contrast, Harris posits an amoral universe—no Nirvana, no ultimate resolution of contradictions, no redemption for the suffering of immiserated populations. History is not unfolding toward some grand triumph (Absolute Freedom/Spirit) according to some rational script. Yet, in this amoral context, meaningful experiences and memories of a social group can be codified and archived, goals can be set, traditions can be built and rebuilt iteratively. We can string along traces, we can build bridges to the future worthy of our heritage/culture. These traces describe the agency of our ancestors; "an image of the future gives the sacrifices of the present a meaning and purpose." Such goals/teloi are not pre-given; they are heuristic devices. Resistance traditions (e.g., Philosophy Born of Struggle) can be built, which offer affectual and intellectual bulwarks that help make sense of our transnational reality and promote ascendency beyond abjection. In a world replete with unnecessary misery and necro-being, Harris marks ascendency with dignity as a praiseworthy target/"telos" and a good reason for creating bridges to the future.

Edward W. Blyden (1832–1912), Pan-African advocate of the concept "African personality" and author of *A Voice from Bleeding Africa on Behalf of Her Exiled Children* (1856), *A Vindication of the African Race Being a Brief Examination of the Arguments in Favor of African Inferiority* (1857), and *Christianity, Islam and the Negro Race* (1887), developed a conception of *telos*, that is, how the present is inclined toward a future purpose. Blyden's conception postulates historically different racial ontological kinds. Each kind authored a particular civilization. There was a natural enmity between racial civilizations, given their conflicting values. Blyden understood the African civilization as quintessentially defined by the "African personality" that was untouched by Asiatic and European influences. Character traits such as being communal, polygamist family units, spontaneity, goodwill, and racial loyalty define authentic African traits that, were they not suppressed by the subjection of foreign forces, especially Christianity and its morally debased interest in wealth and power aggrandizement, would self-realize their own being.[1] That self-realization would be communal in a way that would preclude the development of a bourgeoisie or working class.[2]

The ascendance of Africans from a state of abject racial subordination in the diasporas and colonial oppression in Africa was, for Blyden, Africa's destiny.[3] It was Africa's destiny as a function of providence, history's unfolding, and natural law.[4] African ascendency would be a regeneration of past glory and a realization of the intrinsic virtuous traits of Africans. Blyden believed that once the African civilization achieved equal power with all other civilizations, images of Africans as primitive would dissipate. Africans would then be seen as dignified because they would own and control the land of their birth.

Blyden came to consider Islam's practices preferable to Christian practices because Christian missionaries promoted subservience among their African converts, whereas Islam required the conquered to become dignified. In addition, manumission by conversion was frequently practiced by Muslims, but most European and American Christian slaveholding communities ended manumission by conversion in the mid-eighteenth century. In addition, the practice of *partus sequitur ventrem* (children born of a slave mother inherit her status as slave) guaranteed that slave populations would reproduce themselves and simultaneously fail to form families capable of transferring wealth across generations. Mothers, whether raped, single, or married, produce slaves who produce more slaves. Fathers, unable to determine the status of their wives or children, become, at best, emasculated slave-producing husbands. Ascendency to modernity with dignity was, for Blyden, the telos of Africans (Dorsey 2000; Patterson 1982).

Realization of the character virtues of each civilization's quintessential intrinsic racial and cultural personality was the outcome of history's unfolding, that is, how the present portends the future, and Africa's past progressive character is consonant with the future. Blyden accepted wholeheartedly the assumption, widely held in his lifetime, that mankind is divided into races and that the movement of history and society can only be adequately explained in terms of their interaction.[5] The interaction, following a logic defined by human nature in a moral universe, shapes what can happen. History for Blyden was linear; events were serial moments forming a line from past glory through catastrophe, culminating in grand achievements. The logic of the unfolding of history pointed to the eventual ascendency of African civilization, and providence assured the accomplishment of the African telos. This is Blyden's "theocratic determinism."[6] Consequently, the future was imminent in the present, and the present hid a nascent future.

It is comforting to imagine that each event contributes to the creation of significant future events. It is also comforting to imagine that the future can be predicted by looking at the present. As a metaphor, we can imagine that when one meteor hits another, the impact on the second meteor is recorded as a "memory."[7] If the first meteor is destroyed, all that remains is the trace elements, the first left on the second, the altered path of the second, and the scattered remnants of the first. In this way, each event can be imagined as a record contributing to the outcome of significant events by its trace. Cumulative results can be imagined, coalescing to form a nice, neat bundle of significant moments. Archives can be envisioned as repositories that help form the material trace of a linear history by a set of records capturing the primal essence of the past. Such visions, images, and illusions should be abandoned.

Imagine the following: the universe and human history are amoral. Rather than a perfect memory repository where good is rewarded and evil is punished in an unseen world by unseen forces, imagine that human history is as amoral as the rest of the universe—a universe where neither material nor immaterial phenomena are memory repositories. That is, imagine that individual lives, like a thousand languages, ethnic groups, religious movements, and benevolent societies, have died, leaving no record and no reason to believe that their contributions will be rewarded, their bad acts punished, or their sufferings vindicated. Given this scenario, the impact on the second meteor is a metaphor, not a memory, a trace element, not a record of the first meteor's essence. The trace of the first meteor is imperfect. Analogously, human history is mirrored neither by, nor in, the natural universe as a memory but as a trace element. Given that history is not linear, Blyden's admonitions and their implications—and, possibly, other forms of historical realism that rely on linear accounts that presuppose a moral universe—need reconsideration.

I describe several research activities as ways to consider Blyden's admonitions and their implications for archives. The Philosophy Born of Struggle (PBOS) Archives (www. pbos.com) and the Alain L. Locke Archive at Howard University's Moorland Spingarn Collection are used to help situate the meaning of resistance traditions and their trace.

Resistance traditions are distinguished by a concern with radical social change for the purpose of universal human liberation (Ernest 2004). That concern is often expressed by arguments for justified methods of social action to create change, accounts of why humanity should change, evaluations of conditions of misery, and depictions of unnecessary unjust conditions and explanations as to why they exist.

The secular resistance tradition in African American culture includes traditions of debate, which do not rely on religious authority for their warrant (Allen 1991). Secular resistance traditions are deeply webbed in theological views. That is, they may share concerns, metaphors, and values (Allen 1991; Derrida 1996; Birt 2002; Galston 2011). Yet secular approaches use different argument strategies, terms, references, authority figures, and methods of argument. Secular justifications for social actions, for example, do not require an account of how such actions accord with sacred texts or cherished orally conveyed proverbs. Nor do they require an account of how unwarranted social conditions, such as the suffering of innocent children, accord with the omnipotent and omnibenevolence of deities, sacred texts, or spiritually inspired proverbs. Theological arguments for social change rely on texts or proverbs considered sacred and characteristically provide accounts of why innocent persons suffer that accord with supernatural intentions. The purpose of promoting universal human liberation and applauding heroic figures to enhance a sense of dignity among those suffering abjection, however, is often shared by both secular and sacred traditions within communities of resistance.

Resistance traditions, both secular and sacred, are replete with the belief that our deeds are indelibly etched in human history (Ernest 2004). Actions are normally considered estimable or condemnable, for example, courageous or cowardly, loyal or unfaithful.

Consequently, for the secular and sacred streams of the resistance tradition, how individuals live is often taken to be meaningful in a moral universe—a universe that is structured and embedded with moral meaning etched in human history. Canonical concepts of human teleology in the Abrahamic religious tradition end one's trip through Hades with the reward of eternal life. The End of Days among Christians, for example, results in eternal happiness for all past and future generations, no matter how much misery those lives suffered; for Immanuel Kant, the end of conflict among the civilized portends perpetual peace between stable nations; for Karl Marx, the end of capitalism portends perpetual peace without nations, classes, or races. The telos of the secular and sacred often picture a state that makes the fortunate who live in that state the embodiment of past lives—the heavenly are not burdened with sin; workers in a communist world are not alienated; Africans in a world devoid of colonialism own and control their own resources, such as in J. E. Casely Hayford's *Ethiopia Unbound*.[8] The moral traits idealized by Casely Hayford of benevolence, simplicity of desire, communal egalitarianism, spiritualism, and caretaking of ancestors were exhibited by village inhabitants and never disrupted by animosity toward immigrants or fatigue from working measured hours of routine labor on an assembly line or plantation crew.

A collection of articles by African American philosophers, *Philosophy Born of Struggle: Anthology of Afro-American Philosophy from 1917* (Harris 1983) begins at the point where African Americans developed philosophical arguments in a literate, Christian-dominated tradition—a tradition that has become increasingly secular. In addition, it begins with the significant rise in a sense of peoplehood. African Americans are a raciated ethnicity.[9] That is, they are an ethnic group—a diasporan culturally distinct African people —and also a raciated population (Davis 2001). African Americans are defined and seen as a Black population of persons descended from sub-Saharan Africa, using the "one drop" rule such that one descendent from Africa makes a person a Negro (Davis 2001). In the early period of American history, authors used Negro, African, or colored as identity markers. The ethnogenesis of Black identity as a racial group and African identity as an ethnic group was coterminous (Gomez 1998; Hall 2005). African people in the Americas lost their ethnic community, language, name, and religion; they gained a ubiquitous racial identity and emerging community: Negro.

Beginning in 1994, the Philosophy Born of Struggle Association began sponsoring an annual conference, which J. Everet Green and I initiated at Rockland Community College in New York. The themes of each conference are consonant with themes from *Philosophy Born of Struggle*. Presentations at the conference have addressed themes such as "Explorations in a Black Philosophy of Culture," "Legitimation Crisis in American Philosophy," "Re-Thinking the Intellectual Life," "Philosophy and Liberation," and "Philosophy and the Scientific Spirit." Various presentations are recorded at each conference. Interviews of individuals began in 2004. The PBOS Archives, established in 2009, are located at Purdue University's Black Cultural Center Library. They are the largest digital (DVD) repository of philosophers concerned with issues of race, ethnicity, Black identity, and African heritage; they are the largest digital repository of individual interviews of such philosophers (forty-five interviews) as well as one of the largest repositories of women addressing such issues. It is the only archive dedicated to Africana philosophy. The complete collection is available online at pbos.com.

Philosophy, on my account, is most valuable when its authors and texts are decidedly dedicated to liberation. In the midst of a planet beset with preventable misery, the pursuit of liberation is at least laudable. It is certainly understandable that individual members of populations who are victims of vicious stereotypes would face existential angst when they pursue esoteric interests. It has been argued that the impact of racism frequently tends to function as an impetus for African Americans to search for solutions to social maladies. Their feelings of anguish and angst about interest in esoteric issues, such as the distinction between *a priori* and *a posteriori* logical constructions, as opposed to their feelings about solutions to immediate social maladies, have been well recorded in interviews (Yancy 1998). It is, however, false to say that African American philosophers are necessarily concerned with liberation as the means of overthrowing existing institutions to achieve a conception of freedom, even when they are concerned with immediate social maladies. Those who are concerned with liberation often have radically different views. Contemporary African American philosophers frequently communicate with one another; that communication is made easier than it was in the past because of such organizations as the Caribbean Philosophical Association (www.car ibbeanphilosophicalassociation.org), the Alain Locke Society (www.alain-locke.com), and the Society for the Study of Africana Philosophy (www. africanaphilosophy.weebly. com). African American philosophers in the early twentieth century, however, did not frequently communicate with one another.

Early-twentieth-century African American philosophers such as William T. Fontaine, Cornelius Golightly, Eugene C. Holmes, and Roy Morrison often knew about and communicated with one another regarding possible academic positions. Each addressed issues of racism. However, they almost never debated the warrant of their conflicting philosophies. Fontaine's use of the sociology of knowledge and Golightly's analytic ethics were never addressed by other African American philosophers, and almost no one ever seriously engaged their views. Early-twentieth-century African American philosophers never saw themselves as forming a coherent community but viewed themselves, at best, as a struggling racial aggregation of different persons, always victims of racism.

None of the authors in the anthology *Philosophy Born of Struggle* define themselves in terms of being "postcolonial" or representative of any ethnic group such as Akan or Yoruba. There is no content in the theories produced by authors of the last generation— from 1903 to approximately 1970—covered in *Philosophy Born of Struggle*, other than in the works of Alain Locke, William T. Fontaine, and Angela Davis, that offered well-developed ideas for battling the condition of postcoloniality. In short, their "African" world is a function of race and filiated heritage, not ethnic commitments to a language, religion, or national geographic region. The only "independence" celebrated was American independence from Britain or the ending of slavery in 1865.

In 1983 I looked at this diffuse collection of philosophers from a third-person, objective standpoint and imposed an order.[10] "African American Philosophy," as described in 1983, was considered a history of distinct movements of individual authors that, when viewed from a third-person perspective, could be seen as a coherent intellectual community. I defined that collection as the progenitor of a growing movement; it became the heritage of "African American Philosophy." I described the heritage in the "Introduction" to *Philosophy Born of Struggle* as both an historical fact—a resistance tradition—and a creation.[11] Of the twenty-one authors in the anthology, only three could be described as revolutionary. All the others were at best liberals. All of the authors, including the revolutionaries, were academicians. I described the authors as members of a "resistance tradition," such that "resistance" meant, narrowly, to be against racism. However, its broader connotation meant "revolutionary." "Resistance tradition" thus functioned at least as a double entendre. African American philosophers have struggled to create intellectual niches in a viciously hostile academic community. Black philosophy conferences were held at the University of Illinois, Chicago Circle, in 1971, the Tuskegee Institute in 1973 and 1976, the Wingspread Conference Center in Racine, Michigan, in 1976, Morgan State University in 1979, the University of the District of Columbia in 1980, and the conference on Africana philosophy at Haverford College in 1982. The Robert R. Moton Center for Independent Study under the leadership of philosopher Broadus Butler provided postdoctoral fellowships that facilitated the study of Black philosophy and conference sessions, where senior philosophers such as Eugene C. Holmes were introduced to newly graduated African American philosophers between 1976 and 1977. These historic meetings and programs resulted in the institutionalization of African American philosophy. The Alain L. Locke lecture series at the W. E. B. Du Bois Center for African and African American Research, the annual Locke Lecture at Howard University, the Anna Julia Cooper Fellow faculty position at Penn State University, and the William T. Fontaine Society and fellowship at the University of Pennsylvania are a few of the institutions made possible by conferences and programs that created networks and partnerships. The American Philosophical Association's Committee on Blacks in Philosophy sponsors regular lectures and a newsletter and promotes equity in the profession; the Alain Locke Society sponsors conferences; and the Society for the Study of Africana Philosophy holds regular discussion sessions. Spelman University has an impressive record of graduates who continue on to graduate school, especially at the University of Memphis, which enjoys the National Research Council's highest ranking for diversity. And last but not least, if not a flagship then certainly a leader, the Tuskegee University National Center for Bioethics in Research and Healthcare has a long history of addressing biomedical ethical issues.

"African American Philosophy" is now a recognized area of philosophy by the American Philosophical Association. There are now far more frequent articles about the struggles, sufferings, and accomplishments of African American philosophers than existed in 1983. African American philosophers properly may be seen as agents—not as human monkeys aping Europeans and authors of philosophies—due serious consideration, at least in part, because there is a trace, a record. The existence of an archive is an affirmation that what they have said is worthy of being maintained and being made accessible to others.

The PBOS Archives arguably contribute to shaping a heritage. It does so by making some features of philosophical dialogue present while, unintentionally, fortuitously, leaving other dialogues outside the pale of its collection. It also, by simple virtue of limitations of resources, leaves unrecorded many African Americans in the midst of a racist profession. The PBOS Archives are at best a scratch on the second meteor but not at all a perfect memory. The Alain L. Locke Archive at Howard University is home to the bequest of America's most noted African American philosopher and arguably one of the most noted of African descent. The archive is judiciously maintained by Joellen El Bashir, the daughter of the artist Ed Pryce from Tuskegee, Alabama. Locke (1885–1954) graduated from Harvard University in 1907 with a degree in philosophy. He was the first Black Rhodes scholar, studying at Oxford's Hertford College during 1907–10 and then at the University of Berlin during 1910–11. He worked with Georg Simmel, one of the founders of sociology, and Hugo Münsterberg, a philosopher and psychologist who significantly influenced William James. Locke received his PhD in philosophy from Harvard University in 1918. He taught at Howard University in Washington, DC, for almost forty years until his retirement in 1953, receiving an honorary doctorate from that university in 1954. Locke helped shape classical pragmatism and authored a philosophy: critical pragmatism. He was the principle author of concepts guiding the Harlem Renaissance, a resource for the Black Arts Movement, and a resource for members of the Adult Education movement, which considered cultural learning an educational attainment (Harris and Molesworth 2010).

In 1917, Locke submitted his doctoral thesis to his advisor, Ralph B. Perry (biographer of the noted founder of pragmatism, William James), and graduated with the 1918 class. Locke's submission of his dissertation on September 17, 1917, can be seen as marking a transition in the history of African American philosophy from philosophies steeped in theology to completely secular philosophies. Locke authored a unique philosophy that would have a life within and outside the academy. It also marked a valuable moment in historiography; we know when Locke submitted his dissertation because he saved the comments and letters from his advisor, with handwritten dates and notes on his copy of the dissertation. We do not have this sort of record for any other African American philosopher.

The primary resource for the *Alain L. Locke: The Biography of a Philosopher* (Harris and Molesworth 2010) is Locke's archive. There is only one other biography of an African American philosopher, *Black Philosopher, White Academy: The Career of William Fontaine* (Kuklick 2008), which was written prior to the establishment of Fontaine's scattered records in an archive at the University of Pennsylvania. No Blyden archives exists in Liberia, Sierra Leone, Nigeria, or Trinidad. Like the scattered pieces of a broken meteor, what is left of his records are dispersed, almost exclusively in libraries and private collections in the modern West.

It is possible to discuss the relationship of Locke's philosophy to his life in great detail, as well as to discuss his philosophy independent of his life, because of the great corpus of publications, letters, photographs, and memorabilia he left. There is no evidence that a mysterious hand of history was responsible for the existence of Locke's papers.

The personal papers of the last generation of African American philosophers are rarely recovered. Whatever contribution the last generation made is not only primarily lost, but we only have trace variables to suggest how past generations have caused or shaped present contours of resistance traditions. The idea of a pristine, primal, recordable, nascent future in the present is arguably a misguided way of seeing the present. The present is not a mirror such that its reflection is a precursor or picture of the future.

Archives help shape the kinds of memories we have. Memories do not exist as a neat compendium of facts but, rather, as a compendium of values made real by what becomes untrammeled facts of life. What lives, then, is at least in part decidable in a world of unpredictable future identities and needs. The meaning of "African," for example, is unfinished as described by V. Y. Mudimbe in *The Invention of Africa: Gnosis, Philosophy, and the Order of Knowledge*. The meaning of "African" has a history and is currently shaped by a sense of common geographic ancestry with an undertow of a common ethnic, racial, and cultural kind. It is also trailed by antiblack racism, stereotypes of "uncivilized" agents, dependent beggars, and violent and irrational criminals. Future people will decide what the unfinished "African" will be; existing people will determine how to destroy the degradation, stereotypes, and racist bigotry befalling African people.

It is up to us to finish the "African" to be placed on the stage for future people to reshape, because there is no teleological end as a neat coalescing of untrammeled memories. *Eo ipso*, Mudimbe's "African" is always a subject and an object. The illusion is that it is an object only—a thing waiting to be realized, discovered, and preserved. Rather, realization is the site of simultaneous transposition, momentary stability, and transvaluation. There is no Blyden-type intrinsic logic of history, one that assures regeneration, redemption, vindication, and self-realization as a function of unchanging natures or an imagined destiny that would be a neat negation of existing miseries and satisfy existing ideals of the good. That is the delusion of historicist reason—it offers a logic that will unfold in a history that is driven by reason and natural laws that make for regeneration, redemption, vindication, and self-realization at some point in an imagined future. The absolute villainy of the slave catcher, accountants on slave ships assessing the value of pregnant women raped by sailors, young boys made into eunuchs, colonizers with superior weapons burning villages to make a path for railroad tracks, and merchants of weapons and fatigues selling to the most vicious groups that control itinerate diamond mines are certainly sources causing us to need redemption stories. Such stories make the suffering purposeful; the suffering is imagined as a precursor to a grand redemption and better future.

Trauma is that emotion that grips the spirit when it fully appreciates that there are no regeneration, redemption, vindication, and self-realization stories neatly matching reality. Suffering is real and often without redemption or vindication for those who suffer.

No Nirvana, End of Days, or resolution of contradictions in the future will ever make the misery, pains, senses of degradation, and humiliation suffered by generations disappear. I posit that suffering has no transcendent otherworldly mysterious meaning. There is no transposition; persons who suffered in the past are not relieved of their misery by descendants who give their ancestors' agony voice. Tragedy exists. The dead are not vindicated. Those giving voice may be rejuvenated, elated, or feel that their activities give meaning to the dead, themselves, and others. The dead do not hear the voices of the living. Giving voice to the past may also help make possible socially and existentially beneficial senses of pride in ancestry, or a feeling that the living are executing the will of the deceased. Those sources of self-worth, especially for persons and populations suffering from antiblack racism, provide a sense of inheritance worthy of enhancing our bridge-building. Given that there is no moral universe and that history is not linear, there being only traces, there is ascendency—and that, while not capable of saving all the records of the lives lost, is a goal that makes bridges to the future worthy of our heritage creations and tradition formations.

We need a trace. It is a compelling need. It describes the agency of our ancestors. There is a need to know that our ancestors were agents, whether successful insurrectionists, captured slaves, entrepreneurs, or basket weavers. It is a condition of our being. It is what makes our lives existentially meaningful to us. We record the meaning, not the universe. An image of the future gives the sacrifices of the present a meaning and purpose. One feature of Locke's philosophy provides a way to see why traces, embedded in the records of archives, have an import far beyond the sheer fact of records as memories and why they have that import in a way that has nothing to do with contributing to a linear history in a moral universe.

According to Locke, universally appreciated aesthetic forms of the beautiful are often created from local folk culture. That which is local, provincial, and parochial can become universal. Populations that are the source of cultural goods that convey universal and meritorious traits enhance popular perceptions of that population. They are likely to be perceived as worthy of respect and dignity. Conviviality between the local and the cosmopolitan is created in such cases. Minorities, parochial communities, partisans of ethnic and racial groups across social strata can achieve dignity—a recognition of worth by others as a function of the continual reality of transvaluation, which creates the possibility of the local making its voice universal, not of a static essence, unchanging character trait, or a ubiquitous racial personality. To be dignified or honored is to be shown deference.[12] Deference is accorded because of a person's or group's presumed possession of intrinsic magnanimous goods, such as courage, trustworthiness, or self-discipline. Heroic Africans, like heroic Polynesians or Latin Americans, are always stoic and reserved. These are universal traits defining what it is to be heroic—always with local features that give such traits their texture (Wiredu 1996; Aldridge 2003). And if Locke is right, generalizations such as "heroic" are not terms referring to singular essences, forms, or properties mirrored in the universe but are, rather, complex valuations (Locke 1992). Aesthetic goods such as symmetry or balance, for example, when expressed by parochial cultural formations, whether Yoruba, African American, or Afro-Peruvian, denote traits that elicit deference. Consequently, one import of the sheer existence of archives as repositories is that they are at least in some cases simultaneously local tradition sustainers and crafters, thereby making possible an accord of dignity and honor to the peoples who authored the collection. That is their trace.

Even if citizens are caused to become agents of resistance, their resistance is nonetheless in tandem with the terrain that is not pre-given—their trace. That trace is the consequence of their agency.

"Telos," *circa* presentism and historicism, has been misconceived as a future embedded and discoverable in the present, as well as a projection drawn from the past and cast into the future. The present, however, is not a mirror such that its reflection is a precursor or picture of the future. "Telos" is not pre-given—not in the nature of what comes before, not predetermined, not predestined. A racial kind may dominate *ad infinitum* in any given geography, but it can never remain the same; ethnogenesis and accidents happen. Given limitations of geography, forces such as impacts of new discoveries and the emergence of unanticipated new value categories assure that our present ideals of the good will differ from those of future generations. Cultures are never stable; cultures are always emerging, always fragmented, relatively coherent and contiguous, proprietary-ownership patterned, and influenced by shifting networks of trust, privileges, information, and skills. Transvaluation, migration, incredulity of technology, and instability of ethnic economic niches make the wish-dream of stable needs and ideals of the good that future people will neatly create superfluous. Blyden never imagined that ideals of the good of Africa's exiled children would be diverse— some socialist and others capitalist, some deeply loyal to their nations far more so than caring about the needs of others—anymore than Casely Hayford ever imagined that the children of the community he described would find themselves in tremendously diverse urban centers with marketplaces dominated by malls and warehouses. Our present is not the future Blyden imagined, for example, a future with abortion clinics, interracial marriage, separate African nations, and radical class divides.

Even if the universe were moral, failing absolute providential or some form of material or biological determinism, we would be agents (or acting like we were agents) creating moral codes and norms to promote ascension so long as we are not entrapped in *partus sequitur ventrem*. The norms of regeneration, redemption, vindication, and self-realization—conceived as embedded in the fabric of history such that exiting lives are worthy if they proceed as though they were repairing or vindicating the lives of past generations—make up an approach to the present and to history that we can well do without. One reason for this is because "we are the ones we are waiting for" (Jordan 2005). That is, we are agents, arguably no longer seeking to realize a species being the way nuns, monks, or suicide bombers define their modes of being—being representatives, living vessels, and sacrificial vassals for a future as conceived by the dead or living imaginations.

New forms of being, communication, and communities (e.g., virtual communities) arise as a function of newly created traditions. Therein it is possible to ascend beyond abjection and make sense of a transnational reality that in some ways accord with

Blyden's ideal of Pan-African unity. Blyden's picture of a linear history encoded in a moral universe is an ill-advised guide for archiving, but his desire for ascending with dignity remains a worthy target and a reason for creating bridges to the future.

Notes

1. An early draft of this article was presented at the XIIIth CODESRIA General Assembly Meeting, Rabat, Morocco, December 5–9, 2011, for the panel "Archives of Post-Independence Africa and Its Diaspora: Archiving the African Diaspora." I am deeply indebted to CODESRIA and its Secrétaire Exécutif Ebrima Sall. See Edward W. Blyden, *African Life and Customs* (reprinted from the *Sierra Leone Weekly News*) (London: African Publication Society, 1908); "Edward Wilmot Blyden and the African Personality: A Discourse on African Cultural Identity," in *Racial Structure & Radical Politics in the African Diaspora*, ed. James L. Conyers Jr. (Piscataway, NJ: Transaction, 2009), 143–60; Teshale Tibebu, *Edward Wilmot Blyden and the Racial National Imagination* (Rochester, NY: University of Rochester Press, 2012). It is arguable that Blyden missed an important development, namely, that Europeans suppressed African development by promoting the traits he considered authentic, thereby stifling the growth of modernity represented by the new African elite. See Olúfémi Táíwò, *How Colonialism Preempted Modernity in Africa* (Bloomington: Indiana University Press, 2010).

2. Ibid., 50–1.

3. An example of this is Blyden's "The Call of Providence to the Descendants of Africa in America: A Discourse Delivered to Coloured Congregations in the Cities of New York, Philadelphia, Baltimore, Harrisburg, during the Summer of 1862," in *Liberia's Offering: Being Addresses, Sermons, etc.* (New York: John A. Gray, 1862). Also see Edward Hulmes, "Edward Wilmot Blyden's Understanding of Christianity and Islam as Instruments of Black Emancipation in West Africa," *Islam and Christian–Muslim Relations* 1 (1): 44–65.

4. Such views were also held by other prominent Pan-Africanists. See Delores P. Aldridge and Carlene Young (eds.), *Out of the Revolution: The Development of Africana Studies* (New York: Lexington Books, 2003). Also see Edward W. Blyden, *Christianity, Islam and the Negro Race* (New York: Black Classic Press, 1887), ch. IV; W. E. B. Du Bois, *Souls of Black Folks* (Chicago, IL: A.C. McClurg, 1903), esp. ch. XI on Alexander Crummell.

5. Christopher Fyfe, "Introduction," in *Christianity, Islam and the Negro Race*, ed. Edward W. Blyden (New York: Black Classic Press, 1887), xii.

6. See Tibebu, *Edward Wilmot Blyden and the Racial National Imagination*, 11; Hollis Lynch, *Edward Wilmot Blyden: Pan-Negro Patriot, 1832–1912* (London: Oxford University Press, 1967), 79–80. Blyden's views, like any great thinker, went through phases. In his early intellectual life he was a minister but was deeply critical of missionaries. Then he was deeply critical of Christianity as a religion inclined to be more than an insidious instrument making Africans poor imitations of European culture and supplicants for their interests, especially because of its destruction of the "pure" African Negro. Lastly, he was a free thinker, preferring ethical faith. The demise of African religions, ethnic identities, customs, and languages in proportion to the rise of Christianity, Western dress, products, and norms inclusive of color prejudice substantively influenced his dissatisfaction with religion in general.

7. For discussions of memory, particularly memories of cultural traits and traditions, see Anthony Appiah, "Wole Soyinka and the Myth of an African World," in *Death and the King's Horseman*, ed. Simon Gikandi (New York: W.W. Norton, 2002), 103–12; Wole Soyinka,

The Burden of Memory, the Muse of Forgiveness (New York: Oxford University Press, 1999); Kwame Gyekye, *Tradition and Modernity: Philosophical Reflections on the African Experience* (New York: Oxford University Press, 1997).

8. J. E. Casely Hayford, *Ethiopia Unbound* (London: Cass, [1911] 1969).

9. See "What, Then, Is Racism?" in *Racism*, ed. Leonard Harris (Amherst, NY: Humanity Books, 1999), 437–51. One way to think about the conjunction of race and ethnicity is to note the way Blyden explained the title of an early Pan-Africanist newspaper, the *Negro*, as naming "a peculiar type of humanity, know as the Negro with all its affiliated and collected branches whether on this continent or elsewhere." That peculiar type was simultaneously "African." Hollis Lynch, "The Native Pastorate Controversy and Cultural Ethnocentrism in Sierra Leone, 1971–74," *Journal of African History* 5 (3): 401–2.

10. Leonard Harris, "Introduction," in *Philosophy Born of Struggle: Afro-American Philosophy from 1917* (Dubuque, IA: Kendall Hunt, 2000), second edition, xiii–xxvi.

11. I argue elsewhere that traditions are intrinsically conservative and are inescapably inventions. They can be exceedingly beneficial and earnestly needed. Simultaneously, they are like horror movies. We know, as when we watch such movies, that the characters are not real; traditions are a form of willful bad faith. Tradition should function the way jazz improvisation functions; we need the crucial features of their character to know when and how to make a new contribution. However, we are nonetheless trapped in a particular music form. And like all forms, we have every reason to believe that future generations will create new forms. See Leonard Harris, "Cosmopolitanism and the African Renaissance: Pixley I. Seme and Alain L. Locke," *International Journal of African Renaissance Studies* 4 (2, December 2009): 181–92; "The Great Debate: Alain L. Locke vs. W. E. B. Du Bois," *Philosophia Africana* 7 (1, March 2004): 13–37; "The Harlem Renaissance and Philosophy," in *A Companion to African-American Philosophy*, ed. Tommy L. Lott and John P. Pittman (Oxford: Blackwell, 2003), 381–85; "Prolegomenon to a Tradition: What is American Philosophy?" in *American Philosophies*, ed. Anne S. Waters and Scott Pratt (Oxford: Blackwell, 2002), 5–6; "Introduction," in *Philosophy Born of Struggle: Afro-American Philosophy from 1917* (Dubuque, IA: Kendall Hunt, 2000), second edition, xiii–xxvi; and "The Horror of Tradition or How to Burn Babylon and Build Benin While Reading a *Preface to a Twenty Volume Suicide Note*," republished in *African-American Perspectives and Philosophical Traditions*, ed. John P. Pittman (New York: Routledge, 1997), 94–119.

12. See, for the concept of honor, "Honor, Eunuchs and the Postcolonial Subject," in *Postcolonial African Philosophy*, ed. Emmanuel C. Eze (Cambridge: Blackwell, 1997), 252–9.

References

Aldridge, Delores P., and C. Young, eds. 2003. *Out of the Revolution: The Development of Africana Studies*. New York: Lexington Books.

Allen, Norm R., Jr. 1991. *African-American Humanism*. New York: Prometheus Press.

Appiah, Anthony. 2002. "Wole Soyinka and the Myth of an African World." In *Death and the King's Horseman*, edited by Simon Gikandi, 103–12. New York: W.W. Norton.

Birt, Robert E., ed. 2002. *The Quest for Community and Identity: Critical Essays in Africana Social Philosophy*. Lanham, MD: Rowman & Littlefield.

Blyden, Edward W. 1856. *A Voice from Bleeding Africa on Behalf of Her Exiled Children*. Liberia: G. Killian.

Blyden, Edward W. 1857. *A Vindication of the African Race Being a Brief Examination of the Arguments in Favor of African Inferiority*. Monrovia: G. Killian.

Blyden, Edward W. 1887. *Christianity, Islam and the Negro Race*. New York: Black Classic Press.

Blyden, Edward W. 1908. *African Life and Customs* (reprinted from the Sierra Leone weekly news). London: African Publication Society.

Conyers, James L. 2009. "Edward Wilmot Blyden and the African Personality: A Discourse on African Cultural Identity," in *Racial Structure & Radical Politics in the African Diaspora*, edited by James L. Conyers Jr., 143–60 (cited in full immediately below).

Conyers, James L., Jr., ed. 2009. *Racial Structure & Radical Politics in the African Diaspora*. Piscataway, NJ: Transaction.

Davis, James F. 2001. *Who Is Black?: One Nation's Definition*. University Park: Pennsylvania State University Press.

Derrida, Jacques. 1996. *Archive Fever*. Chicago, IL: University of Chicago Press.

Derrida, Jacques. 2010. *Copy, Archive, Signature*. Translated by Jeff Fort. Stanford, CA: Stanford University Press.

Dorsey, Joseph. 2000. "Women Without History," in *Caribbean Slavery in the Atlantic World*, edited by Hilary Beckles and V. Shepherd, 624–58. Kingston, Jamaica: Ian Randle.

Ernest, John. 2004. *Liberation Historiography*. Chapel Hill: University of North Carolina Press.

Frendel, M. Yu. "Edward Blyden and the Concept of African Personality." *African Affairs* 73 (292, July 1974): 277–89.

Galston, David. 2011. *Archives and the Event of God: The Impact of Michel Foucault on Philosophical Theology*. Montreal: McGill-Queen's University Press.

Gomez, Michael A. 1998. *Exchanging Our Country Marks: The Tranformation of African Identities in the Colonial and Antebellum South*. Chapel Hill: University of North Carolina Press.

Gyekye, Kwame. 1997. *Tradition and Modernity: Philosophical Reflections on the African Experience*. New York: Oxford University Press.

Hall, Gwendolyn M. 2005. *Slavery and African Ethnicities in the Americas: Restoring the Links*. Chapel Hill: University of North Carolina Press.

Harris, Leonard. "The Native Pastorate Controversy and Cultural Ethnocentrism in Sierra Leone, 1971–74." ' *Journal of African History* 5 (3): 401–2.

Harris, Leonard. 1983. *Philosophy Born of Struggle: Afro-American Philosophy from 1917*. Dubuque, IA: Kendall Hunt.

Harris, Leonard. 1997. "Honor, Eunuchs and the Postcolonial Subject." In *Postcolonial African Philosophy: A Critical Reader*, edited by Emmanuel C. Eze, 252–9. Cambridge: Blackwell.

Harris, Leonard. 1997. "The Horror of Tradition or How to Burn Babylon and Build Benin While Reading a *Preface to a Twenty Volume Suicide Note*." Republished in *African-American Perspectives and Philosophical Traditions*, edited by John P. Pittman, 94–119. New York: Routledge.

Harris, Leonard. 1999. "What, Then, Is Racism?," in *Racism*, edited by Leonard Harris, 437–51. Amherst, NY: Humanity Books.

Harris, Leonard. 2002. "Prolegomenon to a Tradition: What Is American Philosophy?" In *American Philosophies*, edited by Anne S. Waters and Scott Pratt, 5–6. Oxford: Blackwell.

Harris, Leonard. 2003. "The Harlem Renaissance and Philosophy." In *A Companion to African-American Philosophy*, edited by Tommy L. Lott and John P. Pittman, 391–5. Oxford: Blackwell.

Harris, Leonard. "The Great Debate: Alain L. Locke vs. W. E. B. Du Bois." *Philosophia Africana* 7 (1, March 2004): 13–37.

Harris, Leonard. "Cosmopolitanism and the African Renaissance: Pixley I. Seme and Alain L. Locke." *International Journal of African Renaissance Studies* 4 (2, December 2009): 181–92.

Harris, Leonard, and C. Molesworth. 2010. *Alain L. Locke: The Biography of a Philosopher.* Chicago, IL: University of Chicago Press.

Jordan, June. 2005. "Poem for South African Women" (c. 1980). In *Directed by Desire: The Collected Poems of June Jordan,* edited by Jan Heller Levi and Sara Miles, 279. Port Townsend, WA: Copper Canyon Press.

Kuklick, Bruce. 2008. *Black Philosopher, White Academy: The Career of William Fontaine.* Philadelphia: University of Pennsylvania Press.

Locke, Alain. 1992. "The Contribution of Race to Culture." In *The Philosophy of Alain Locke: Harlem Renaissance and Beyond,* edited by Leonard Harris, 202–3. Philadelphia, PA: Temple University Press.

Lynch, Hollis. 1964. *Edward W. Blyden, 1832–1912 and Pan-Negro Nationalism.* London: University of London.

Lynch, Hollis. 1967. *Edward Wilmot Blyden: Pan-Negro Patriot, 1832–1912.* Oxford University Press.

Mudimbe, V. Y. 1988. *The Invention of Africa: Gnosis, Philosophy, and the Order of Knowledge.* Bloomington: Indiana University Press.

Mudimbe, V. Y. 1994. *The Idea of Africa.* Bloomington: Indiana University Press.

Patterson, Orlando. 1982. *Slavery and Social Death: A Comparative Study.* Cambridge, MA: Harvard University Press.

Soyinka, Wole. 1999. *The Burden of Memory, the Muse of Forgiveness.* New York: Oxford University Press.

Táíwò, Olúfémi. 2010. *How Colonialism Preempted Modernity in Africa.* Bloomington: Indiana University Press.

Tibebu, Teshale. 2012. *Edward Wilmot Blyden and the Racial Imagination.* Rochester, NY: University of Rochester Press.

Wiredu, Kwasi. 1980. *Philosophy and an African Culture.* Cambridge: Cambridge University Press.

Wiredu, Kwasi. 1996. *Cultural Universals and Particulars: An African Perspective.* Bloomington: Indiana University Press.

Yancy, George, ed. 1998. *African-American Philosophers: 17 Conversations.* New York: Routledge.

INDEX

Index

Index

Index

Index

multiple identities 64
  locations 221

natally alienated 102, 104, 115
national identities 57
  national unity 57
  race-based nations 57
natural responses 168
natural universe 275
naturalism 46
  naturalist 45
naturalization of epistemology 179
nature of being 255, 267
  benign nativism 256
  conception of life 253
  nature of life 253
  ontological essence 44, 78, 255
  species character 256
nature of humans 100, 225
  explicit 225
  implicit 225
natures 48, 59, 63, 74, 80, 104, 226, 227, 236,
    261, 280
Neal, Anthony 33
Necro-being 15, 69–73, 77, 86, 88, 91,
    92, 198
  living death 71
necro-tragedy 15, 30, 69, 70
Negro 139, 146
  as a singular kind 146
nepotism 59, 74, 75, 82, 155
network of meanings 238
Nietzsche, Friedrich 26, 130, 254
  Nietzschean 72, 84, 206
nihilists 268, 269
Nishida, Kitaro 22
Nkrumah, Kwame 57
nonideal 52
nonracist world 58, 82–4, 91, 217
normative 19–22, 27, 71, 76, 120, 191, 198, 199,
    243, 254
  resources 181
norms 15, 20, 27, 33, 90, 116, 123, 185, 197, 243,
    253, 261, 282
Nussbaum, Martha 166

obedience 21, 114, 153, 167, 168
objective
  objective realism 43
  objectively true 130
  objectivism 45, 60
  objectivist 44, 46, 47, 50, 60, 61, 63–5
  universal truth 22, 45
obligation 59, 62, 65, 136, 137, 197, 220
Omi, Michael 49

omnipotent 19, 238, 275
ontological
  being 28, 44, 100
  character of persons 100
  elements 60
  entities 30, 45, 60, 138, 139, 166, 178, 180, 186,
      219, 223, 224, 227, 232
  essences 44
  merit 104
  nature 100
ontologically stable 44, 51, 80, 140
ontology 22, 31, 51, 75, 77, 78, 232, 253
  see collective entity; race
oppositional 31, 46, 51, 75
oppression 14, 33, 52, 58, 63, 65, 66, 72, 121, 126,
    135, 137, 146, 165–7, 172, 179, 186, 203,
    217, 274
  oppressed 30, 31, 28, 59, 63, 65, 80, 83, 87, 105,
      166, 183, 217, 221, 228, 229
  oppressor 58, 80, 83, 217, 232
  theory of 167
organic vitalist fallacy 150
organistic vitalism 148, 149
origin in struggle to destroy boundaries 198
Oruka, Henry Odera 27
other 31, 109, 238
  absolute 48
  Manichean 224, 233
Outlaw Jr., Lucius T. 50
overpoliced 230
ownership 17, 52, 59, 62, 65, 77, 80, 133, 135, 137–9,
    170, 182, 183, 216, 220, 225, 230, 242–4, 282

panopticon 237, 245
paradigm for slavery 237
paradox
  disability paradox 89
  happiness paradox 89
  Hispanic paradox 88
Parks, Robert 78
particularity 22, 215–18, 251
paternalistic 102, 154
patience 21, 129, 134, 153
patriarchy 82, 178
Patterson, Orlando 115, 200
peership 108, 154, 216
Peirce, Charles S. 264
Perry, Ralph B. 191, 279
person
  as agents due dignity 155
  category of 168
  excluded from 252
  full human beings 163
  innocent 275
  normal 85, 148

Index

Index